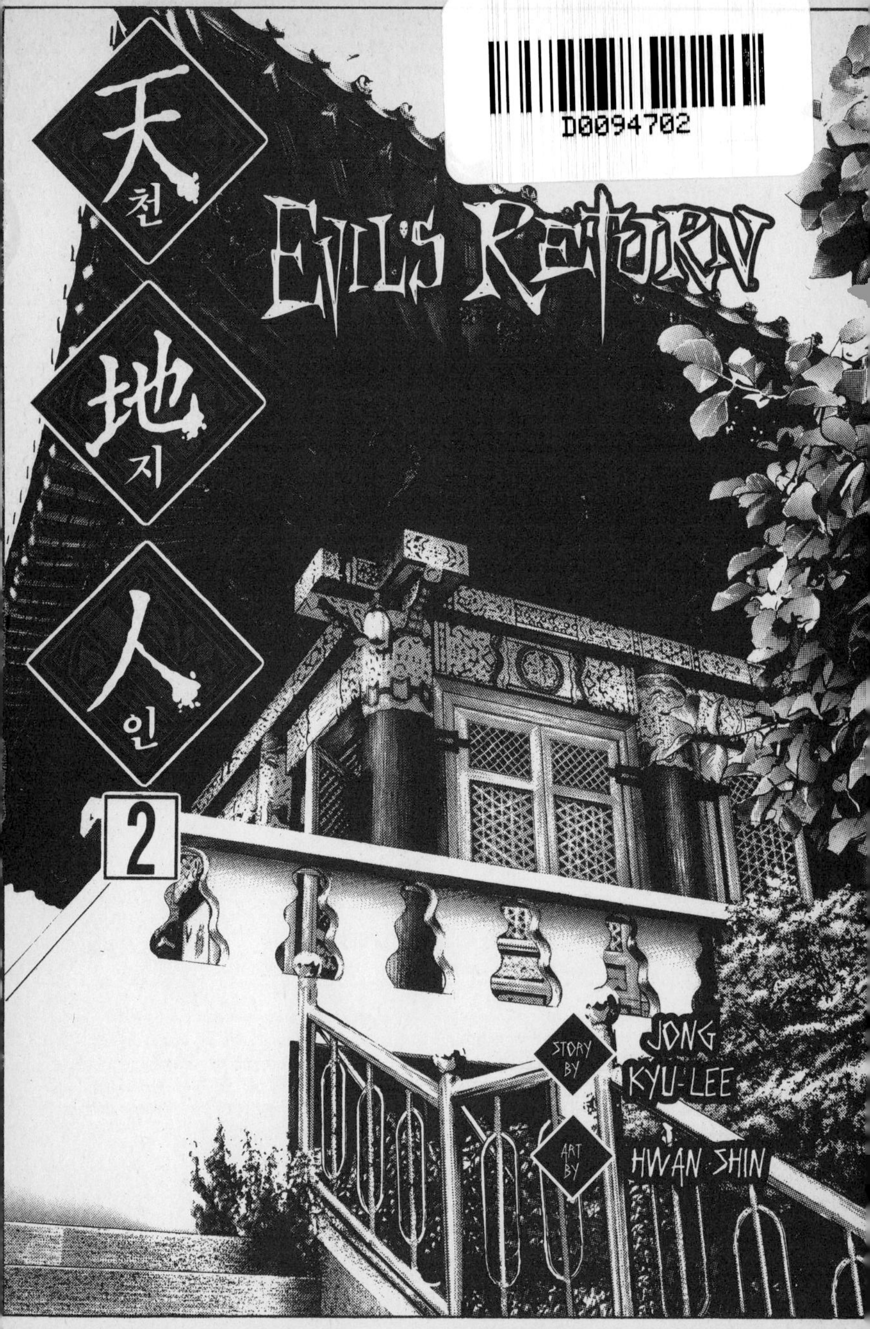
天
천
地
지
人
인
EVIL'S RETURN
2
STORY BY
JONG KYU-LEE
ART BY
HWAN SHIN

Evil's Return Vol. 2

written by Jong Kyu-Lee
illustrated by Hwan Shin

Translation - Seung-Ah Lee
Associate Editor - Wendy Hunter
Retouch and Lettering - Vicente Rivera, Jr.
Production Artist - James Dashiell
Cover Design - Patrick Hook

Editor - Luis Reyes
Digital Imaging Manager - Chris Buford
Pre-Press Manager - Antonio DePietro
Production Managers - Jennifer Miller and Mutsumi Miyazaki
Art Director - Matt Alford
Managing Editor - Jill Freshney
VP of Production - Ron Klamert
President and C.O.O. - John Parker
Publisher and C.E.O. - Stuart Levy

A  Manga

TOKYOPOP Inc.
5900 Wilshire Blvd. Suite 2000
Los Angeles, CA 90036

E-mail: info@TOKYOPOP.com
Come visit us online at www.TOKYOPOP.com

ISBN: 1-59182-785-X

First TOKYOPOP printing: October 2004
10 9 8 7 6 5 4 3 2 1
Printed in the USA

EVIL'S RETURN™

VOLUME 2

ART BY: HWAN SHIN
WRITTEN BY: JONG KYU-LEE

HAMBURG // LONDON // LOS ANGELES // TOKYO

EVIL'S RETURN

STORY SO FAR...

SEO YUMI'S FIRST PERIOD SIGNALED TO LEGIONS
OF DEMONS THAT SHE, THE PROPHESIED MOTHER
OF HELL, WAS READY TO MOTHER THE HELLISH
HORRORS OF ANY DEMON THAT COULD GET ITS
HANDS ON HER. BUDDHIST DISCIPLE AND STUDENT
BODY PRESIDENT SUNWOO HYUN WAS HER FIRST
LINE OF DEFENSE AGAINST THE EVIL FORCES.
BUT WHEN HOTHEADED AND HEAD-OVER-HEELS IN
LOVE FRESHMAN TAE CHAIL CHALLENGED HYUN
TO A DUEL OVER YUMI'S LOVE, THE FRIGHTENED
YOUNG WOMAN WAS LEFT ALONE TO DEAL WITH A
HORDE OF POSSESSED STUDENTS SWARMING THE
SCHOOL GROUNDS. AFTER DEFEATING CHAIL, HYUN
RUSHED TO HER SIDE, ONLY TO BE KNOCKED COLD.
THINGS LOOKED BLEAK UNTIL CHAIL SHOWED UP
SWINGING, READY TO DIE FOR YUMI.

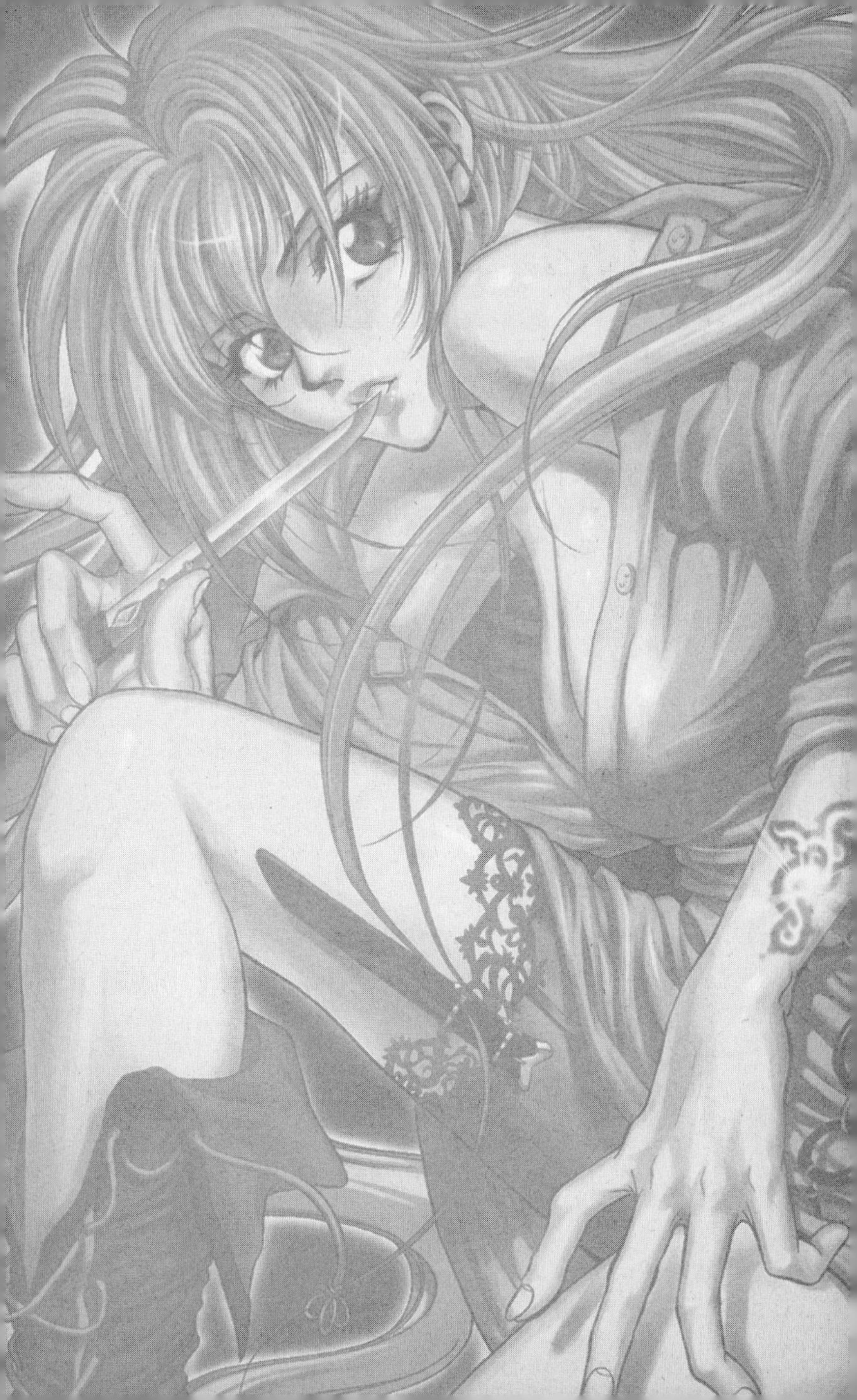

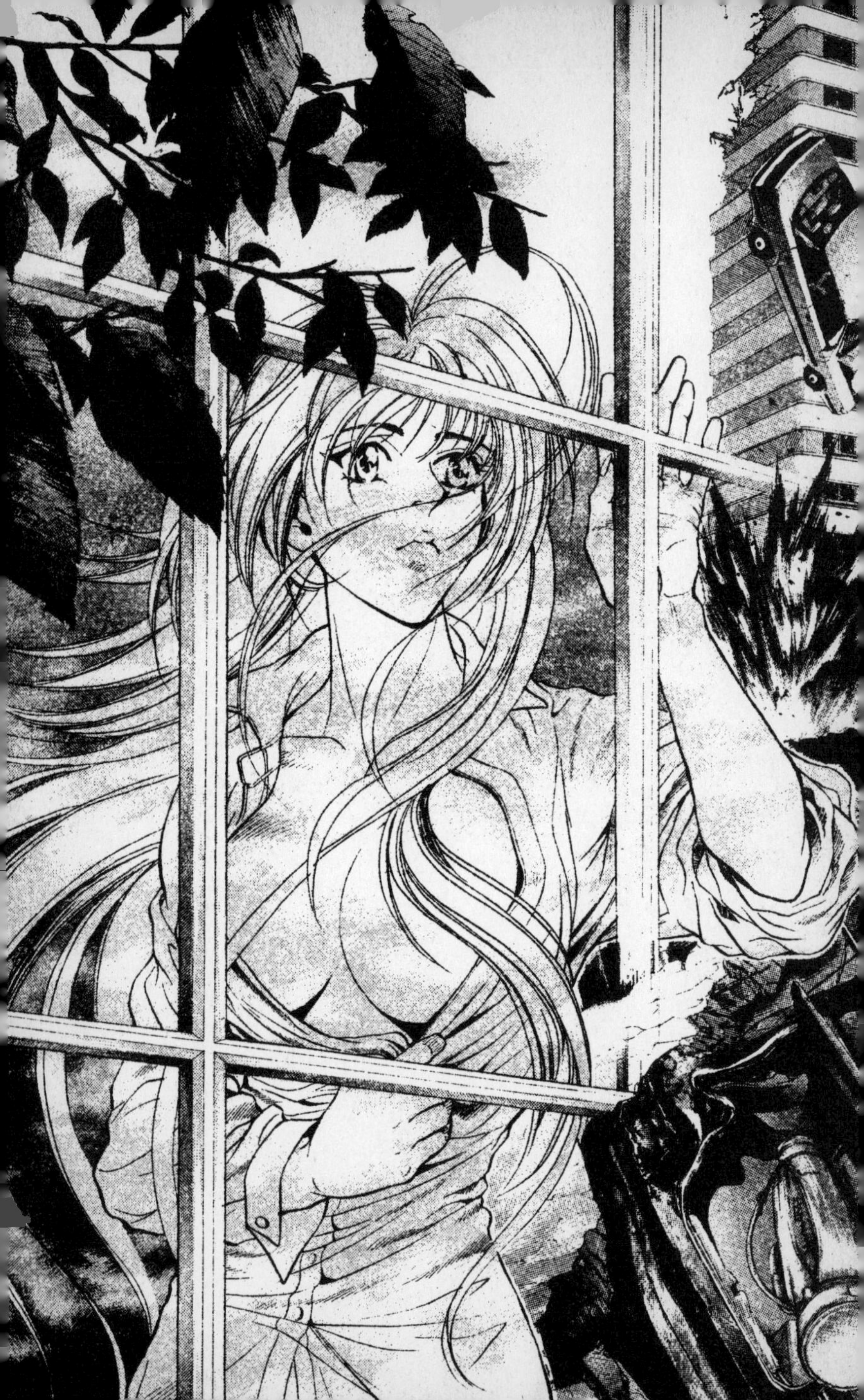

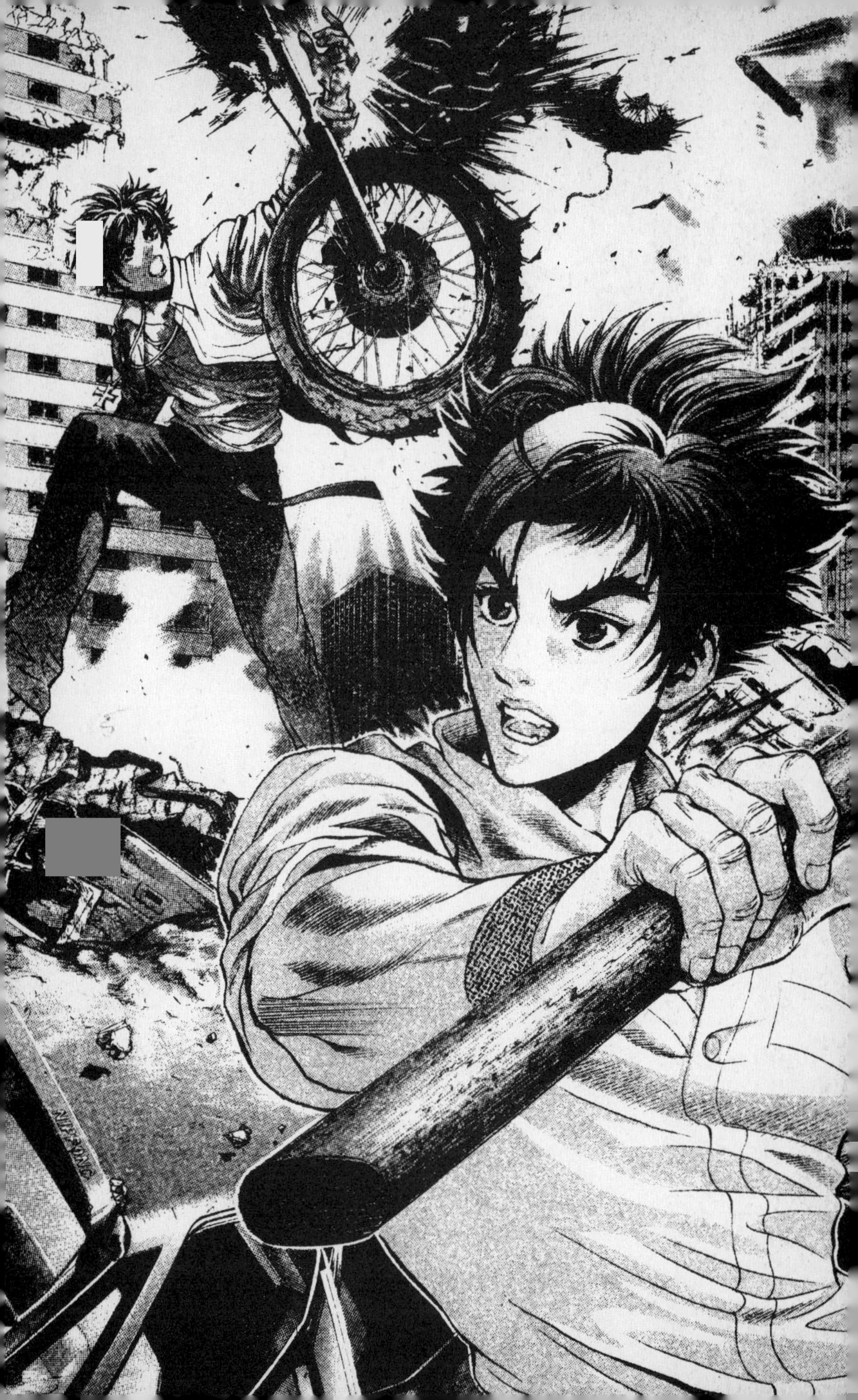

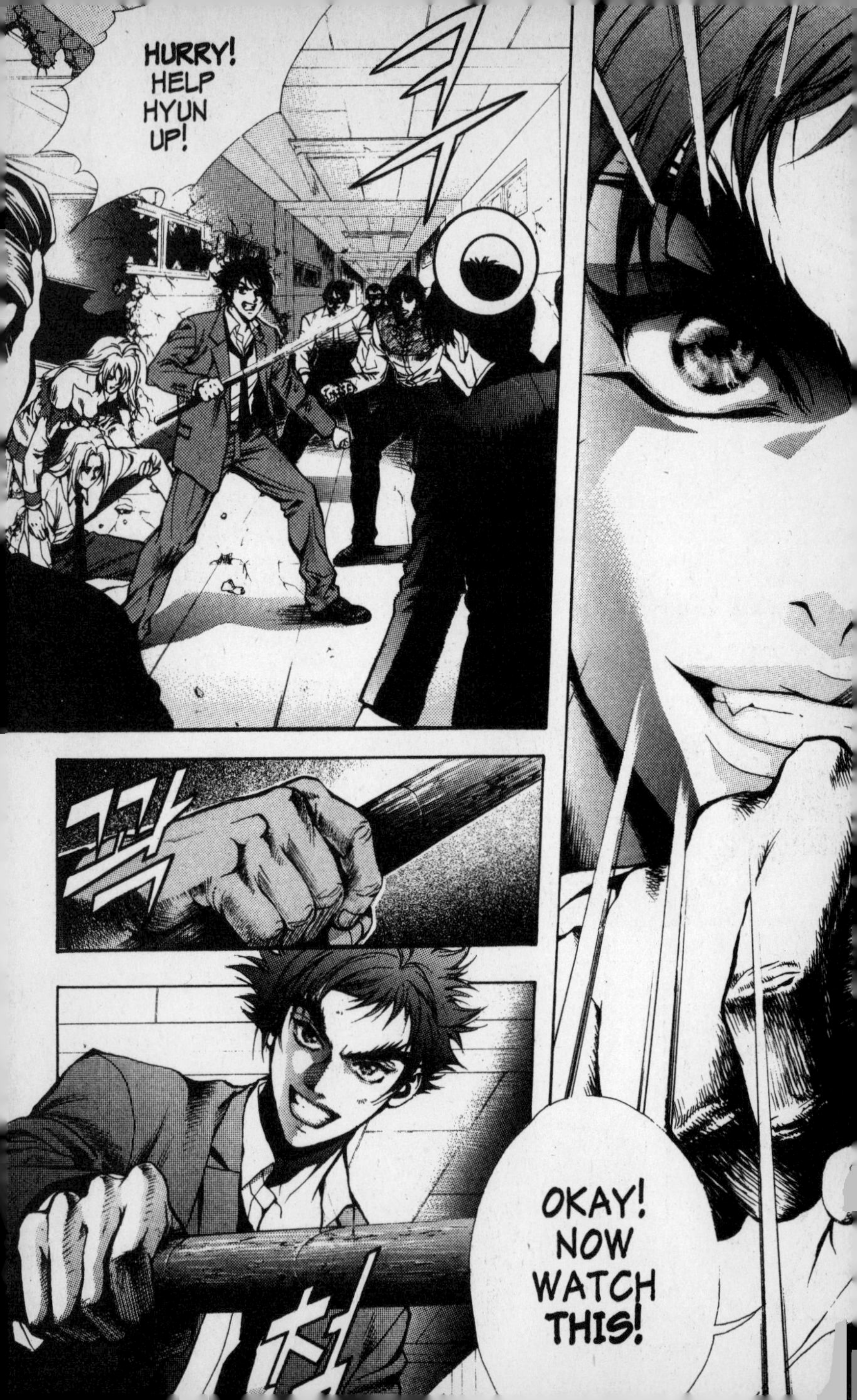
HURRY! HELP HYUN UP!
OKAY! NOW WATCH THIS!

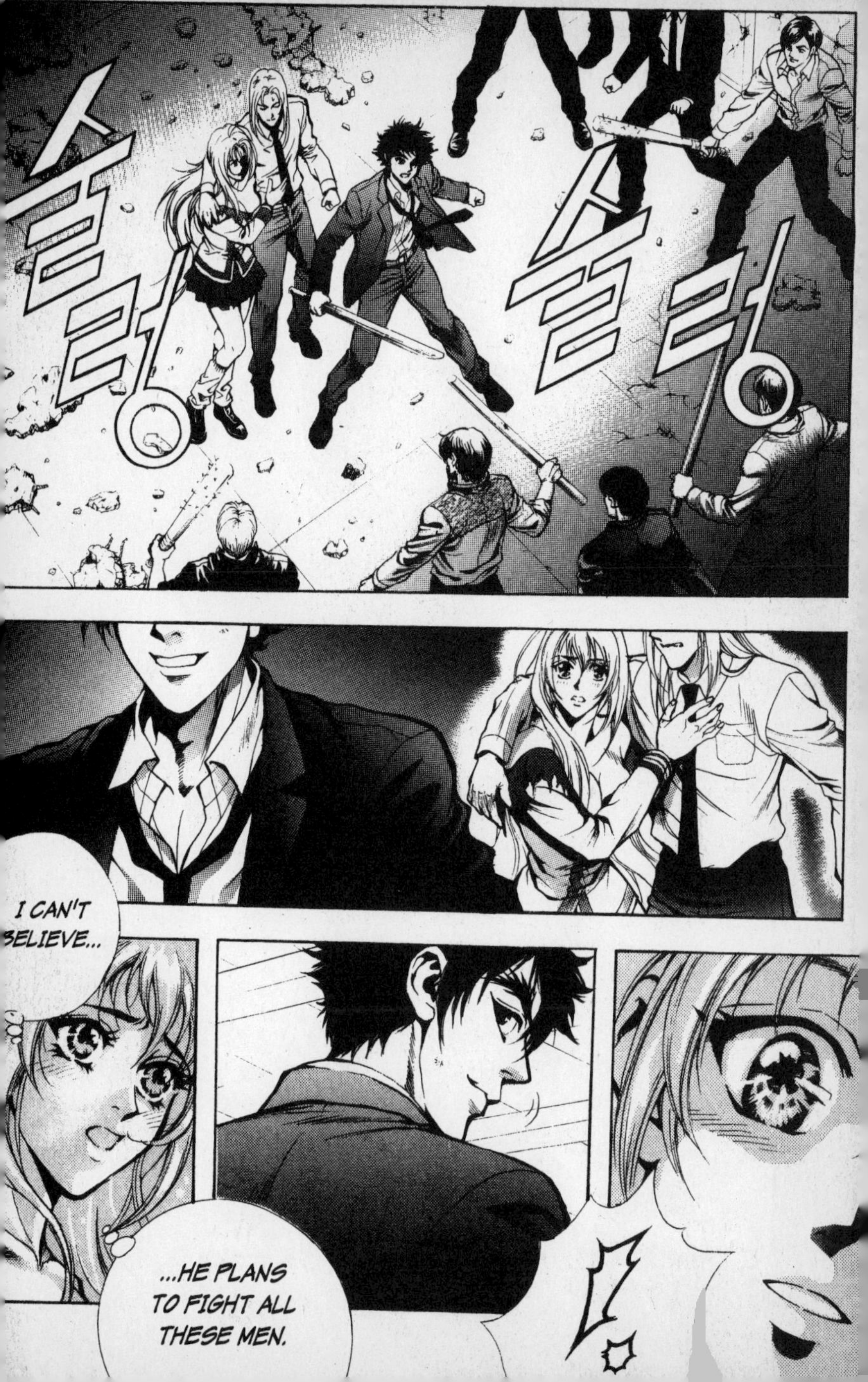

I CAN'T BELIEVE...
...HE PLANS TO FIGHT ALL THESE MEN.

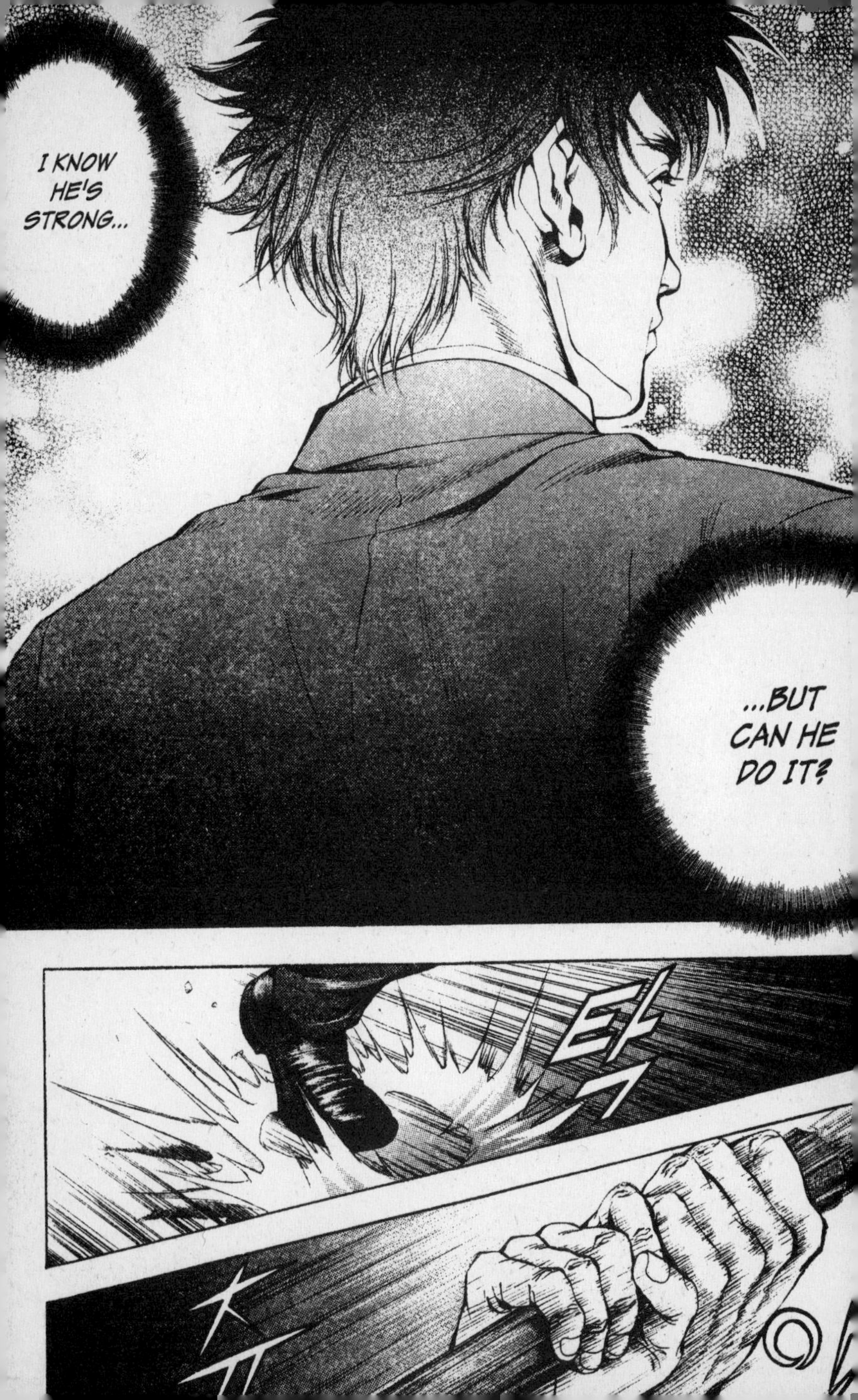
I KNOW HE'S STRONG...
...BUT CAN HE DO IT?

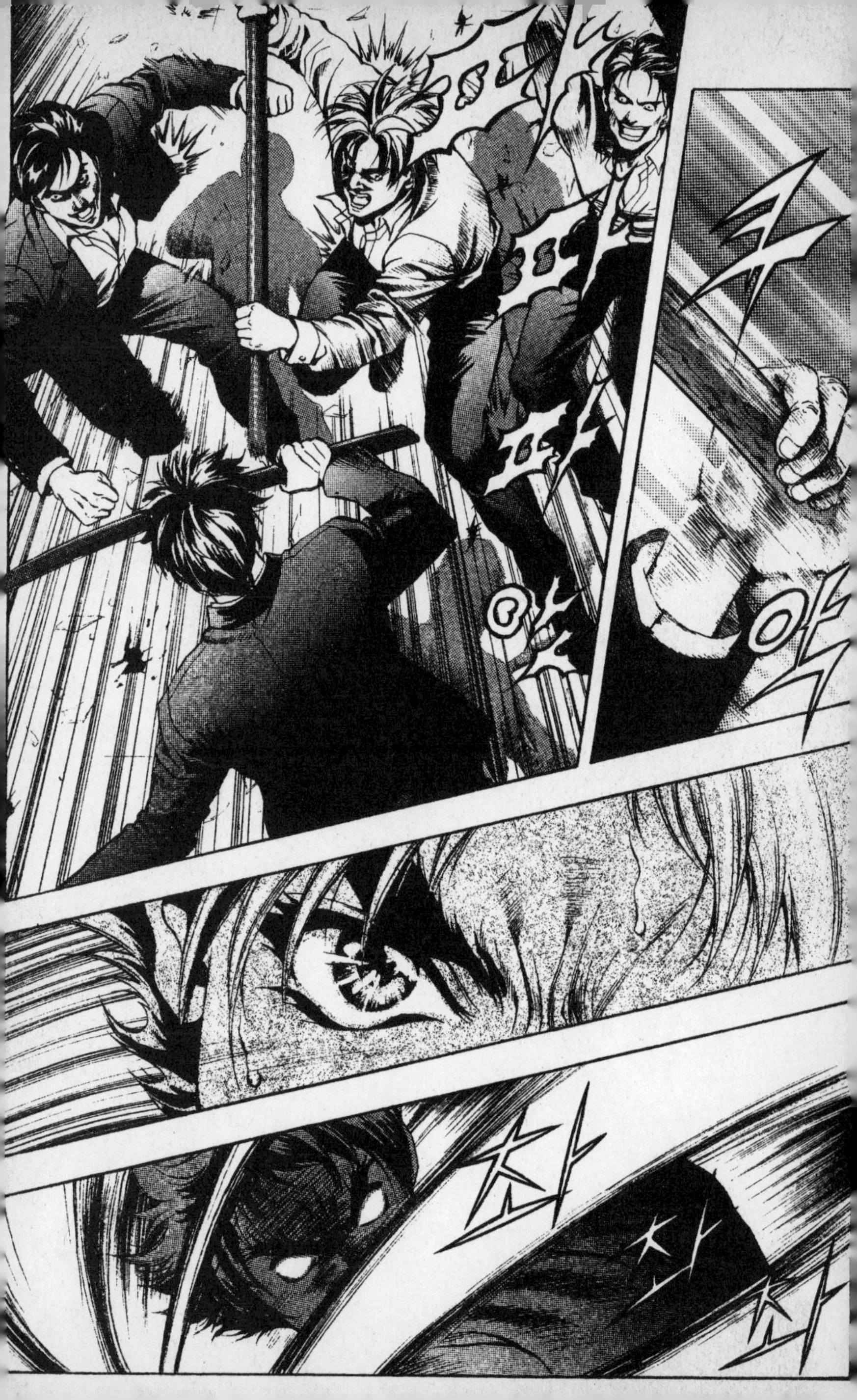

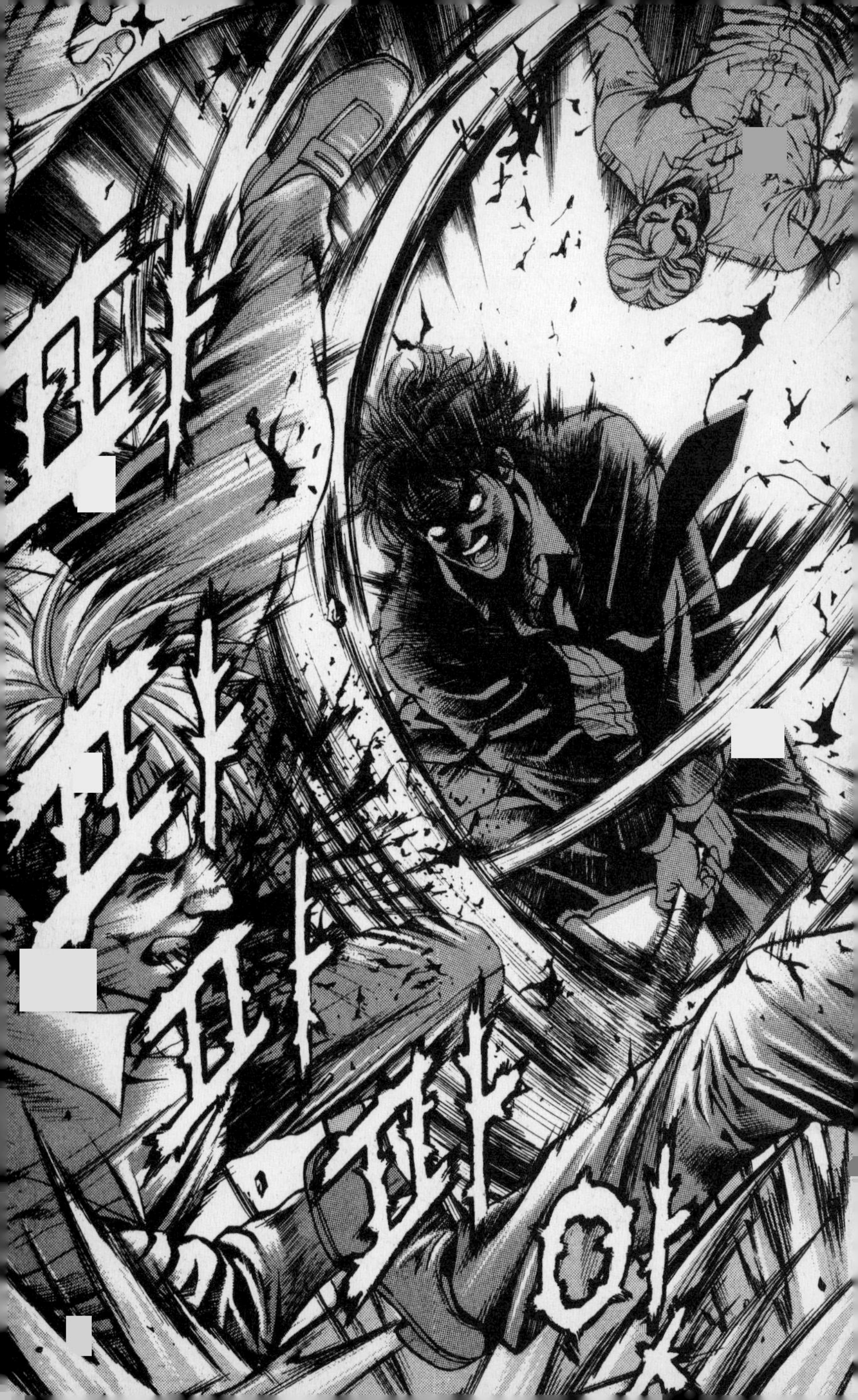

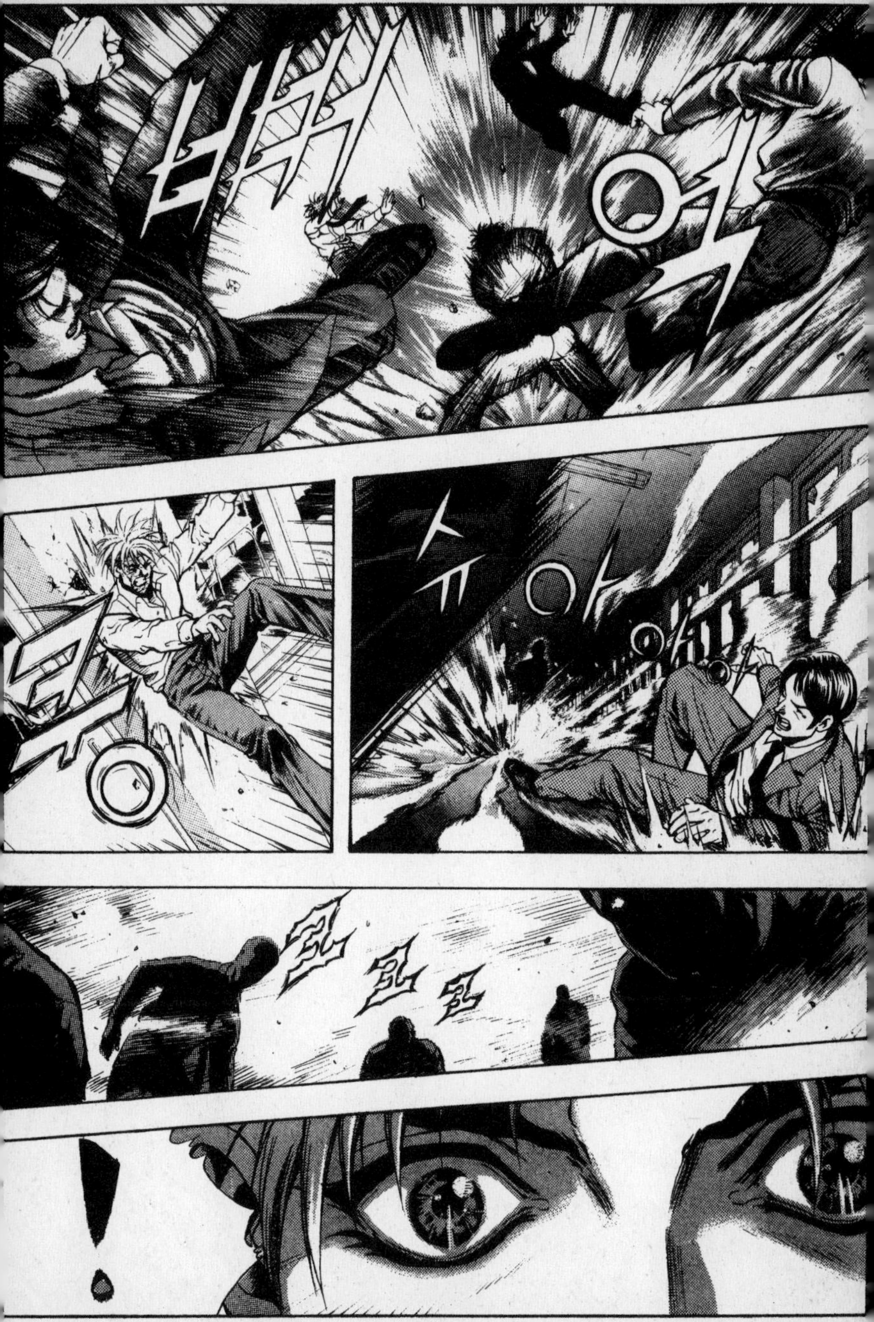
뻐억
!

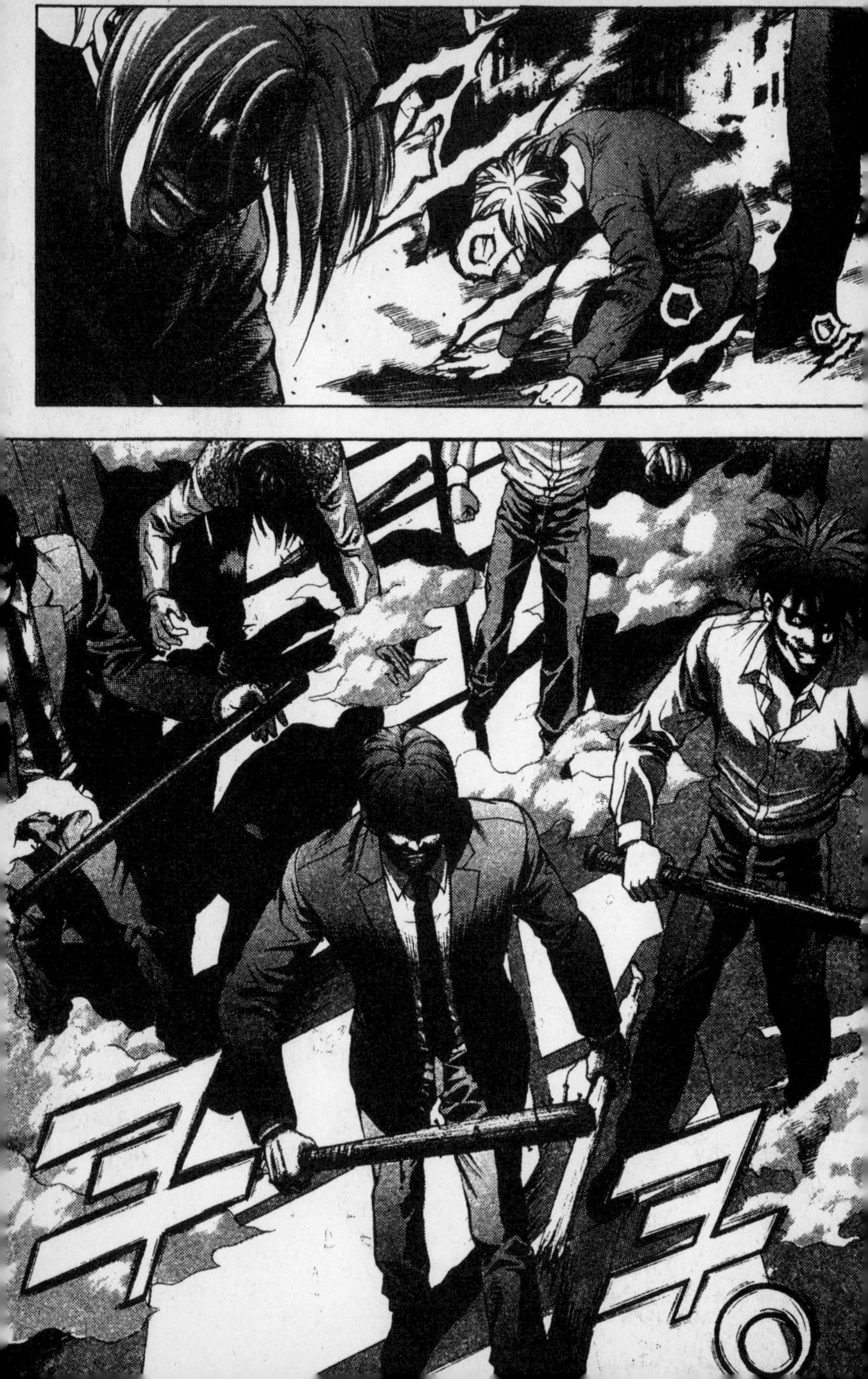
ニヤ

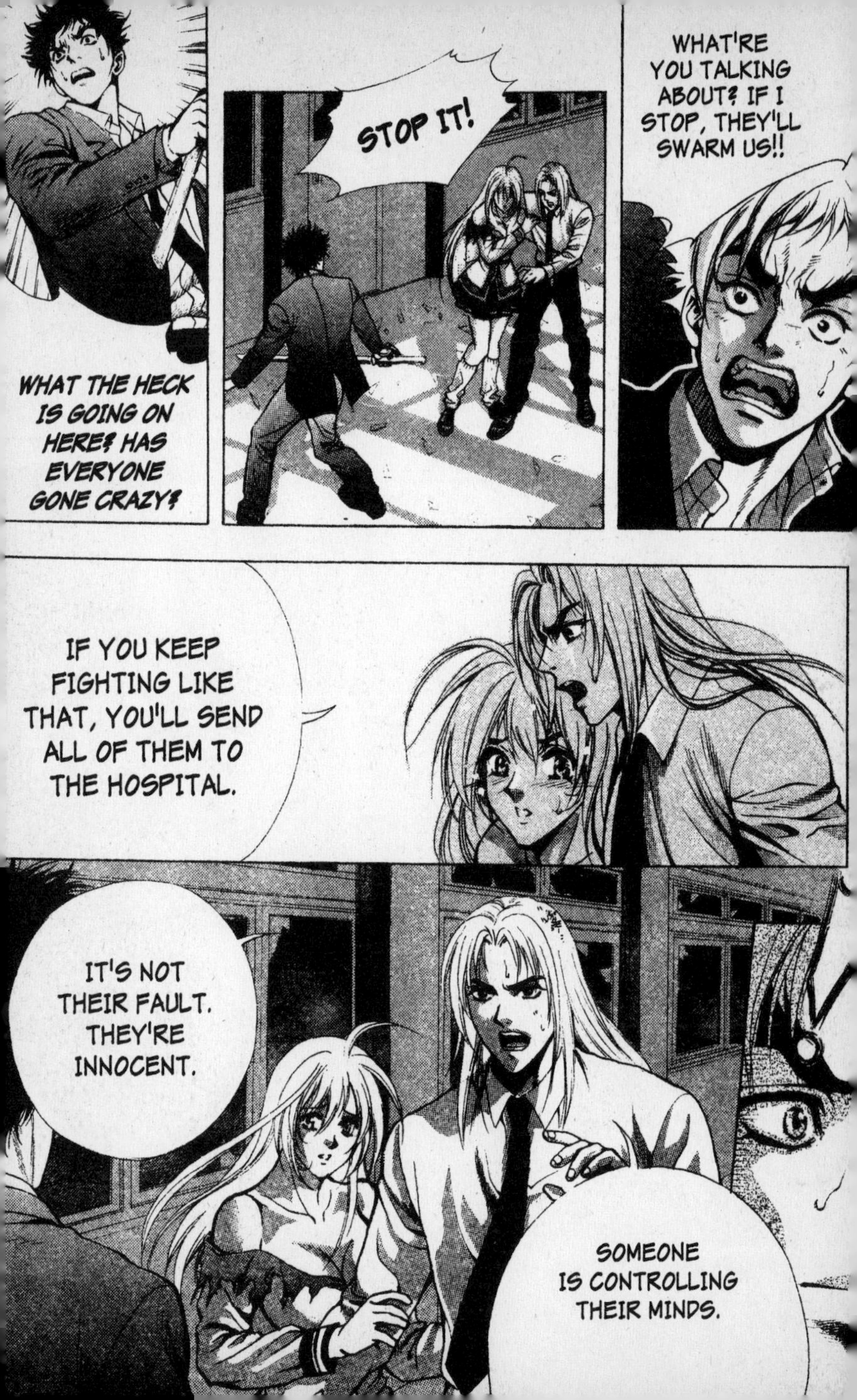
WHAT THE HECK IS GOING ON HERE? HAS EVERYONE GONE CRAZY?
STOP IT!
WHAT'RE YOU TALKING ABOUT? IF I STOP, THEY'LL SWARM US!!
IF YOU KEEP FIGHTING LIKE THAT, YOU'LL SEND ALL OF THEM TO THE HOSPITAL.
IT'S NOT THEIR FAULT. THEY'RE INNOCENT.
SOMEONE IS CONTROLLING THEIR MINDS.

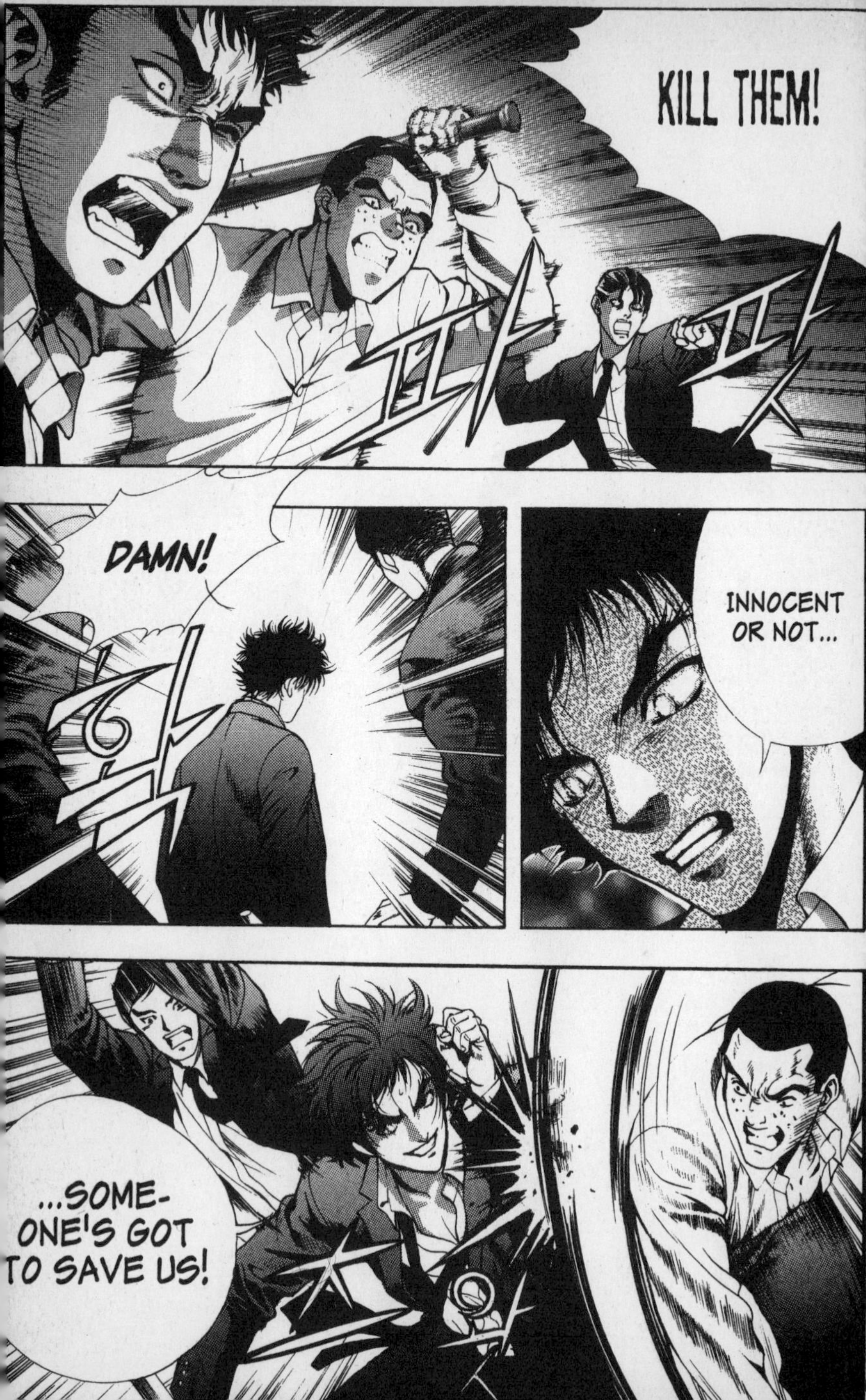
KILL THEM!
DAMN!
INNOCENT OR NOT...
...SOME-ONE'S GOT TO SAVE US!

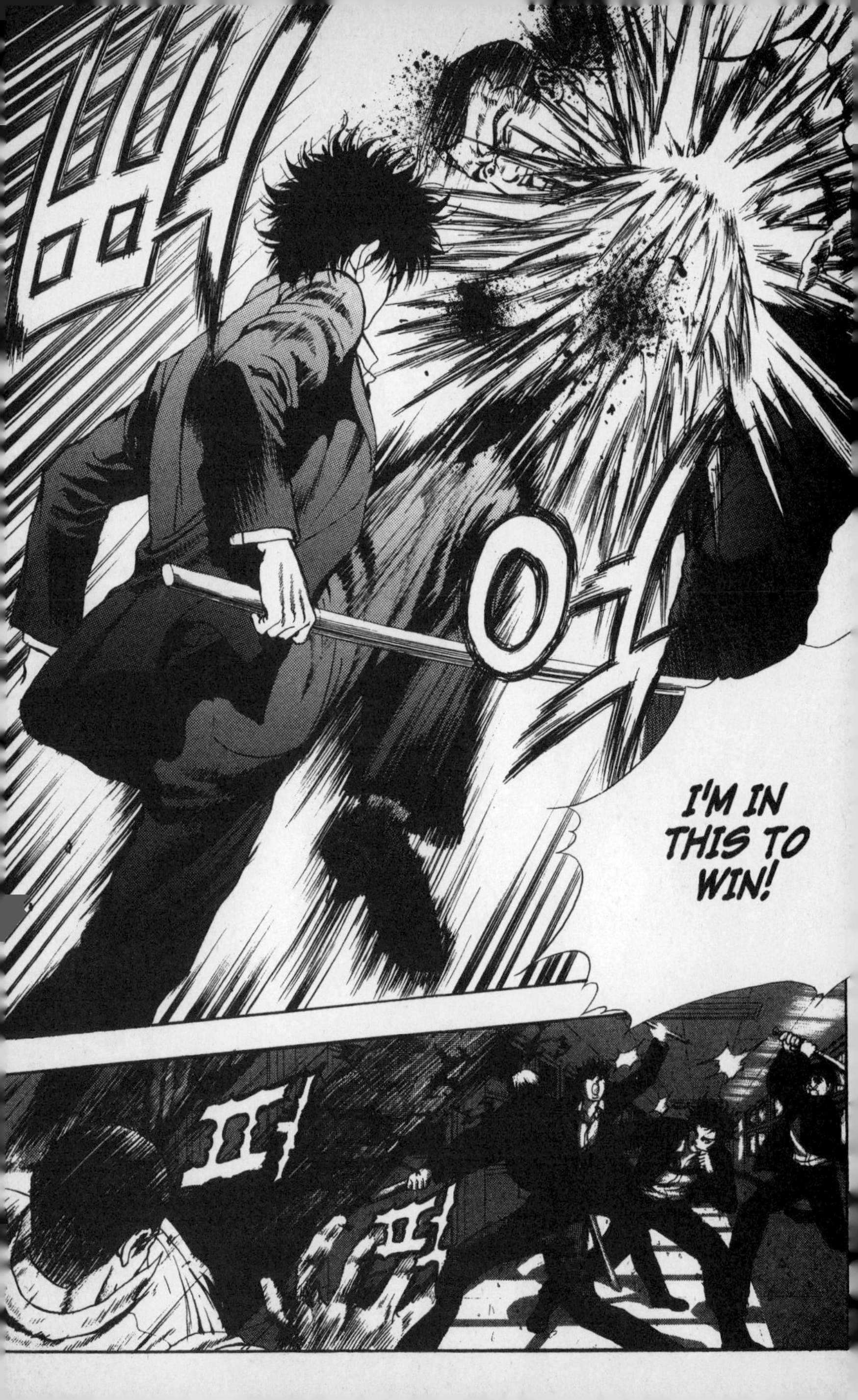
I'M IN THIS TO WIN!

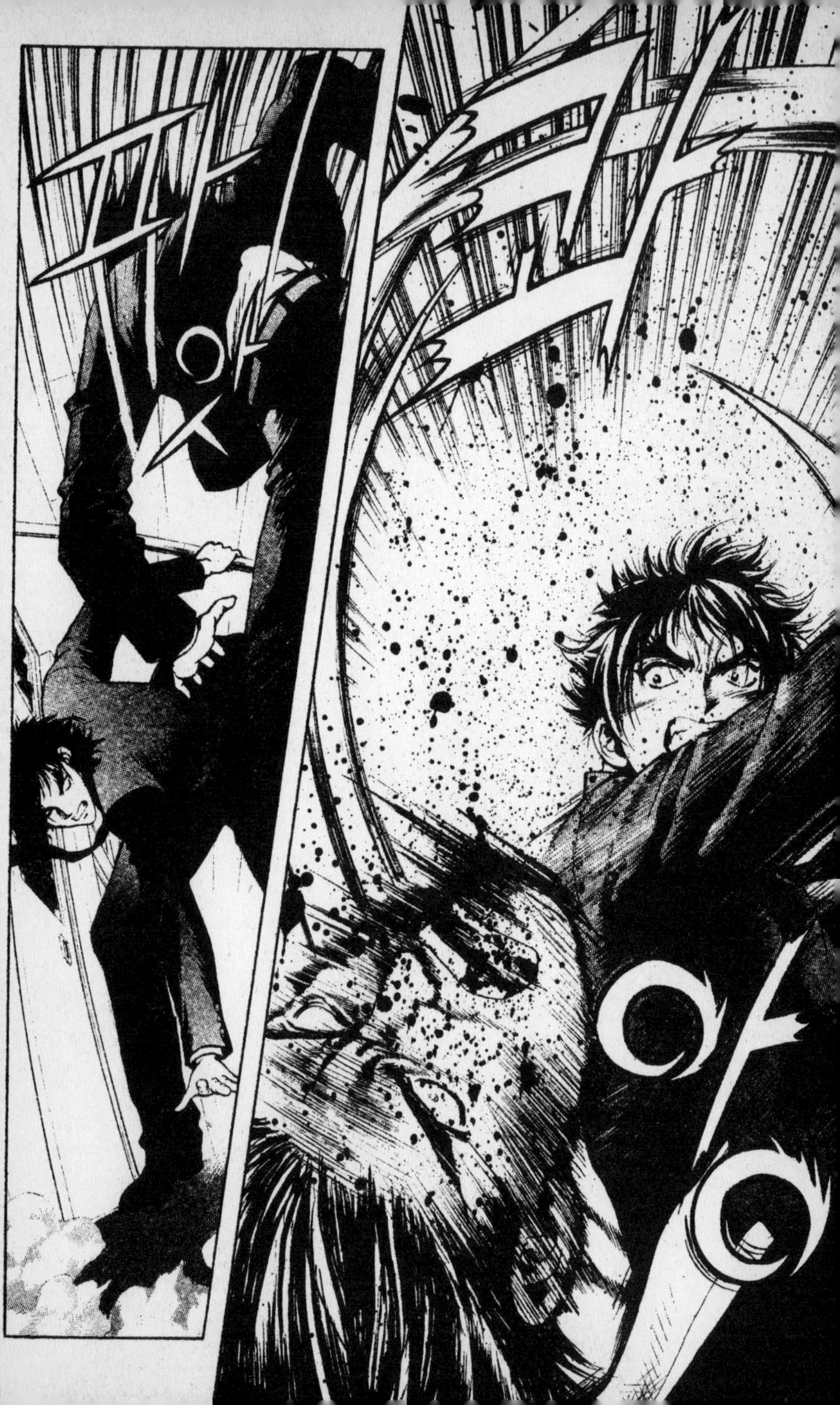

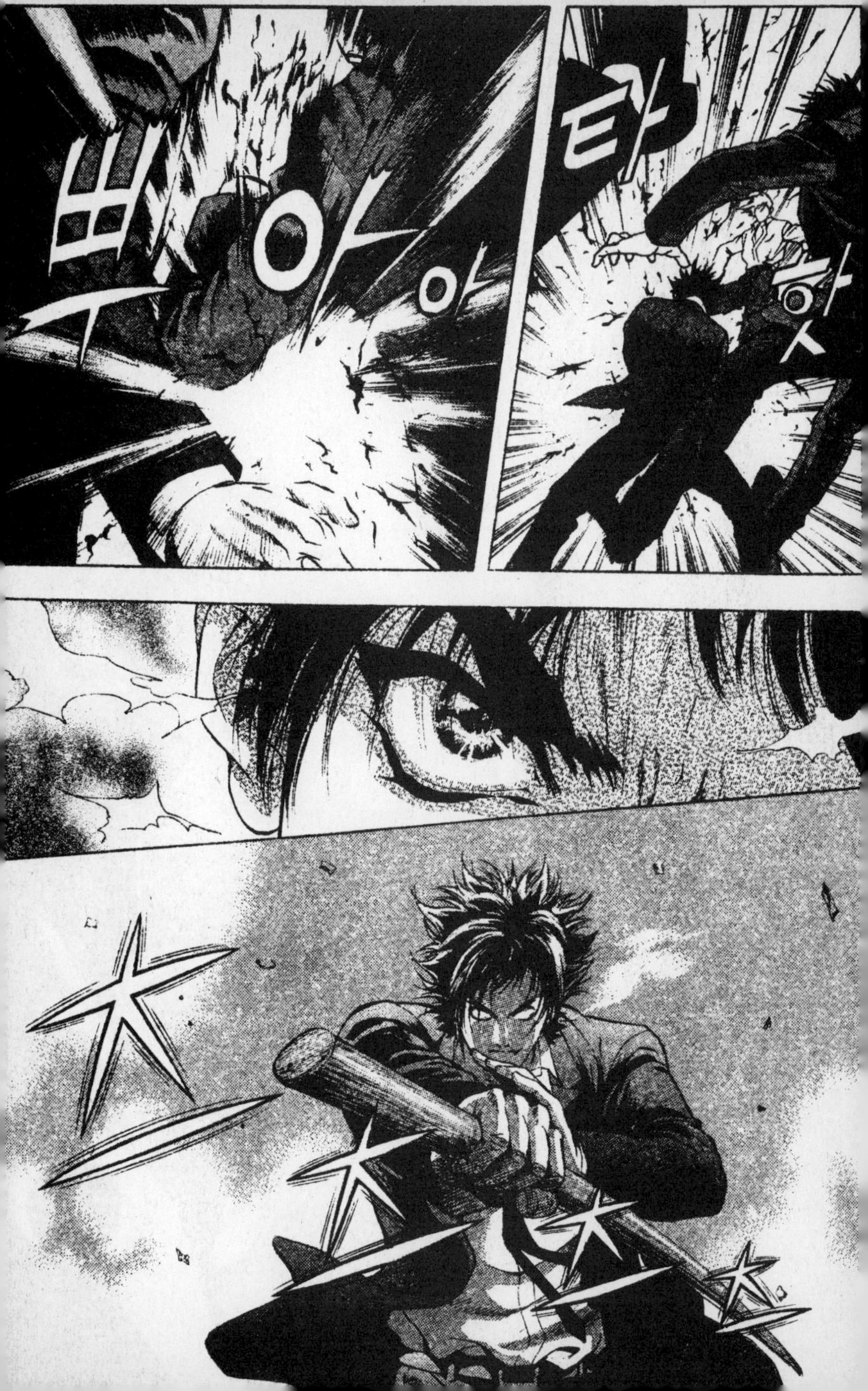
타앗
뿌아아

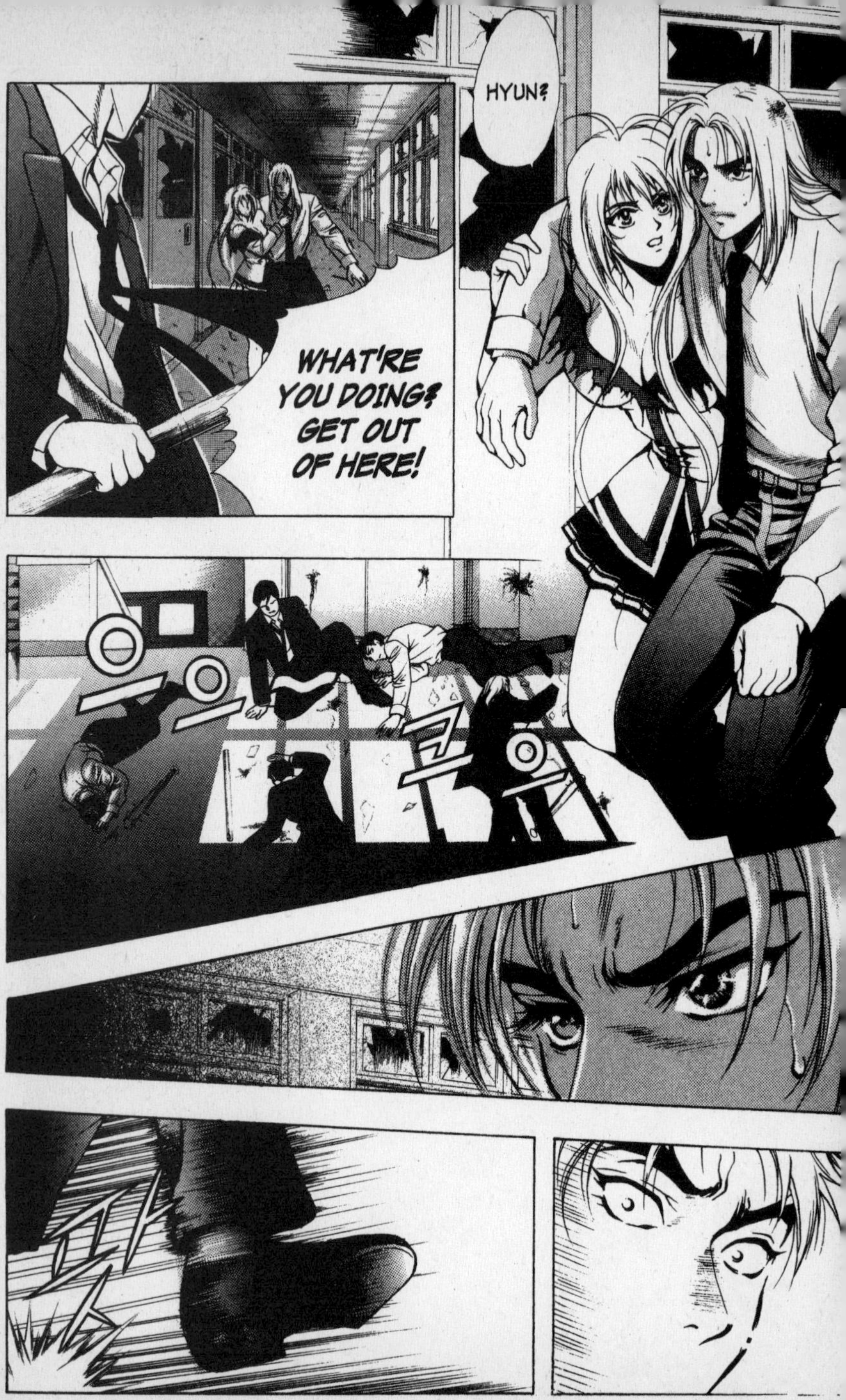
HYUN?
WHAT'RE YOU DOING? GET OUT OF HERE!

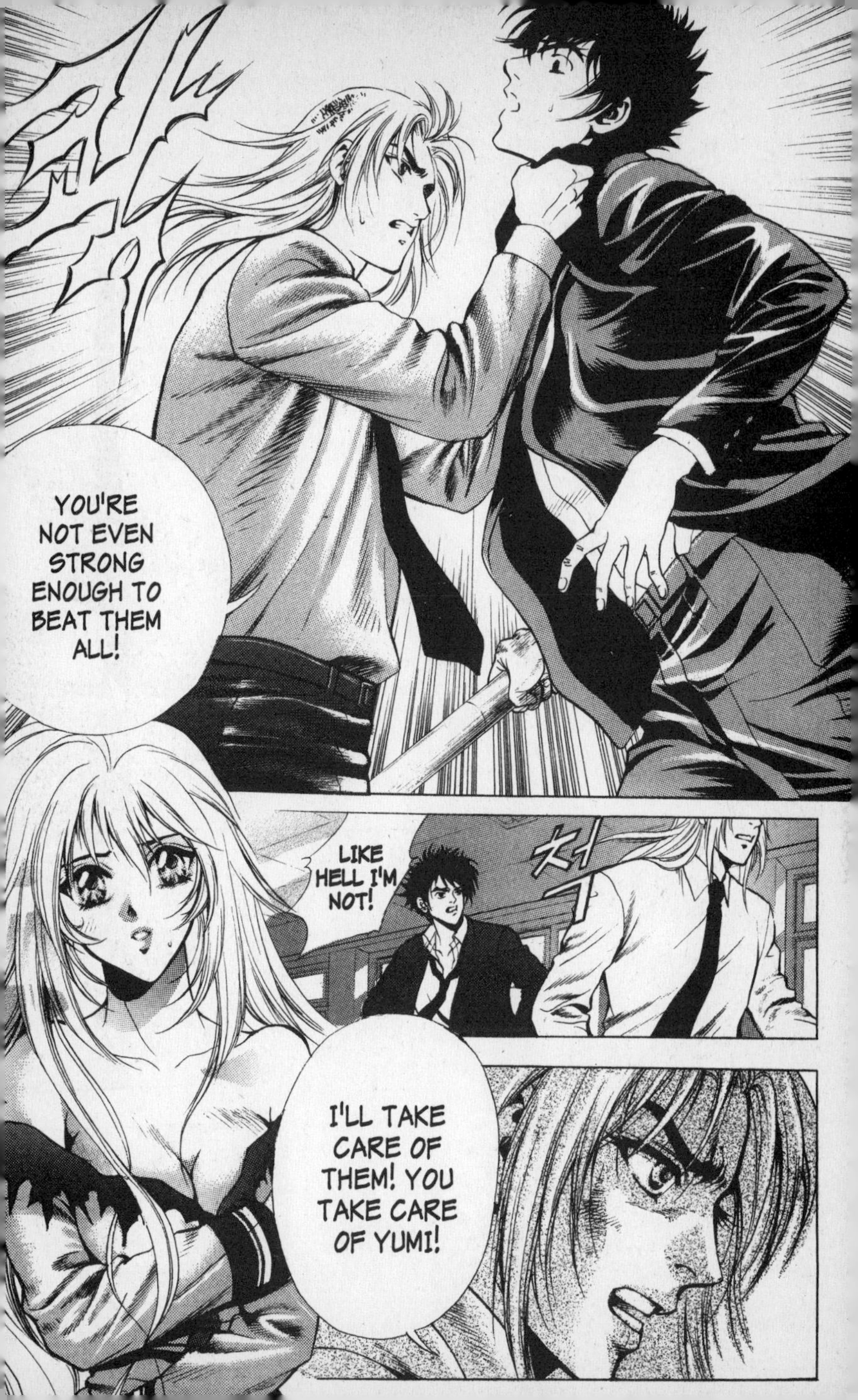
YOU'RE NOT EVEN STRONG ENOUGH TO BEAT THEM ALL!
LIKE HELL I'M NOT!
I'LL TAKE CARE OF THEM! YOU TAKE CARE OF YUMI!

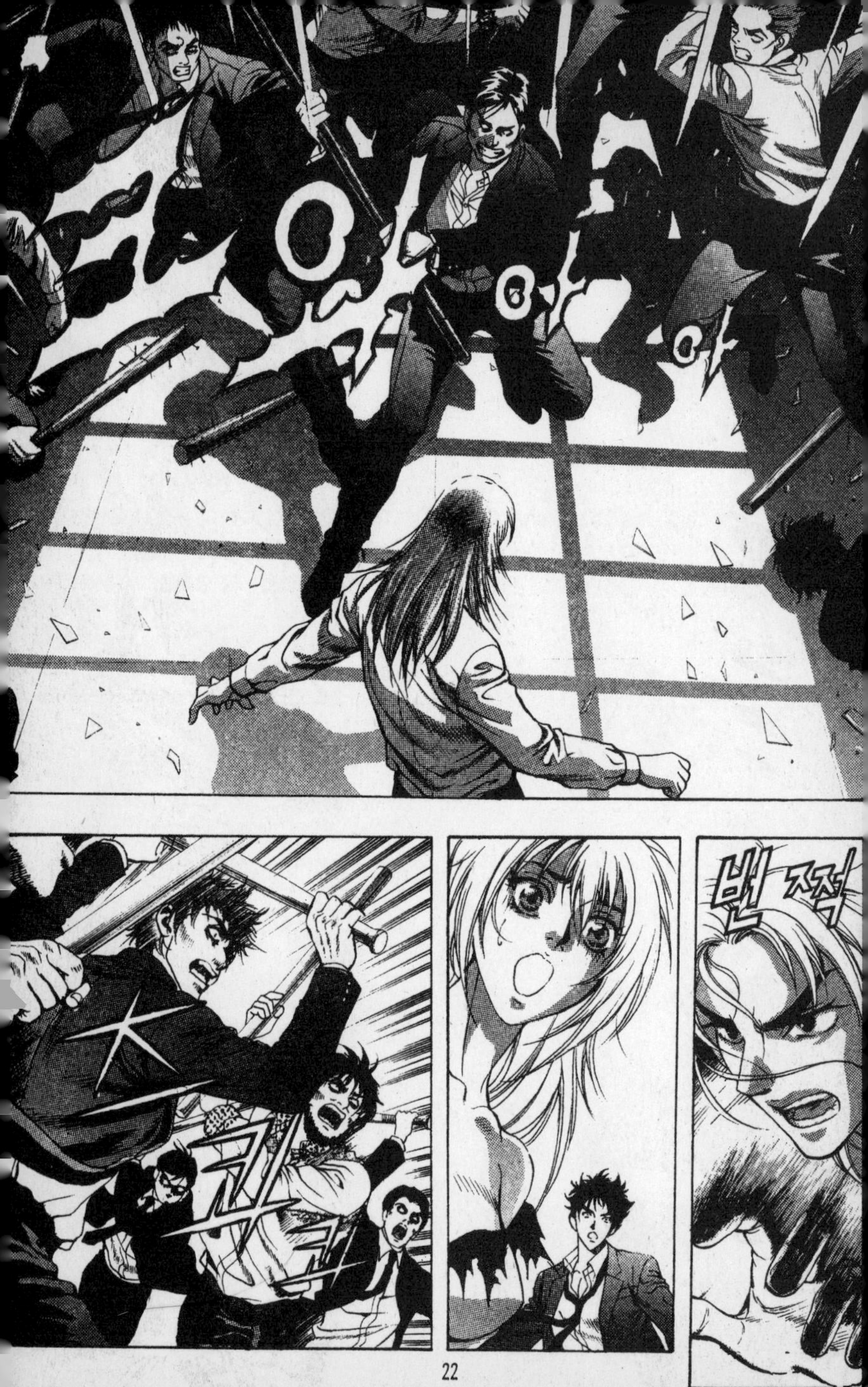
번쩍

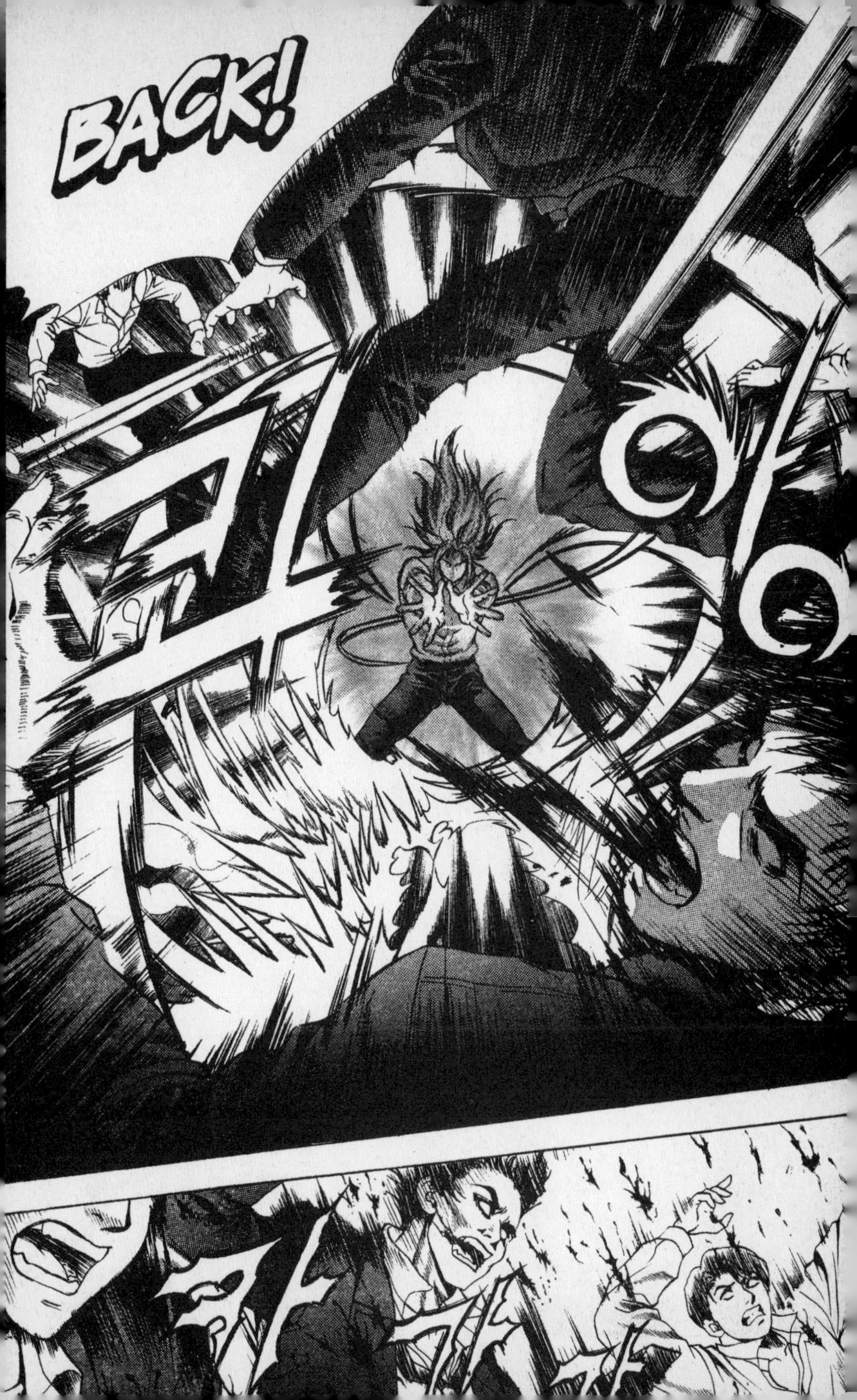

BACK!

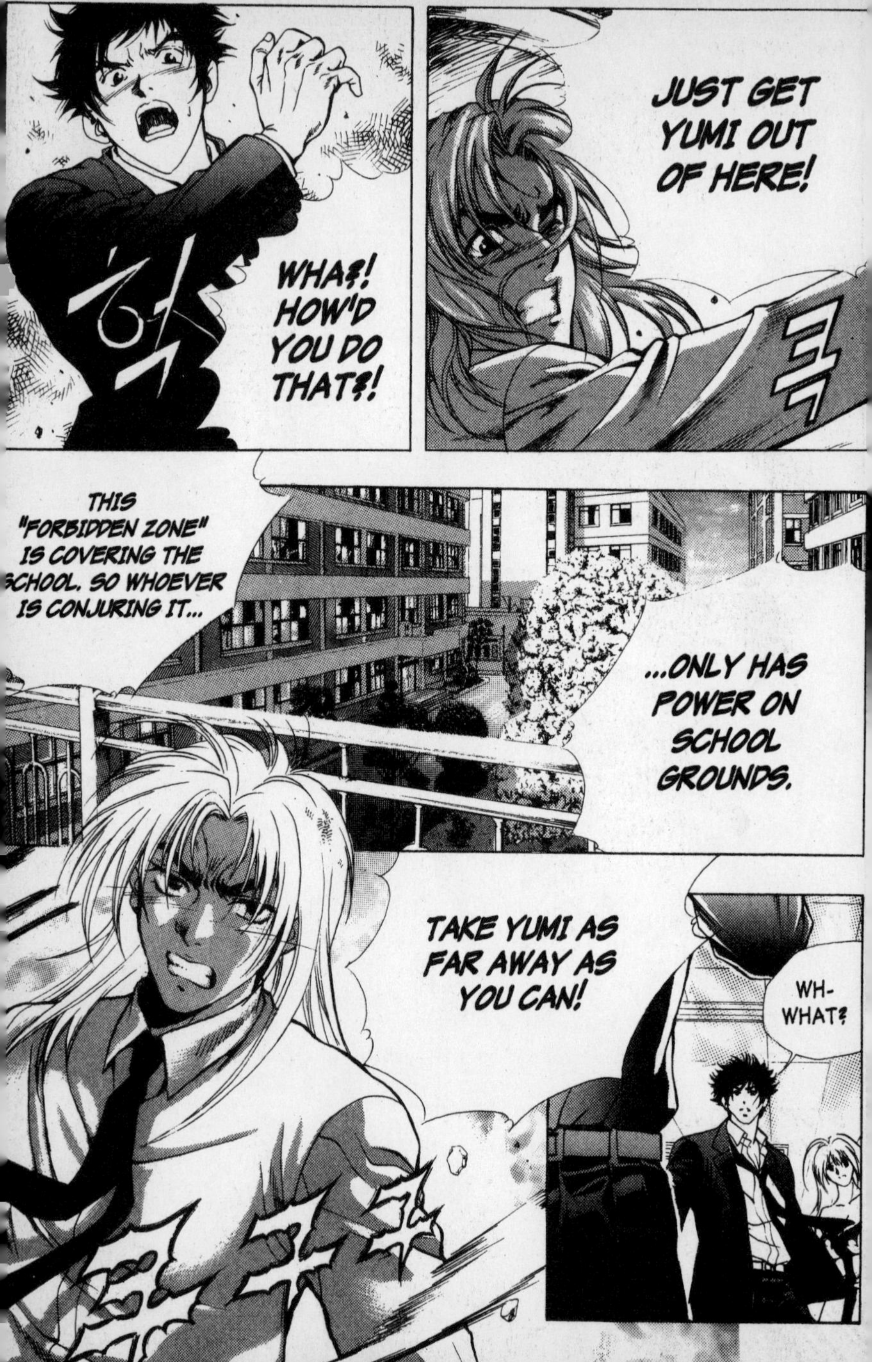
JUST GET YUMI OUT OF HERE!
WHA?! HOW'D YOU DO THAT?!
THIS "FORBIDDEN ZONE" IS COVERING THE SCHOOL. SO WHOEVER IS CONJURING IT...
...ONLY HAS POWER ON SCHOOL GROUNDS.
WH- WHAT?
TAKE YUMI AS FAR AWAY AS YOU CAN!

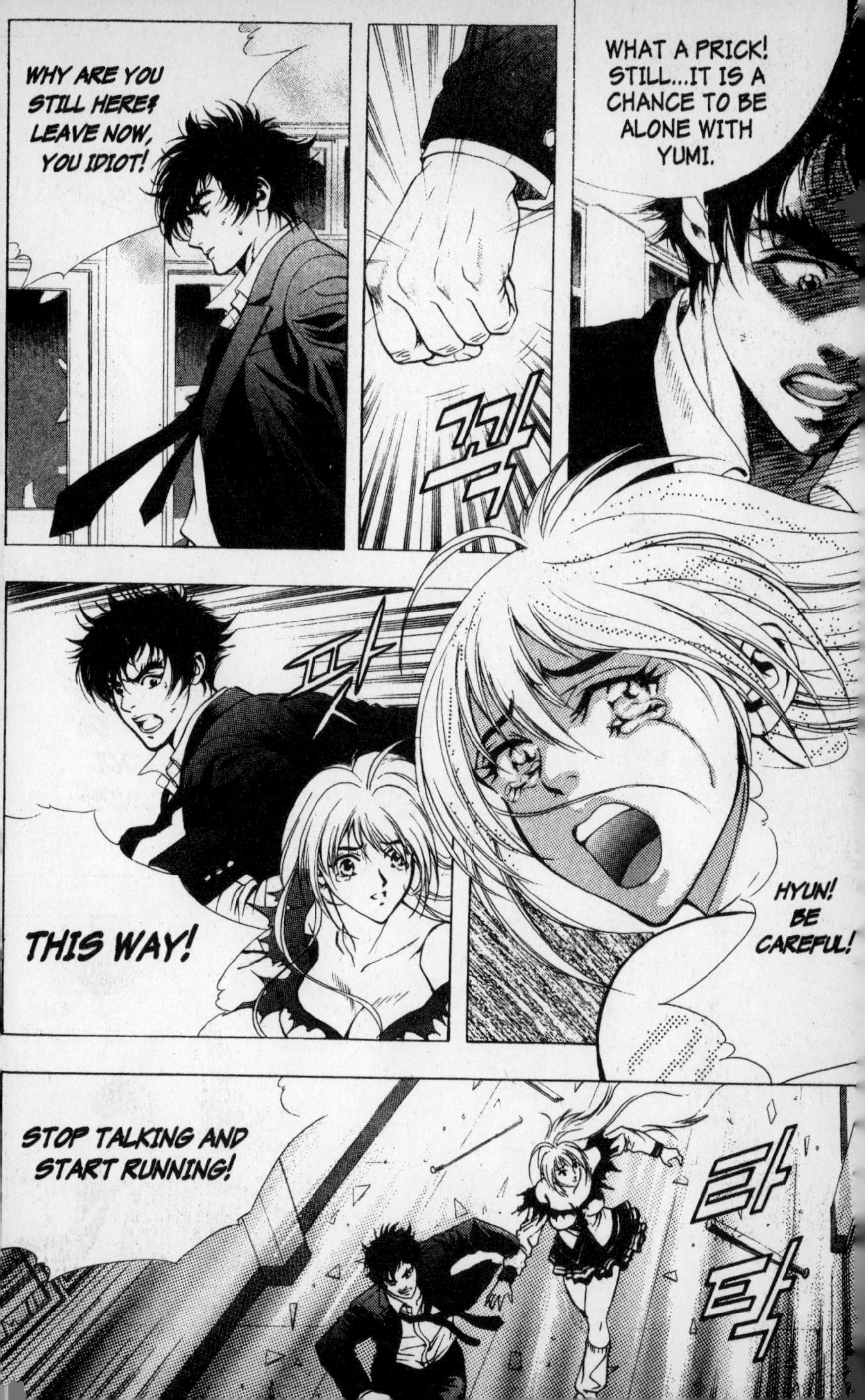
WHY ARE YOU STILL HERE? LEAVE NOW, YOU IDIOT!
WHAT A PRICK! STILL...IT IS A CHANCE TO BE ALONE WITH YUMI.
THIS WAY!
HYUN! BE CAREFUL!
STOP TALKING AND START RUNNING!

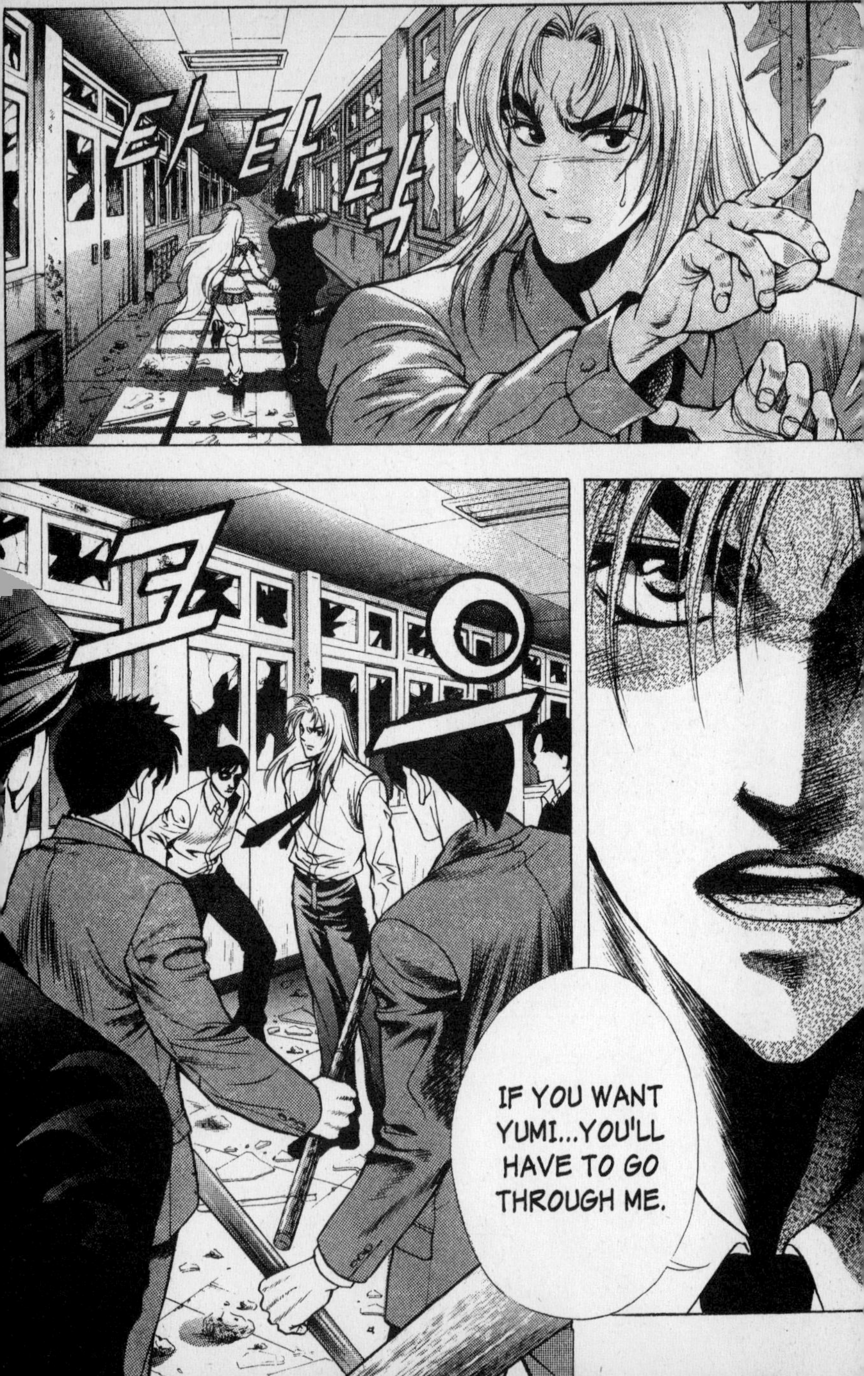
IF YOU WANT YUMI...YOU'LL HAVE TO GO THROUGH ME.

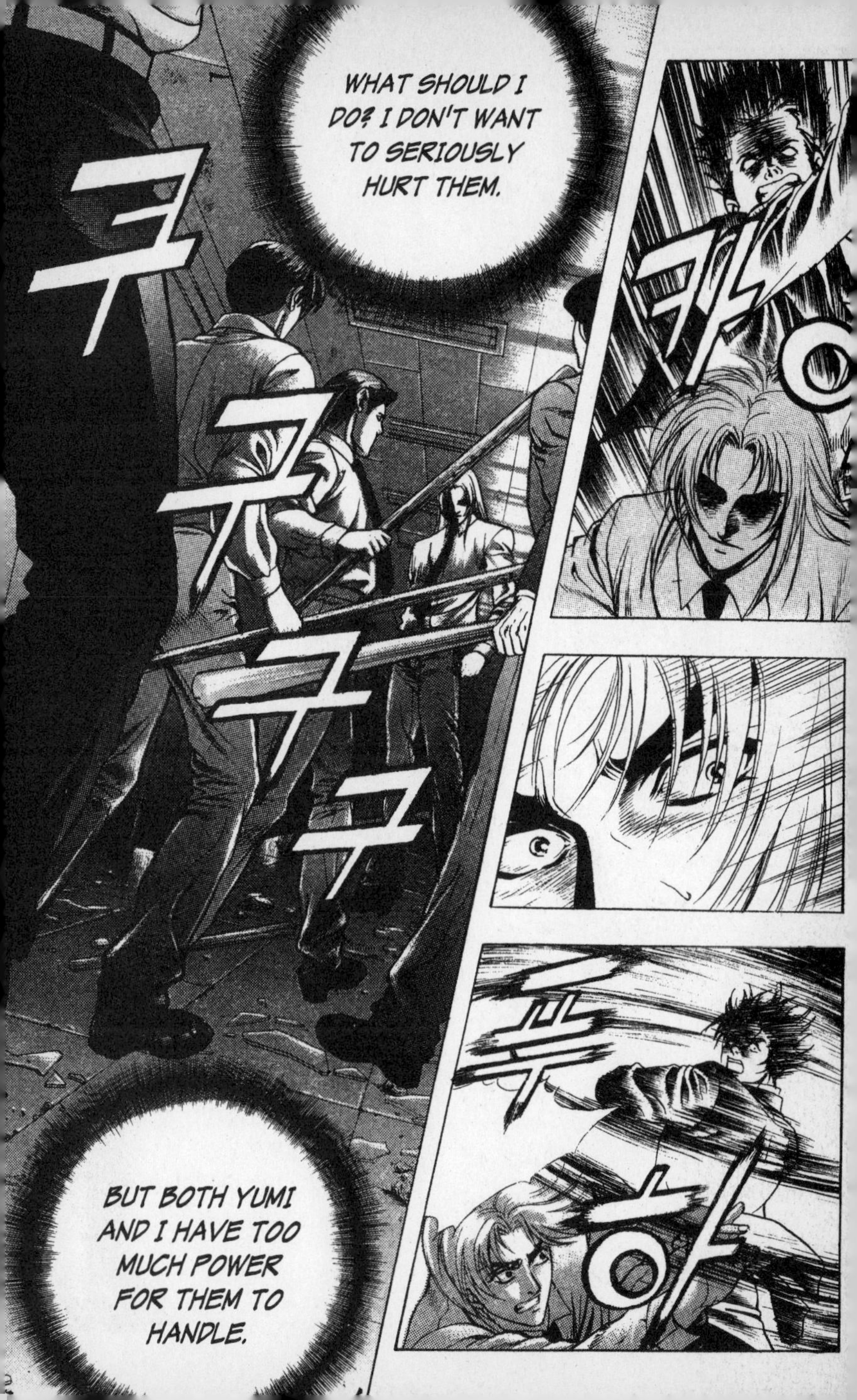
WHAT SHOULD I DO? I DON'T WANT TO SERIOUSLY HURT THEM.
BUT BOTH YUMI AND I HAVE TOO MUCH POWER FOR THEM TO HANDLE.

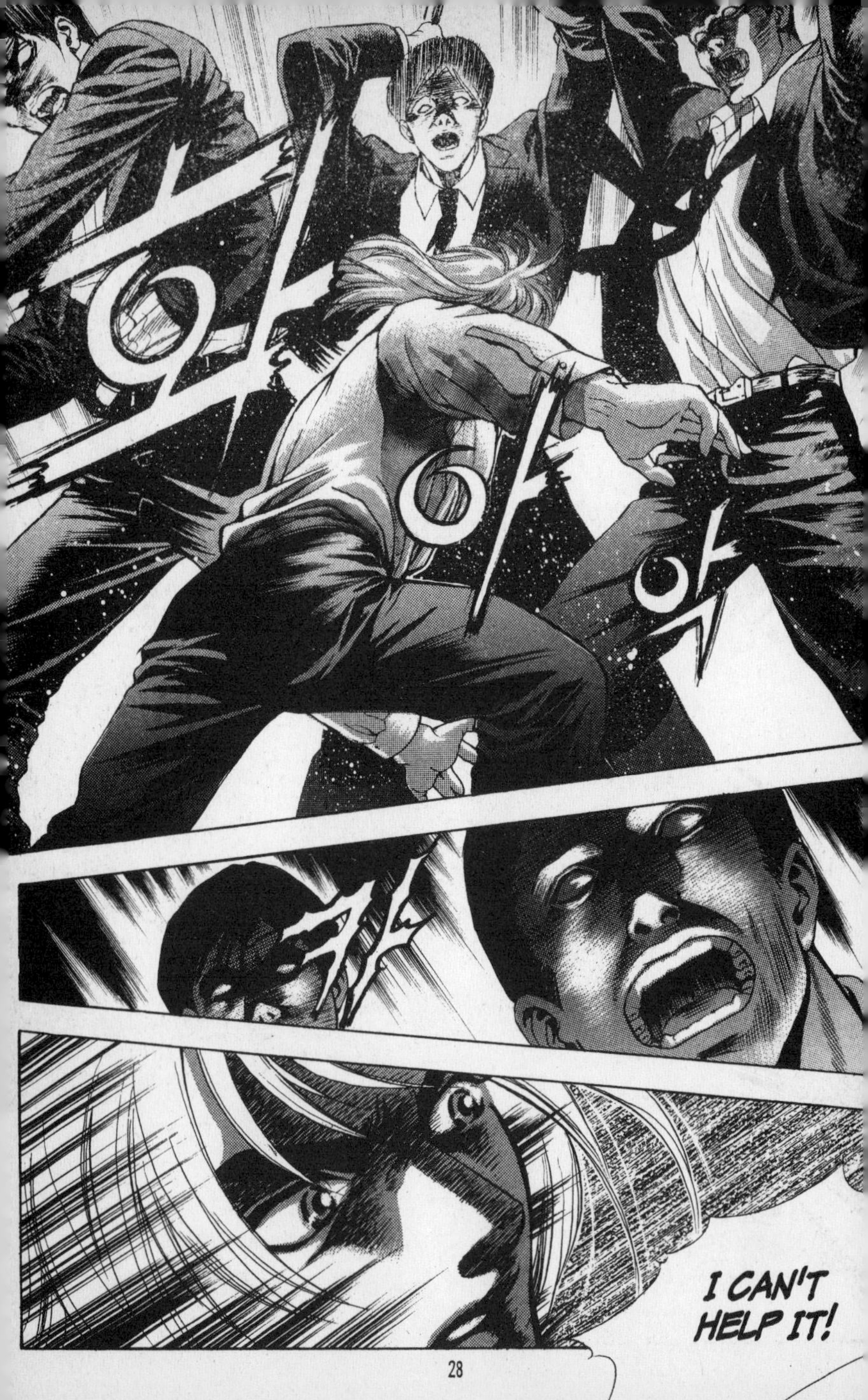
I CAN'T HELP IT!

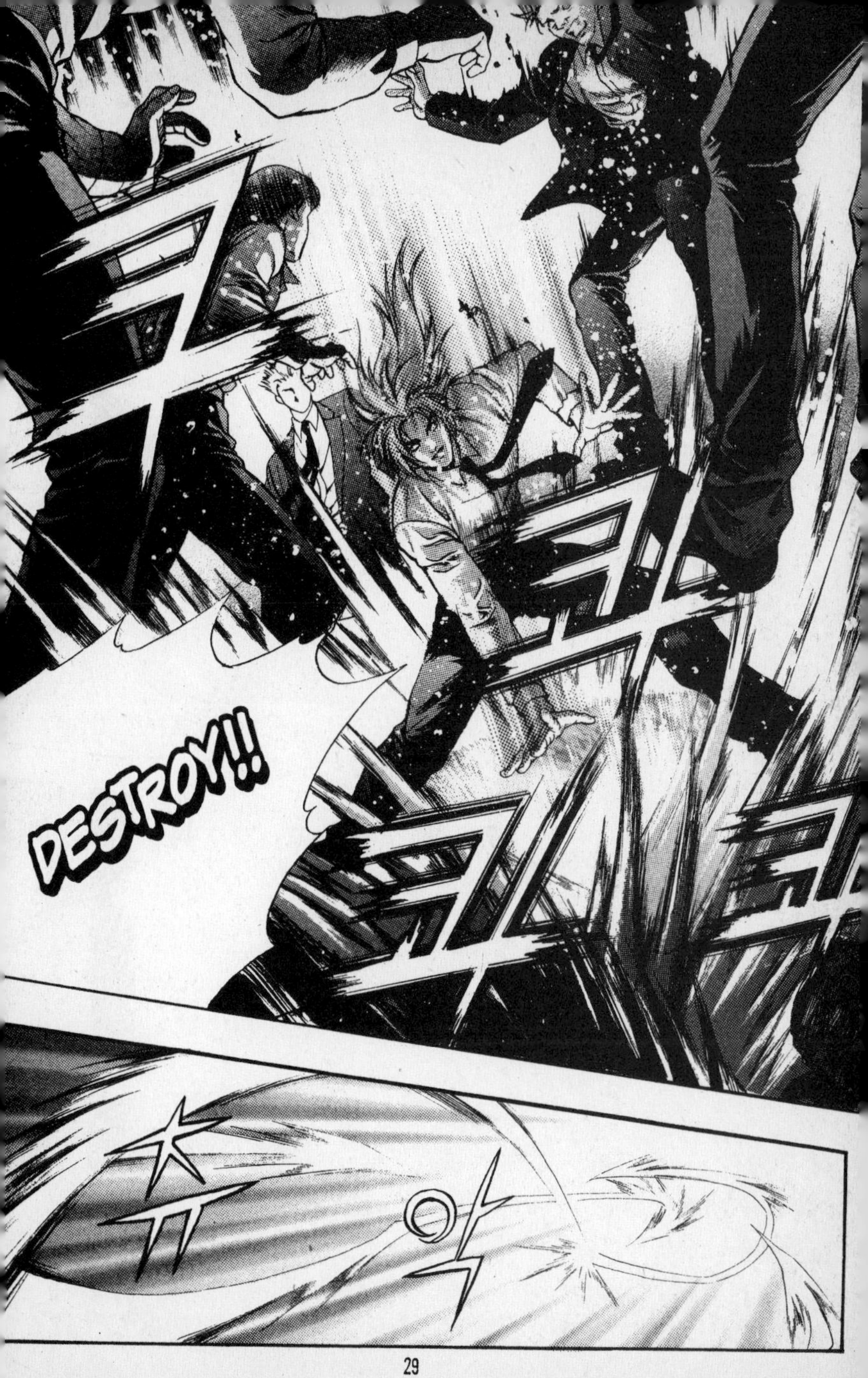
DESTROY!!

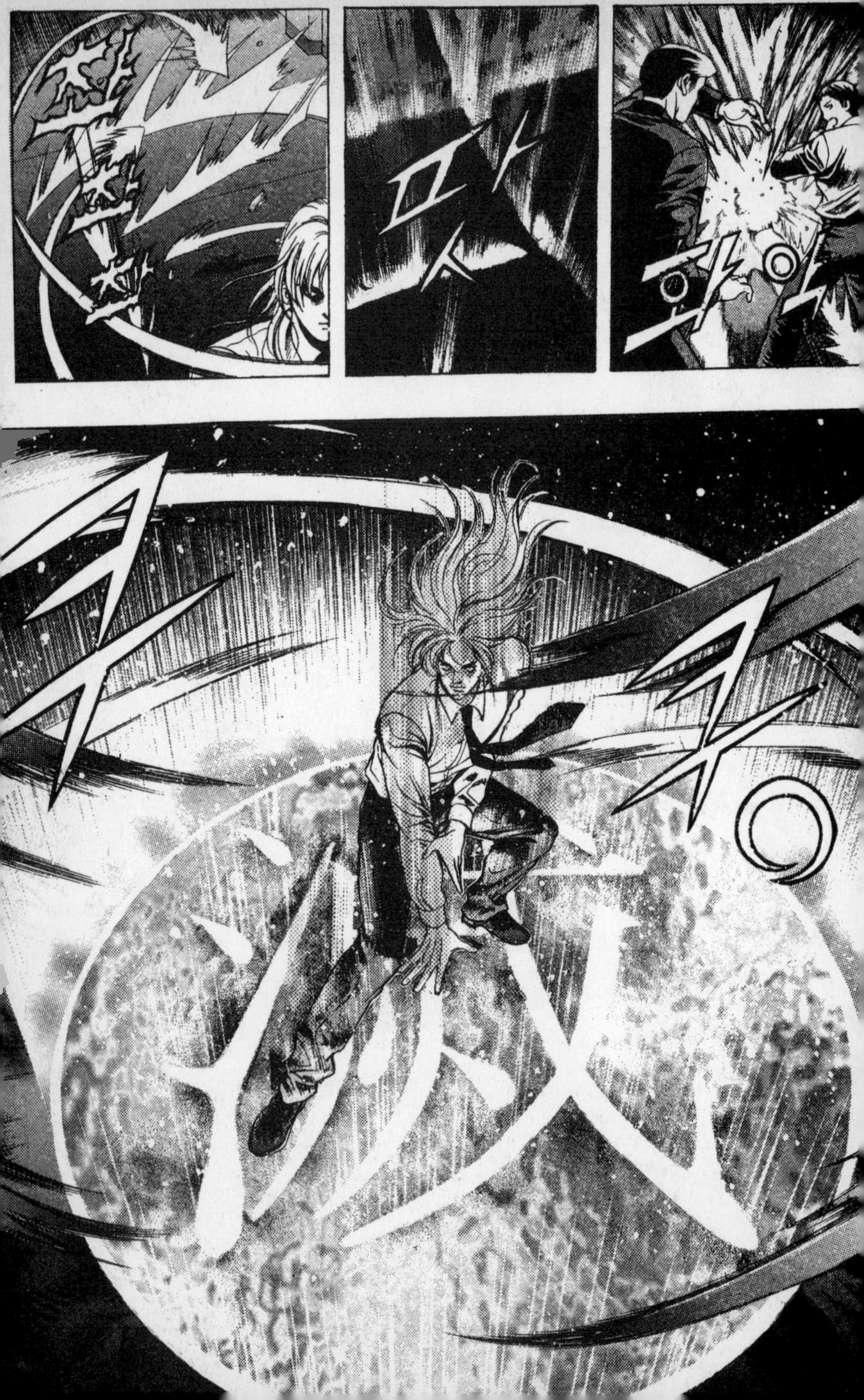

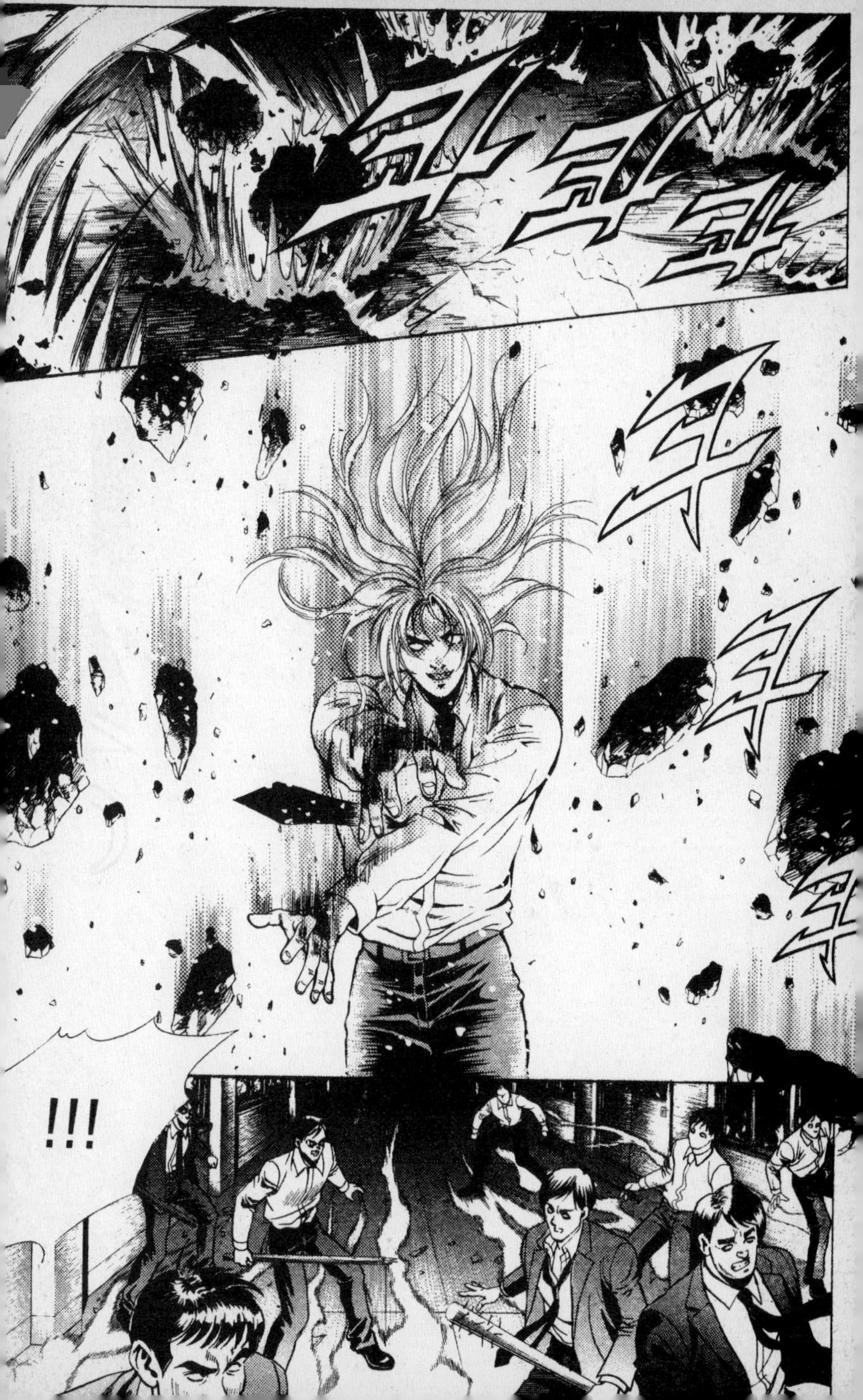
!!!

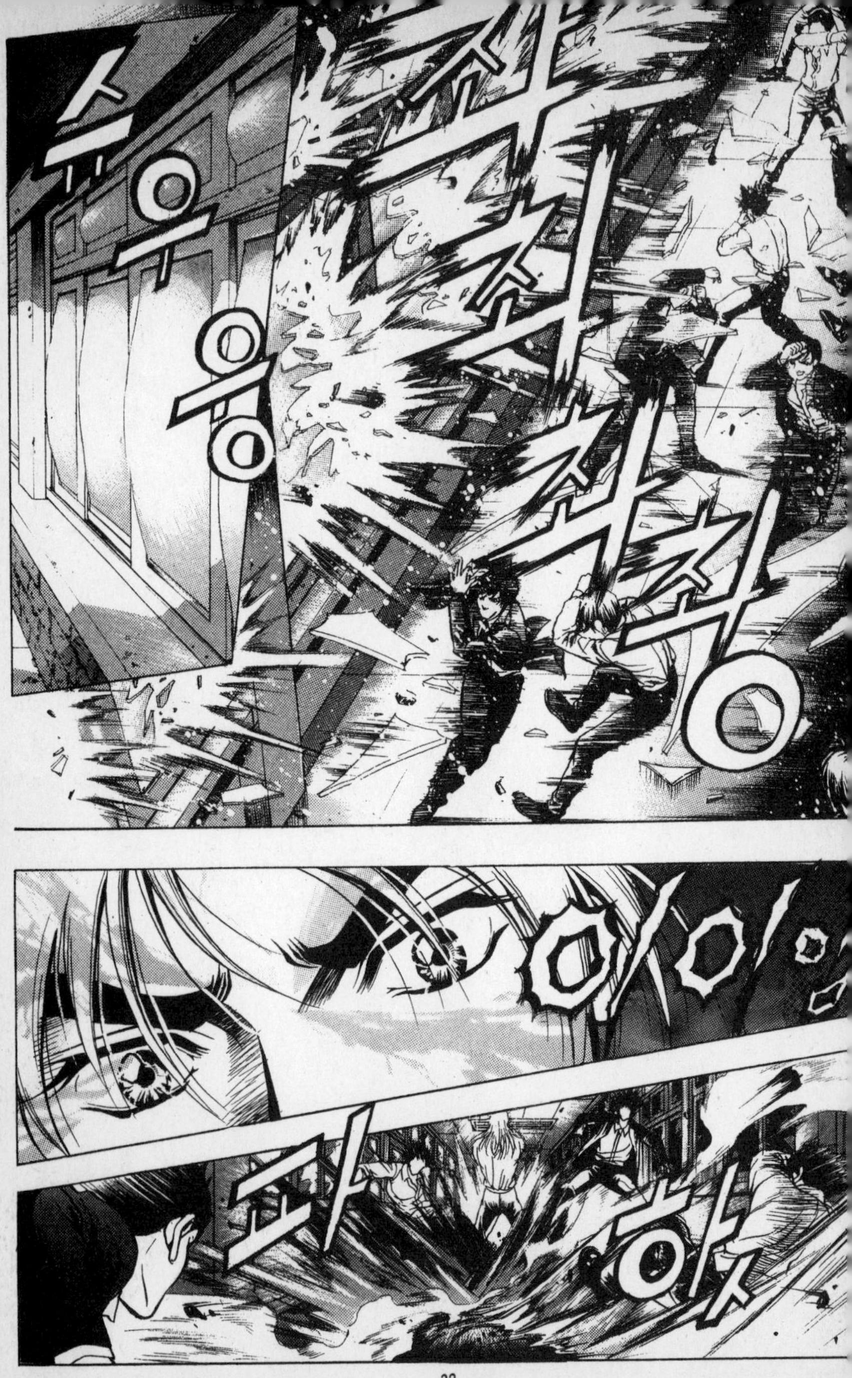
아아!?

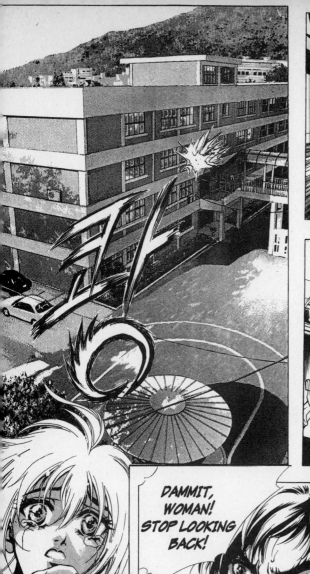

DAMMIT, WOMAN! STOP LOOKING BACK!

HYUN!

HURRY UP!

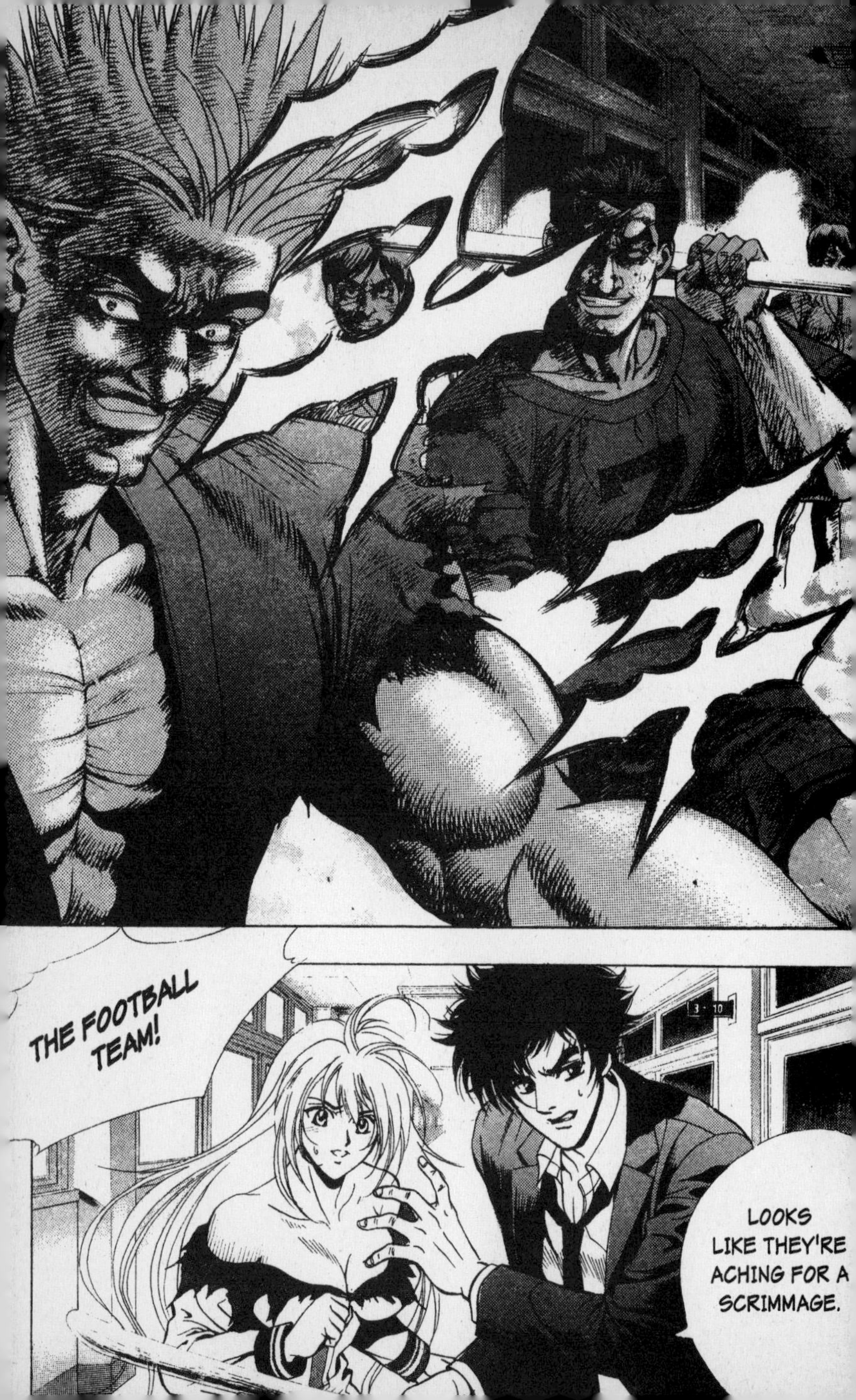
THE FOOTBALL TEAM!
LOOKS LIKE THEY'RE ACHING FOR A SCRIMMAGE.
3-10

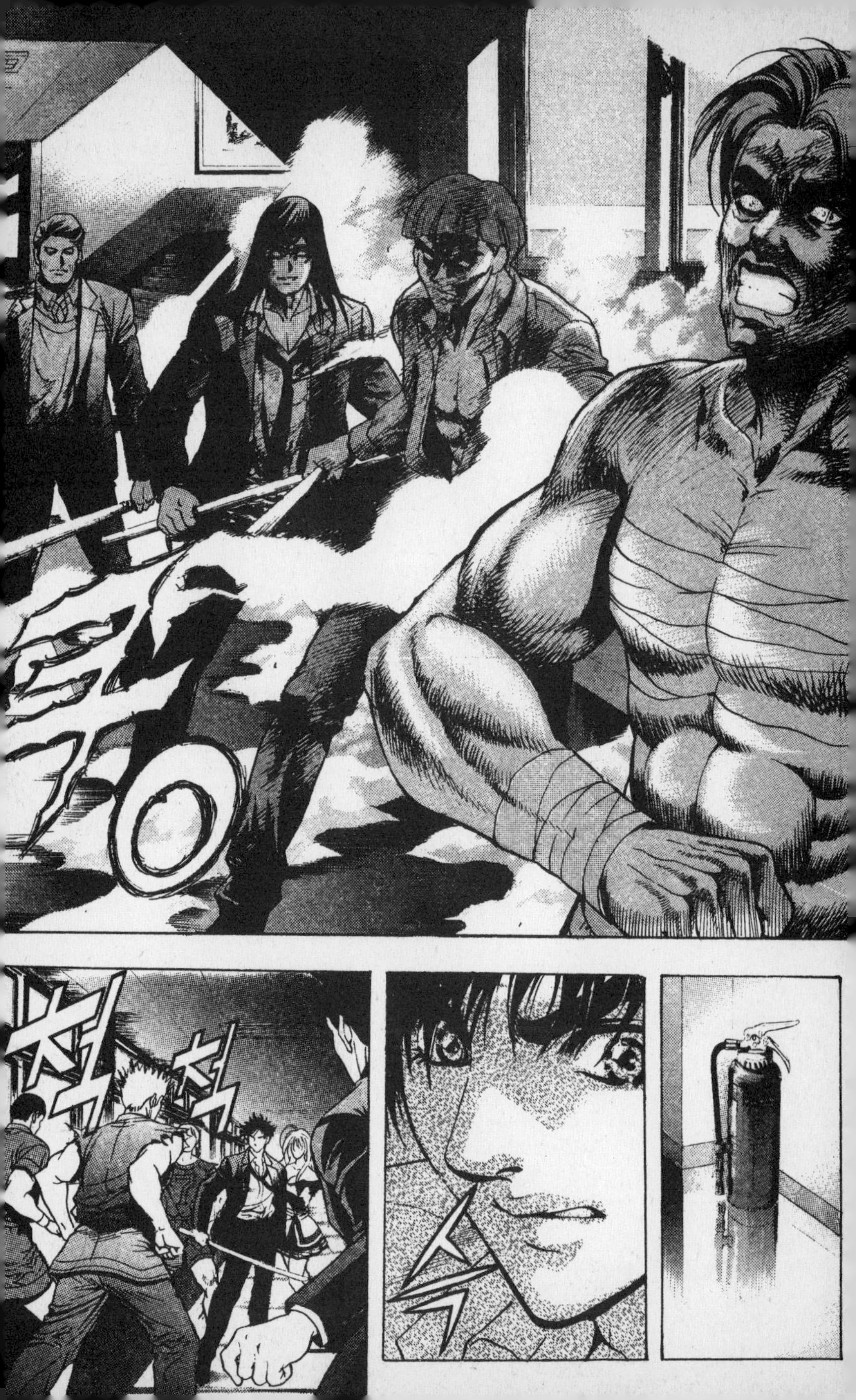

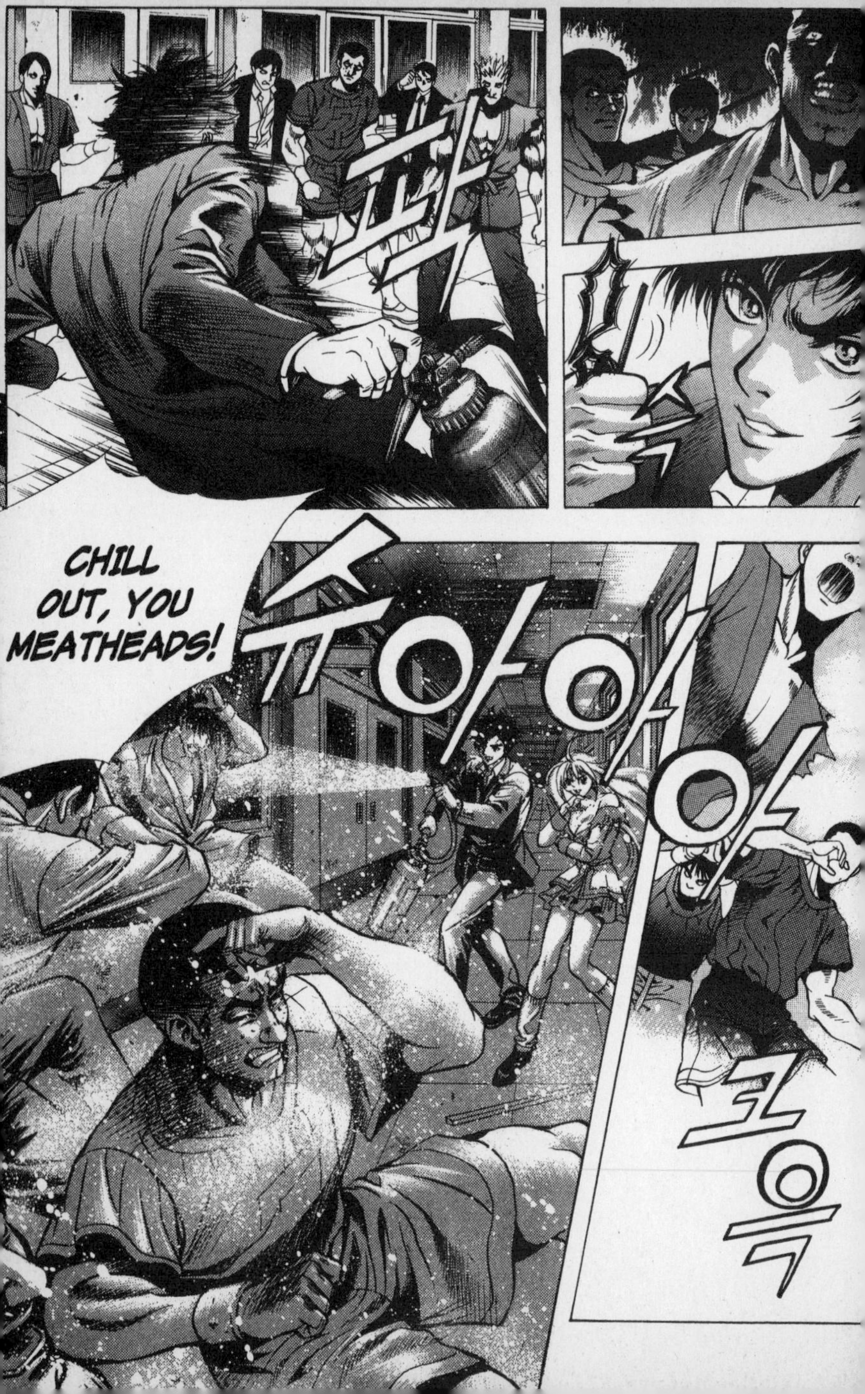
CHILL OUT, YOU MEATHEADS!

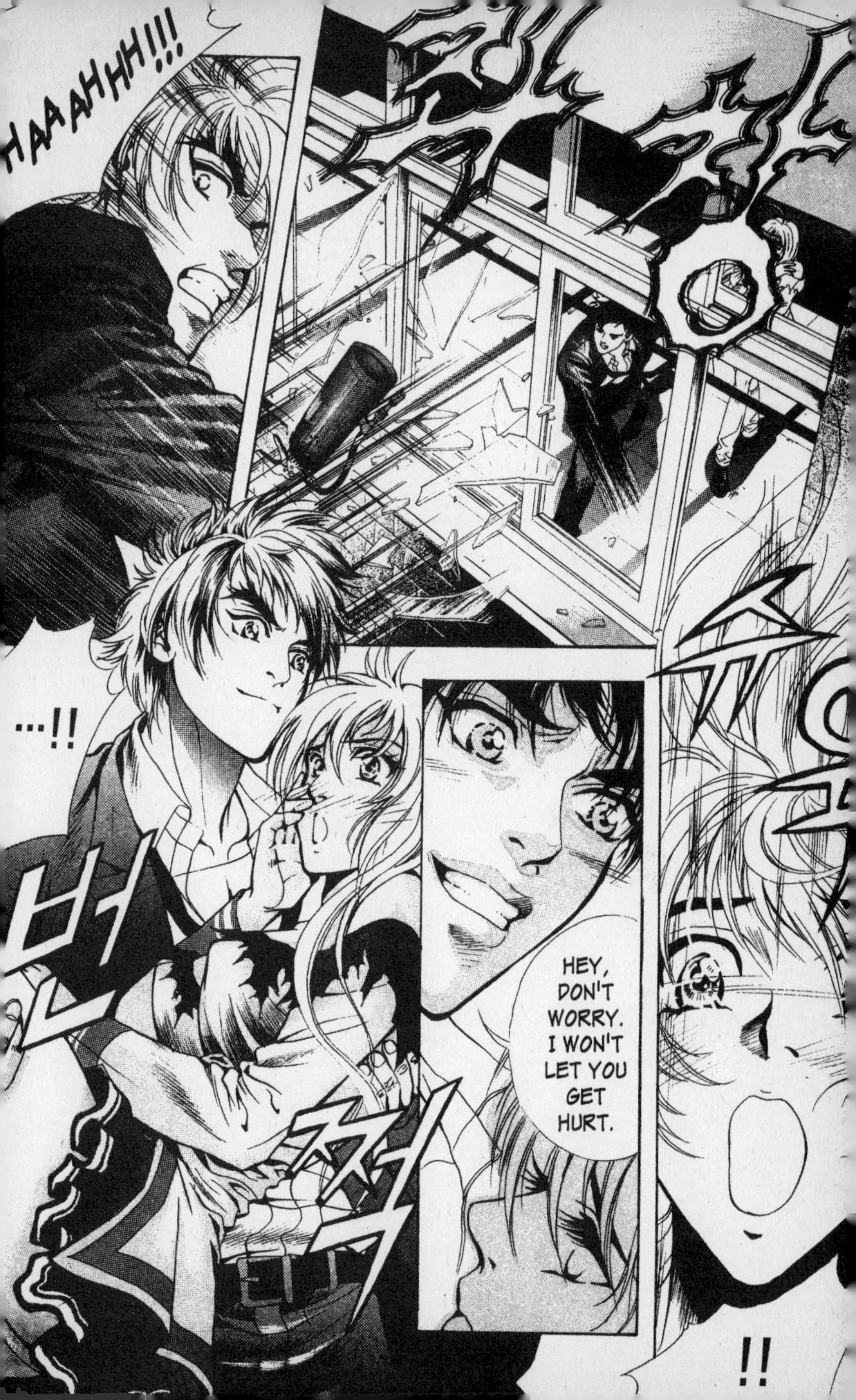
HAAAHHH!!!
...!!
HEY, DON'T WORRY. I WON'T LET YOU GET HURT.
!!

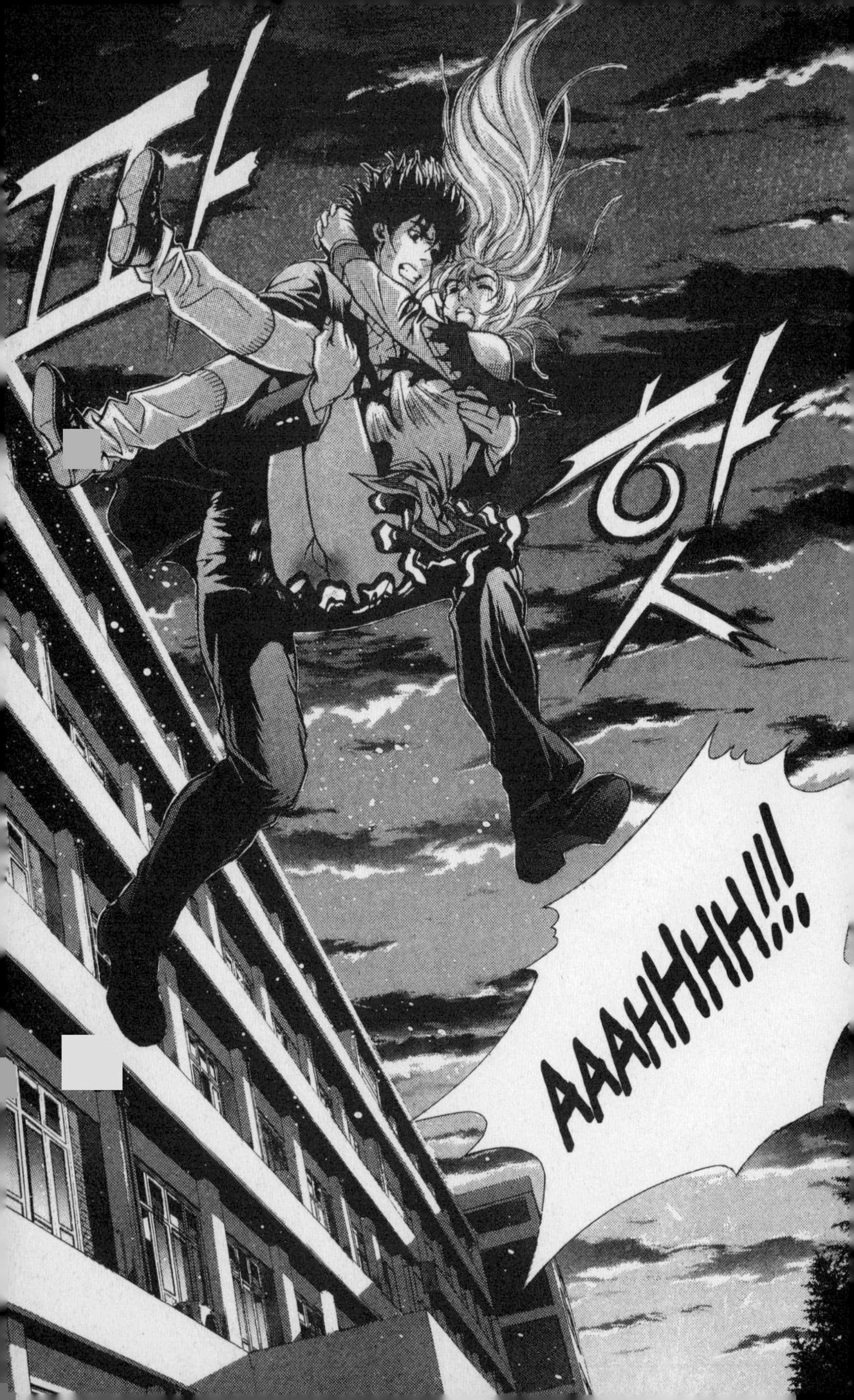
AAHHHH!!!

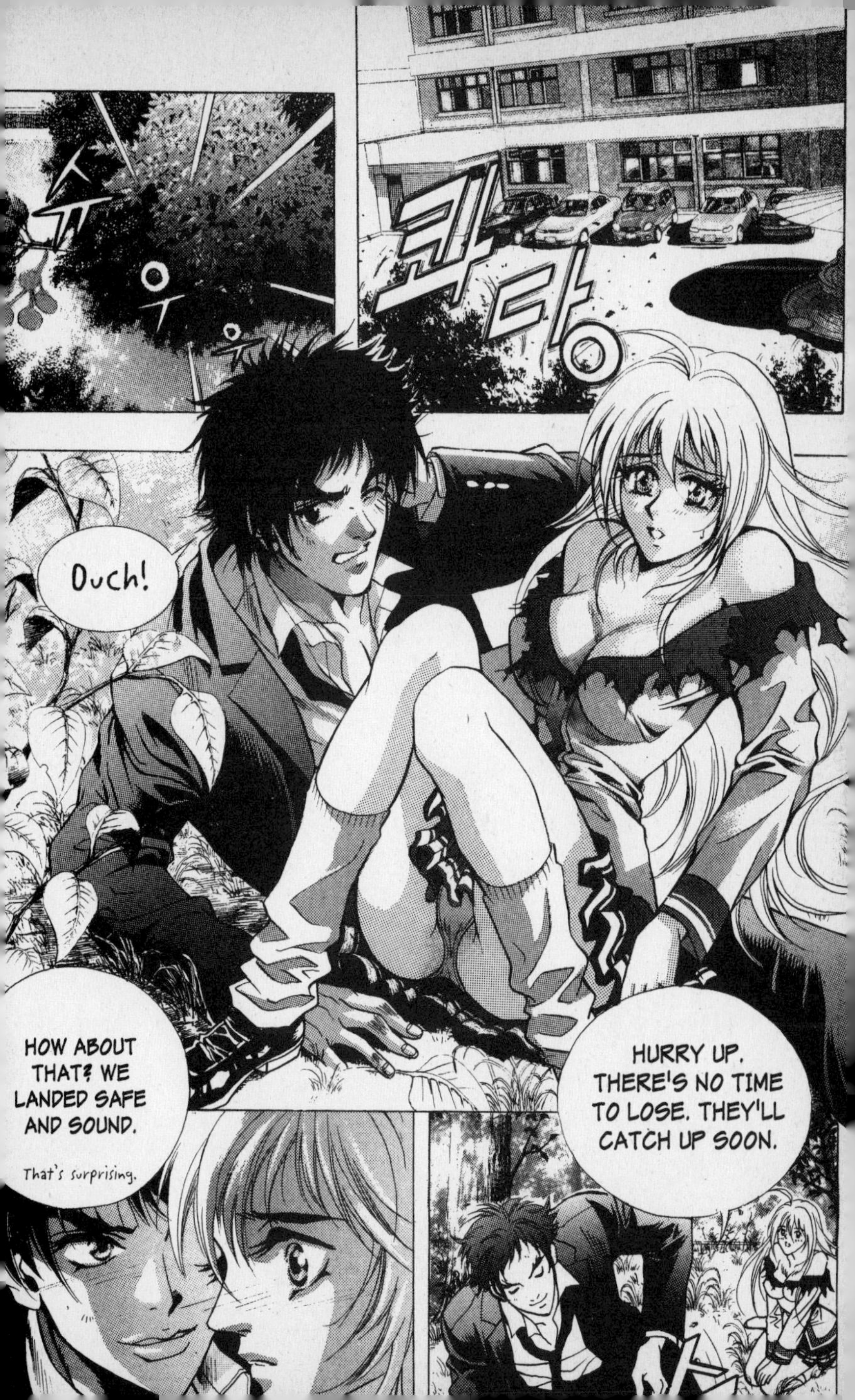
콰당
Ouch!
HOW ABOUT THAT? WE LANDED SAFE AND SOUND.
That's surprising.
HURRY UP. THERE'S NO TIME TO LOSE. THEY'LL CATCH UP SOON.

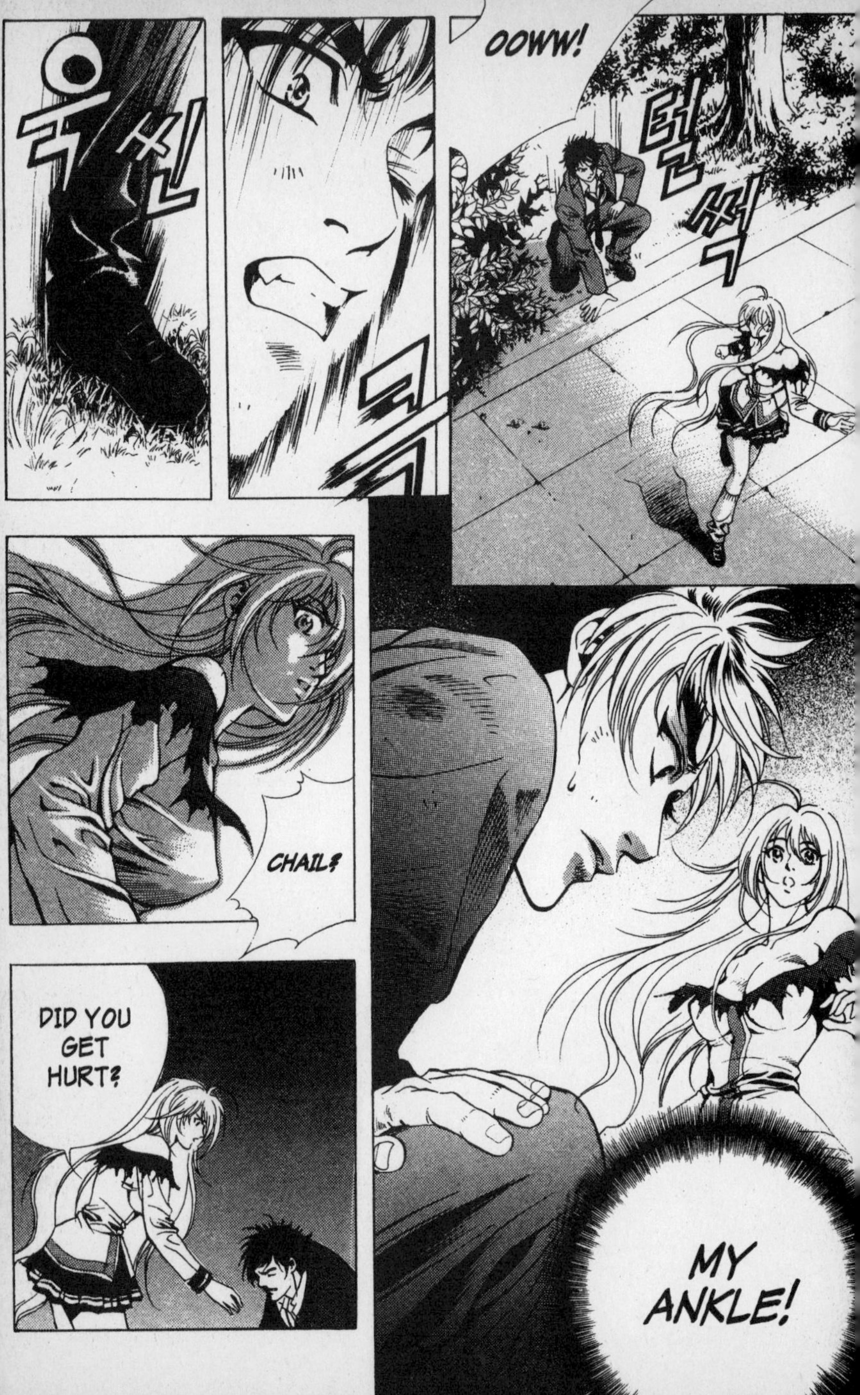

욱씬
OOWW!
털썩
CHAIL?
DID YOU GET HURT?
MY ANKLE!

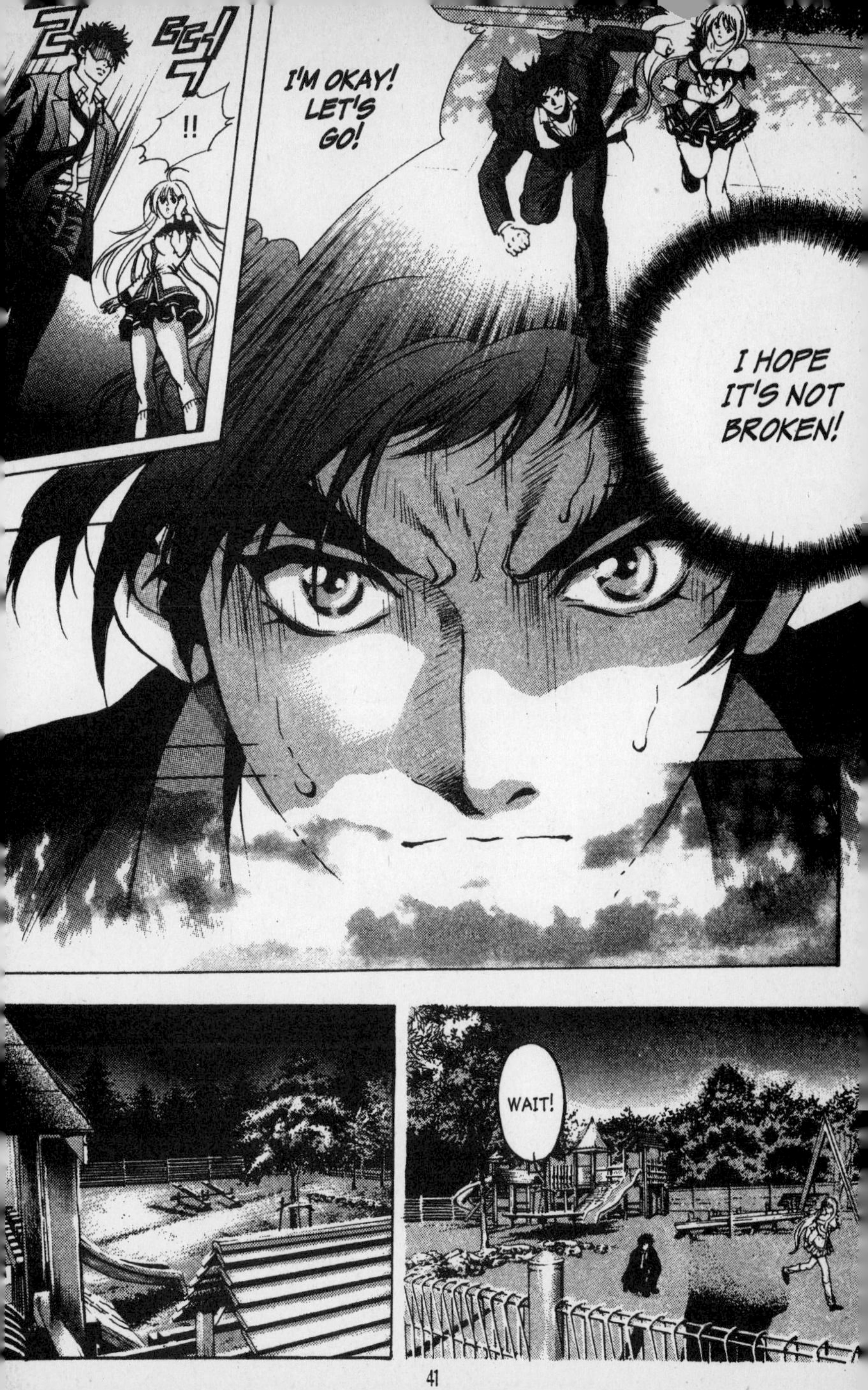
!!
I'M OKAY! LET'S GO!
I HOPE IT'S NOT BROKEN!
WAIT!

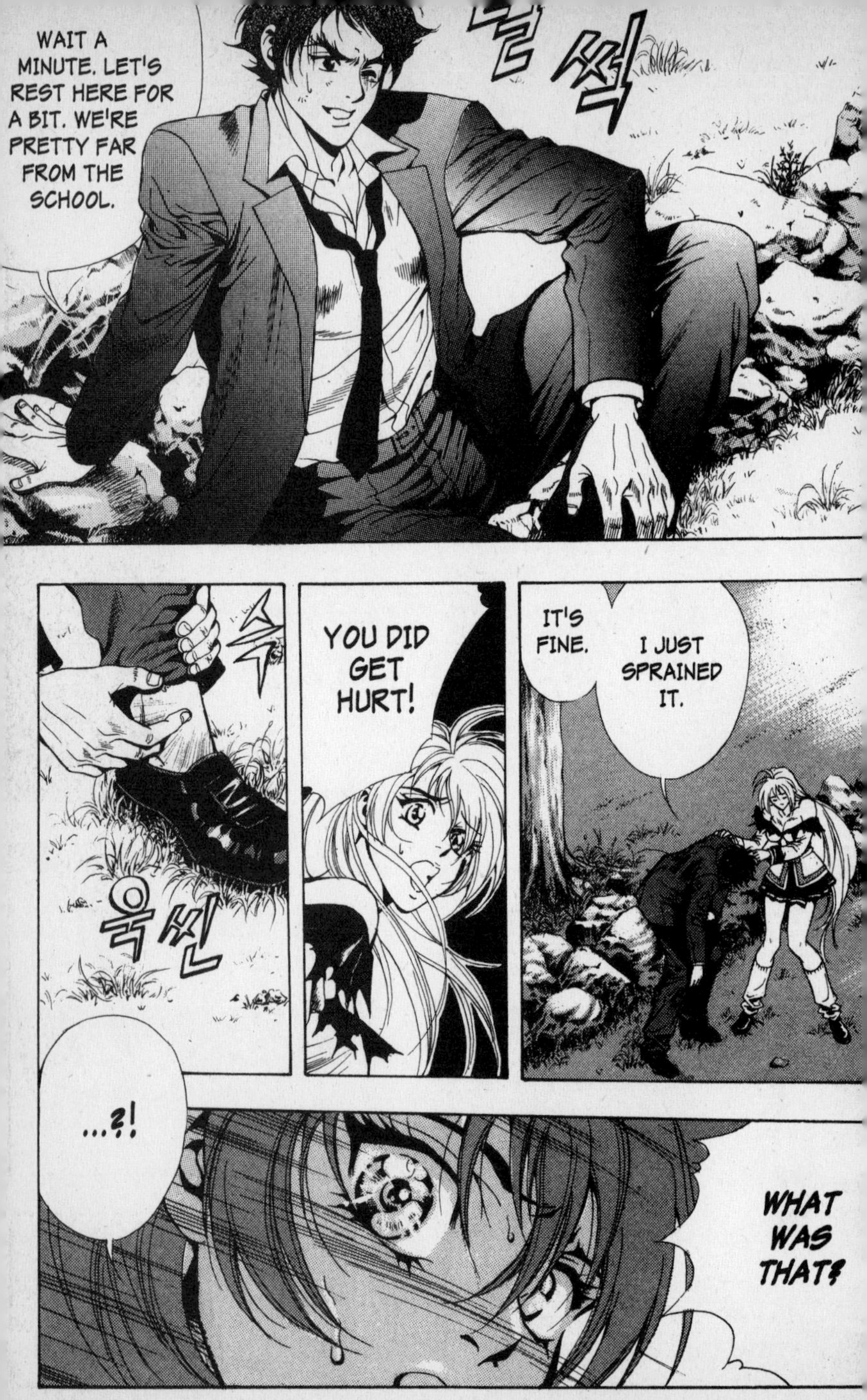

WAIT A MINUTE. LET'S REST HERE FOR A BIT. WE'RE PRETTY FAR FROM THE SCHOOL.
털썩
YOU DID GET HURT!
IT'S FINE.
I JUST SPRAINED IT.
...?!
WHAT WAS THAT?

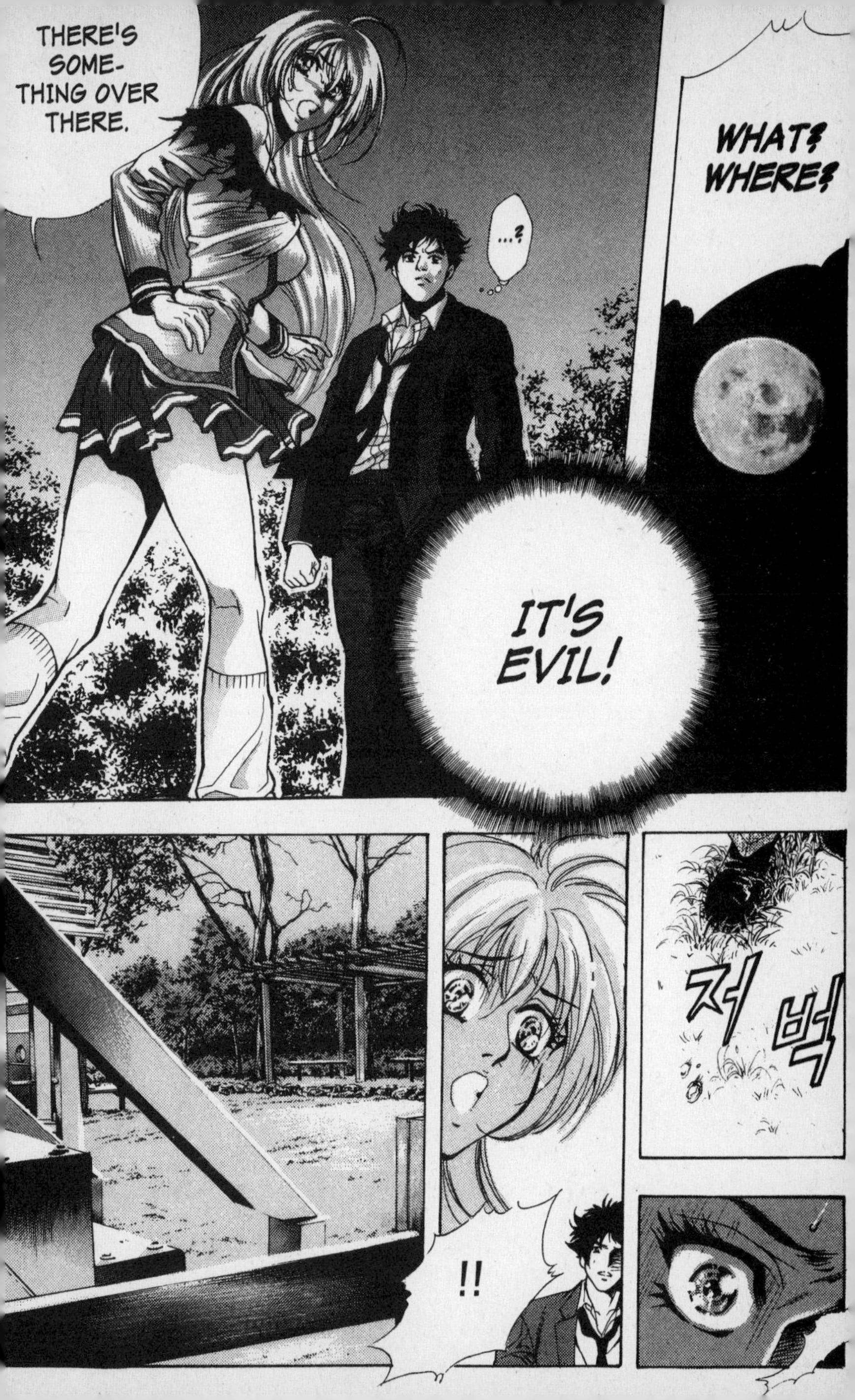
WHAT? WHERE?
THERE'S SOME-THING OVER THERE.
...?
IT'S EVIL!
저벅
!!

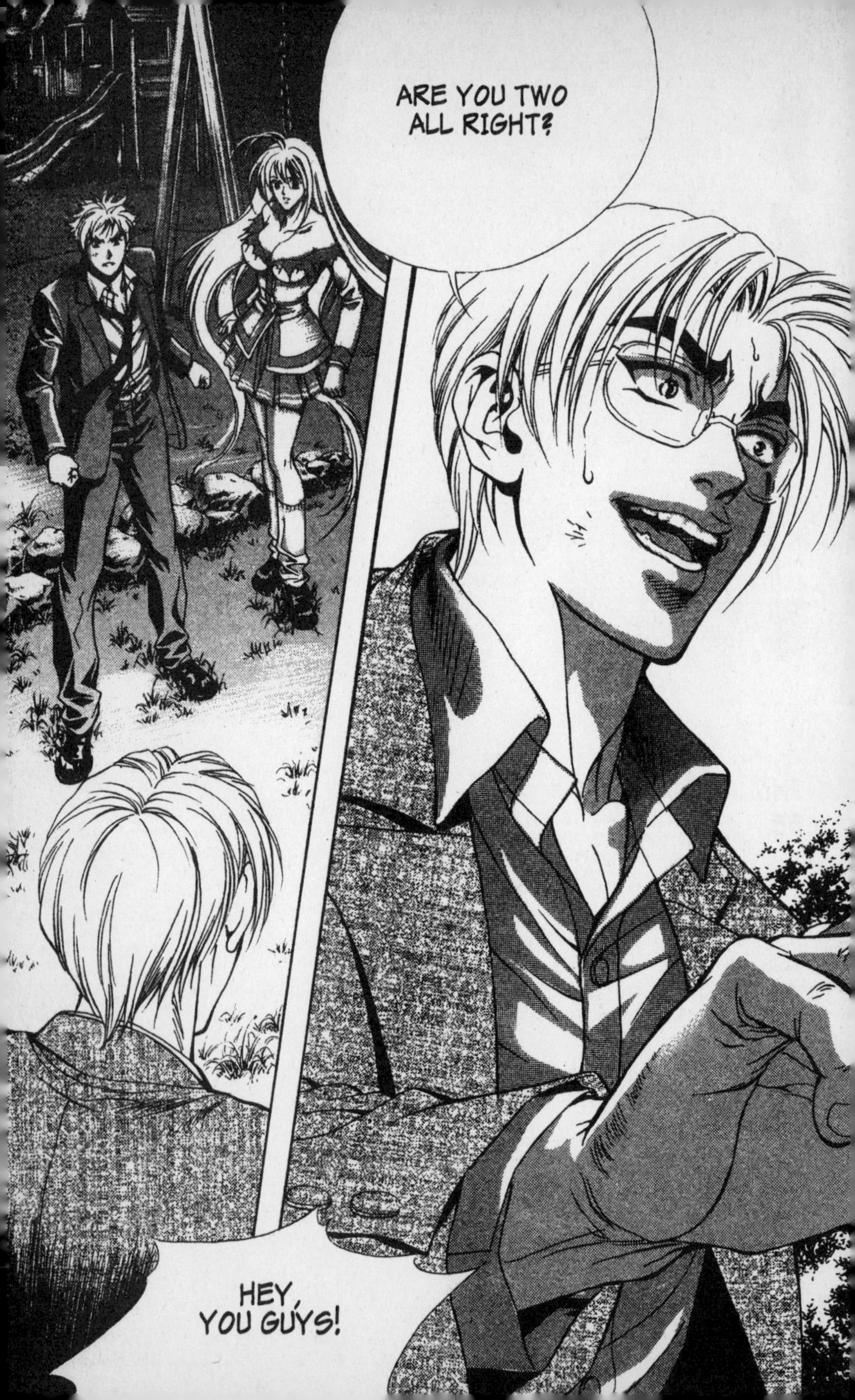
ARE YOU TWO
ALL RIGHT?
HEY,
YOU GUYS!

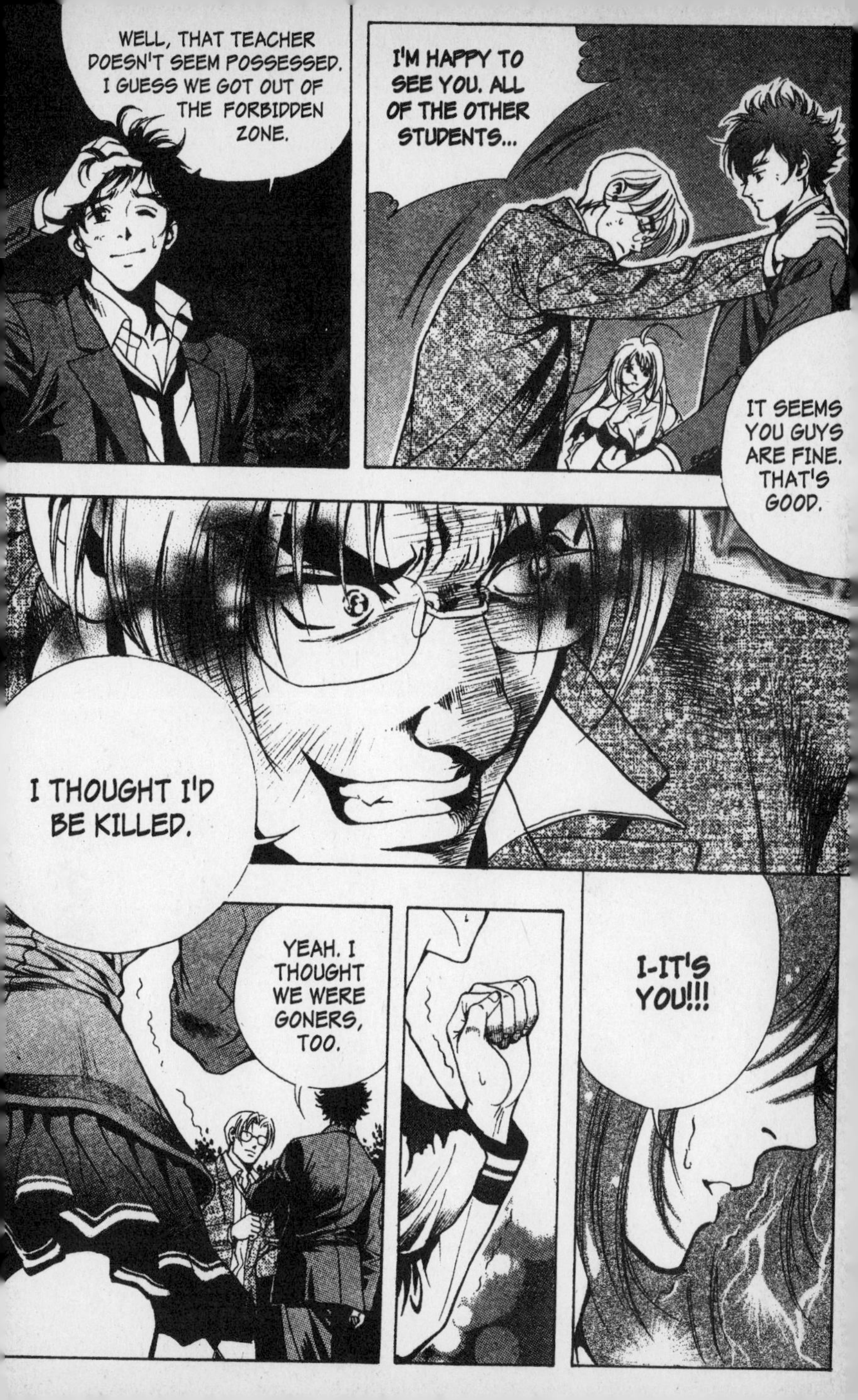
WELL, THAT TEACHER DOESN'T SEEM POSSESSED. I GUESS WE GOT OUT OF THE FORBIDDEN ZONE.
I'M HAPPY TO SEE YOU. ALL OF THE OTHER STUDENTS...
IT SEEMS YOU GUYS ARE FINE. THAT'S GOOD.
I THOUGHT I'D BE KILLED.
YEAH. I THOUGHT WE WERE GONERS, TOO.
I-IT'S YOU!!!

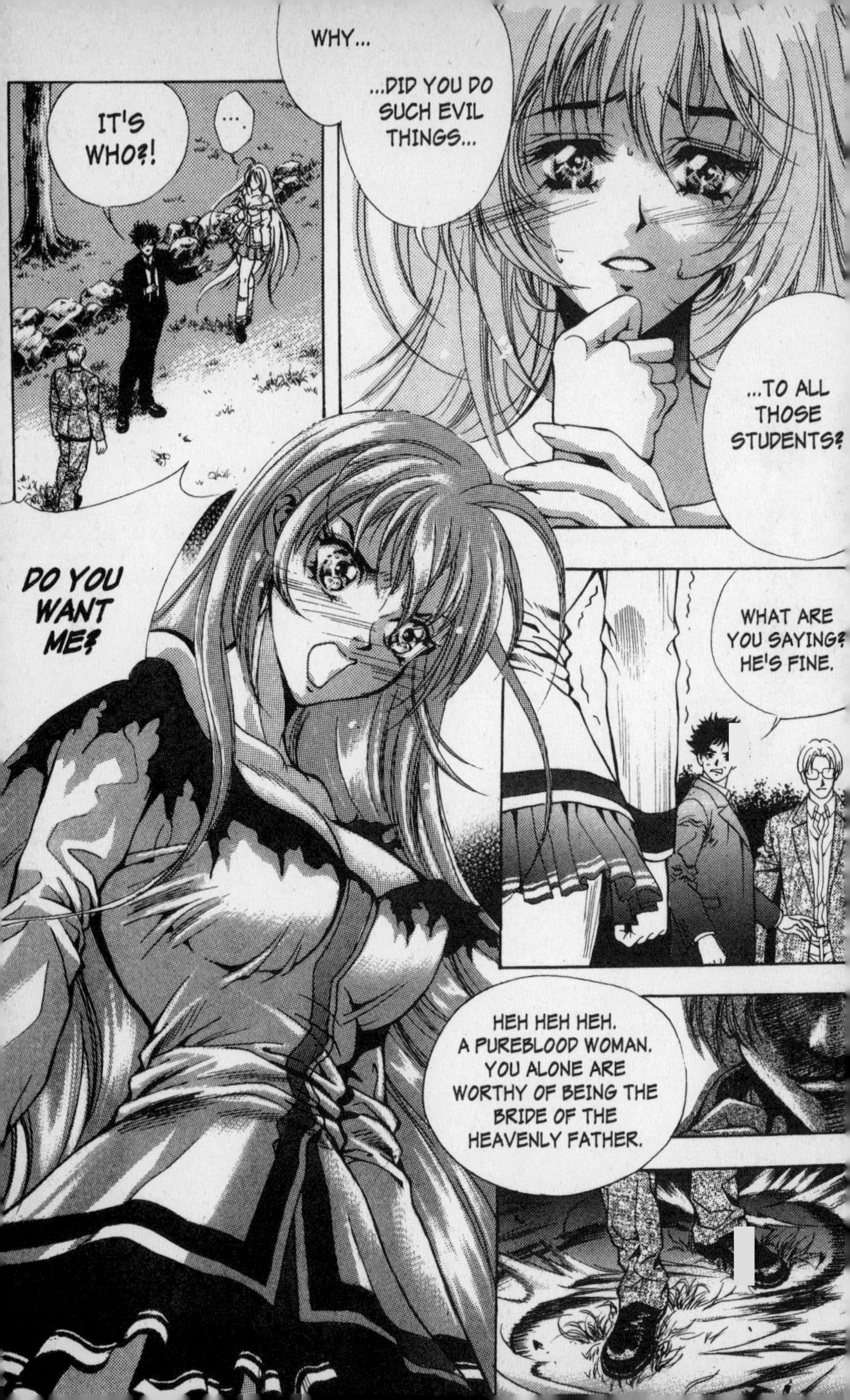
IT'S WHO?!
....
WHY...
...DID YOU DO SUCH EVIL THINGS...
...TO ALL THOSE STUDENTS?
WHAT ARE YOU SAYING? HE'S FINE.
DO YOU WANT ME?
HEH HEH HEH. A PUREBLOOD WOMAN. YOU ALONE ARE WORTHY OF BEING THE BRIDE OF THE HEAVENLY FATHER.

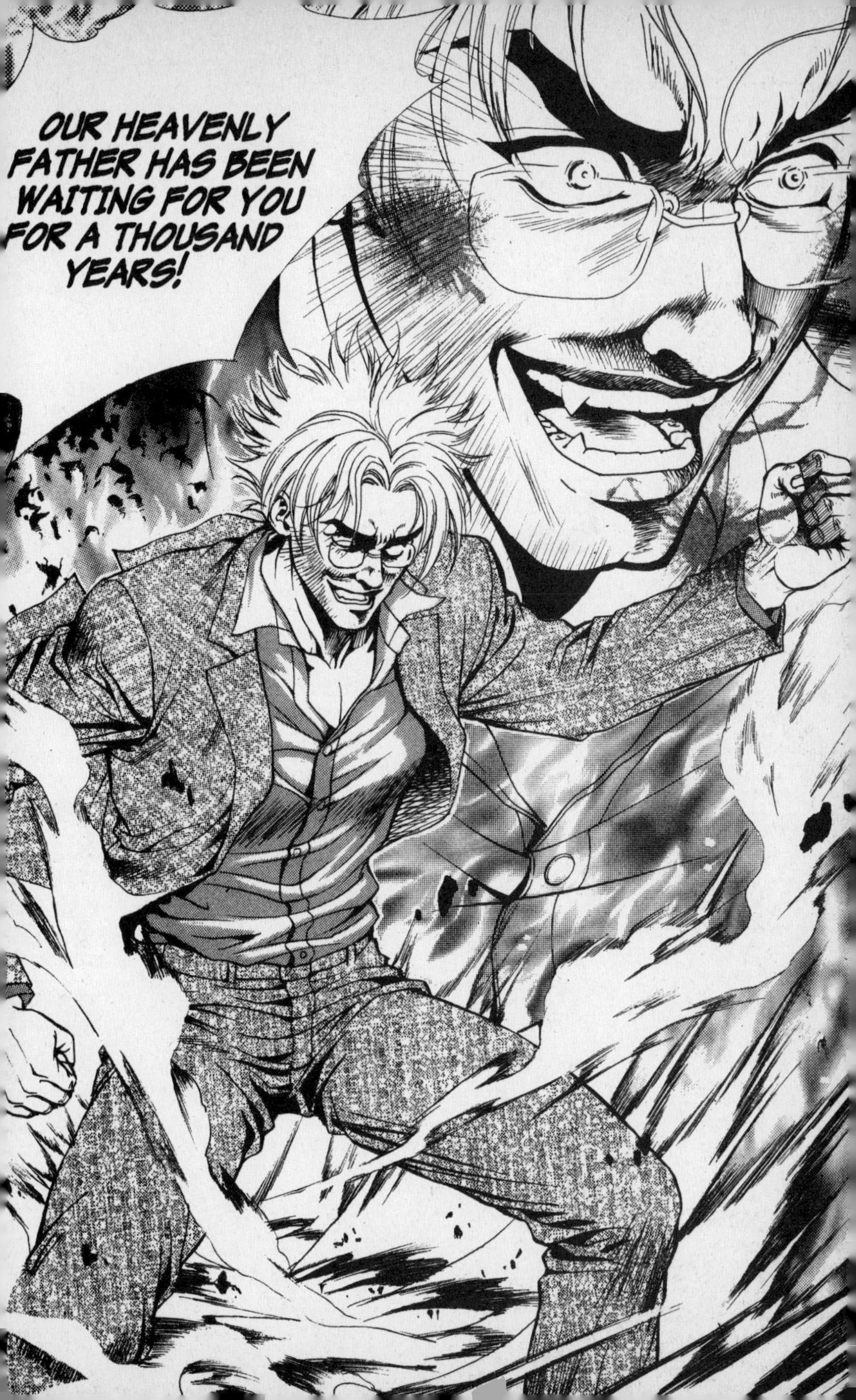
OUR HEAVENLY FATHER HAS BEEN WAITING FOR YOU FOR A THOUSAND YEARS!

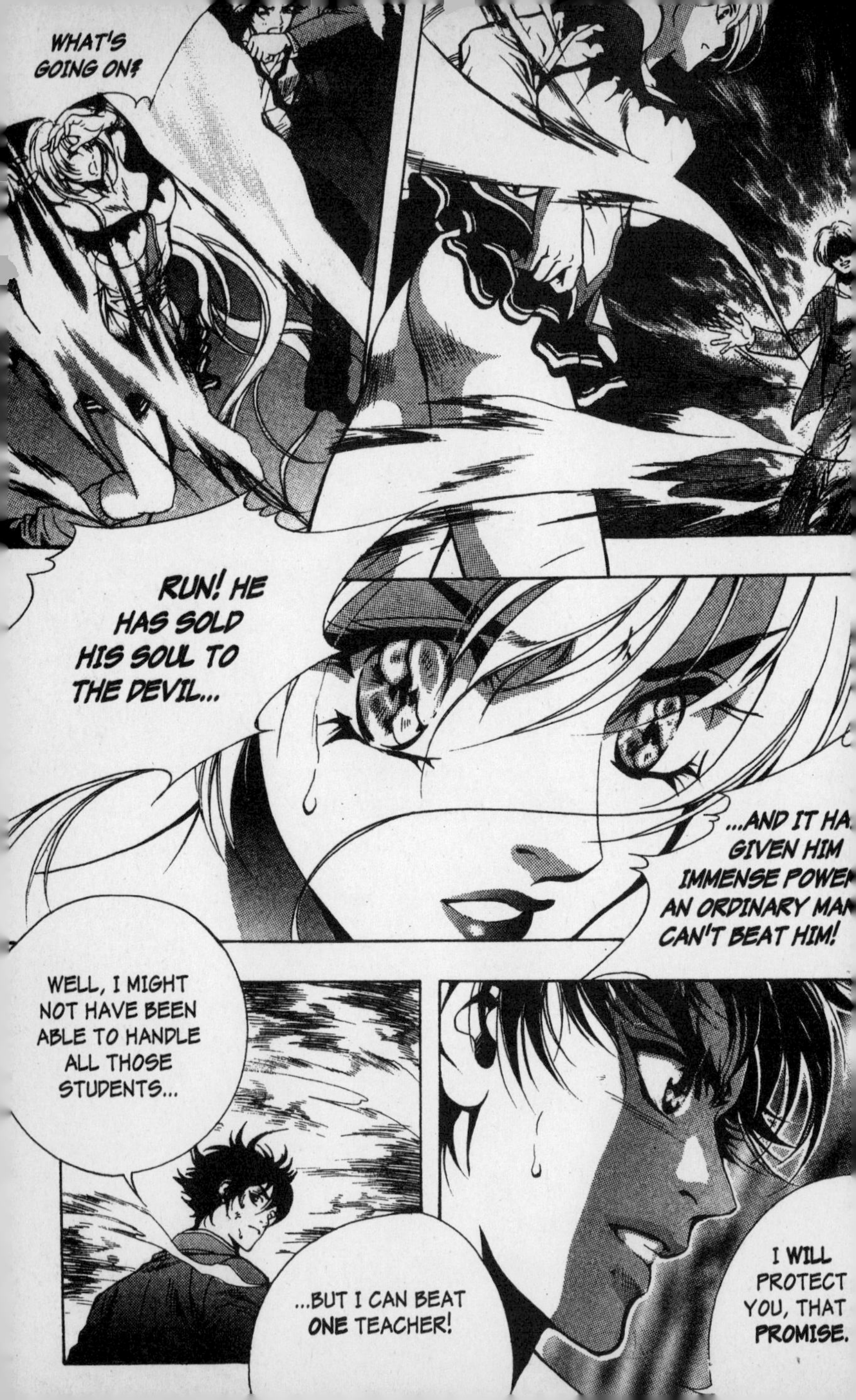
WHAT'S GOING ON?
RUN! HE HAS SOLD HIS SOUL TO THE DEVIL...
...AND IT HA GIVEN HIM IMMENSE POWE AN ORDINARY MA CAN'T BEAT HIM!
WELL, I MIGHT NOT HAVE BEEN ABLE TO HANDLE ALL THOSE STUDENTS...
...BUT I CAN BEAT ONE TEACHER!
I WILL PROTECT YOU, THAT PROMISE.

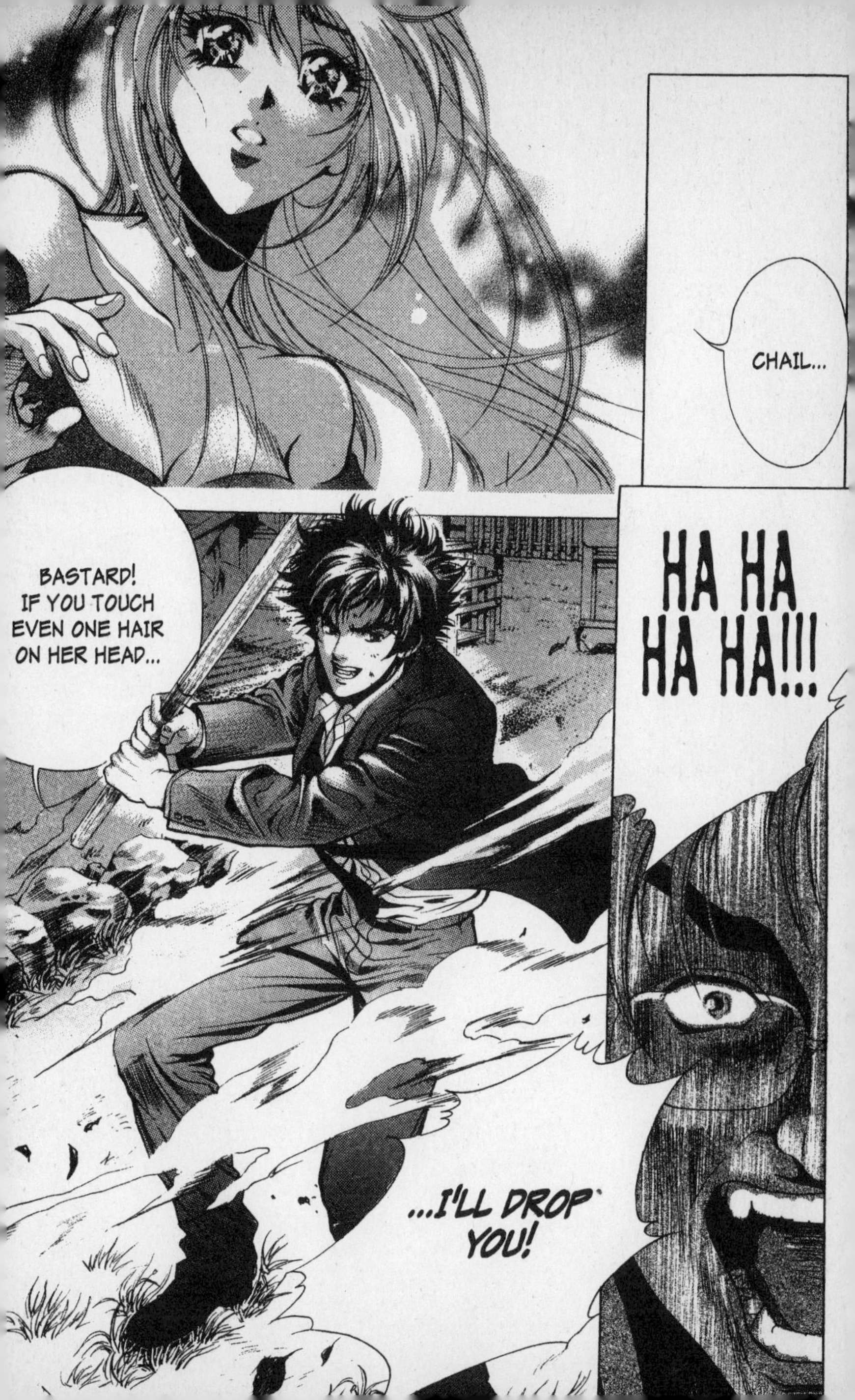
CHAIL...
HA HA HA HA!!!
BASTARD! IF YOU TOUCH EVEN ONE HAIR ON HER HEAD...
...I'LL DROP YOU!

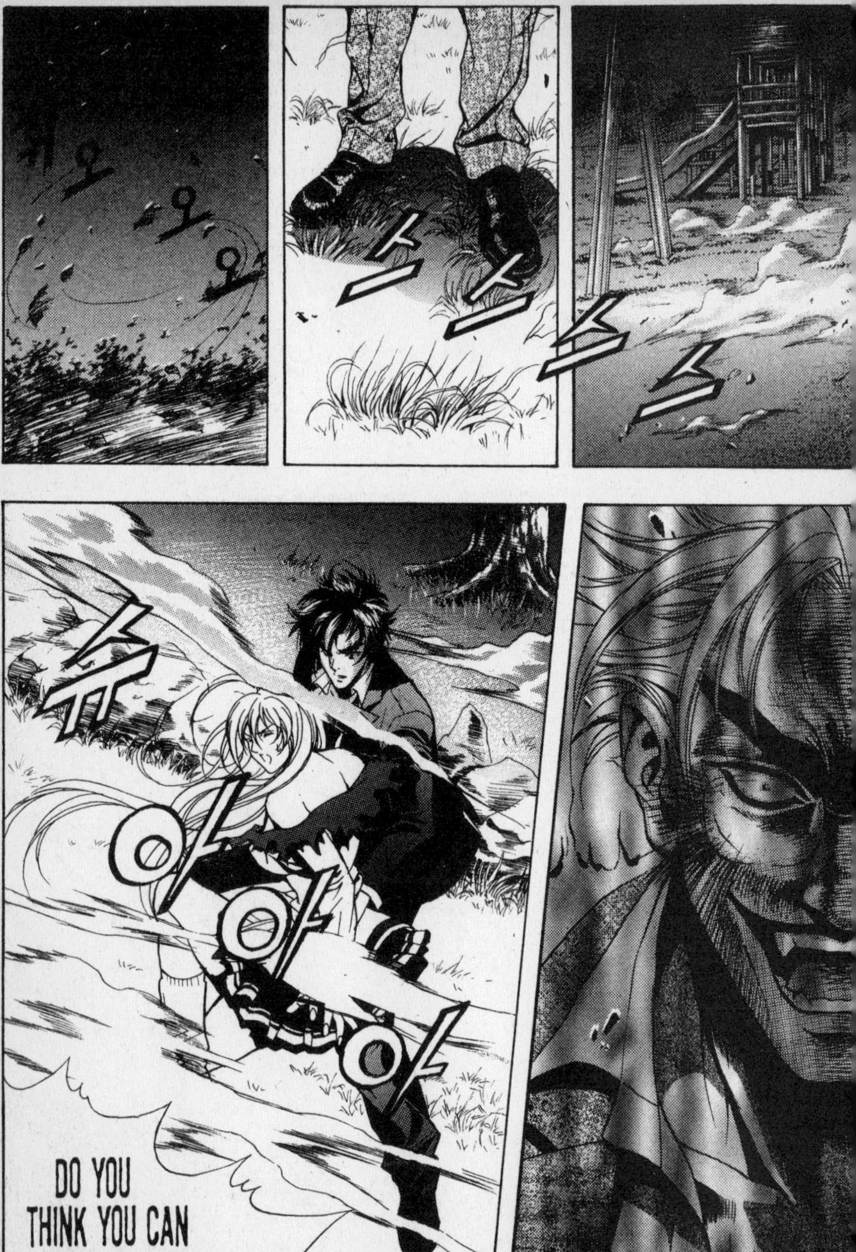
DO YOU THINK YOU CAN PROTECT HER?

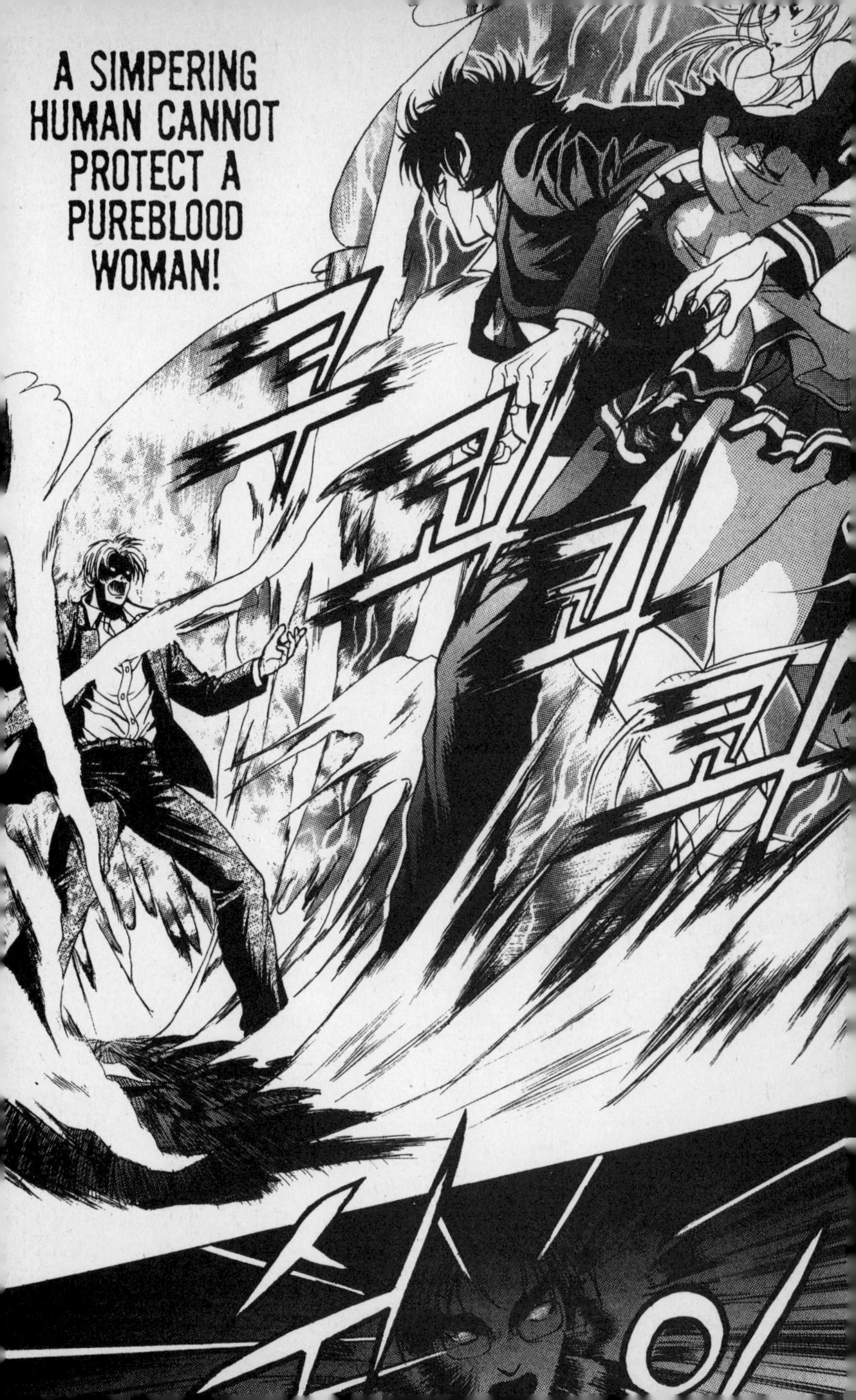
A SIMPERING HUMAN CANNOT PROTECT A PUREBLOOD WOMAN!

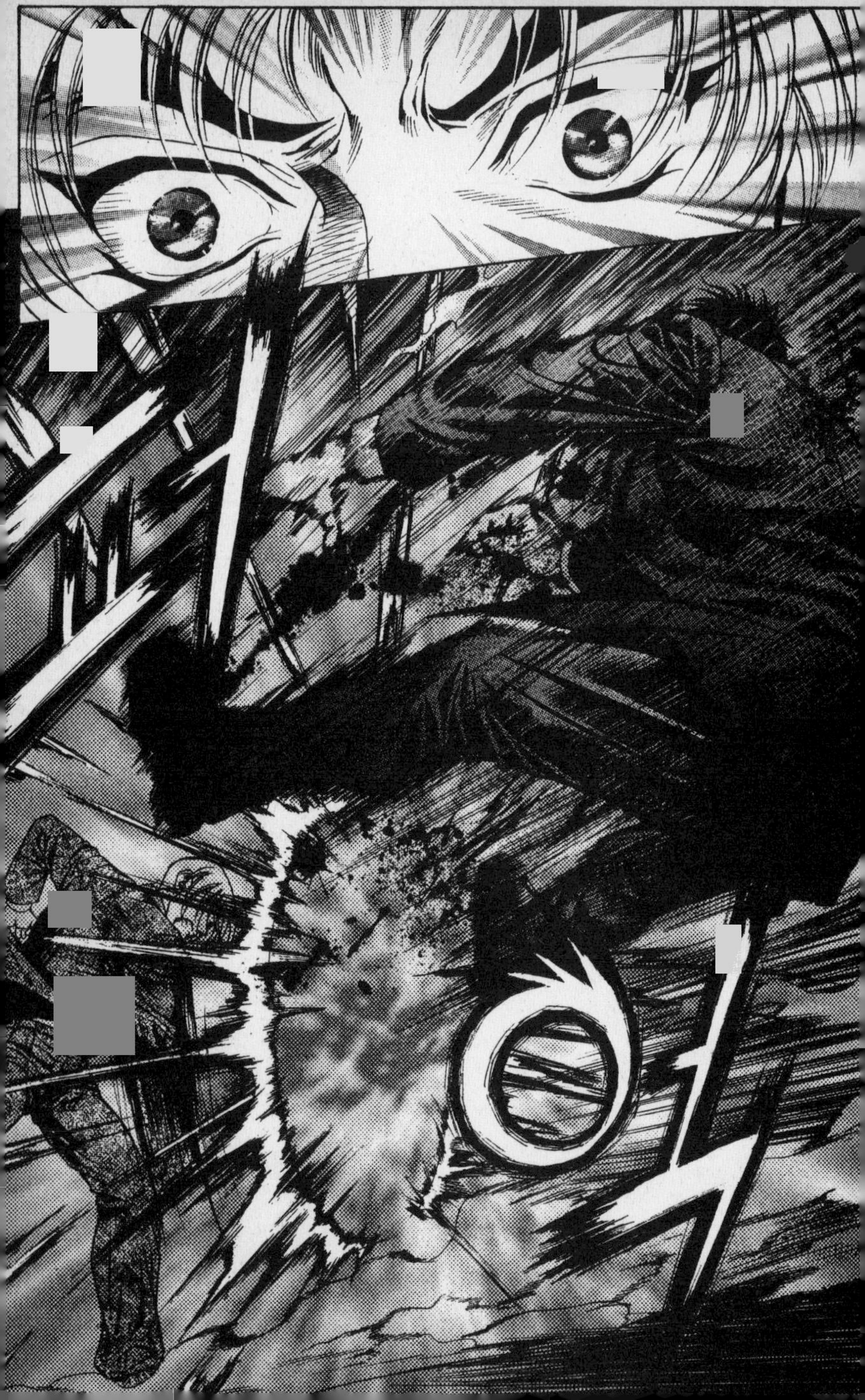

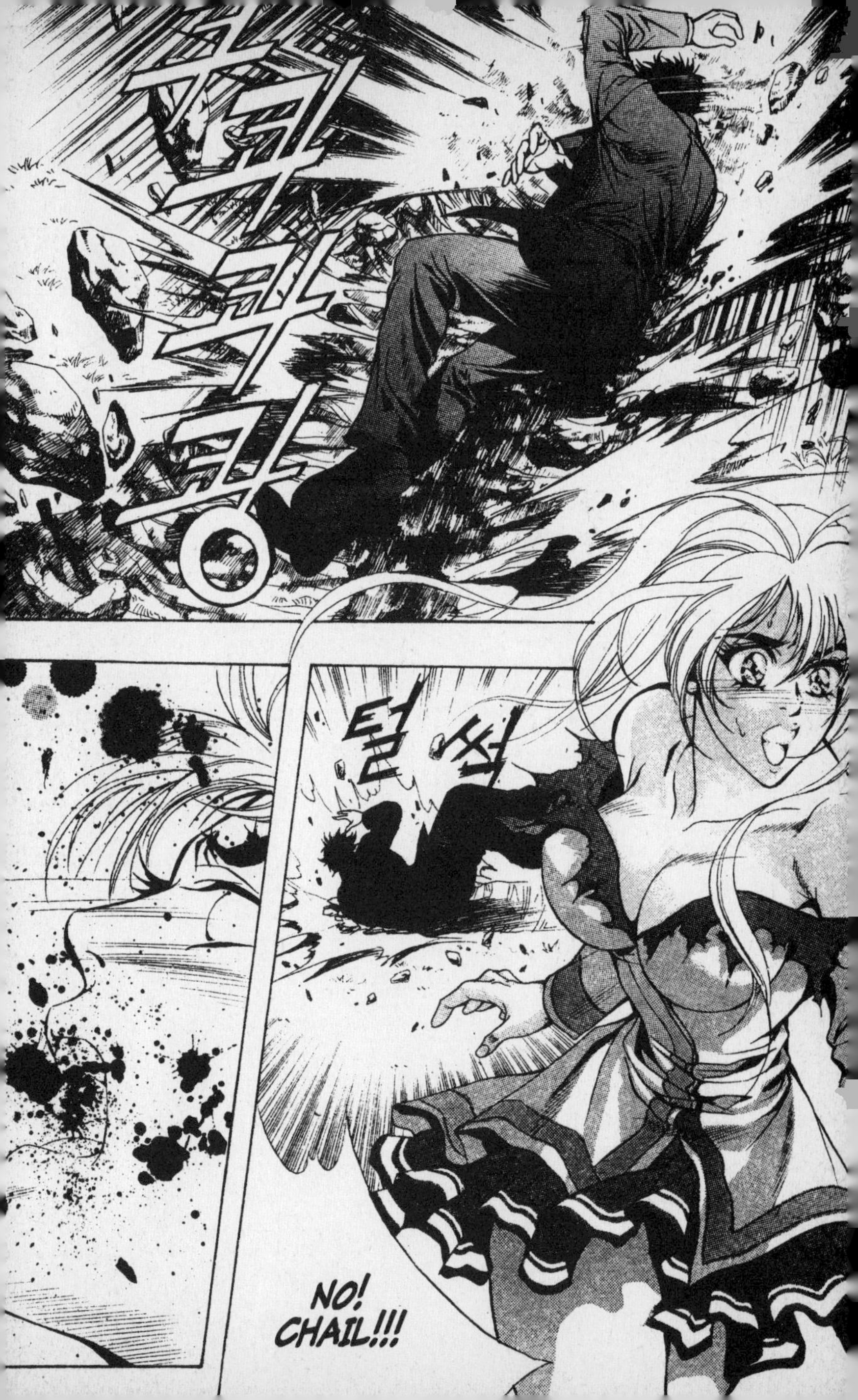
털썩
NO! CHAIL!!!

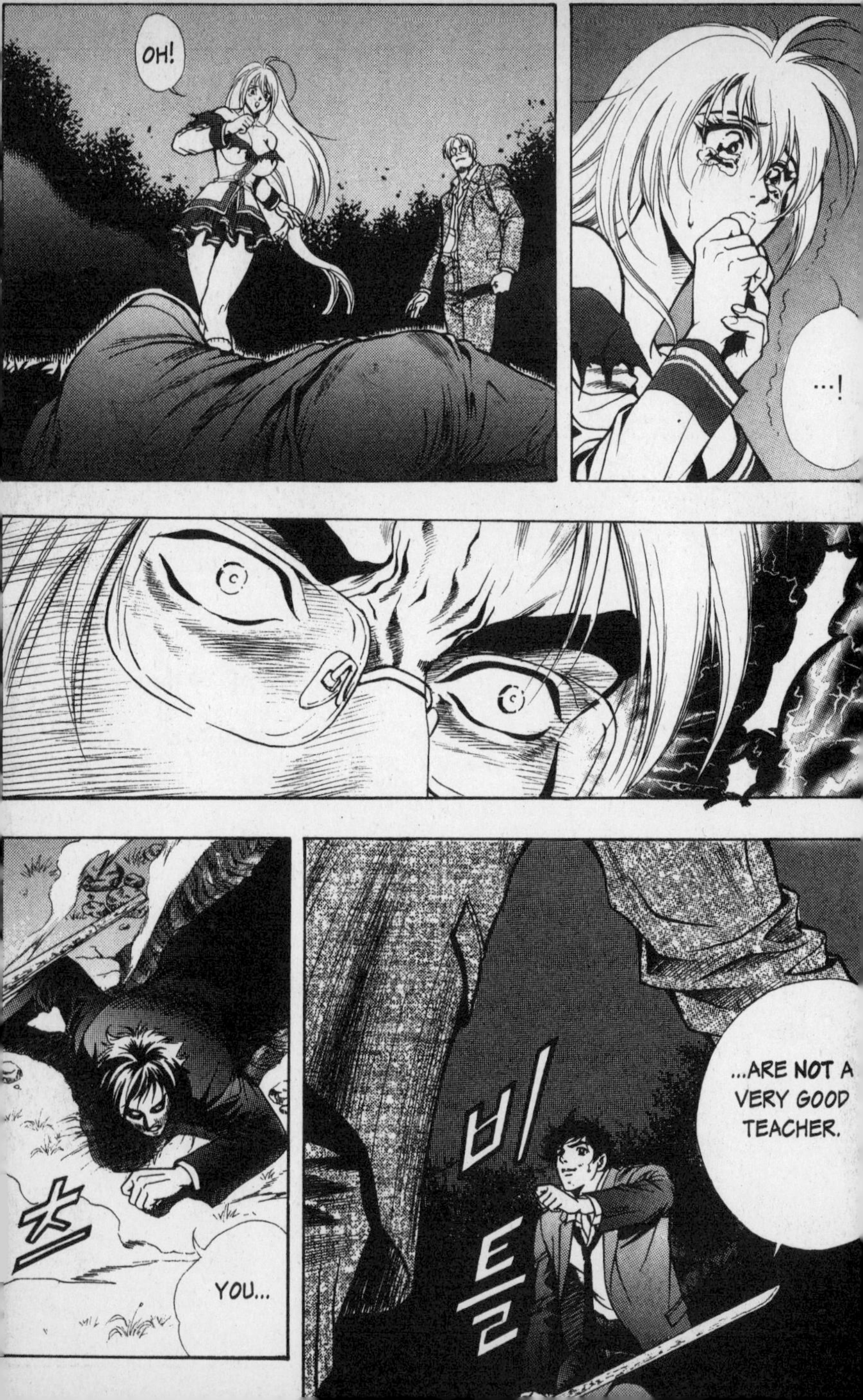
OH!
...!
YOU...
...ARE NOT A VERY GOOD TEACHER.

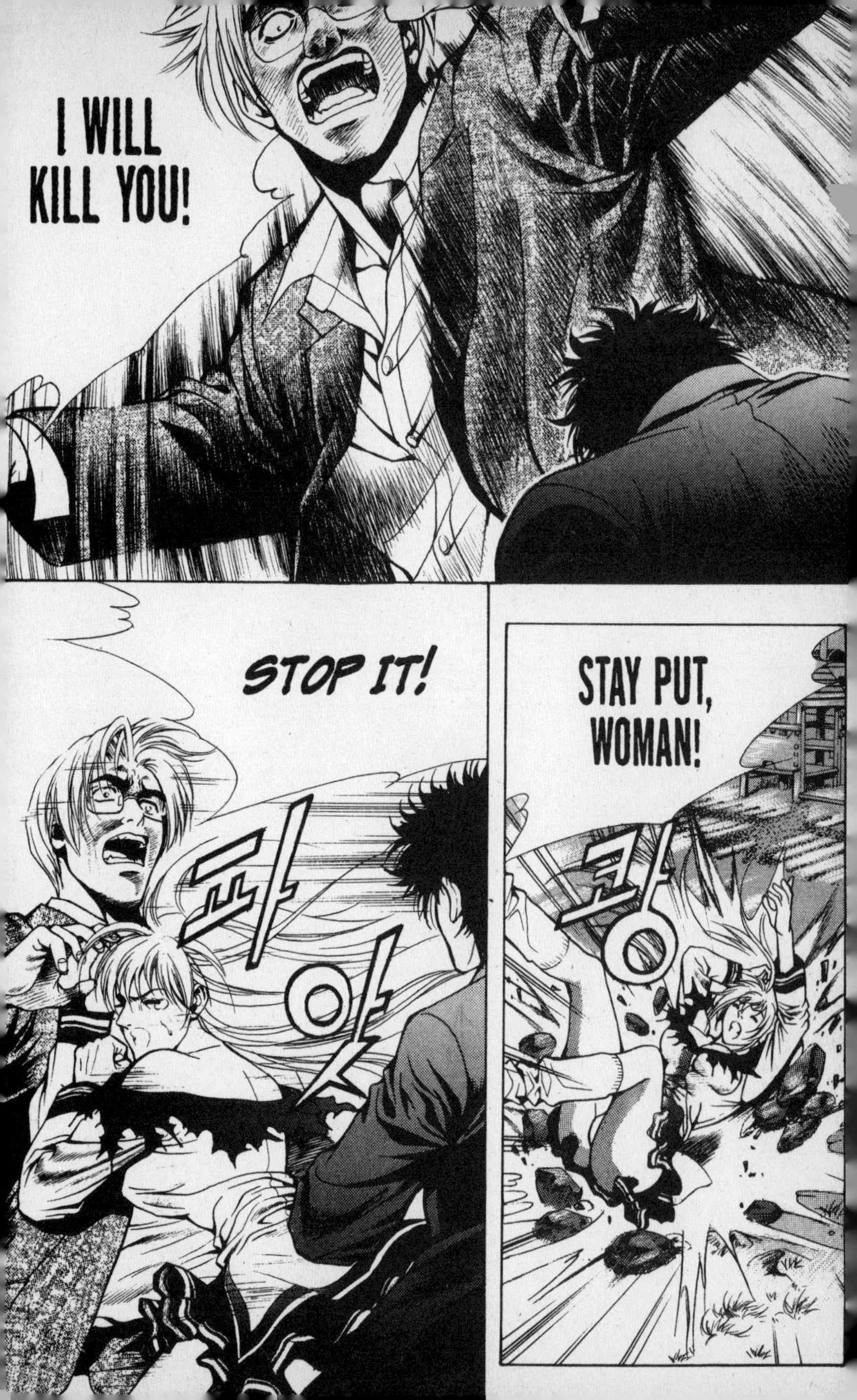

I WILL KILL YOU!
STOP IT!
STAY PUT, WOMAN!

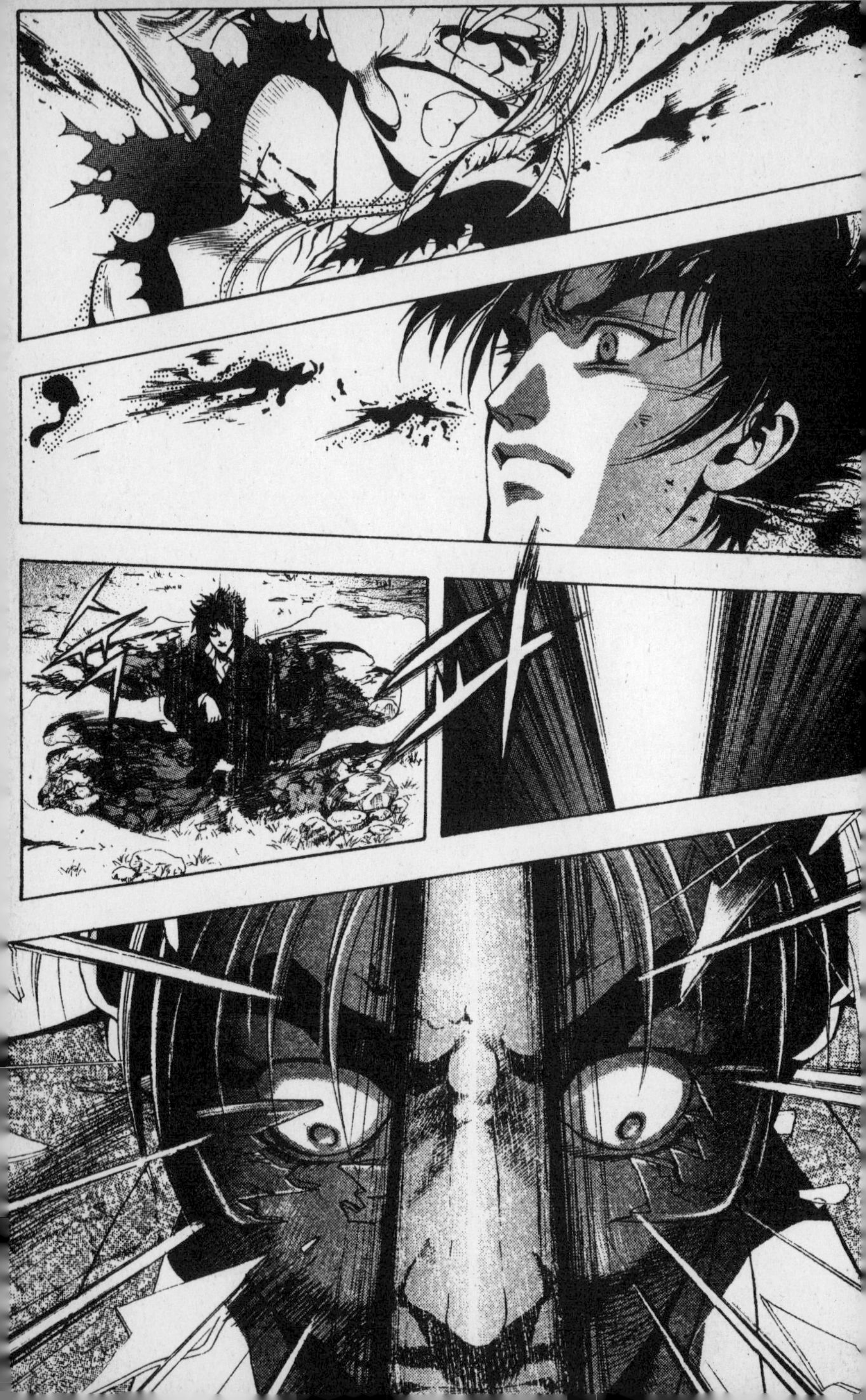

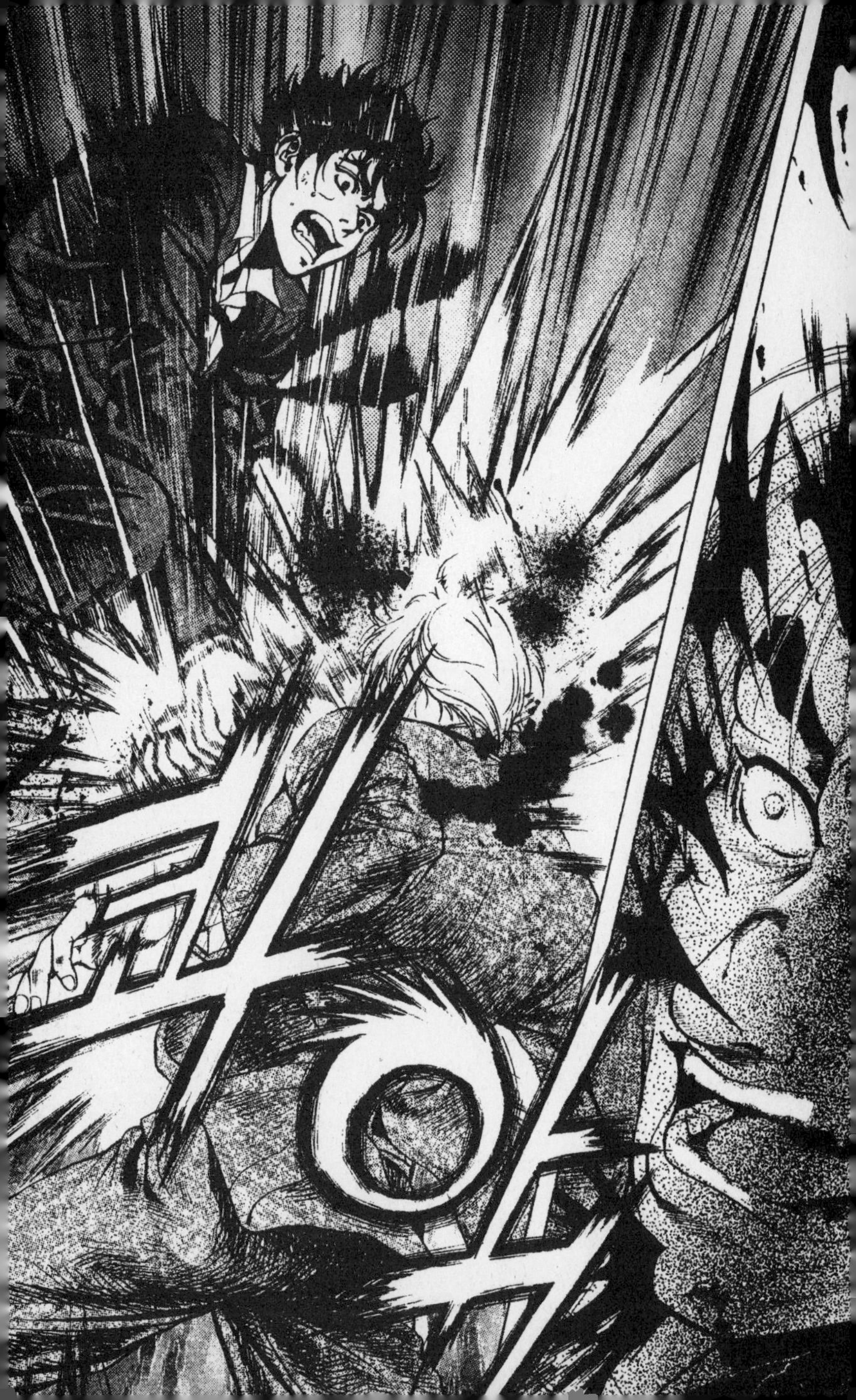

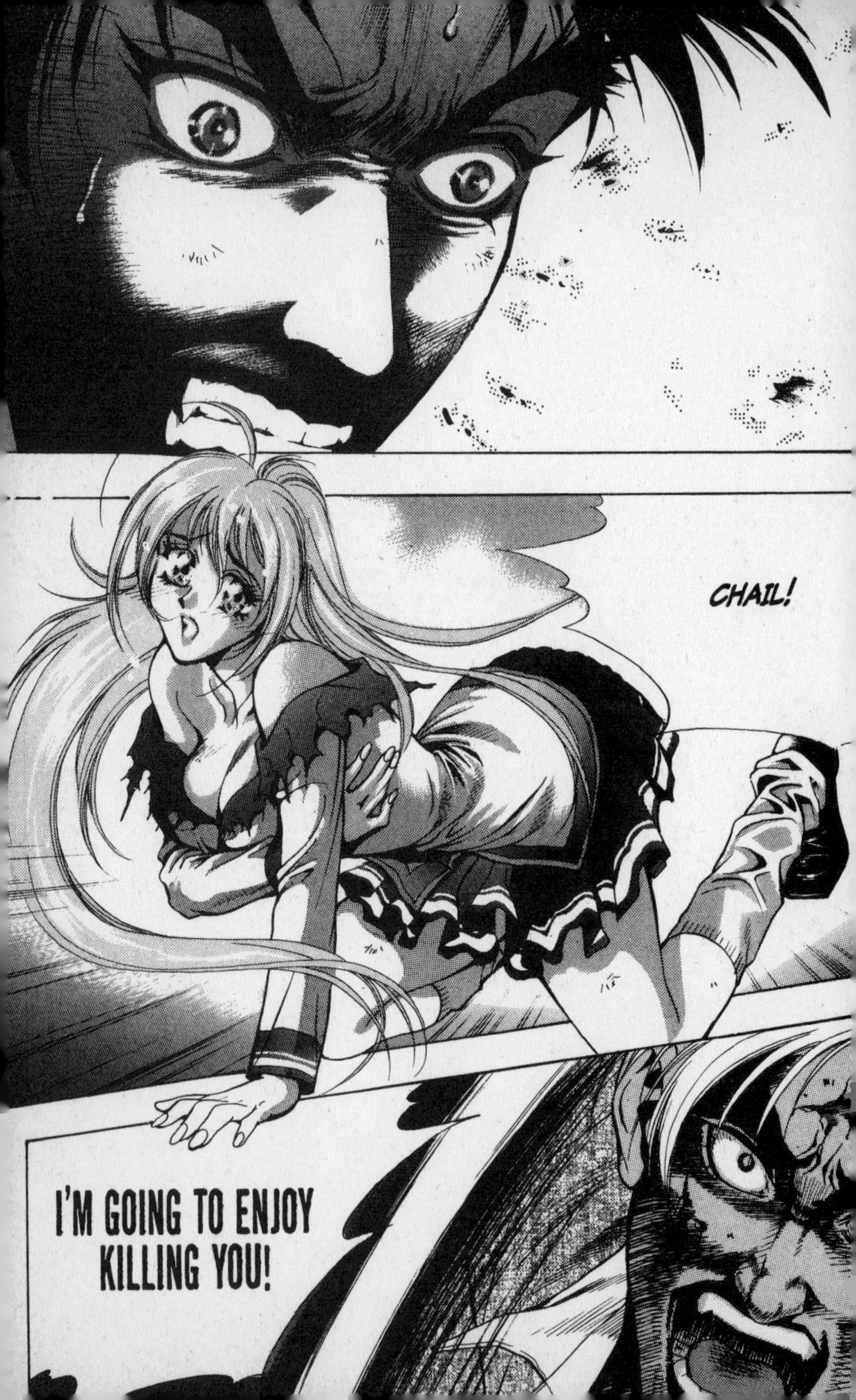
CHAIL!
I'M GOING TO ENJOY KILLING YOU!

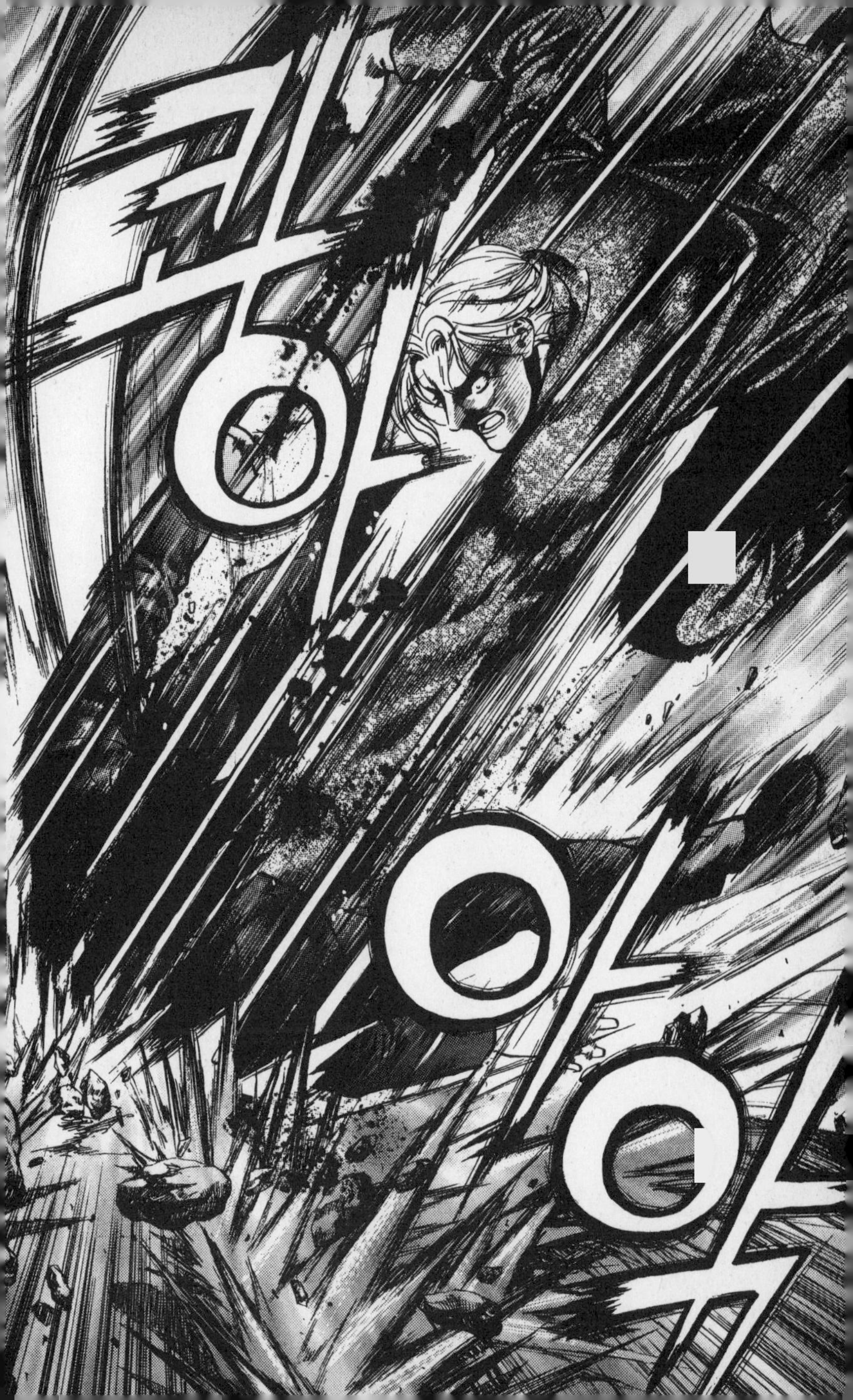

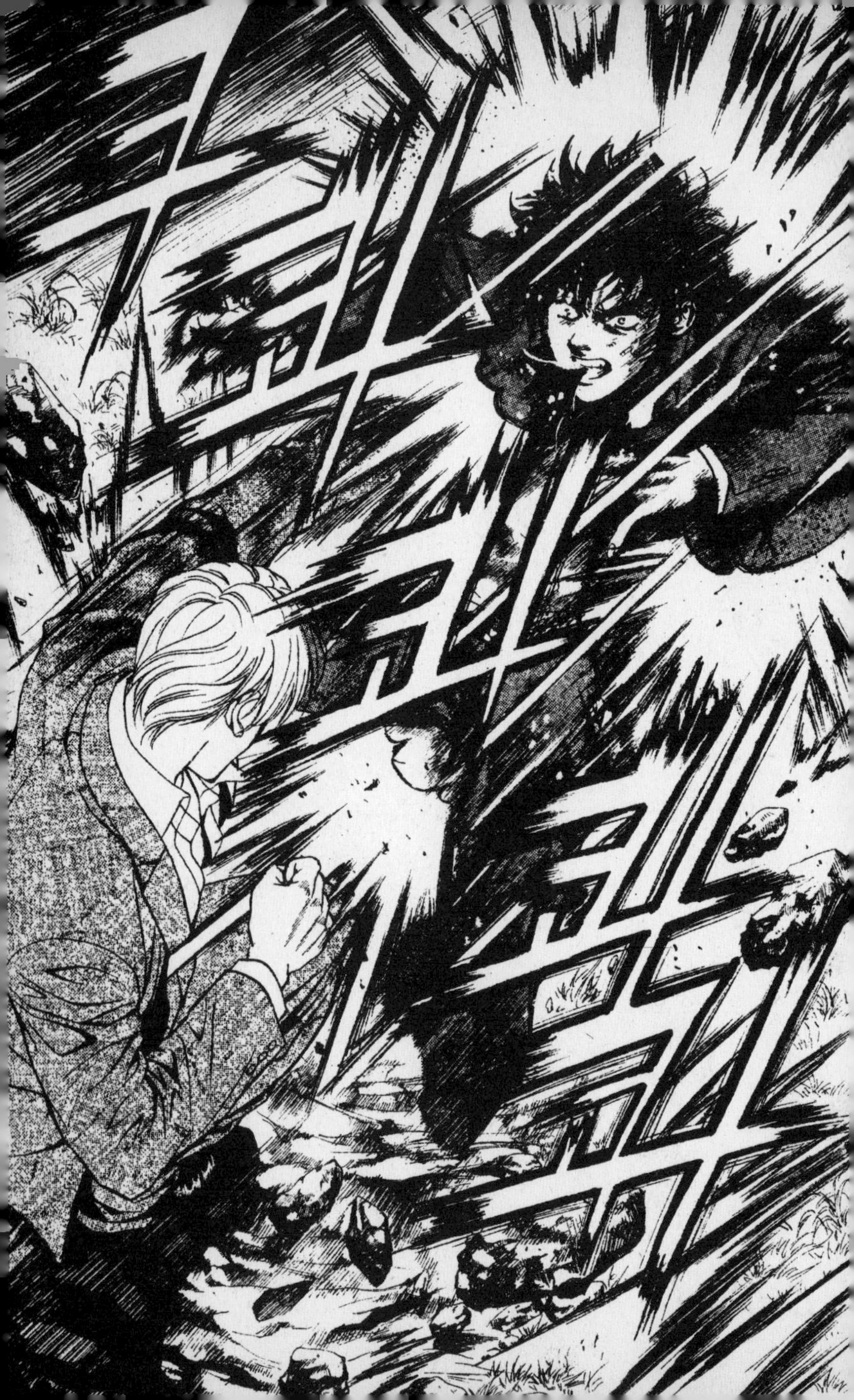

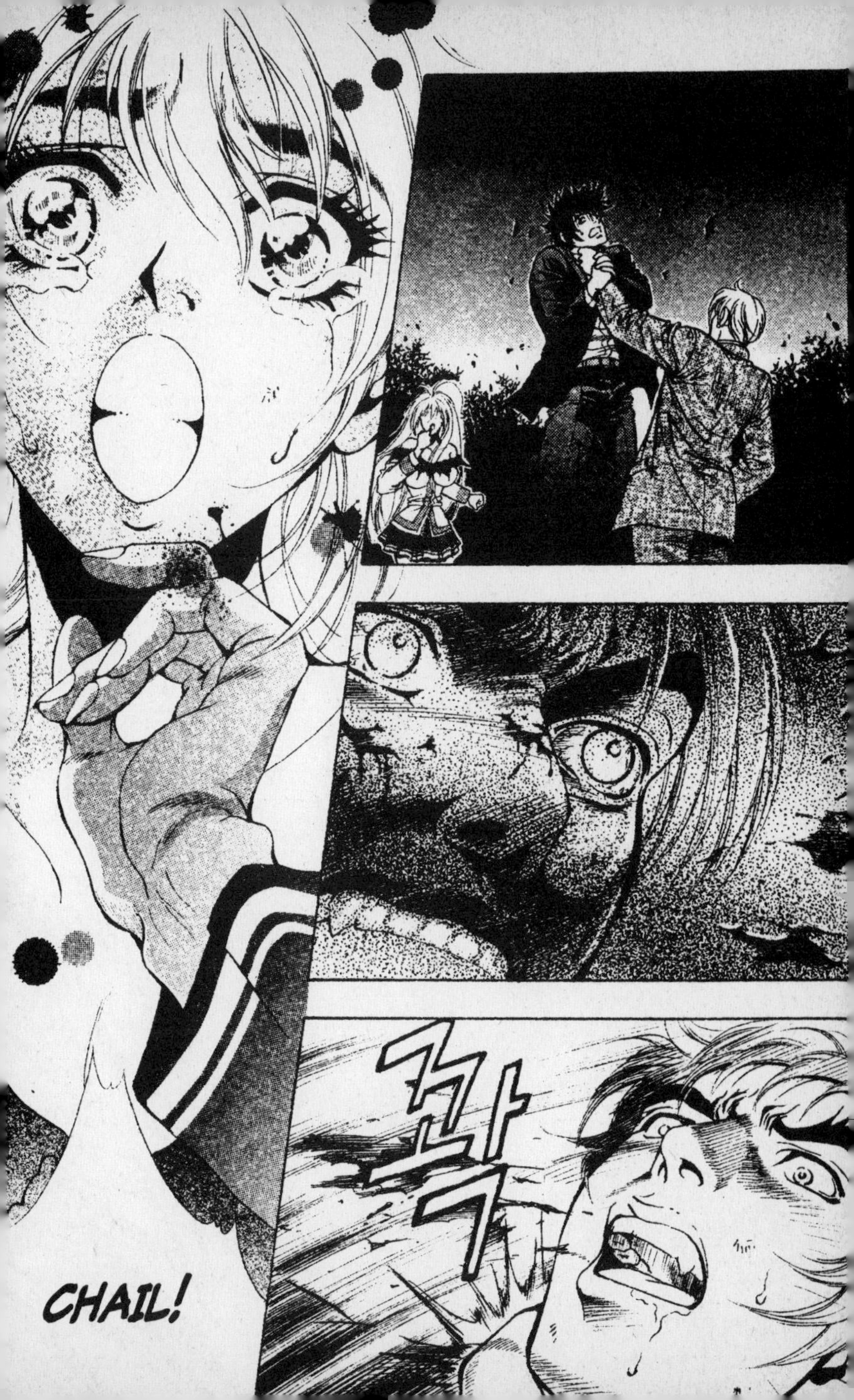
CHAIL!

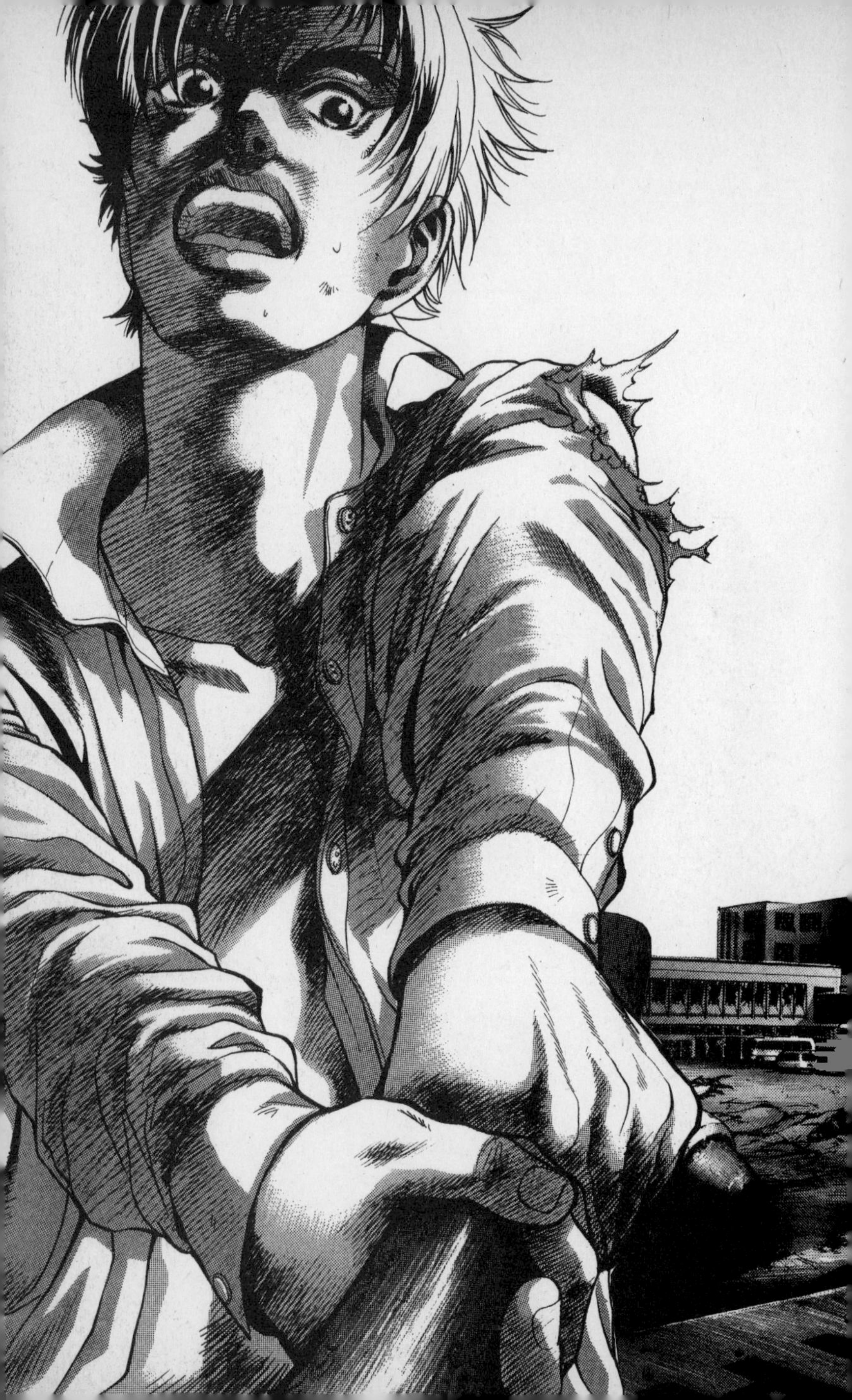

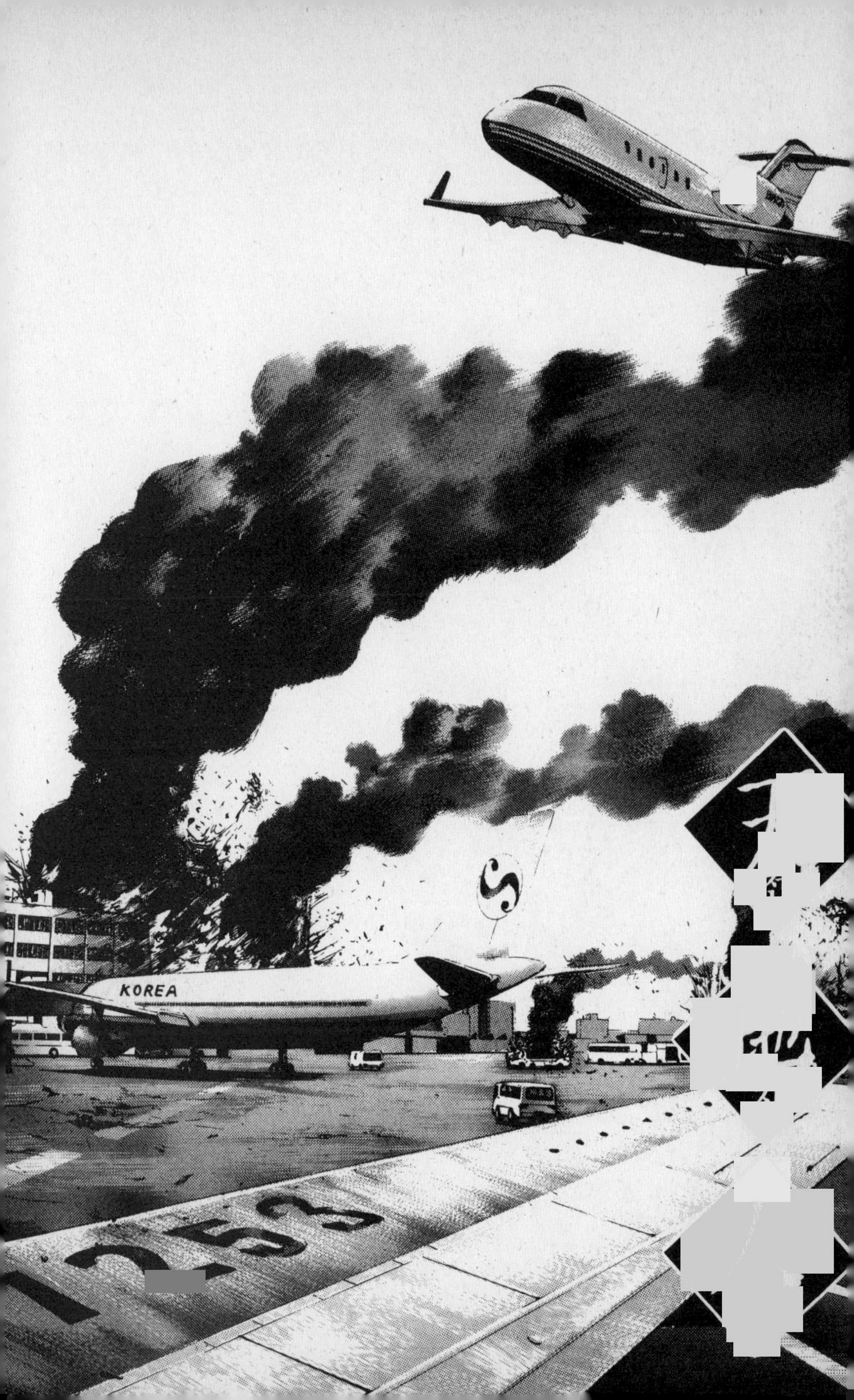
KOREA

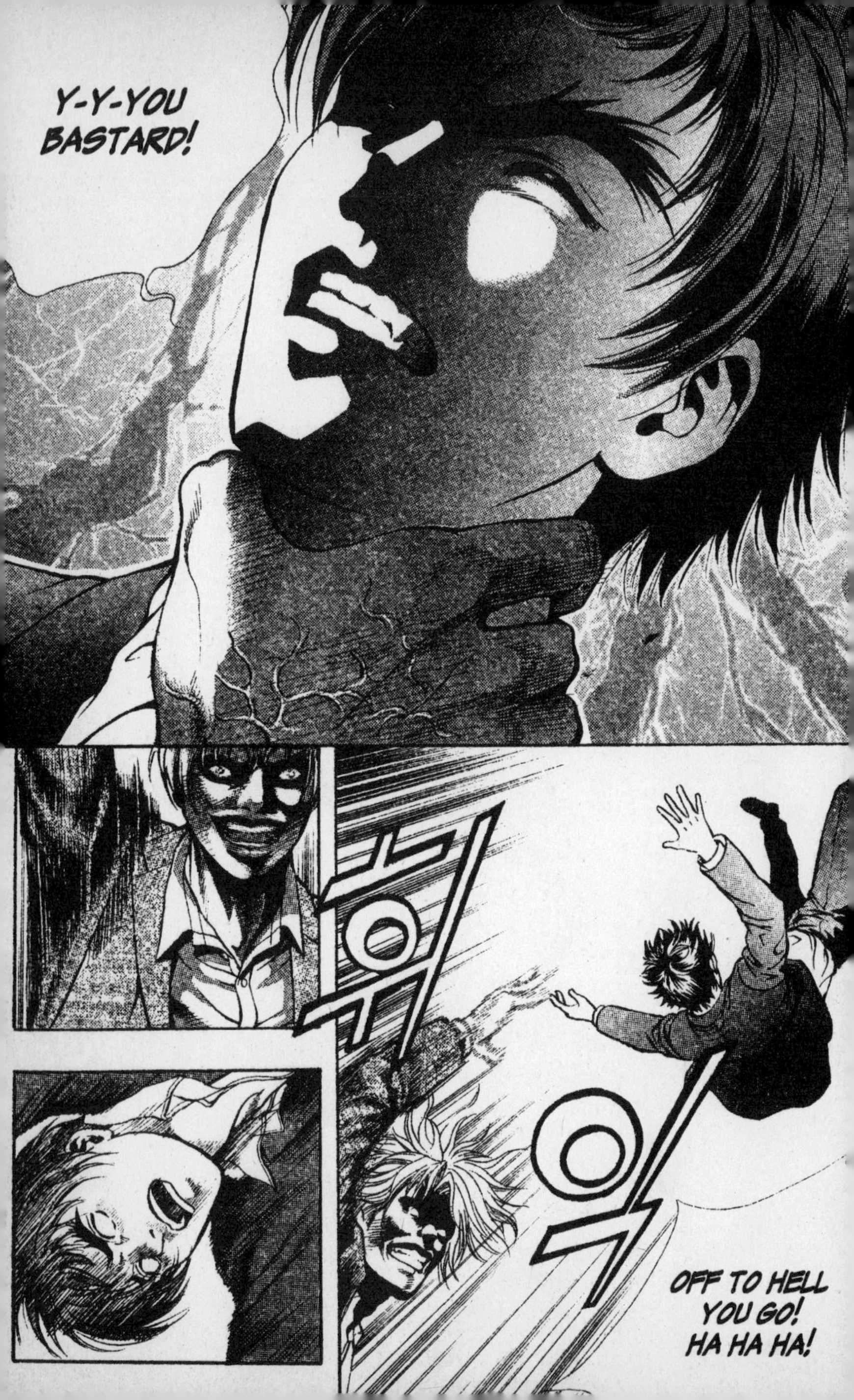
Y-Y-YOU BASTARD!
OFF TO HELL YOU GO! HA HA HA!

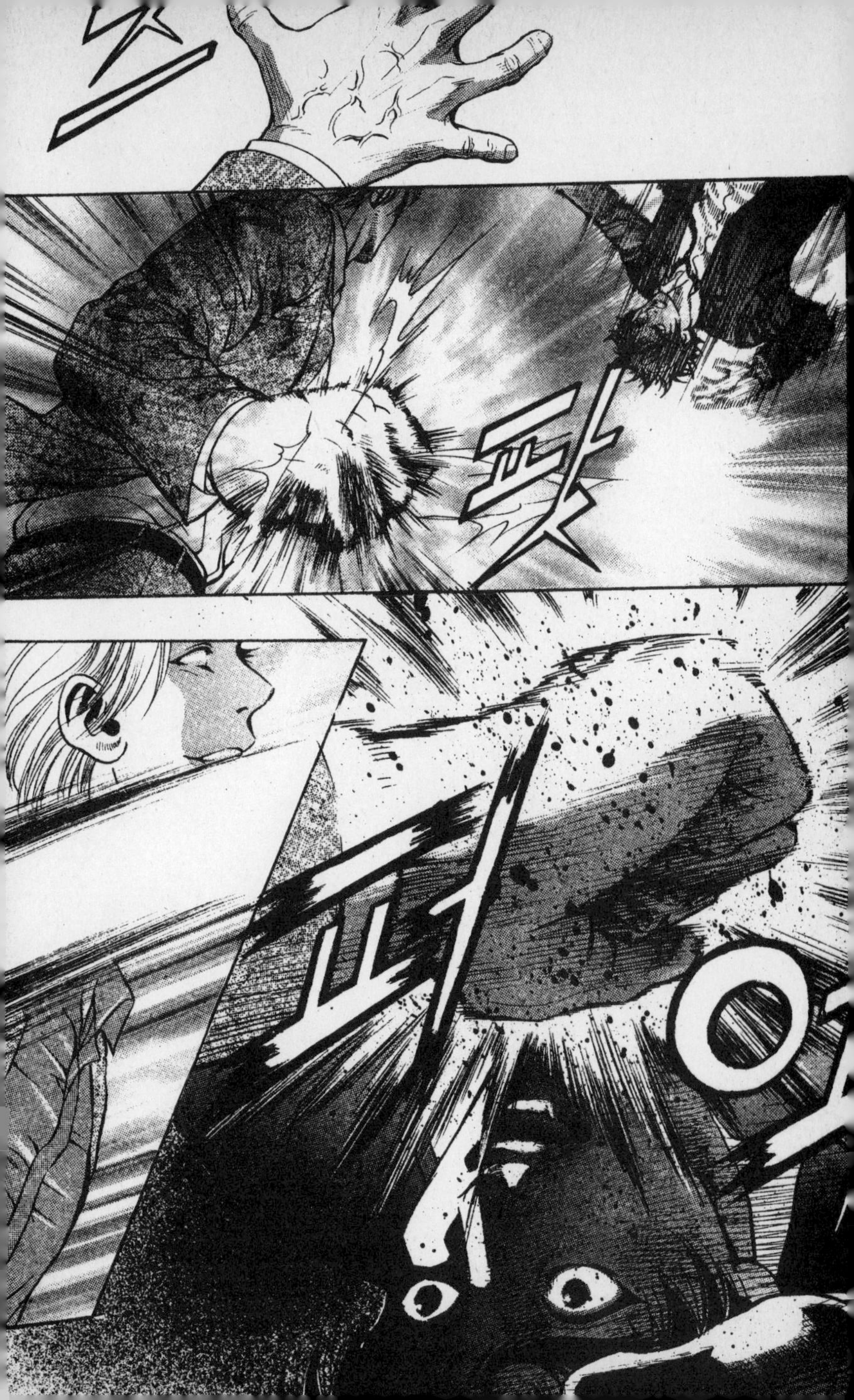

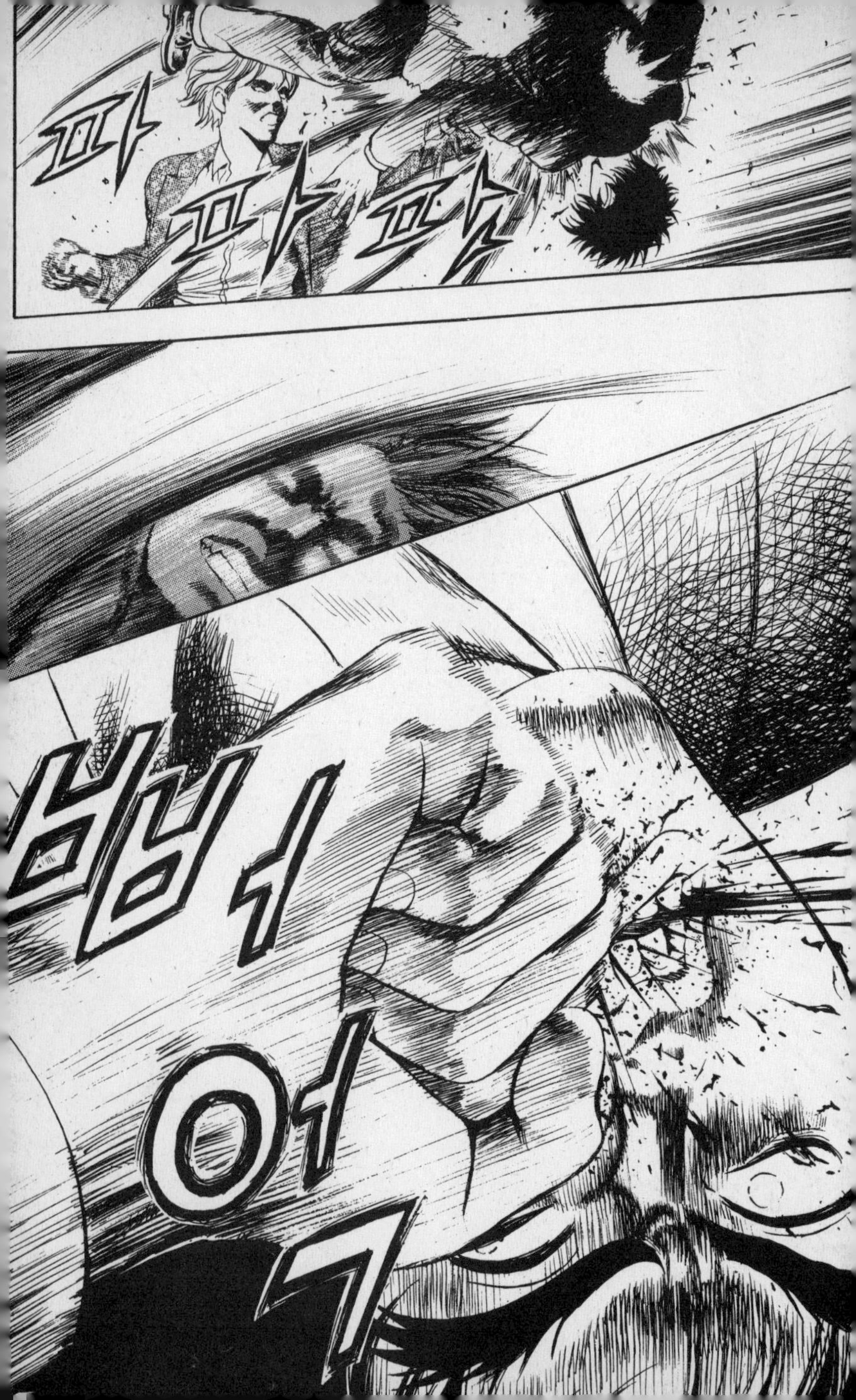
파
파 팍
뻐억

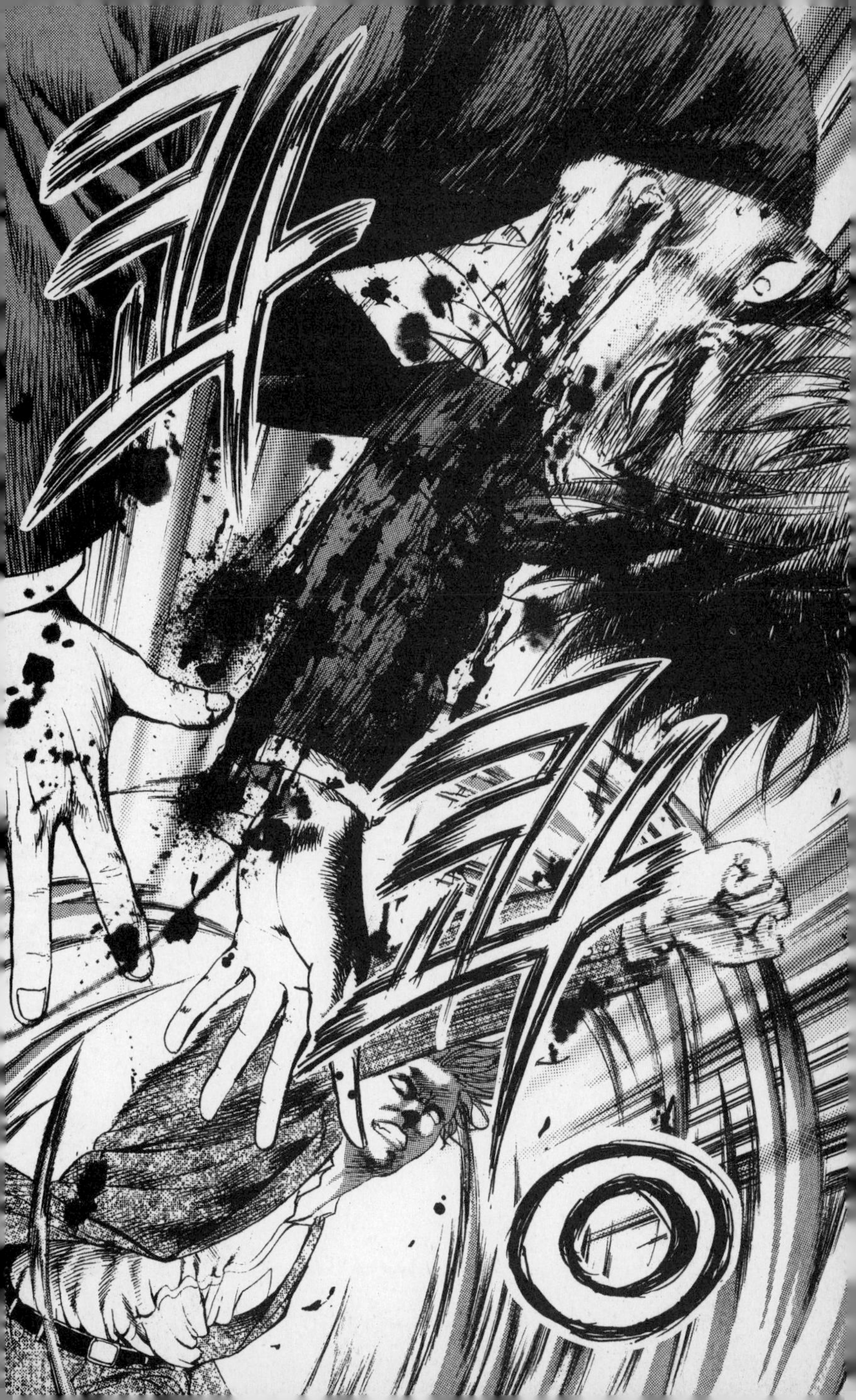

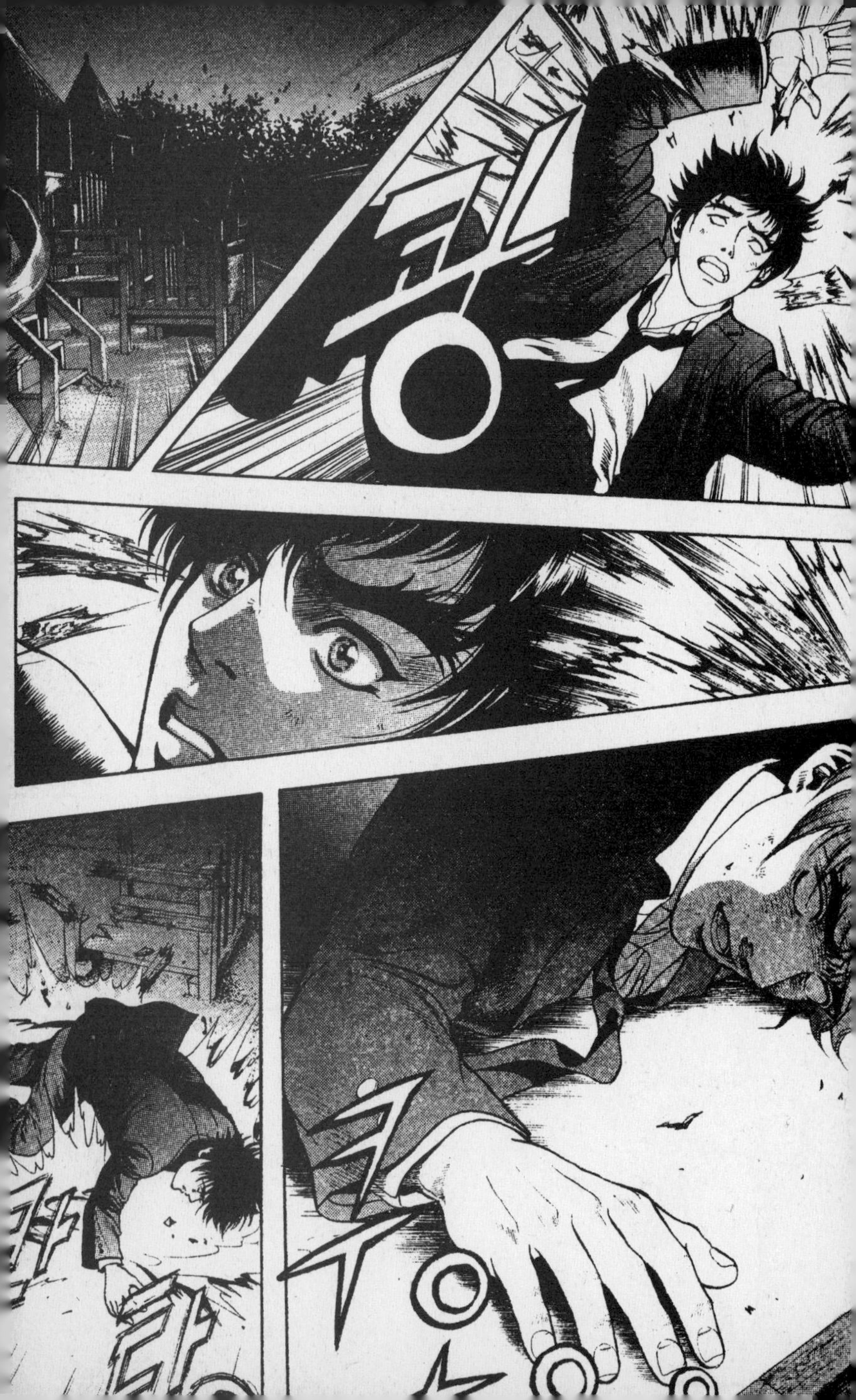

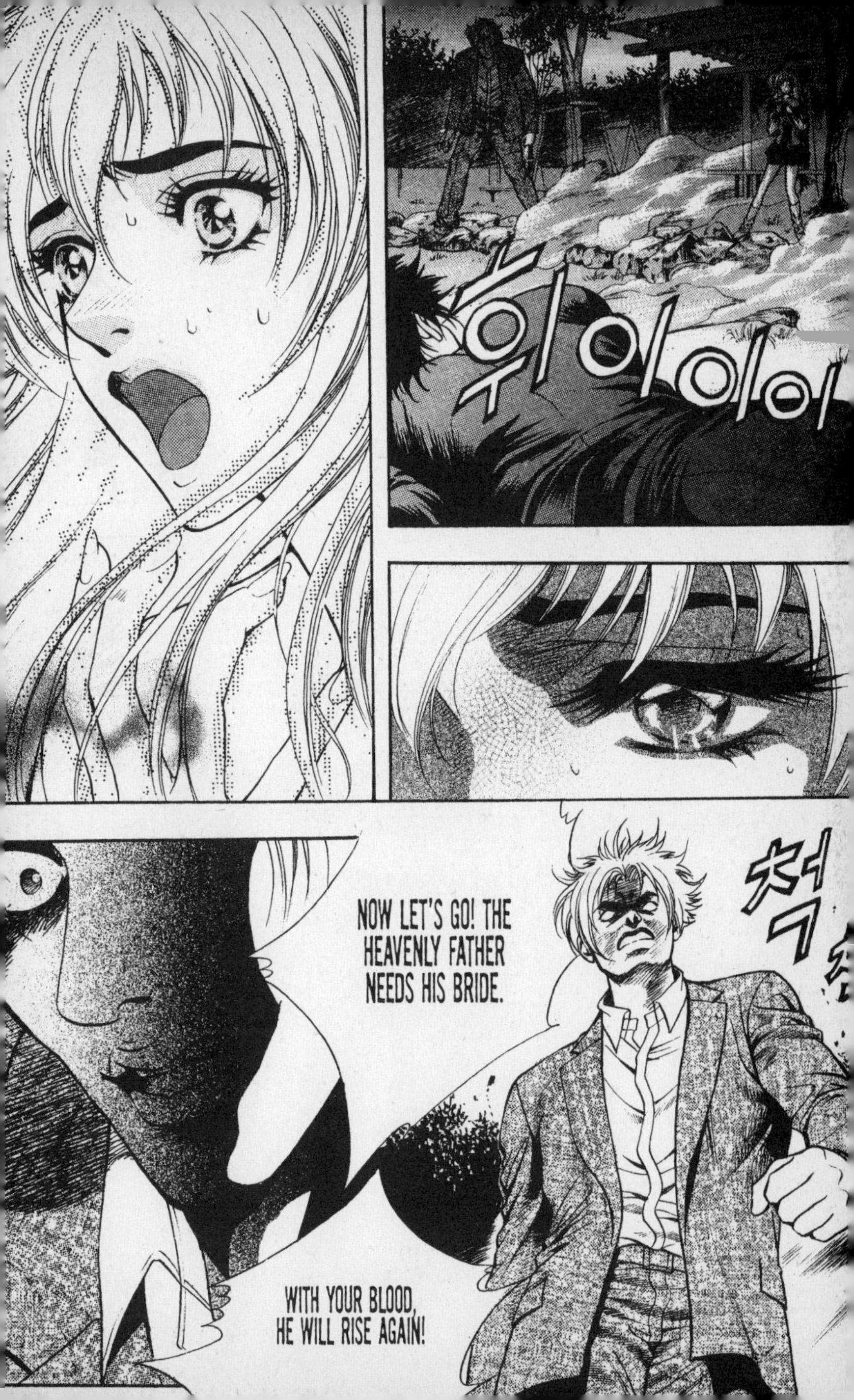
NOW LET'S GO! THE HEAVENLY FATHER NEEDS HIS BRIDE.
WITH YOUR BLOOD, HE WILL RISE AGAIN!

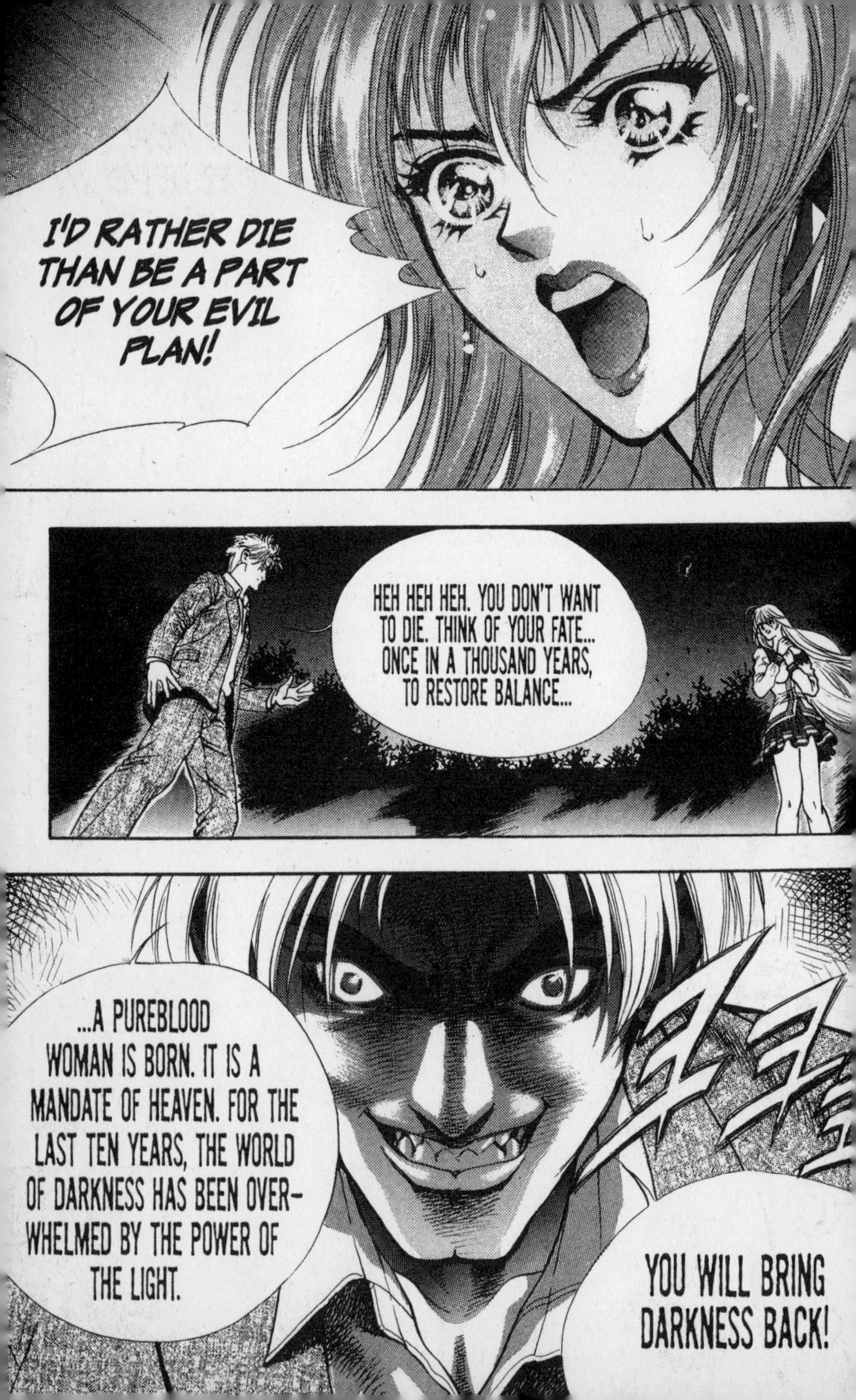
I'D RATHER DIE THAN BE A PART OF YOUR EVIL PLAN!
HEH HEH HEH. YOU DON'T WANT TO DIE. THINK OF YOUR FATE... ONCE IN A THOUSAND YEARS, TO RESTORE BALANCE...
...A PUREBLOOD WOMAN IS BORN. IT IS A MANDATE OF HEAVEN. FOR THE LAST TEN YEARS, THE WORLD OF DARKNESS HAS BEEN OVER-WHELMED BY THE POWER OF THE LIGHT.
YOU WILL BRING DARKNESS BACK!

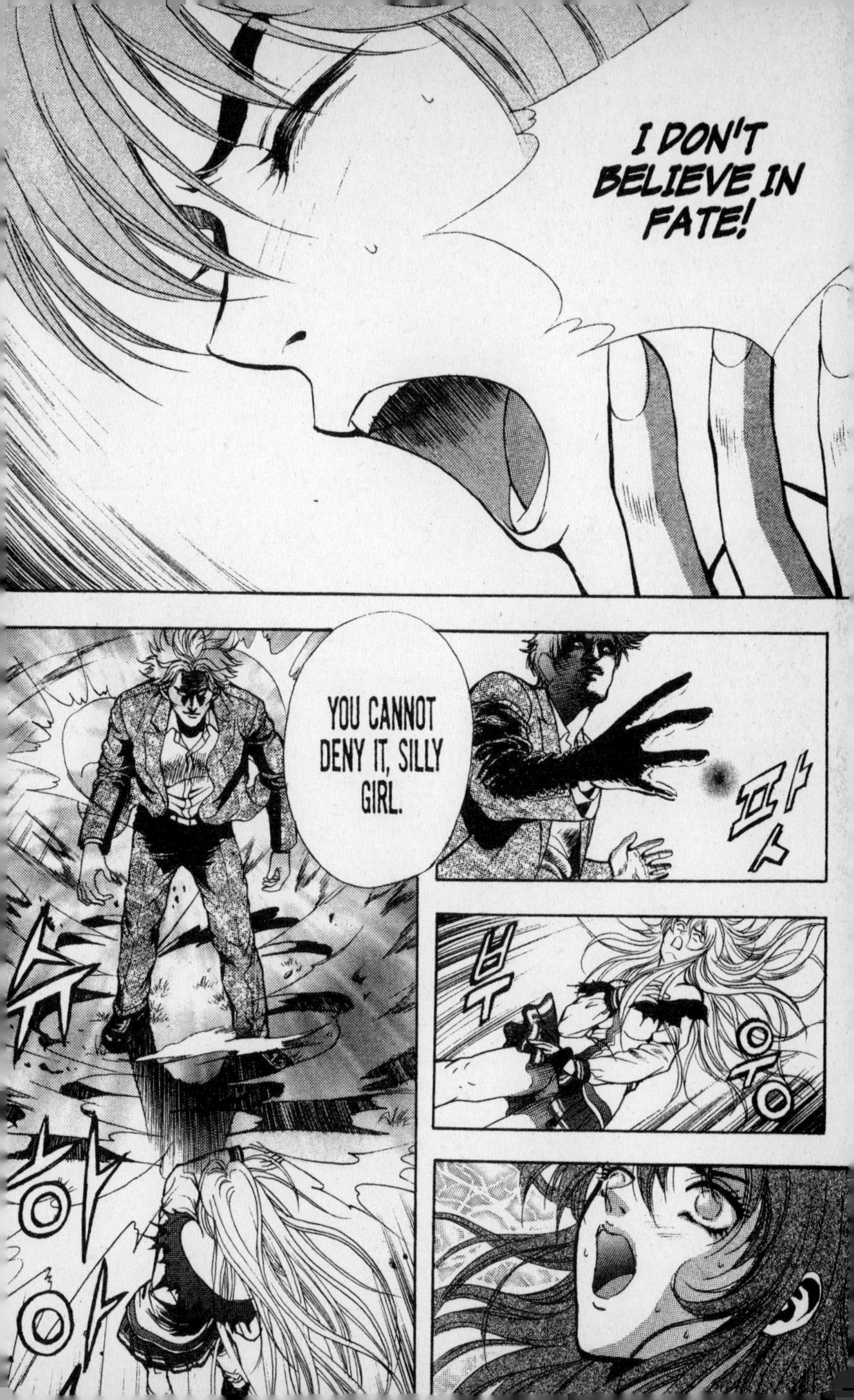
I DON'T BELIEVE IN FATE!
YOU CANNOT DENY IT, SILLY GIRL.

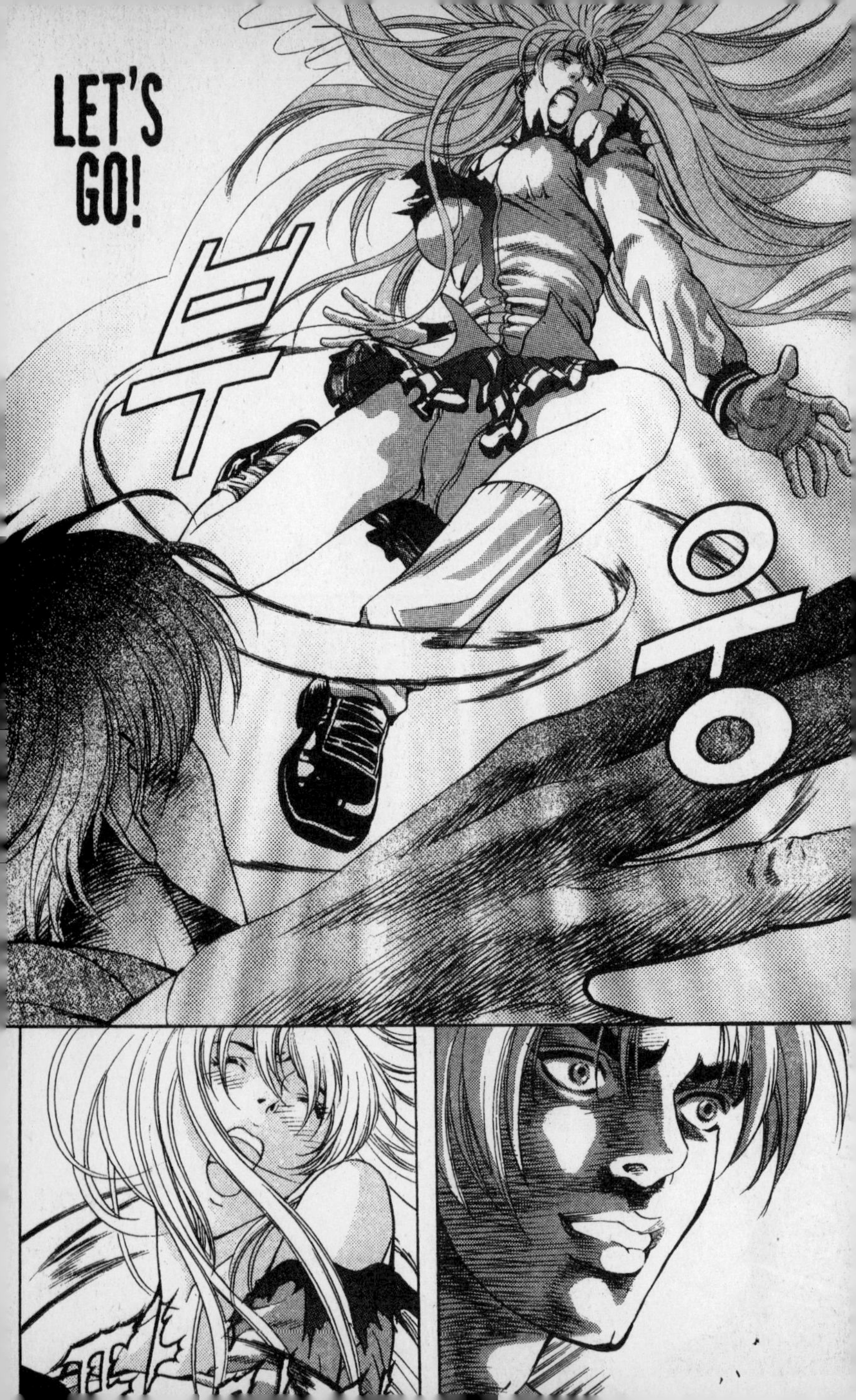
LET'S GO!

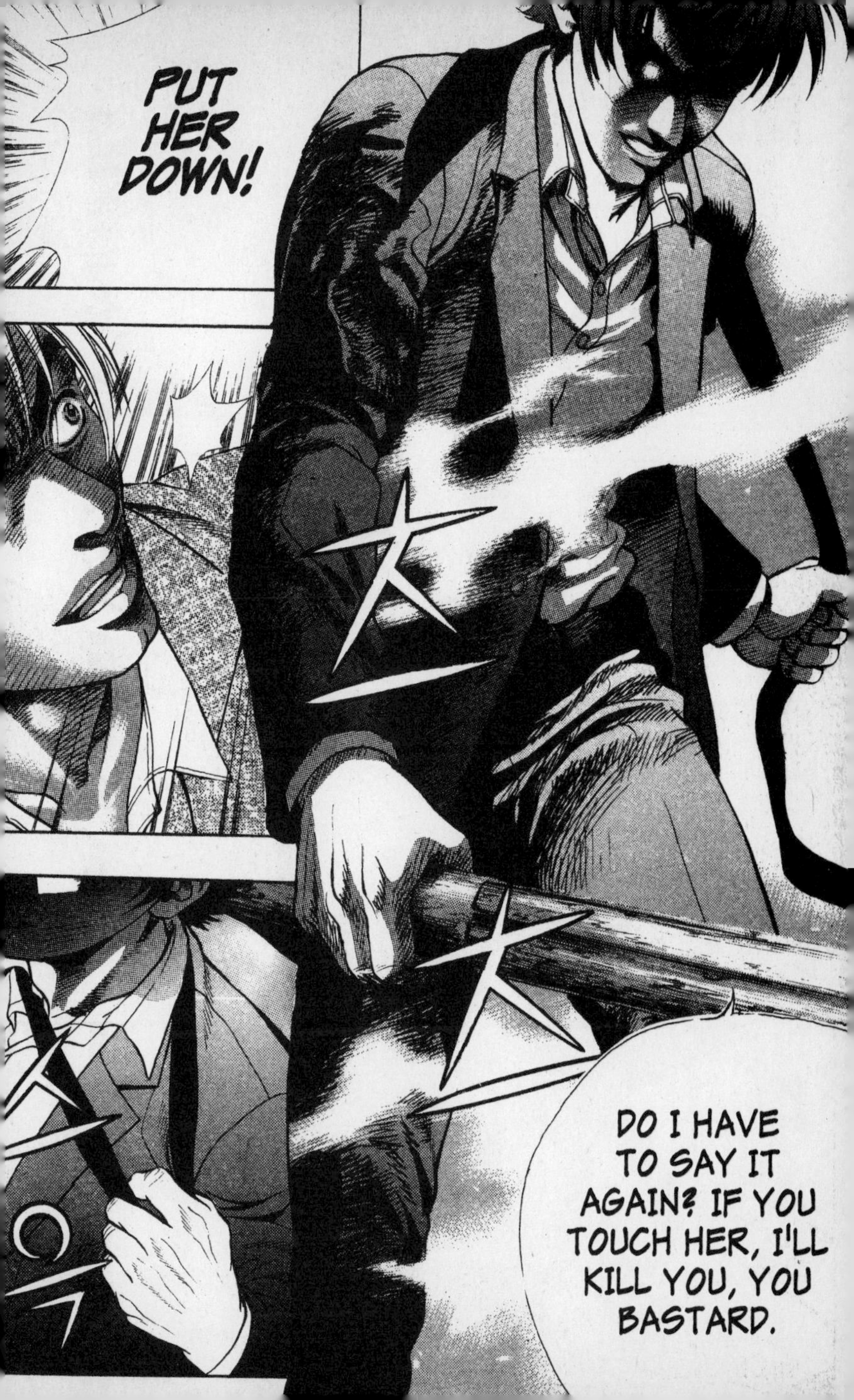
PUT HER DOWN!
DO I HAVE TO SAY IT AGAIN? IF YOU TOUCH HER, I'LL KILL YOU, YOU BASTARD.

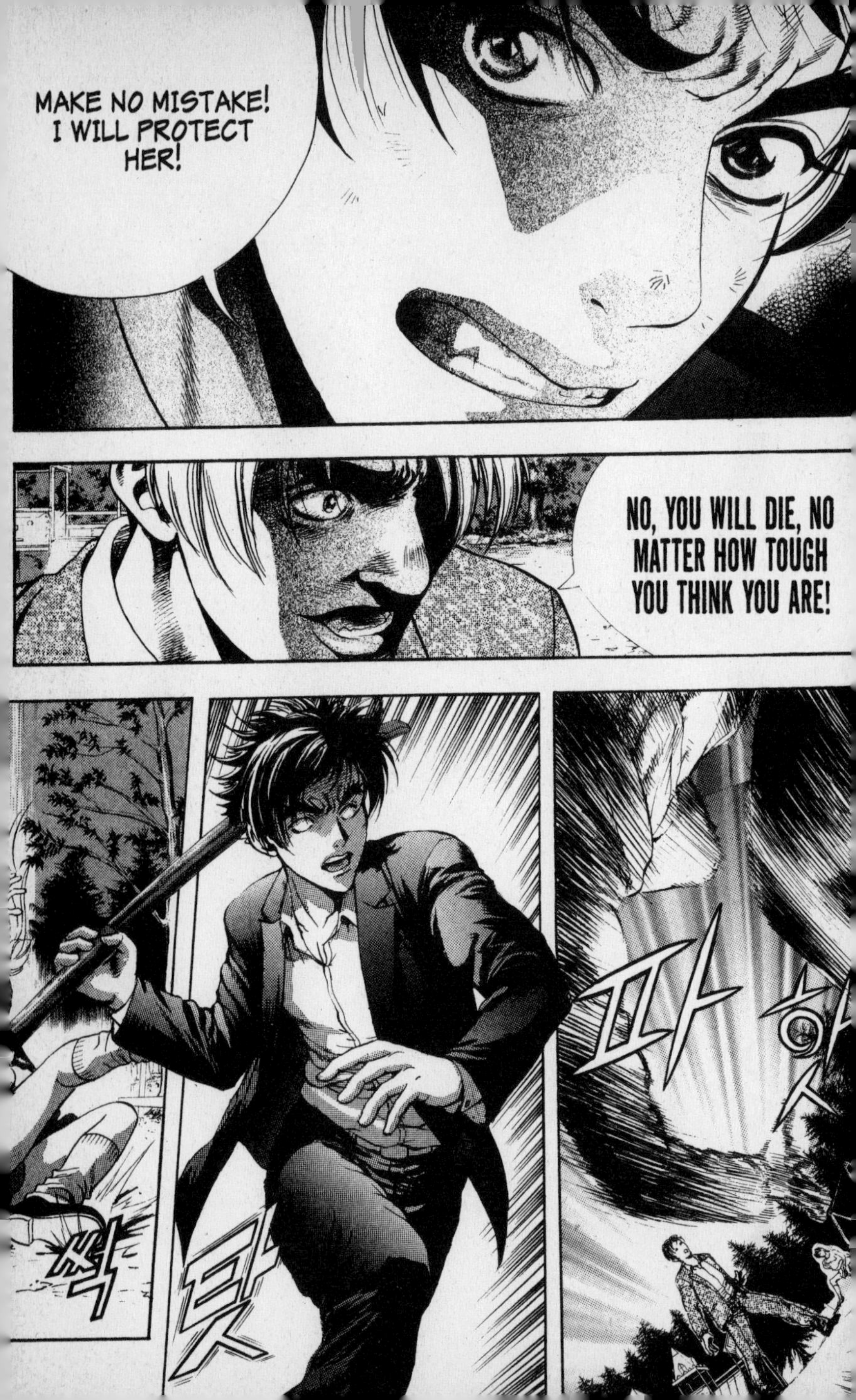
MAKE NO MISTAKE! I WILL PROTECT HER!
NO, YOU WILL DIE, NO MATTER HOW TOUGH YOU THINK YOU ARE!

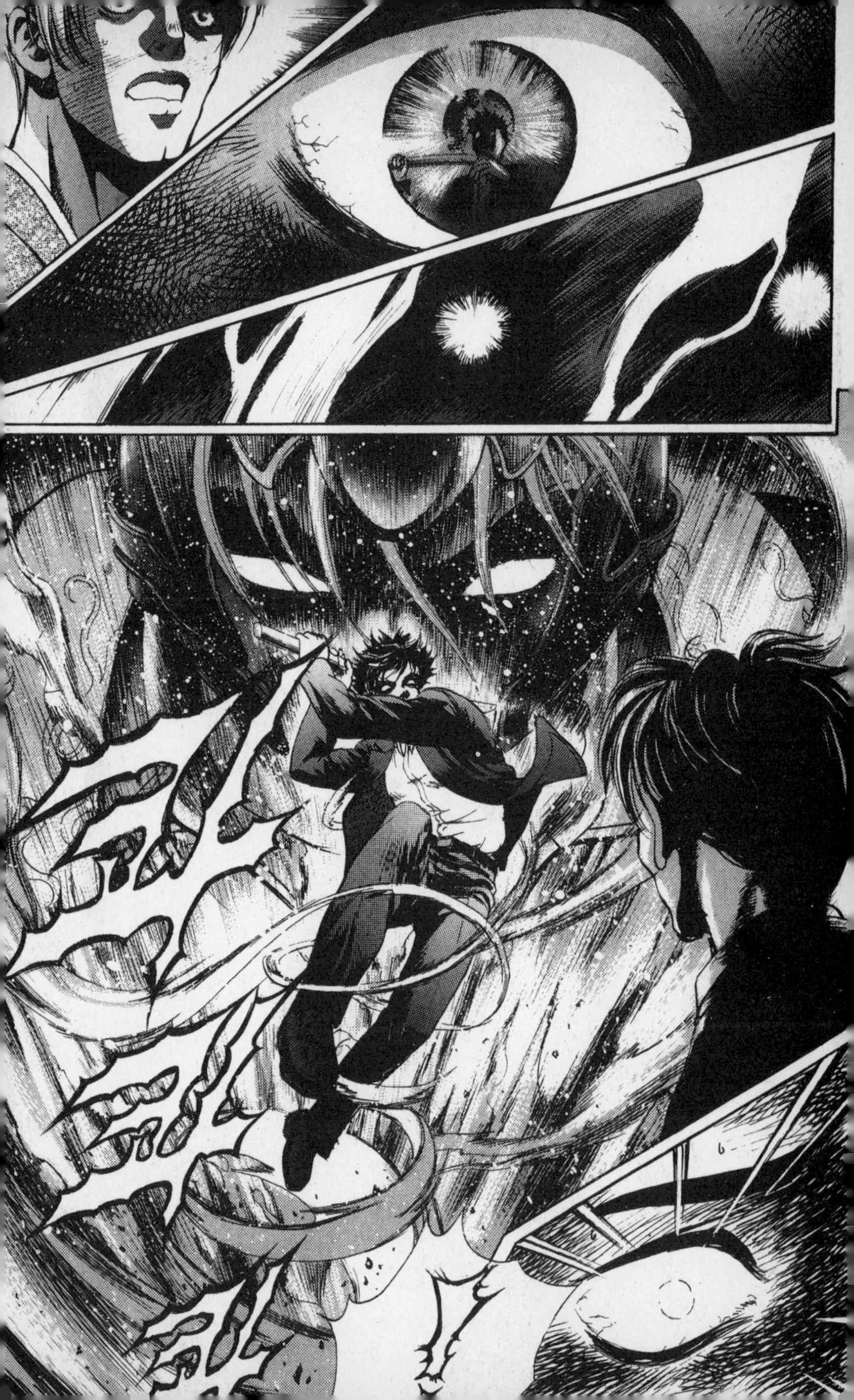

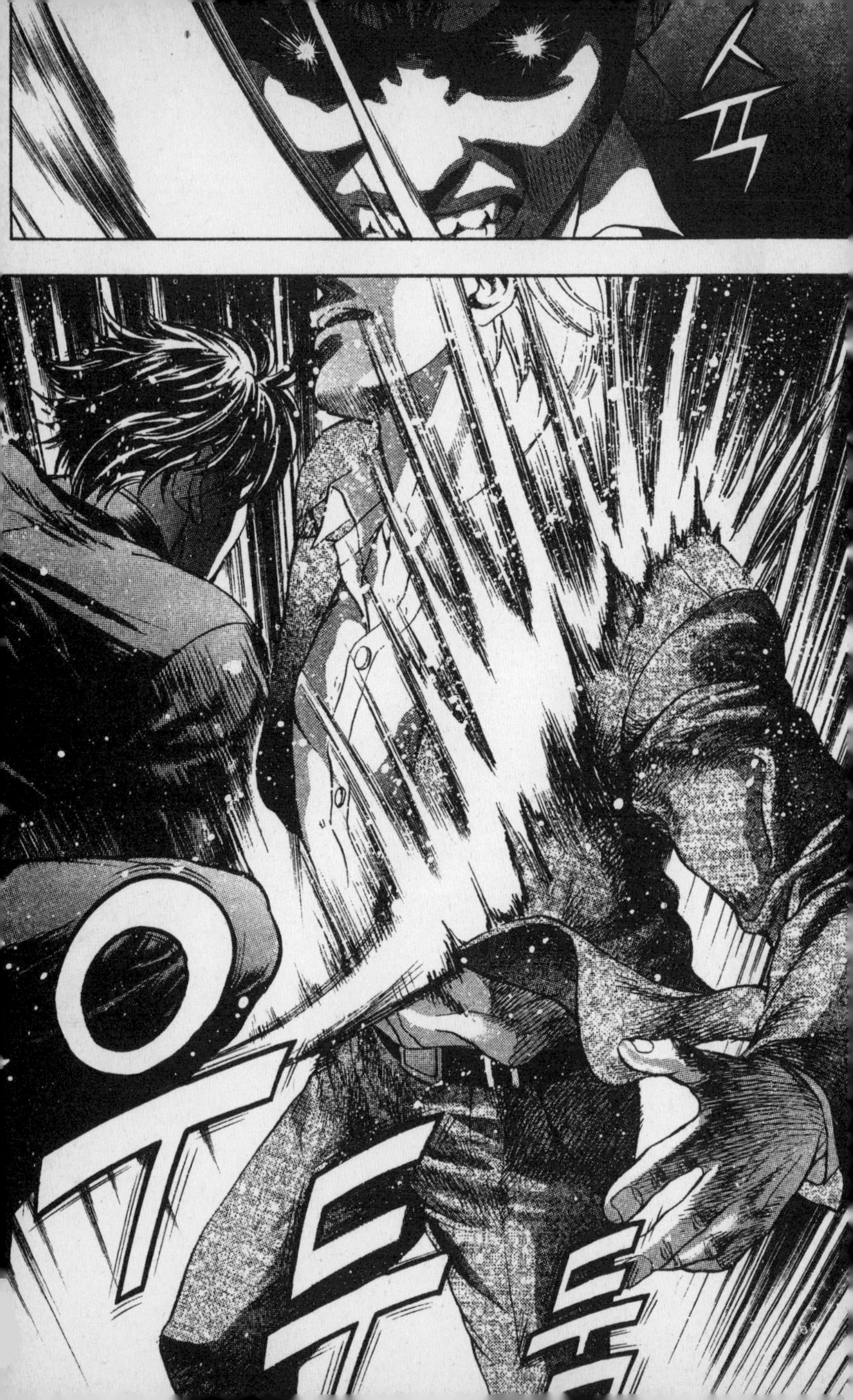

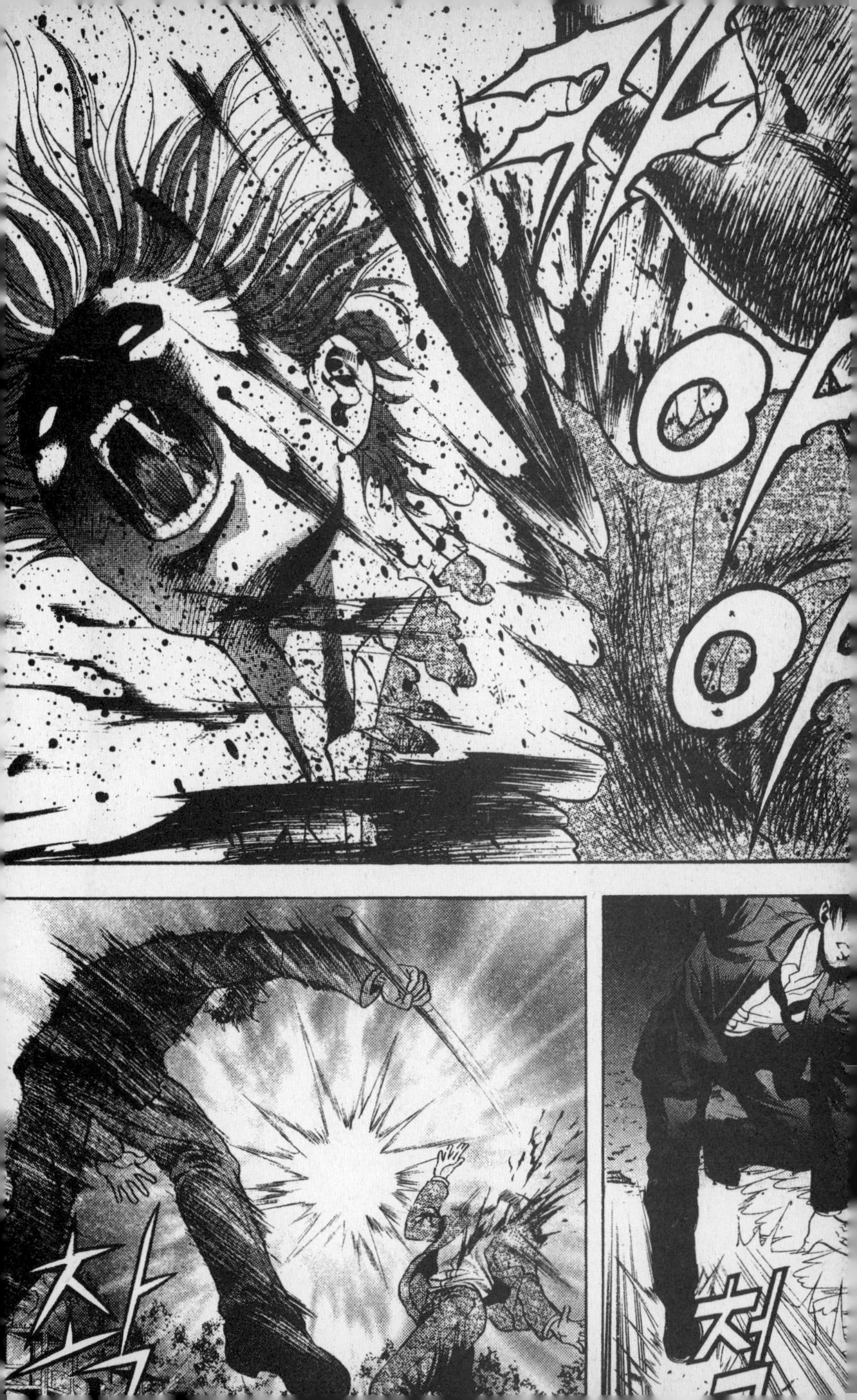

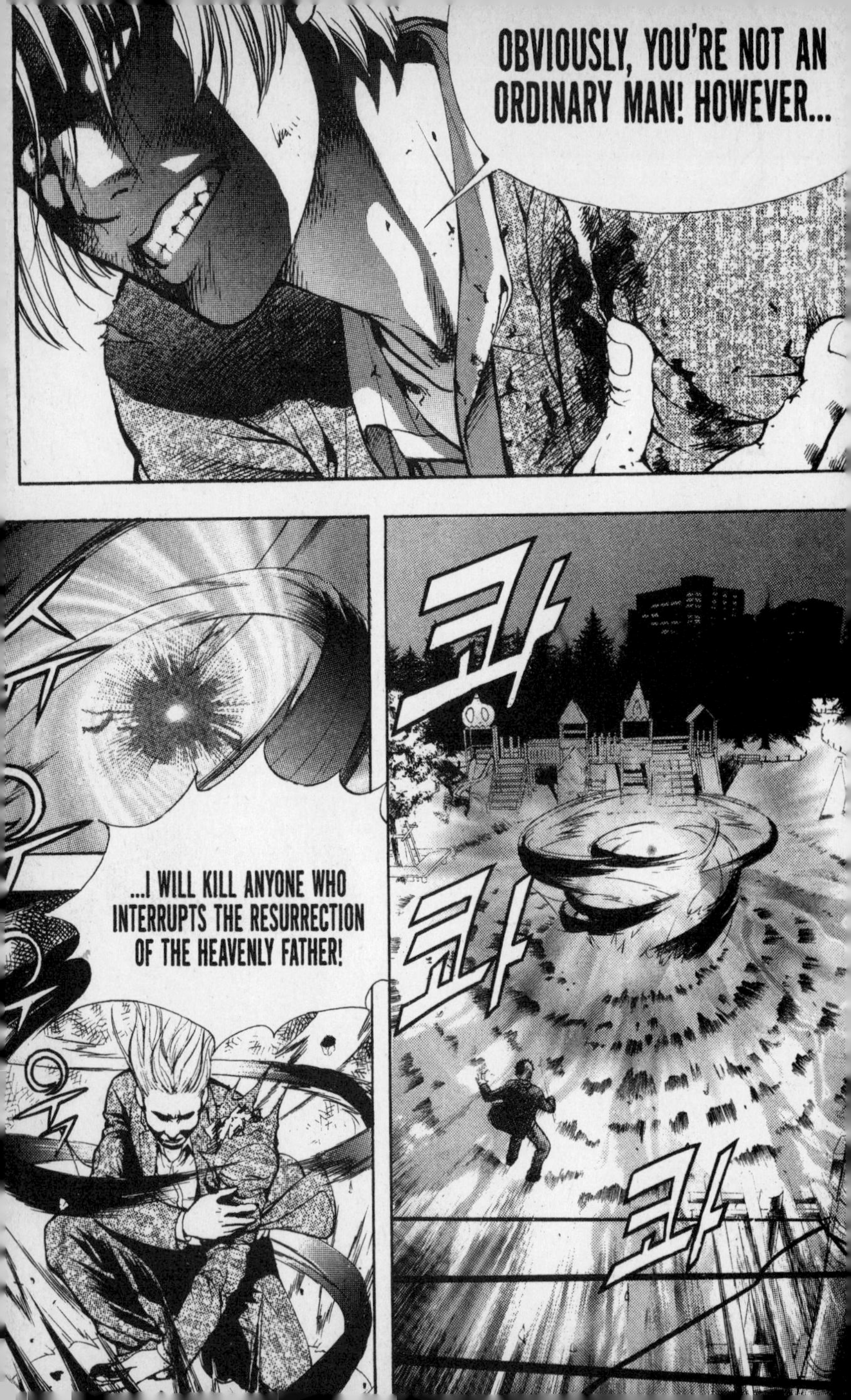
OBVIOUSLY, YOU'RE NOT AN ORDINARY MAN! HOWEVER...
...I WILL KILL ANYONE WHO INTERRUPTS THE RESURRECTION OF THE HEAVENLY FATHER!

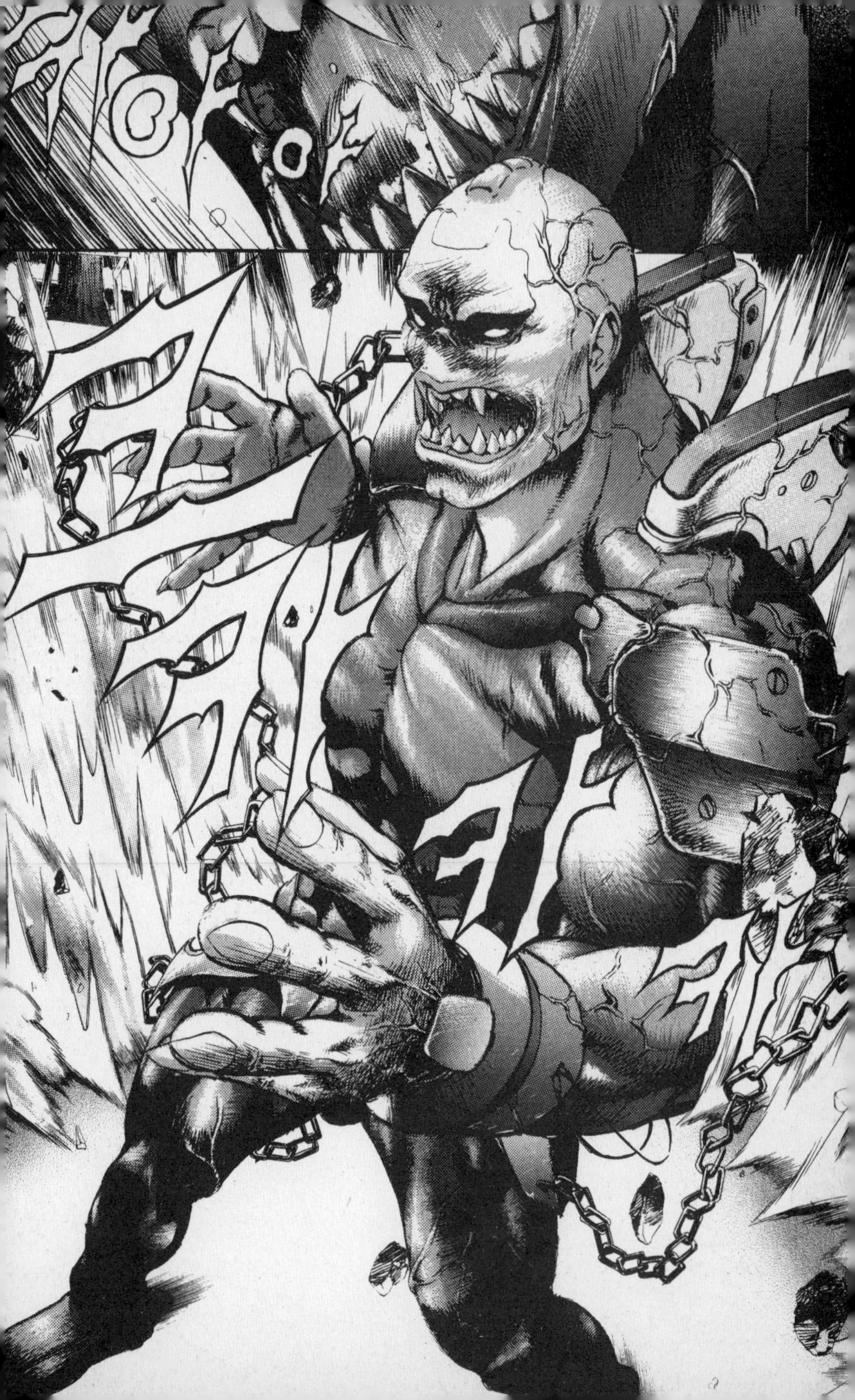

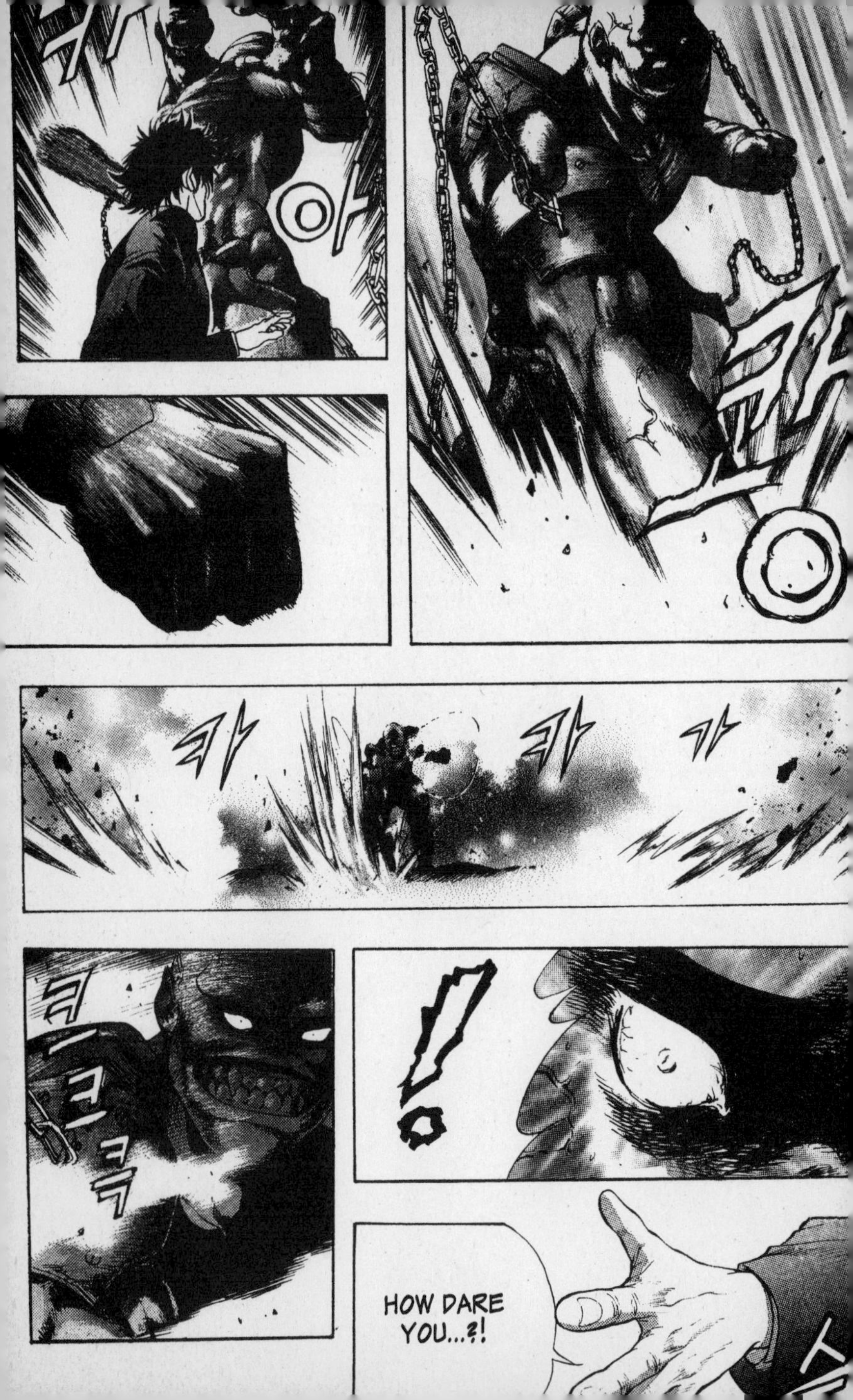
HOW DARE YOU...?!

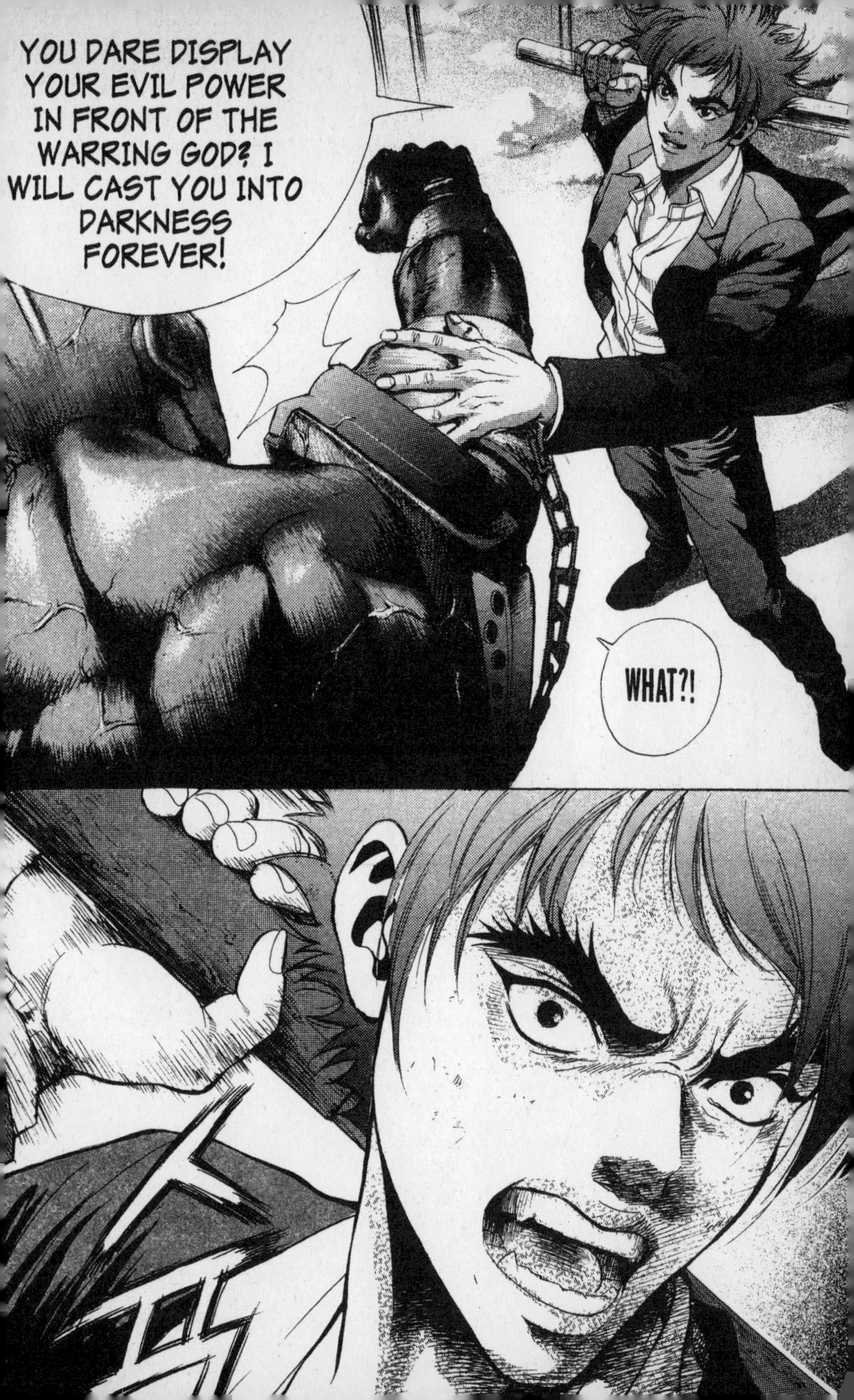
YOU DARE DISPLAY YOUR EVIL POWER IN FRONT OF THE WARRING GOD? I WILL CAST YOU INTO DARKNESS FOREVER!
WHAT?!

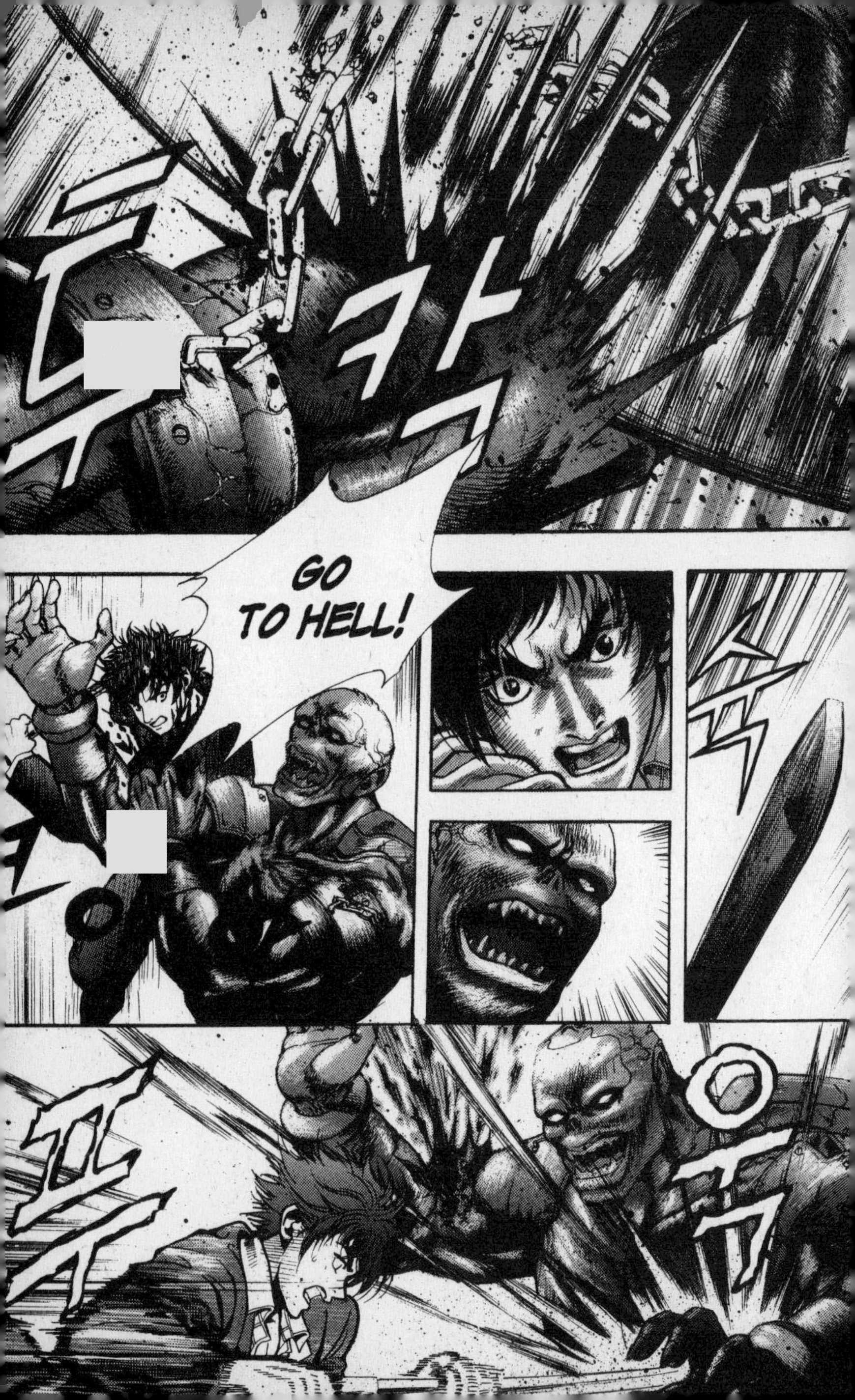
GO TO HELL!

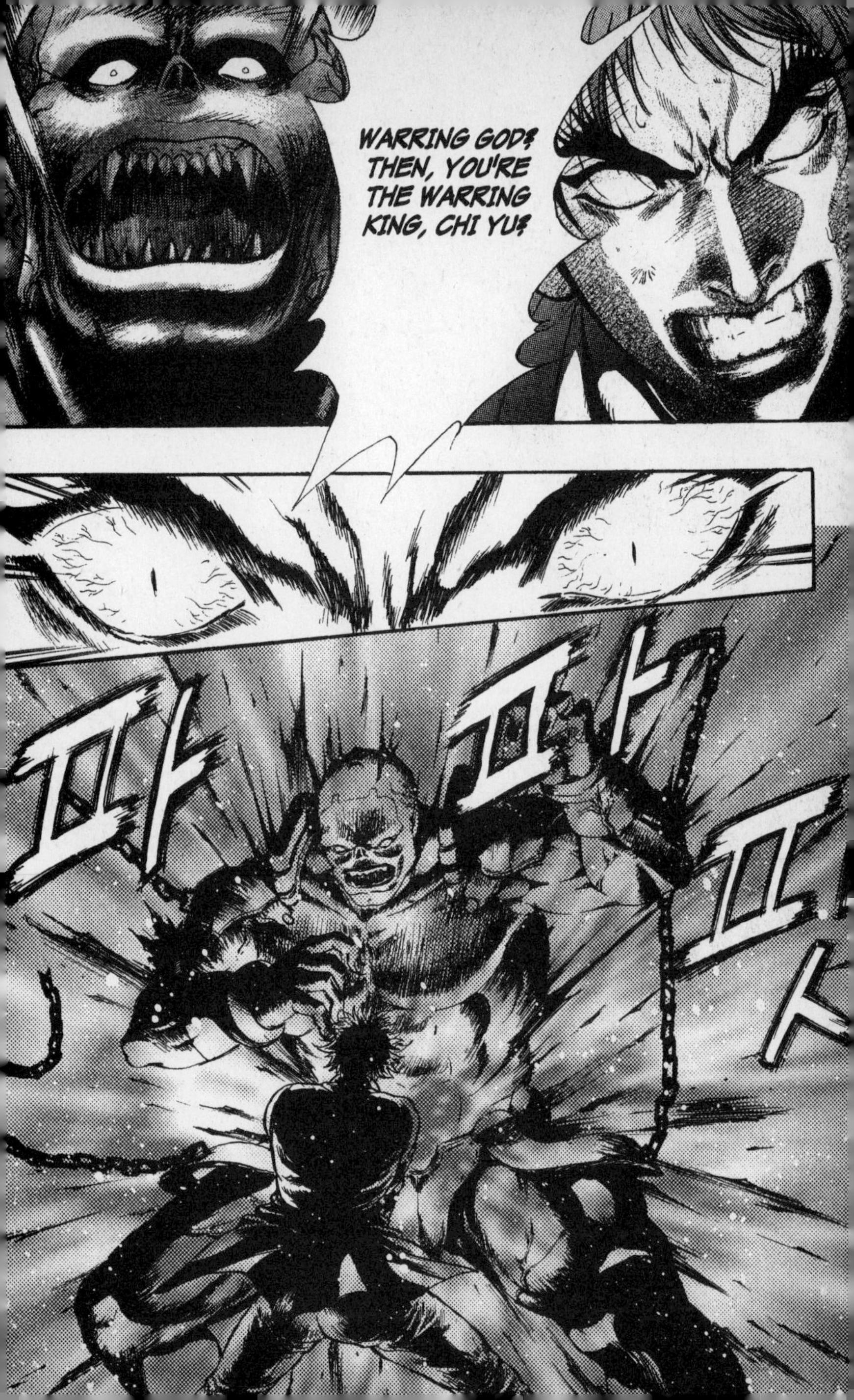
WARRING GOD? THEN, YOU'RE THE WARRING KING, CHI YU?
파
파
파

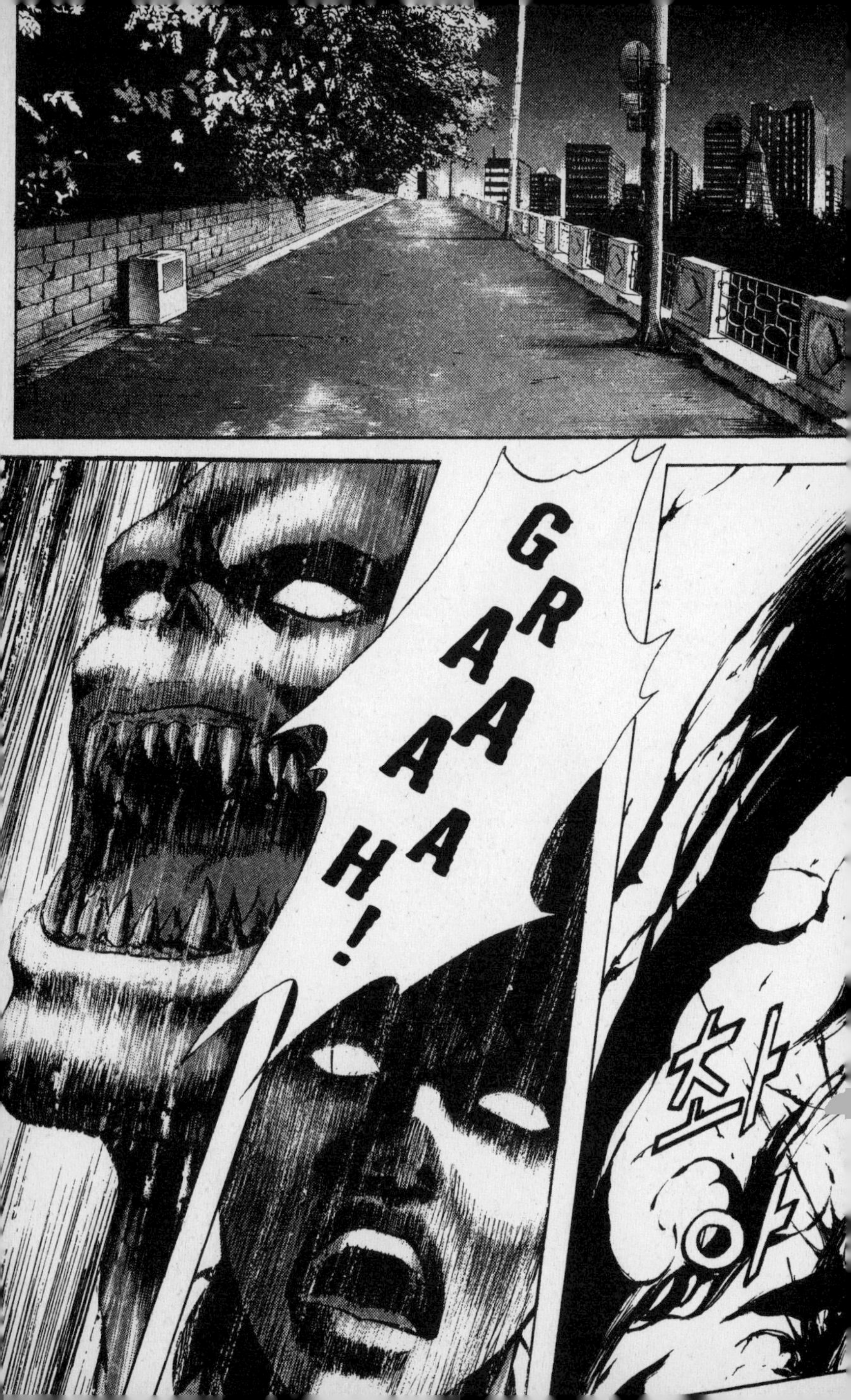
GRAAAAH!

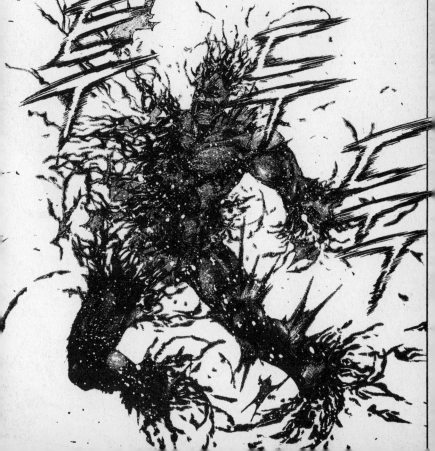

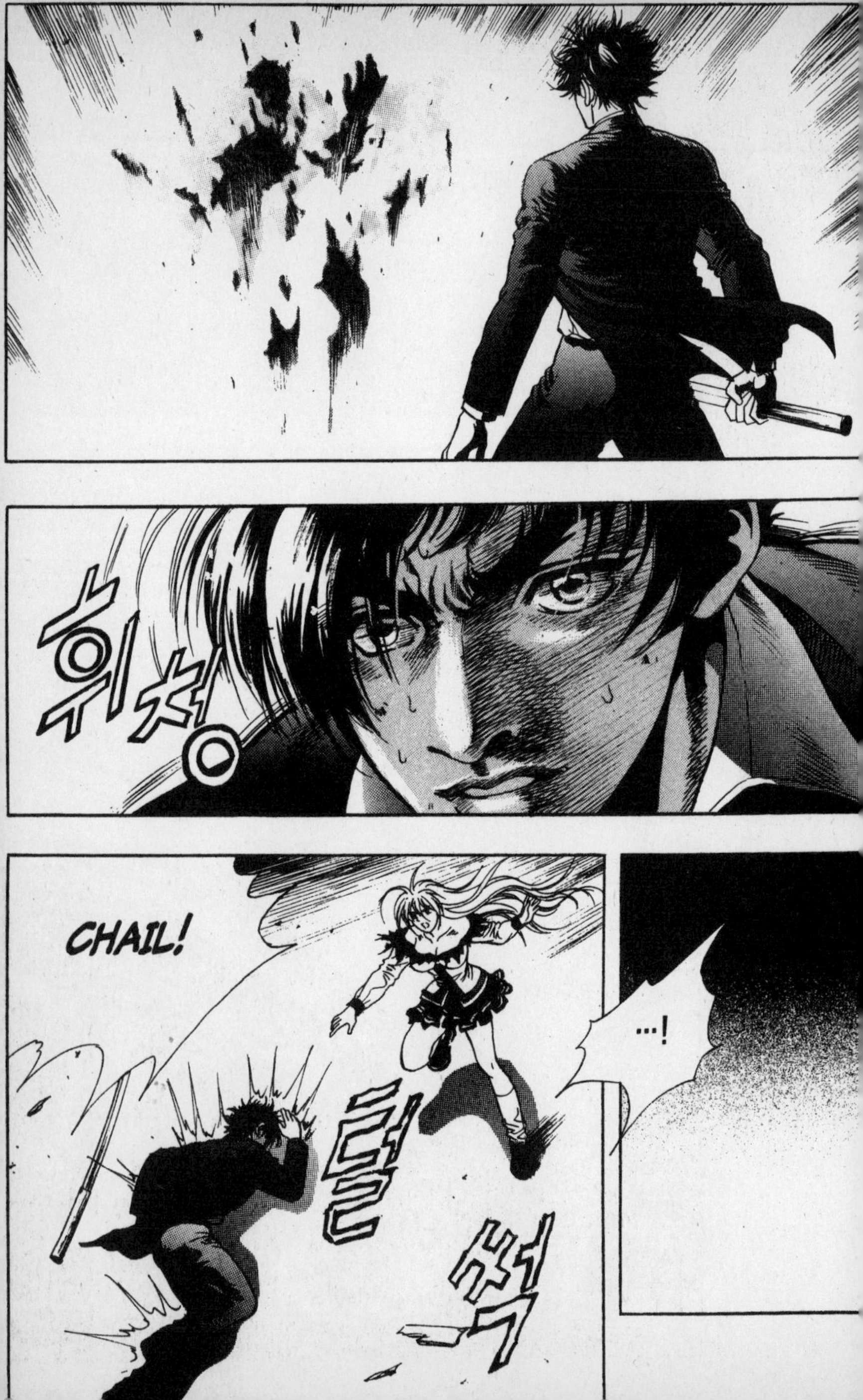
CHAIL!
...!

地

人

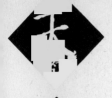

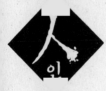

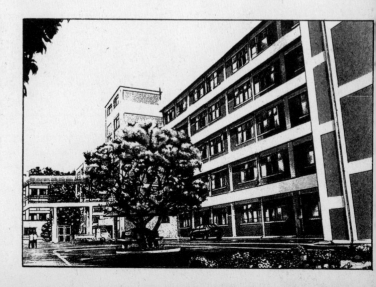

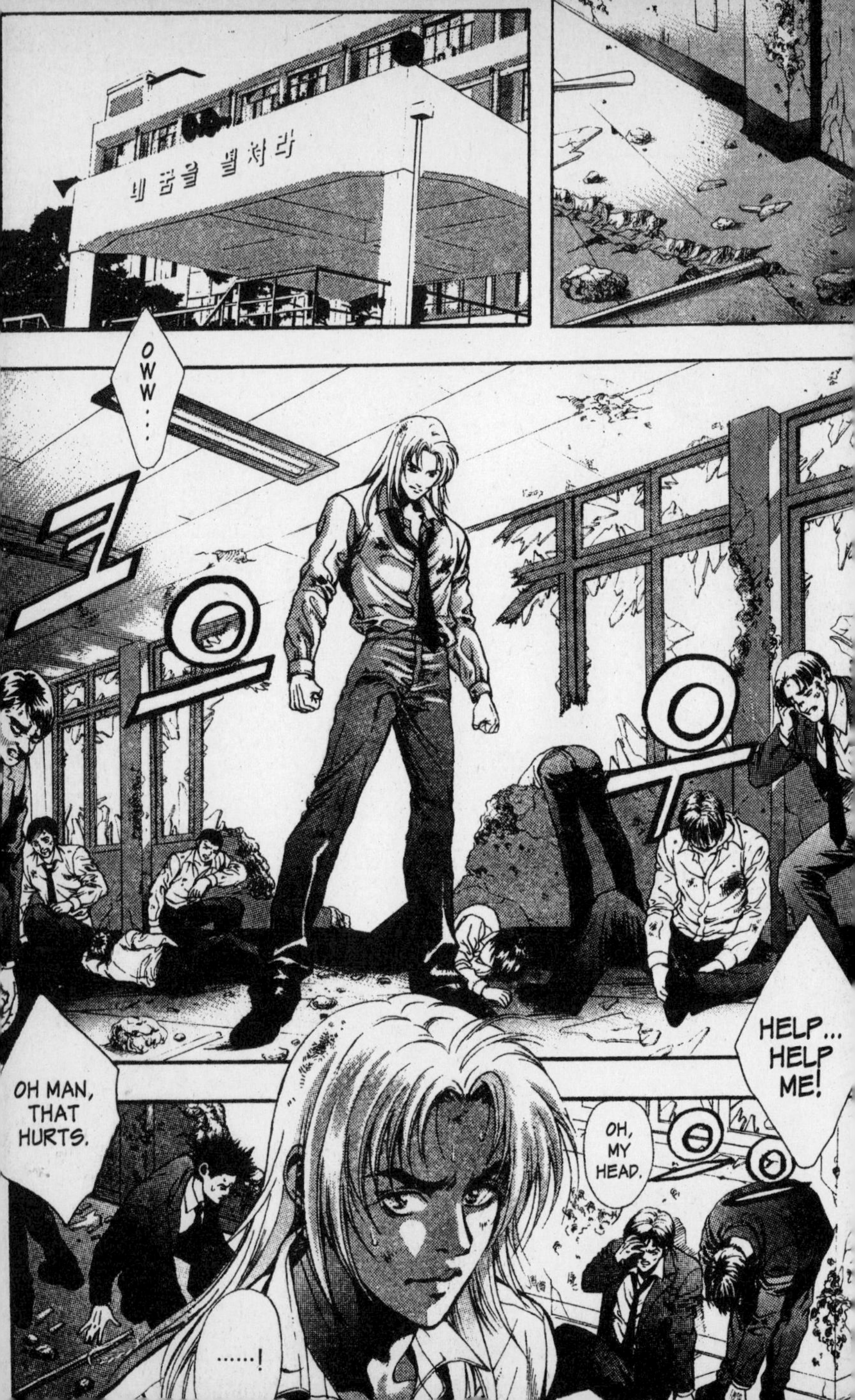

OWW...
OH MAN, THAT HURTS.
OH, MY HEAD.
HELP... HELP ME!
......!

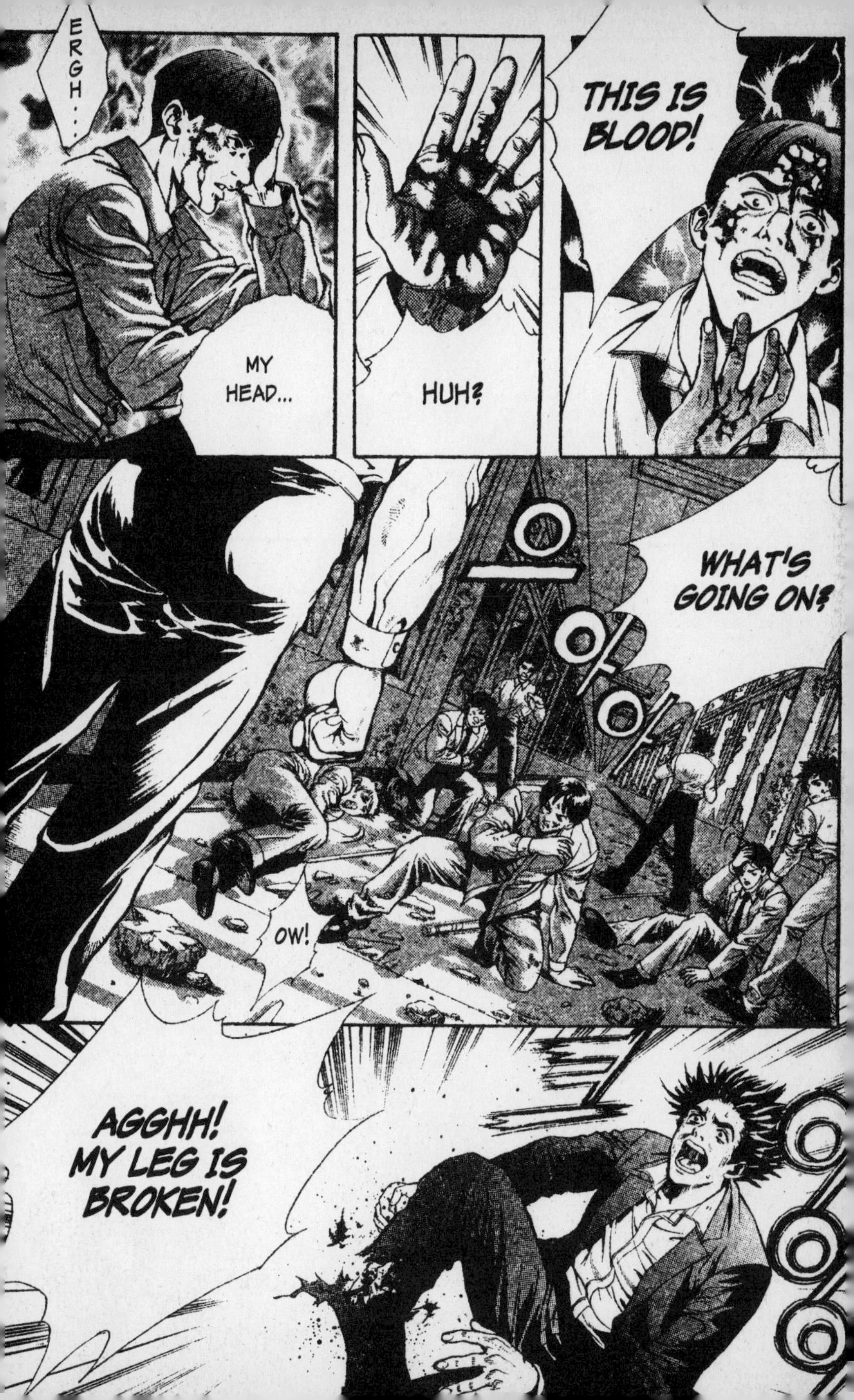

ERGH...
MY HEAD...
HUH?
THIS IS BLOOD!
WHAT'S GOING ON?
OW!
AGGHH! MY LEG IS BROKEN!

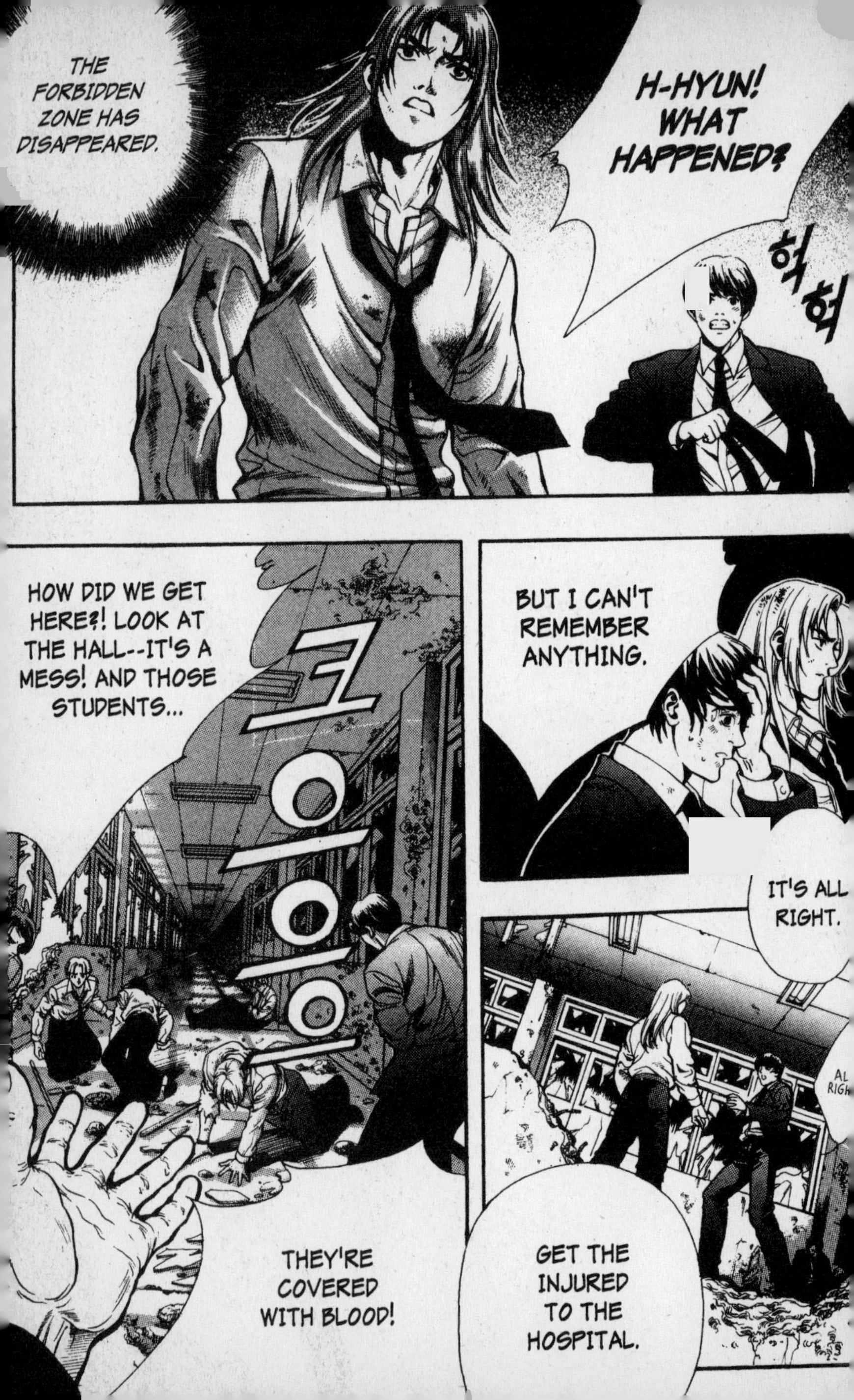
THE FORBIDDEN ZONE HAS DISAPPEARED.
H-HYUN! WHAT HAPPENED?
헉 헉
HOW DID WE GET HERE?! LOOK AT THE HALL--IT'S A MESS! AND THOSE STUDENTS...
THEY'RE COVERED WITH BLOOD!
BUT I CAN'T REMEMBER ANYTHING.
IT'S ALL RIGHT.
GET THE INJURED TO THE HOSPITAL.

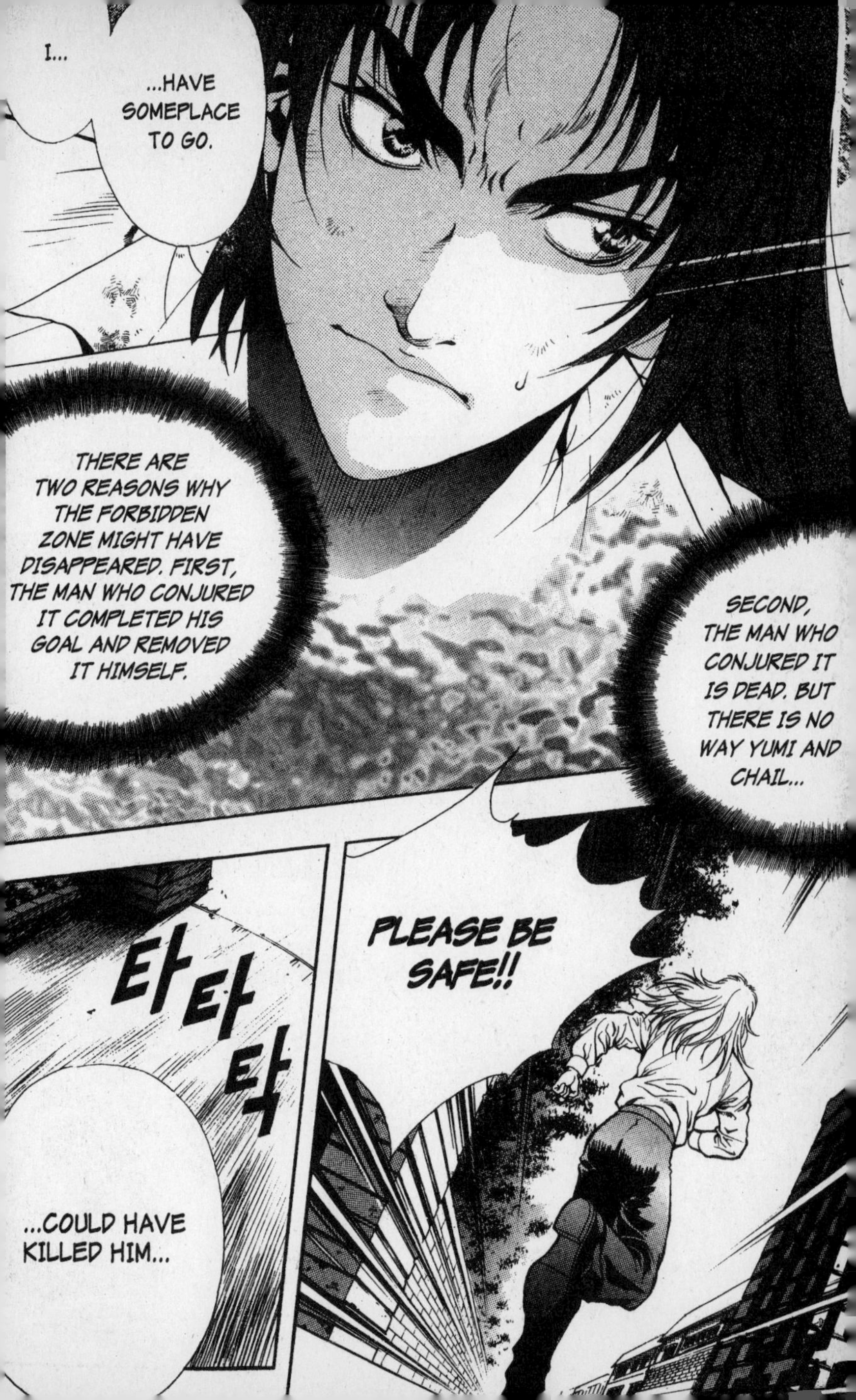
I...
...HAVE SOMEPLACE TO GO.
THERE ARE TWO REASONS WHY THE FORBIDDEN ZONE MIGHT HAVE DISAPPEARED. FIRST, THE MAN WHO CONJURED IT COMPLETED HIS GOAL AND REMOVED IT HIMSELF.
SECOND, THE MAN WHO CONJURED IT IS DEAD. BUT THERE IS NO WAY YUMI AND CHAIL...
...COULD HAVE KILLED HIM...
타 타 타
PLEASE BE SAFE!!

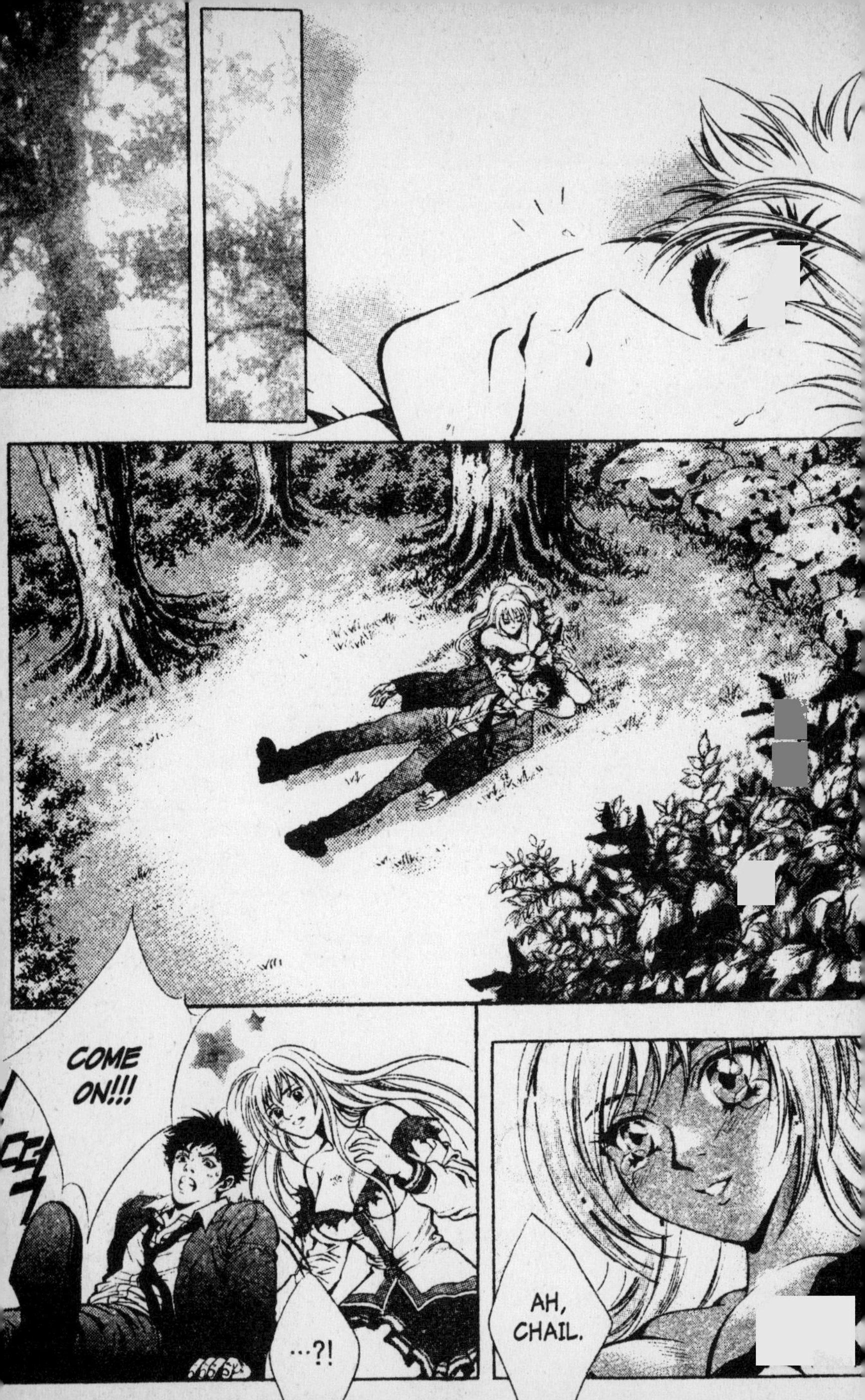
AH, CHAIL.
COME ON!!!
...?!

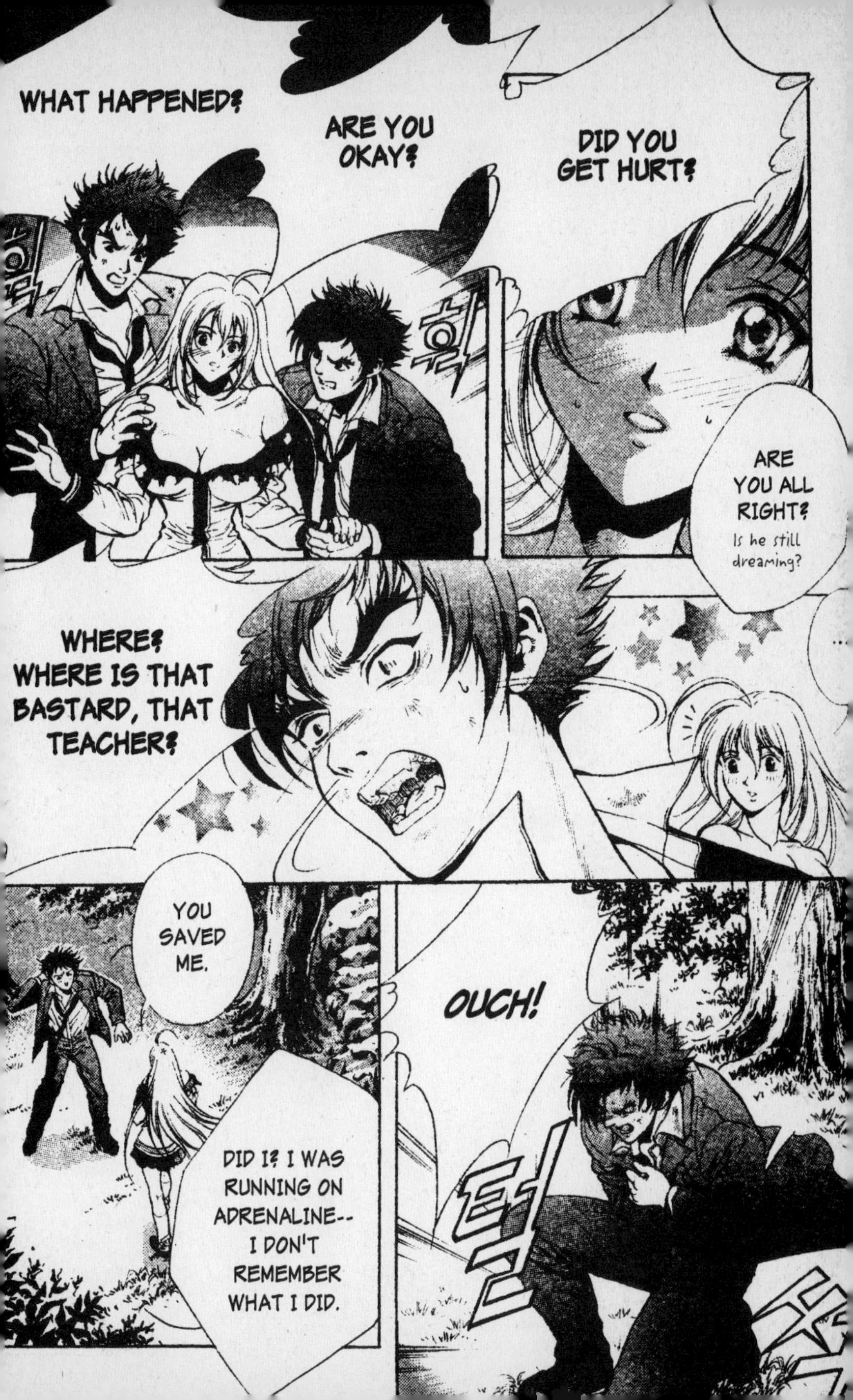
WHAT HAPPENED?
ARE YOU OKAY?
DID YOU GET HURT?
ARE YOU ALL RIGHT?
Is he still dreaming?
WHERE? WHERE IS THAT BASTARD, THAT TEACHER?
YOU SAVED ME.
DID I? I WAS RUNNING ON ADRENALINE-- I DON'T REMEMBER WHAT I DID.
OUCH!

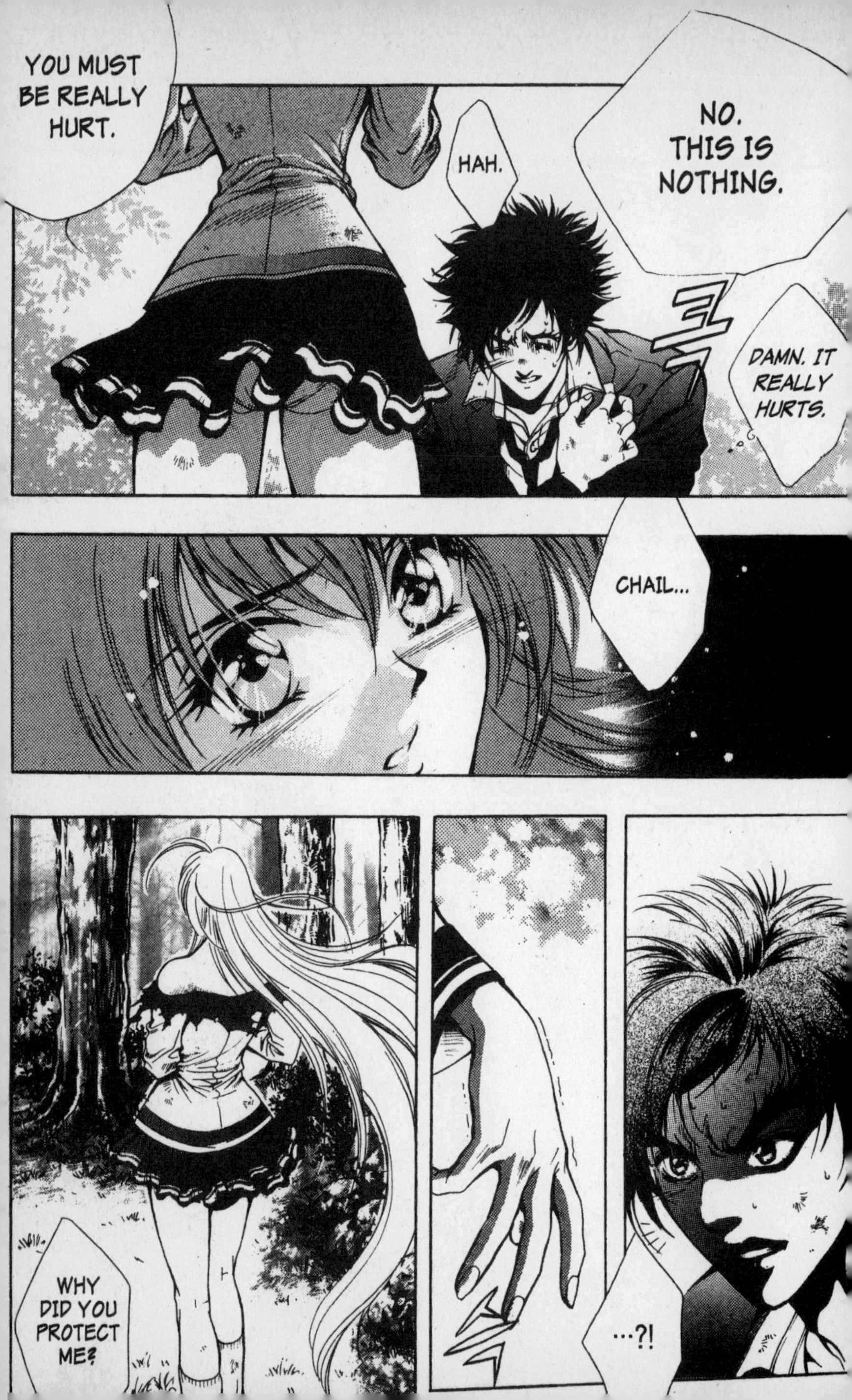
YOU MUST BE REALLY HURT.
HAH.
NO. THIS IS NOTHING.
DAMN. IT REALLY HURTS.
CHAIL...
WHY DID YOU PROTECT ME?
...?!

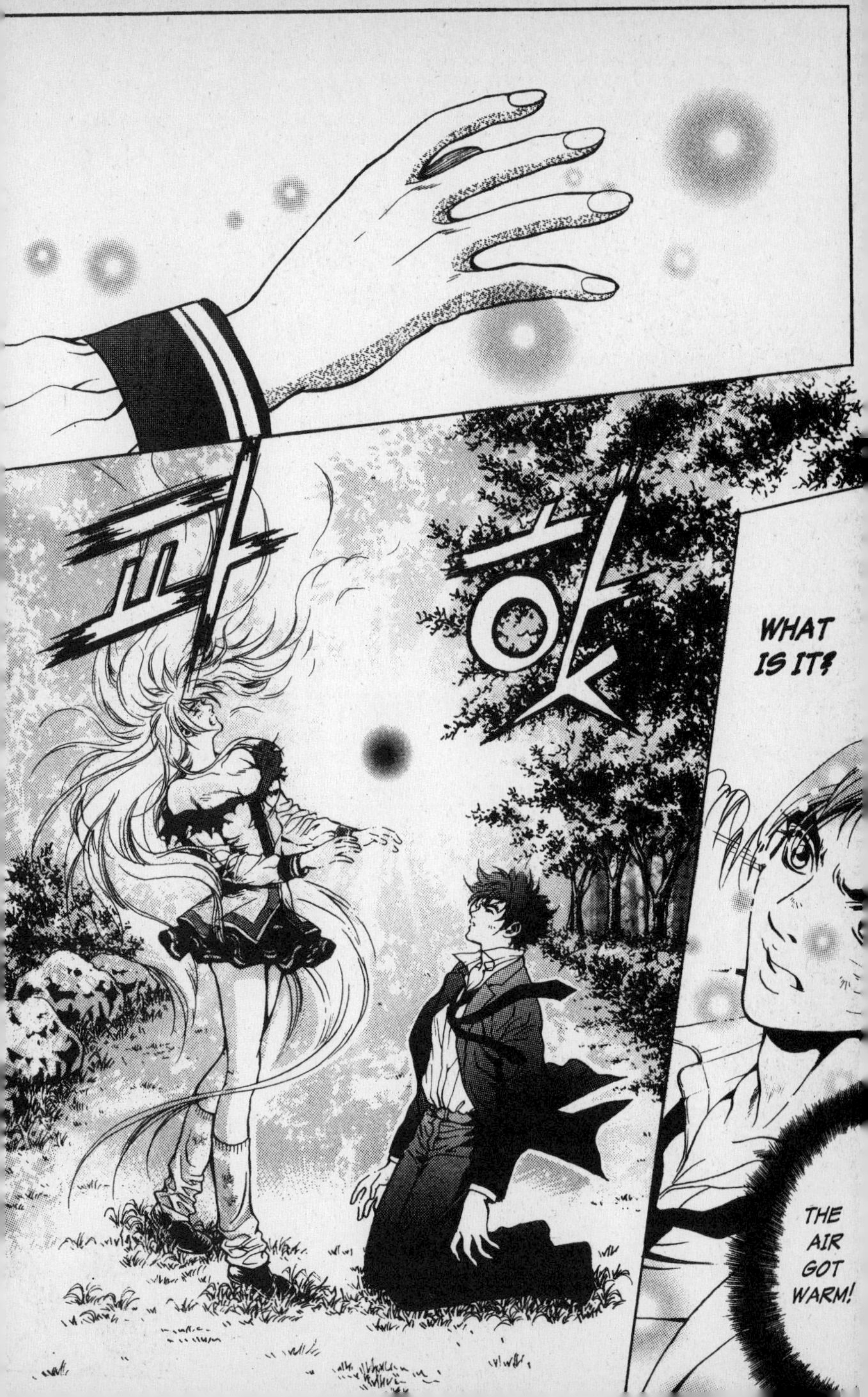
WHAT IS IT?
THE AIR GOT WARM!

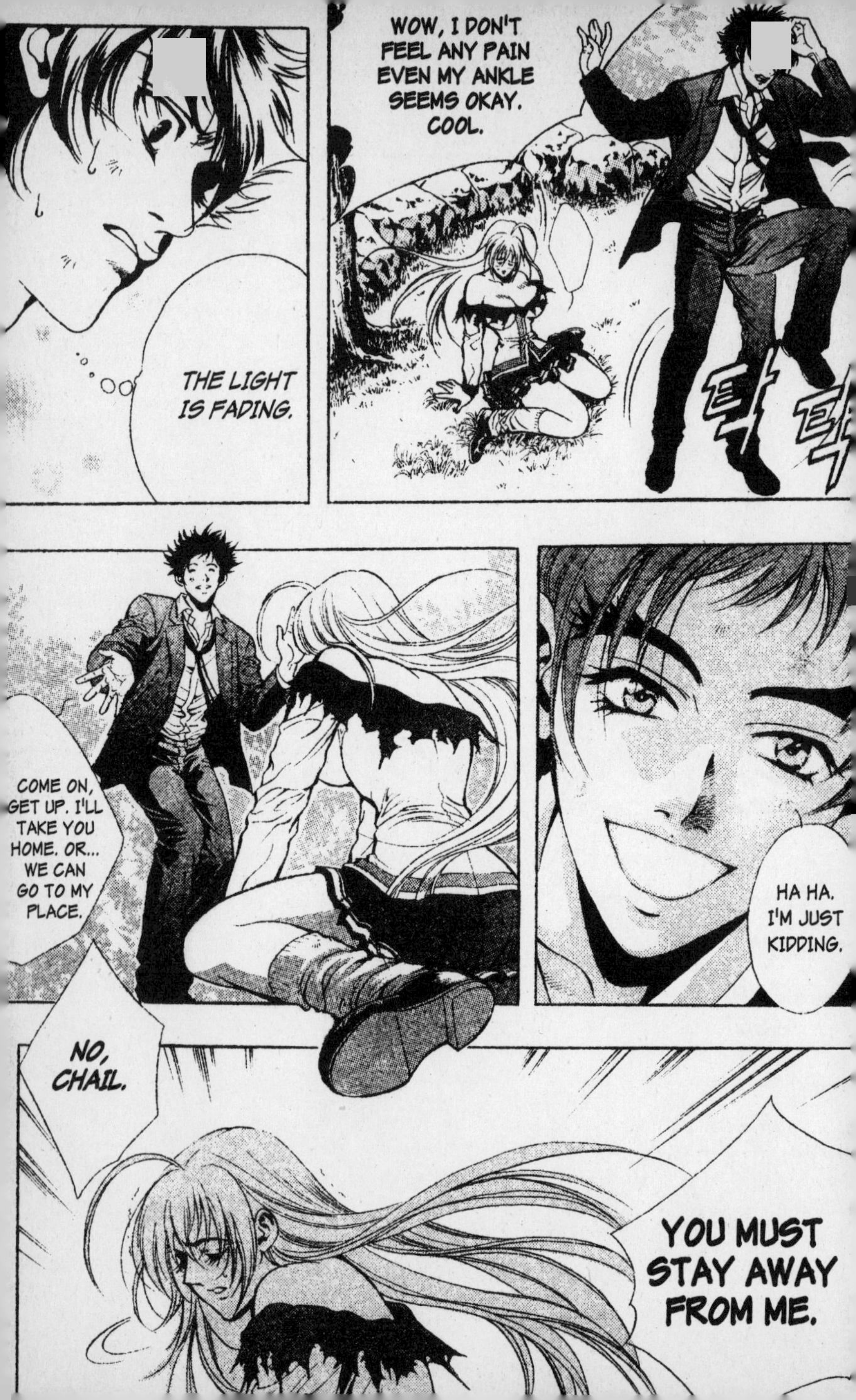
THE LIGHT IS FADING.
WOW, I DON'T FEEL ANY PAIN EVEN MY ANKLE SEEMS OKAY. COOL.
COME ON, GET UP. I'LL TAKE YOU HOME. OR... WE CAN GO TO MY PLACE.
HA HA. I'M JUST KIDDING.
NO, CHAIL.
YOU MUST STAY AWAY FROM ME.

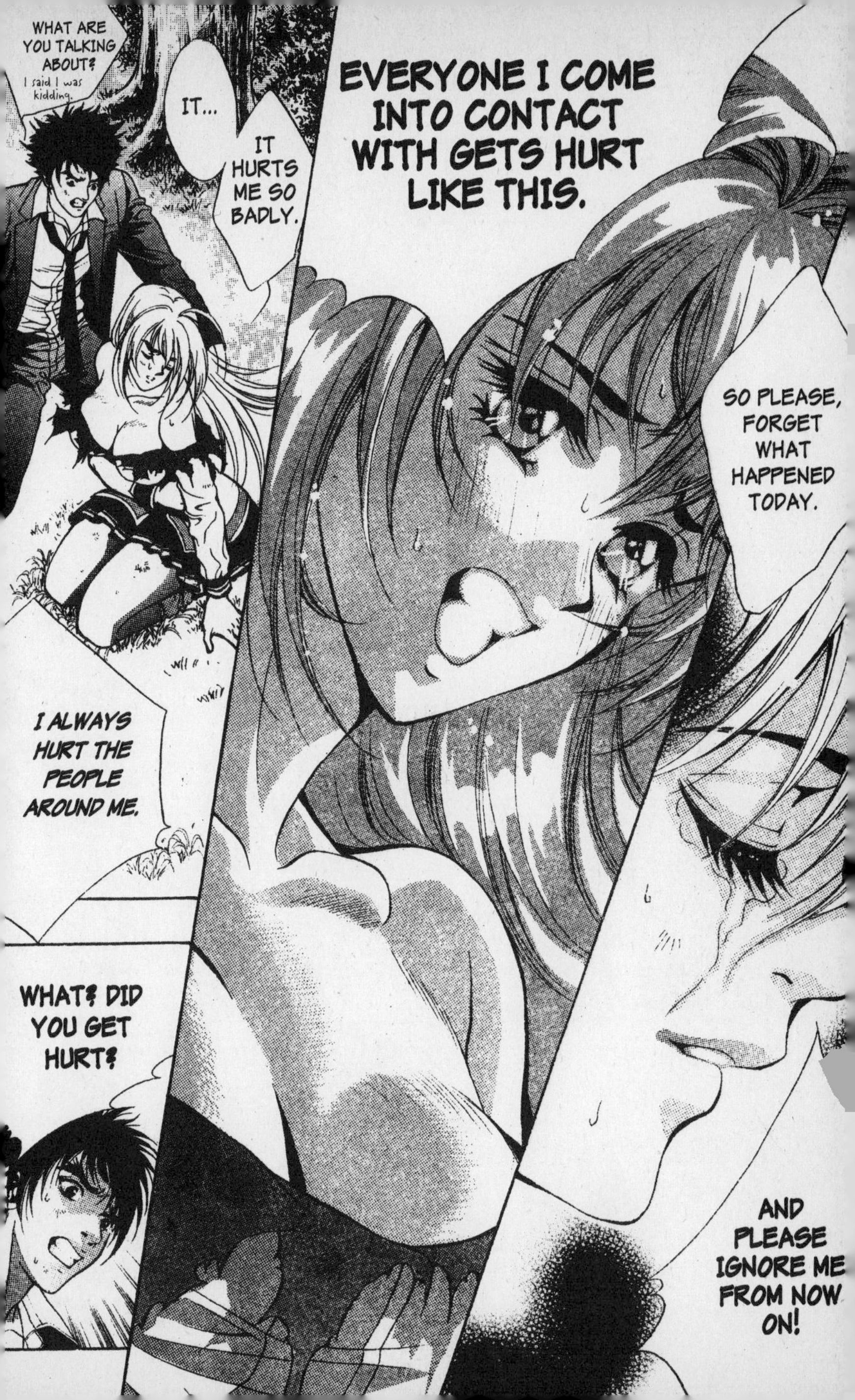

EVERYONE I COME INTO CONTACT WITH GETS HURT LIKE THIS.
IT...
IT HURTS ME SO BADLY.
WHAT ARE YOU TALKING ABOUT?
I said I was kidding.
SO PLEASE, FORGET WHAT HAPPENED TODAY.
I ALWAYS HURT THE PEOPLE AROUND ME.
AND PLEASE IGNORE ME FROM NOW ON!
WHAT? DID YOU GET HURT?

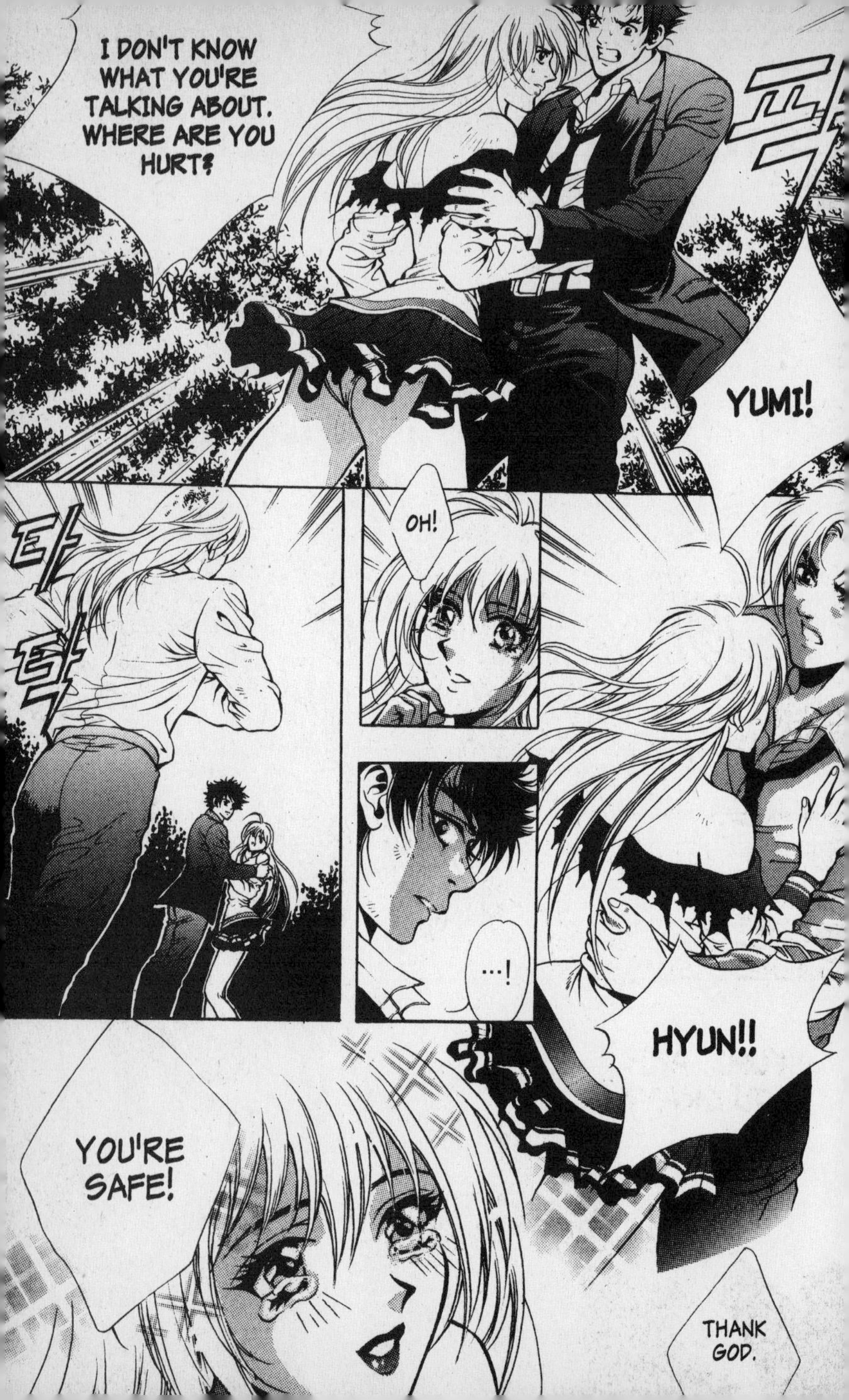
I DON'T KNOW WHAT YOU'RE TALKING ABOUT. WHERE ARE YOU HURT?
YUMI!
OH!
...!
HYUN!!
YOU'RE SAFE!
THANK GOD.

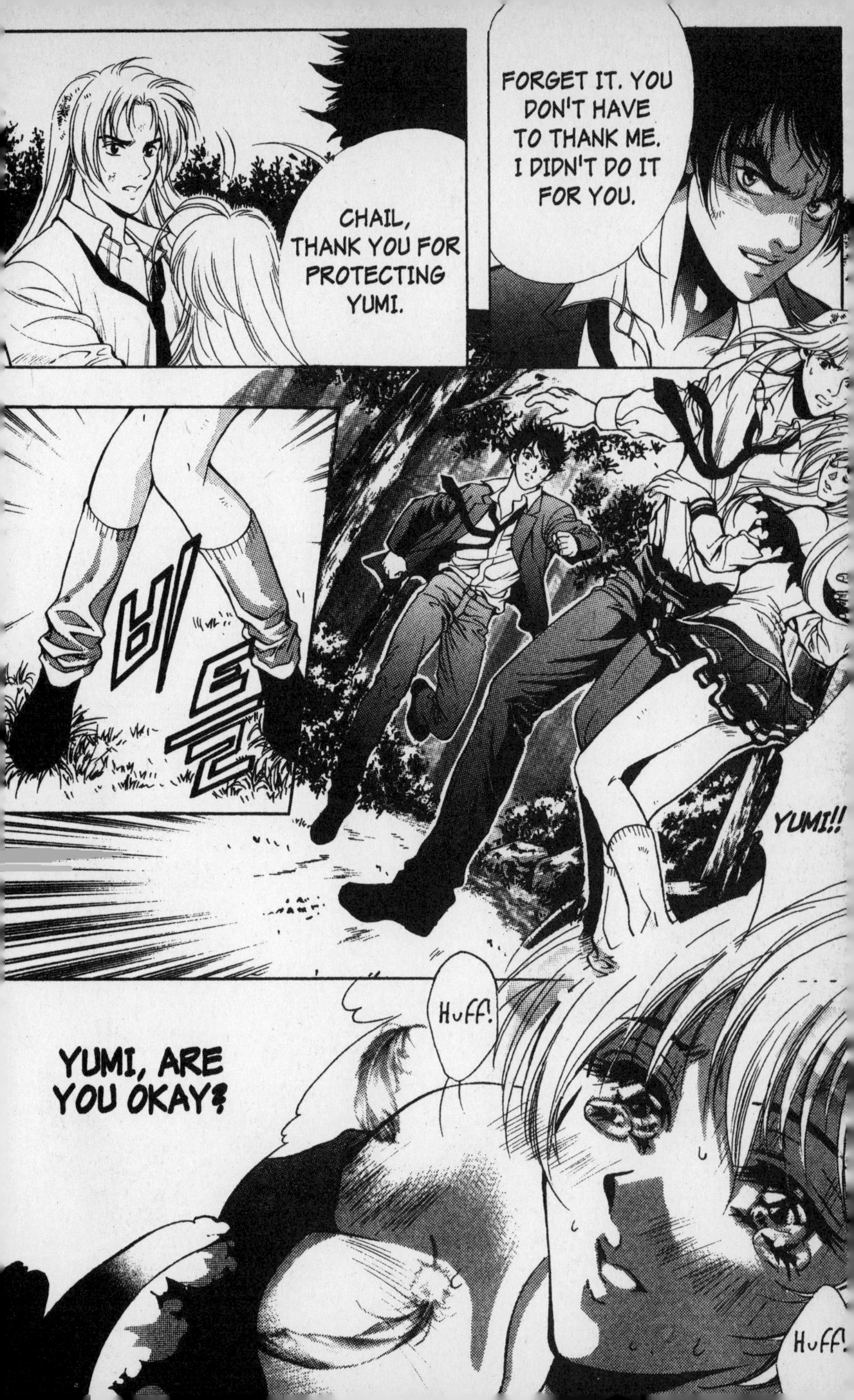
CHAIL, THANK YOU FOR PROTECTING YUMI.
FORGET IT. YOU DON'T HAVE TO THANK ME. I DIDN'T DO IT FOR YOU.
YUMI!!
YUMI, ARE YOU OKAY?
Huff!
Huff!

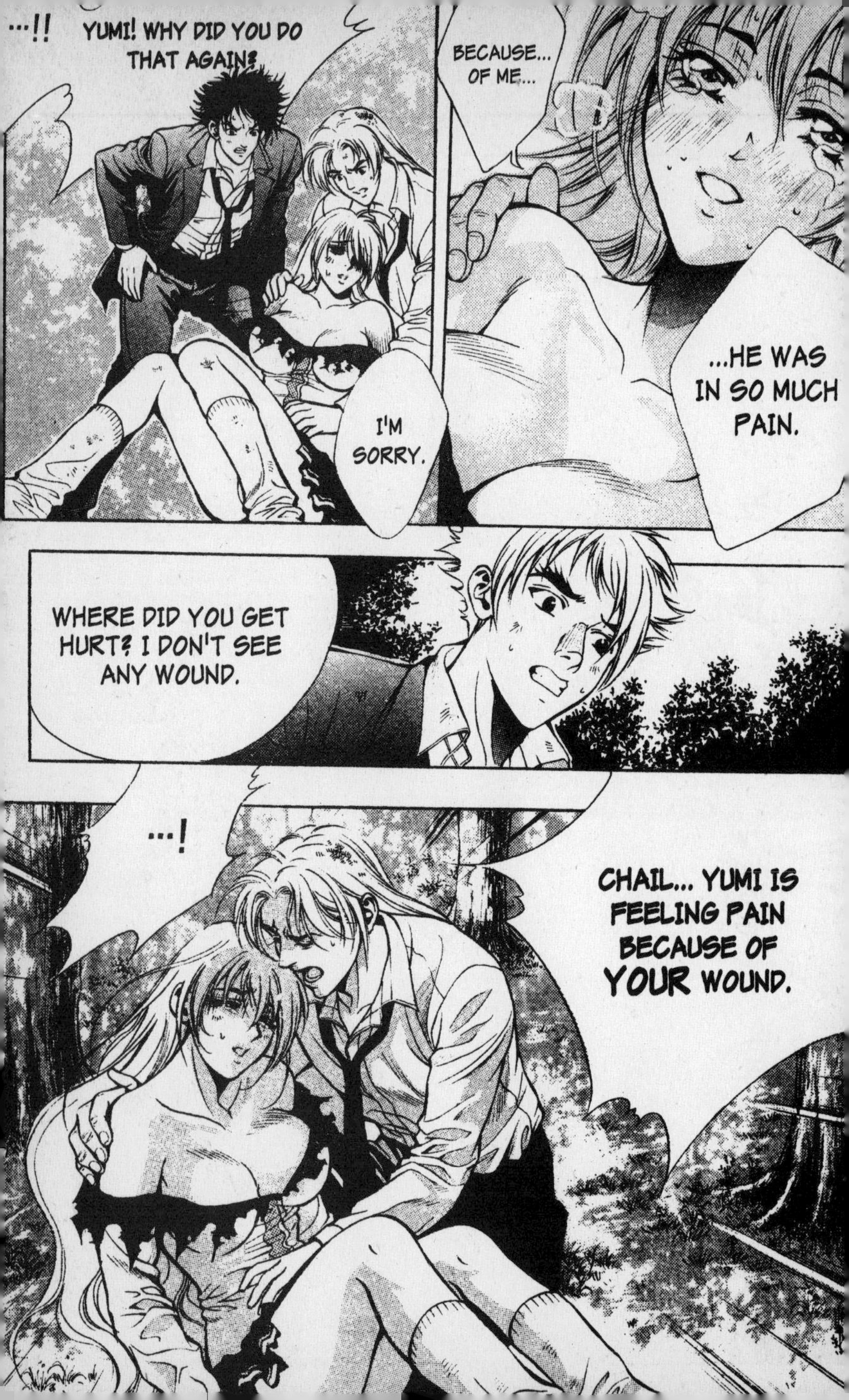
...!!
YUMI! WHY DID YOU DO THAT AGAIN?
I'M SORRY.
BECAUSE... OF ME...
...HE WAS IN SO MUCH PAIN.
WHERE DID YOU GET HURT? I DON'T SEE ANY WOUND.
...!
CHAIL... YUMI IS FEELING PAIN BECAUSE OF YOUR WOUND.

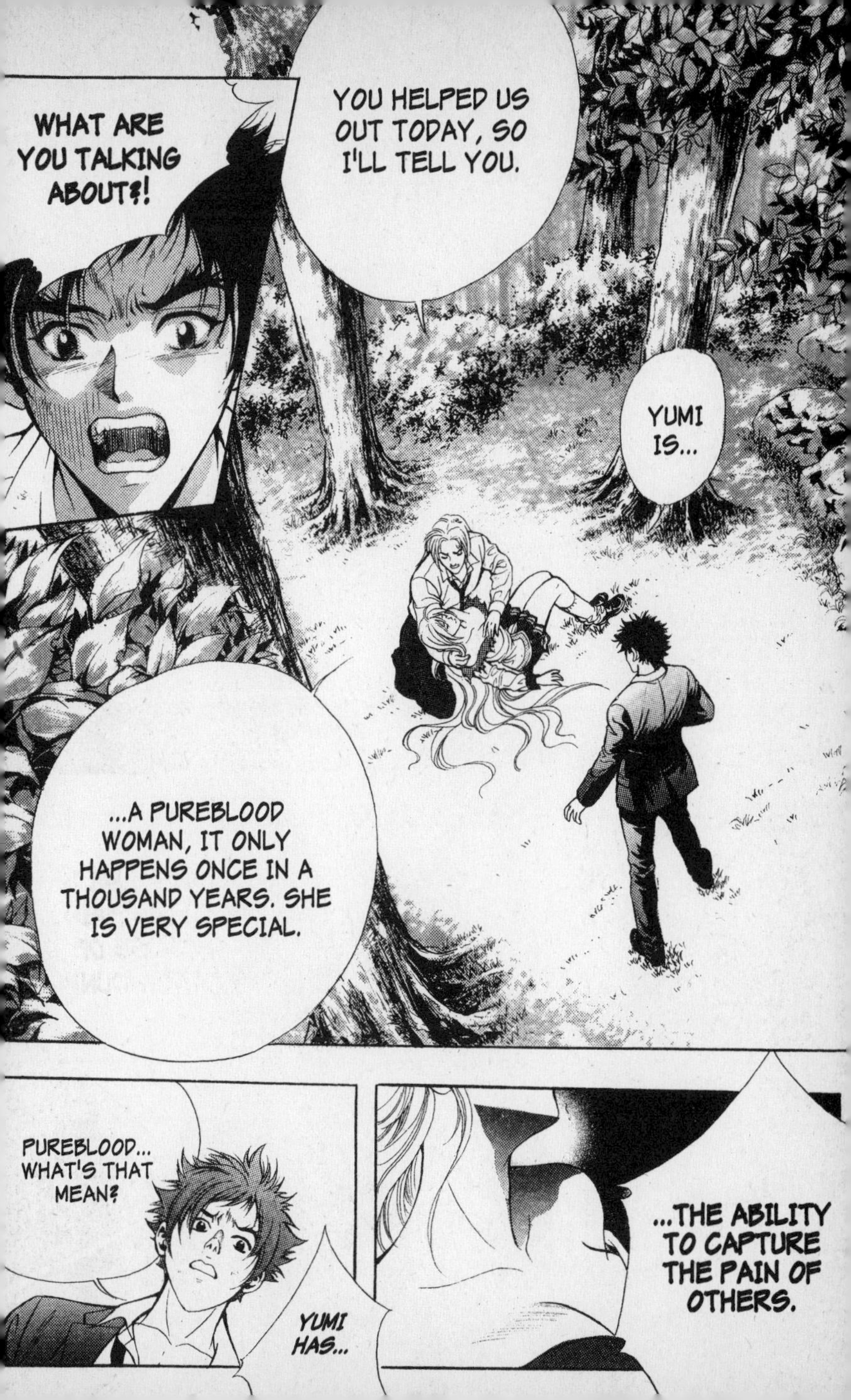
WHAT ARE YOU TALKING ABOUT?!
YOU HELPED US OUT TODAY, SO I'LL TELL YOU.
YUMI IS...
...A PUREBLOOD WOMAN, IT ONLY HAPPENS ONCE IN A THOUSAND YEARS. SHE IS VERY SPECIAL.
PUREBLOOD... WHAT'S THAT MEAN?
YUMI HAS...
...THE ABILITY TO CAPTURE THE PAIN OF OTHERS.

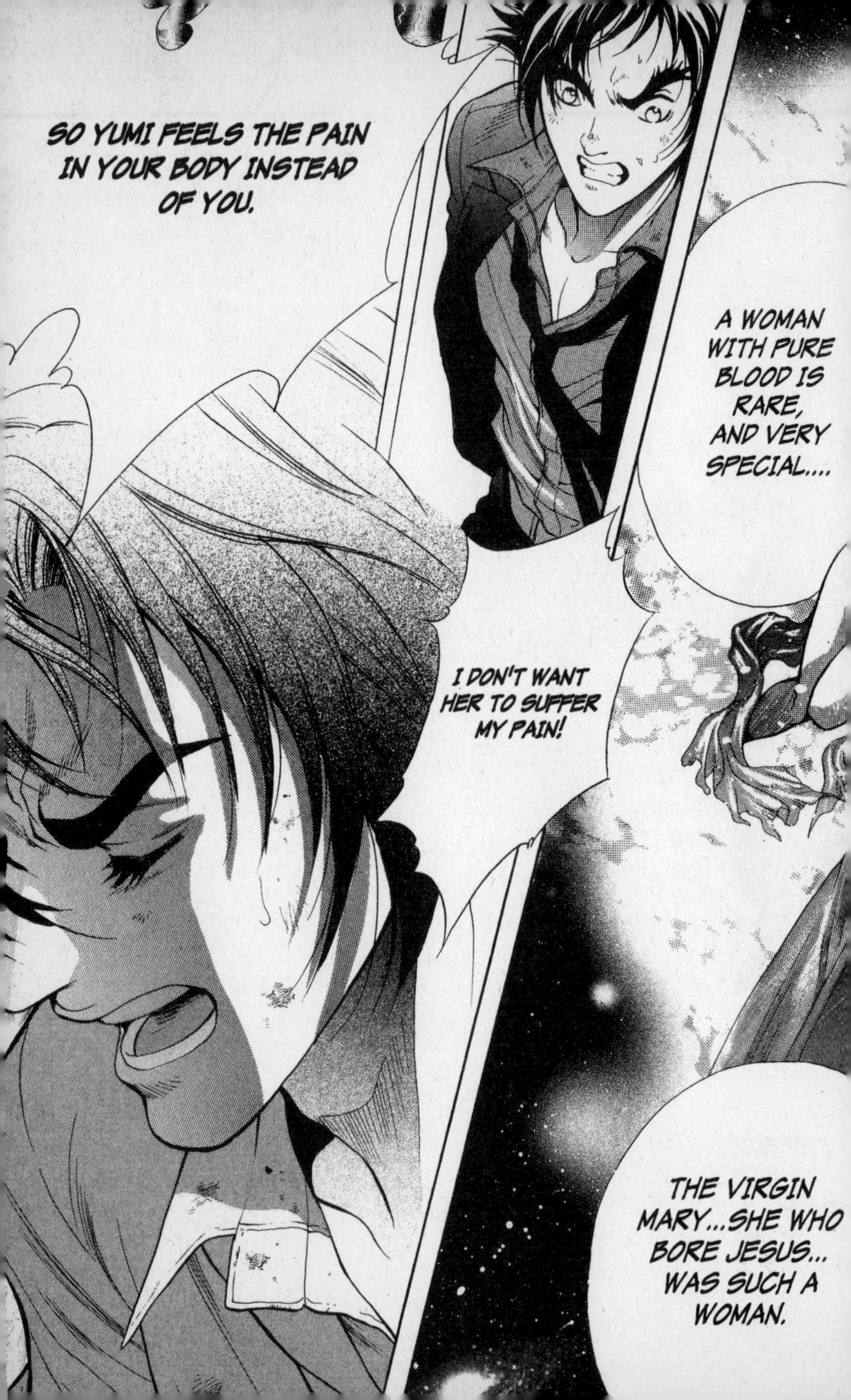
SO YUMI FEELS THE PAIN IN YOUR BODY INSTEAD OF YOU.
A WOMAN WITH PURE BLOOD IS RARE, AND VERY SPECIAL....
I DON'T WANT HER TO SUFFER MY PAIN!
THE VIRGIN MARY...SHE WHO BORE JESUS... WAS SUCH A WOMAN.

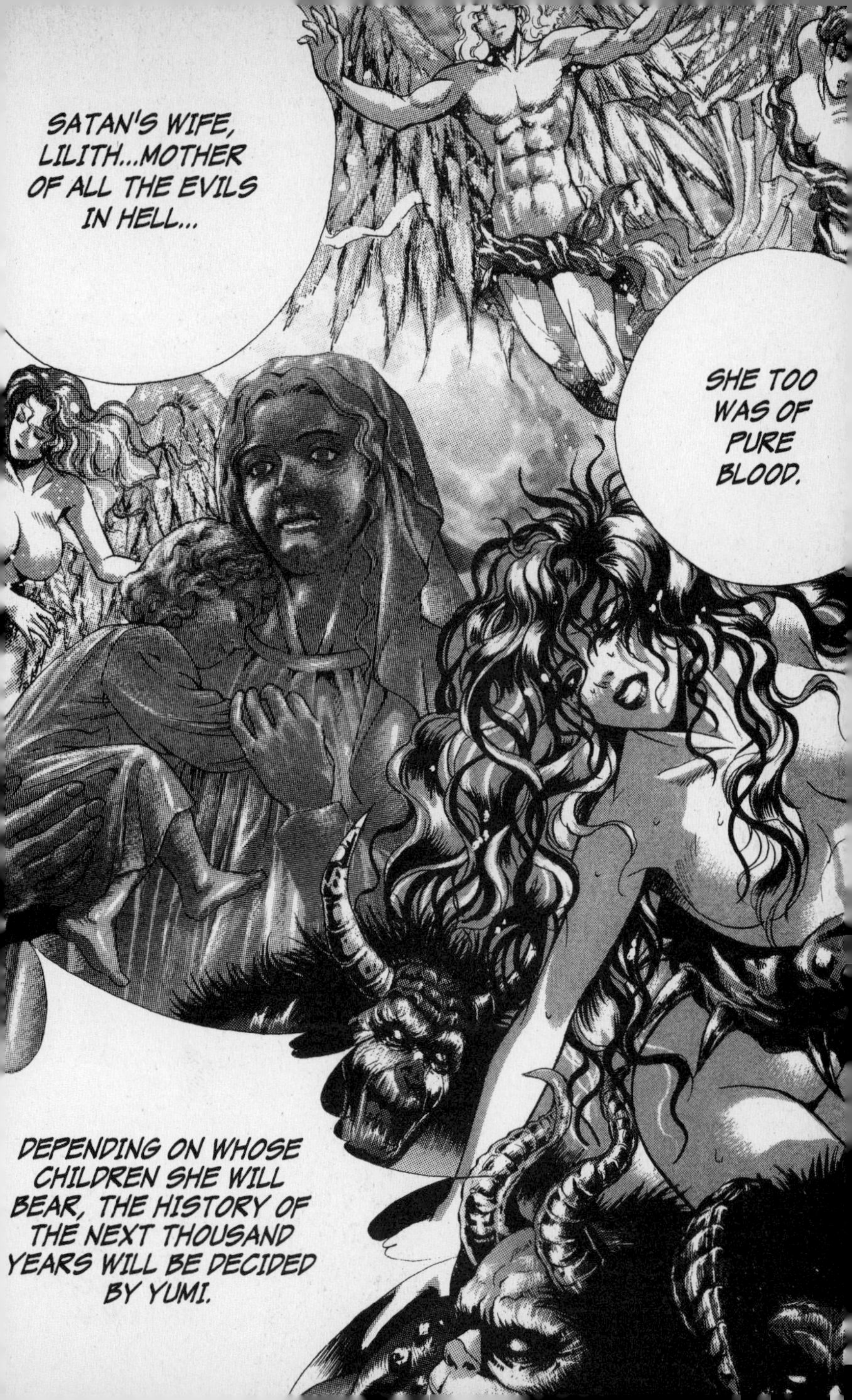
SATAN'S WIFE, LILITH...MOTHER OF ALL THE EVILS IN HELL...
SHE TOO WAS OF PURE BLOOD.
DEPENDING ON WHOSE CHILDREN SHE WILL BEAR, THE HISTORY OF THE NEXT THOUSAND YEARS WILL BE DECIDED BY YUMI.

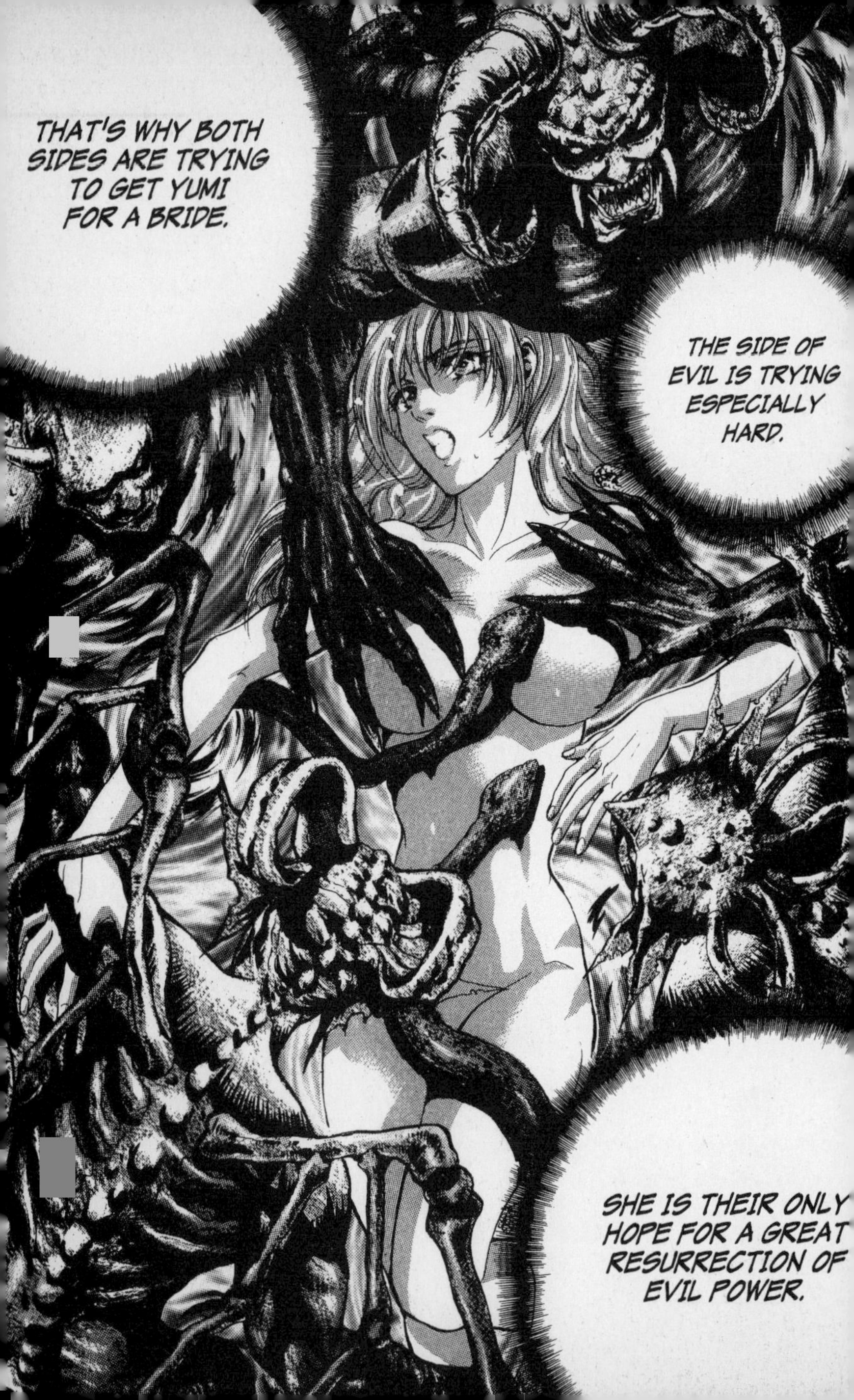
THAT'S WHY BOTH SIDES ARE TRYING TO GET YUMI FOR A BRIDE.
THE SIDE OF EVIL IS TRYING ESPECIALLY HARD.
SHE IS THEIR ONLY HOPE FOR A GREAT RESURRECTION OF EVIL POWER.

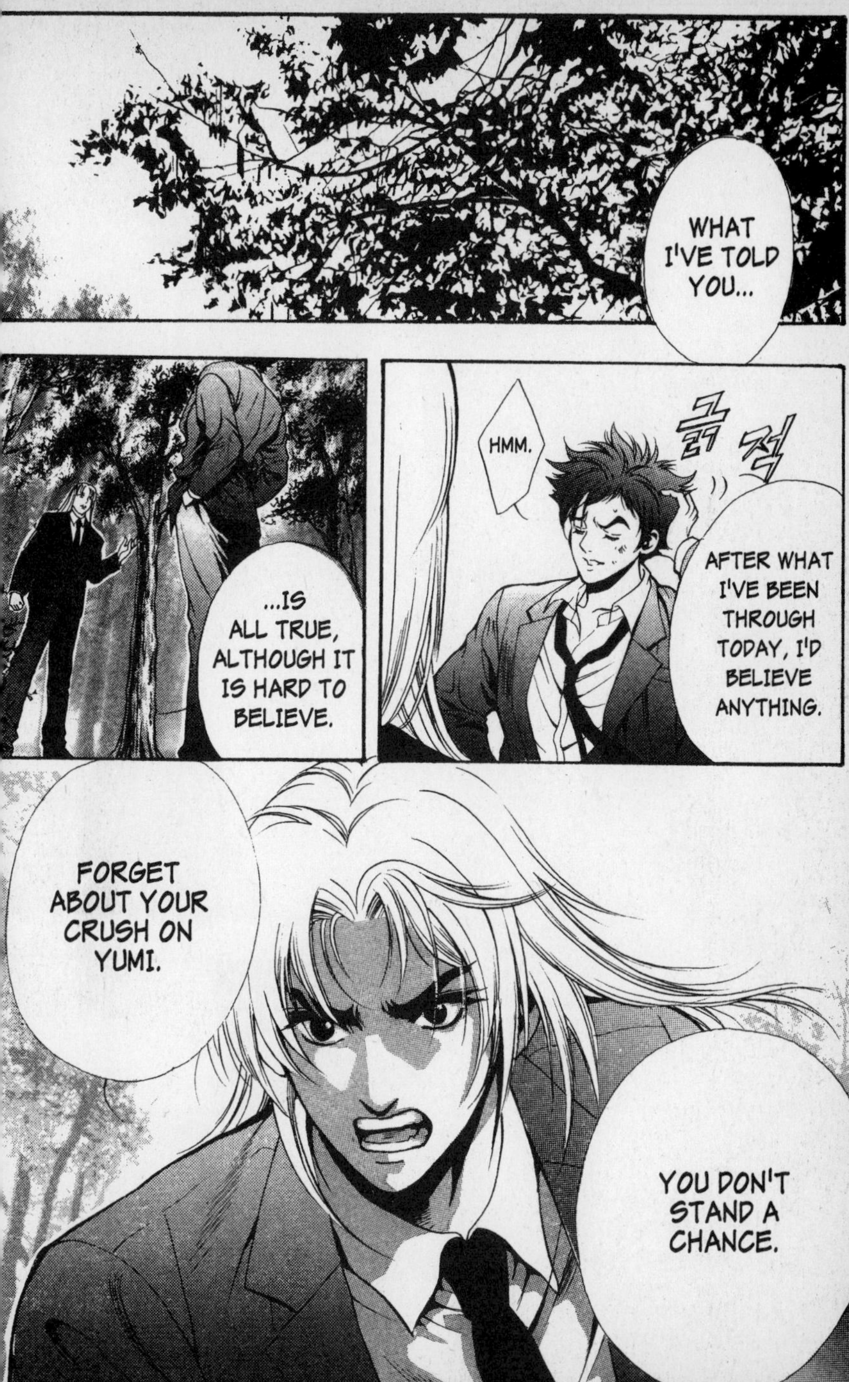
WHAT I'VE TOLD YOU...
...IS ALL TRUE, ALTHOUGH IT IS HARD TO BELIEVE.
HMM.
긁적
AFTER WHAT I'VE BEEN THROUGH TODAY, I'D BELIEVE ANYTHING.
FORGET ABOUT YOUR CRUSH ON YUMI.
YOU DON'T STAND A CHANCE.

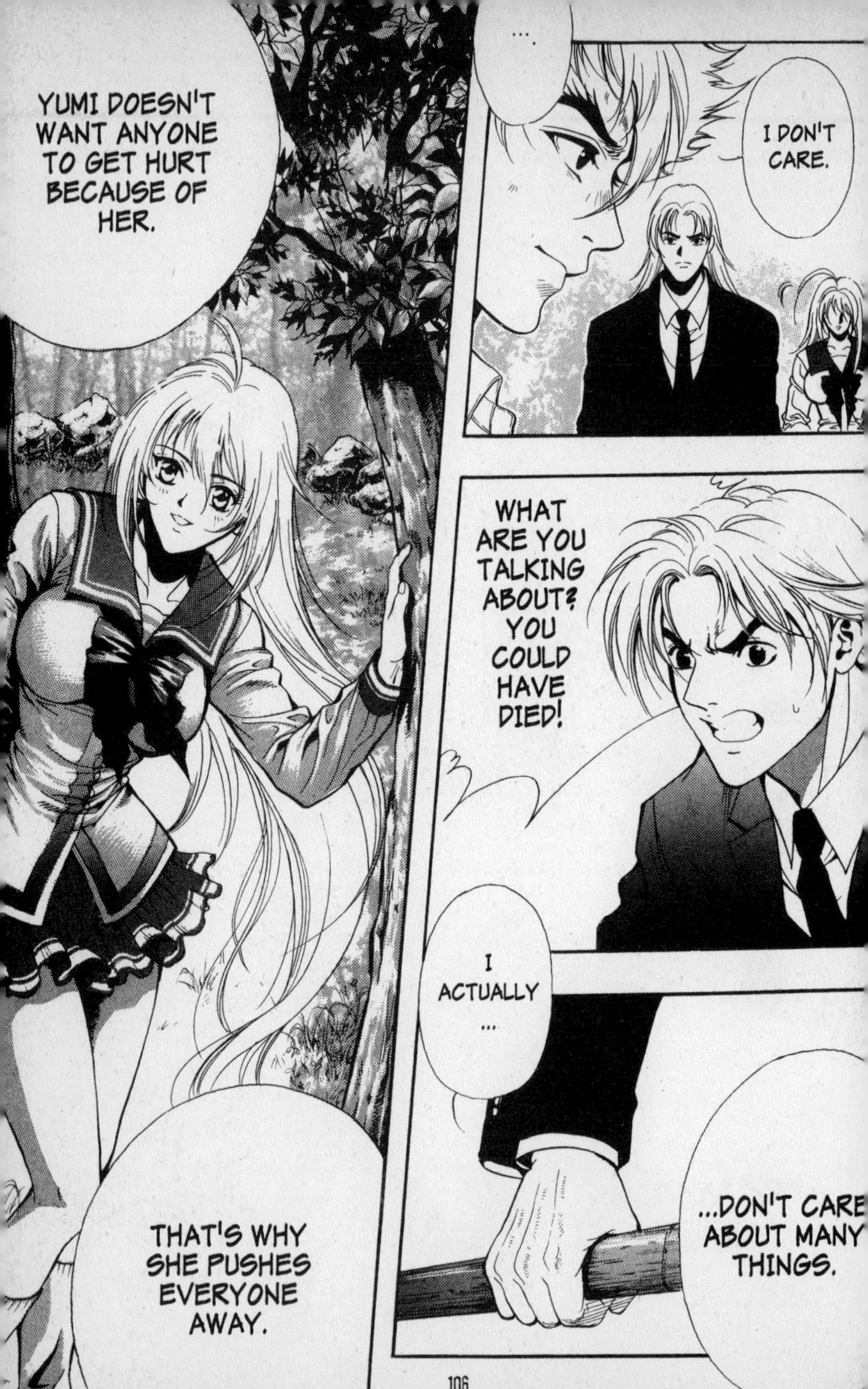
YUMI DOESN'T WANT ANYONE TO GET HURT BECAUSE OF HER.
THAT'S WHY SHE PUSHES EVERYONE AWAY.
...
I DON'T CARE.
WHAT ARE YOU TALKING ABOUT? YOU COULD HAVE DIED!
I ACTUALLY ...
...DON'T CARE ABOUT MANY THINGS.

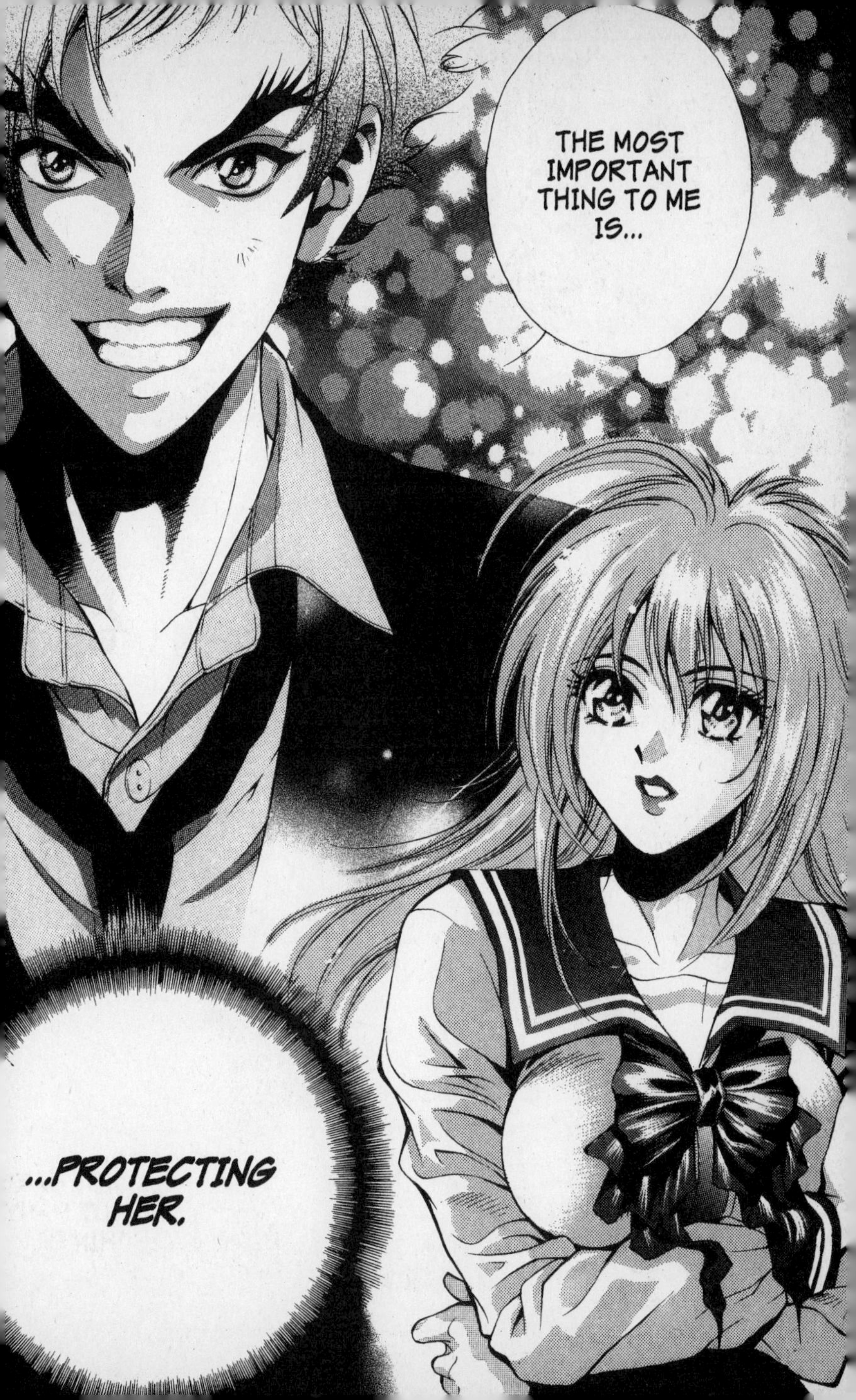
THE MOST IMPORTANT THING TO ME IS...
...PROTECTING HER.

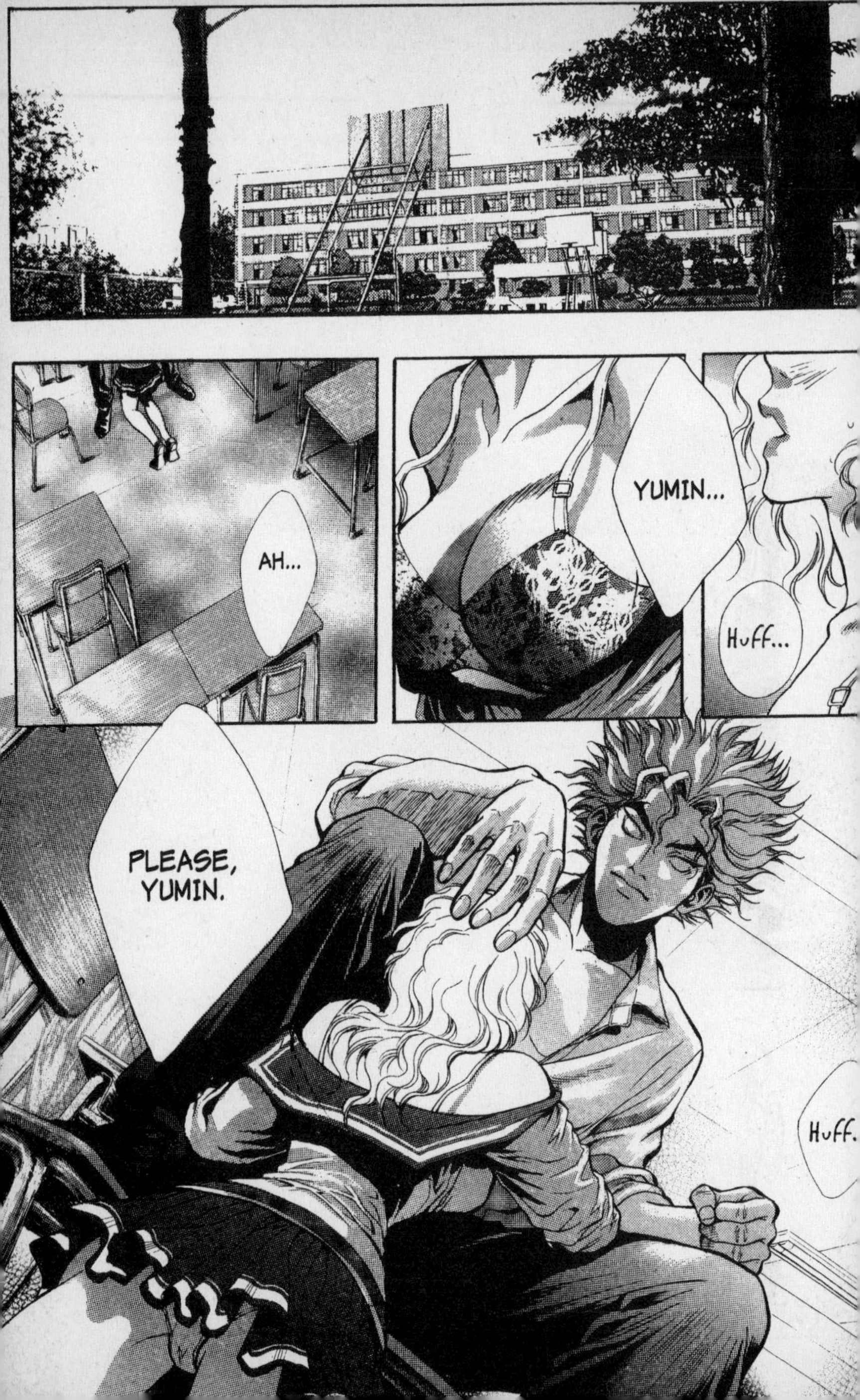

Huff...
YUMIN...
AH...
PLEASE, YUMIN.
Huff.

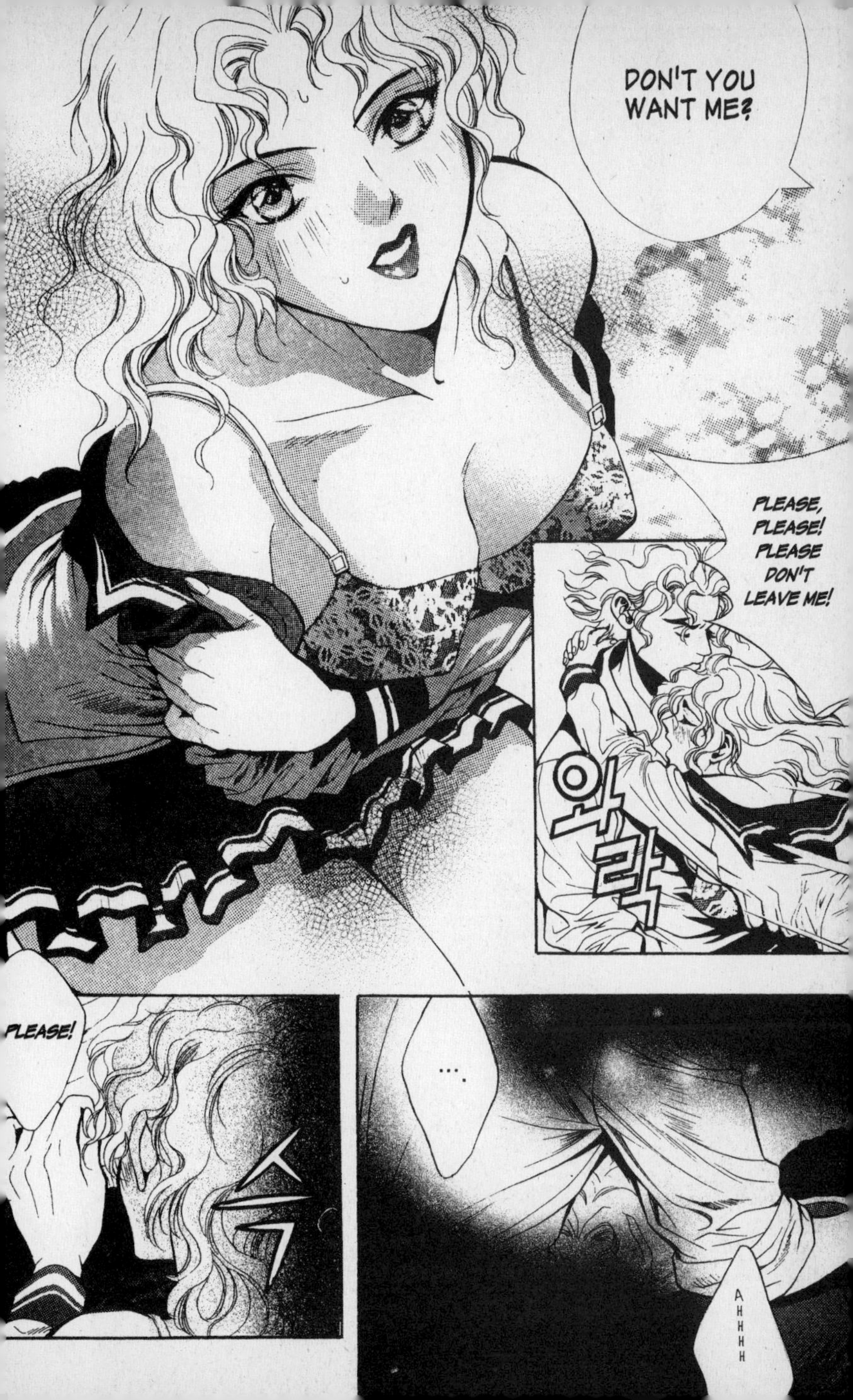
DON'T YOU WANT ME?
PLEASE, PLEASE! PLEASE DON'T LEAVE ME!
와락
PLEASE!
....
AHHHH

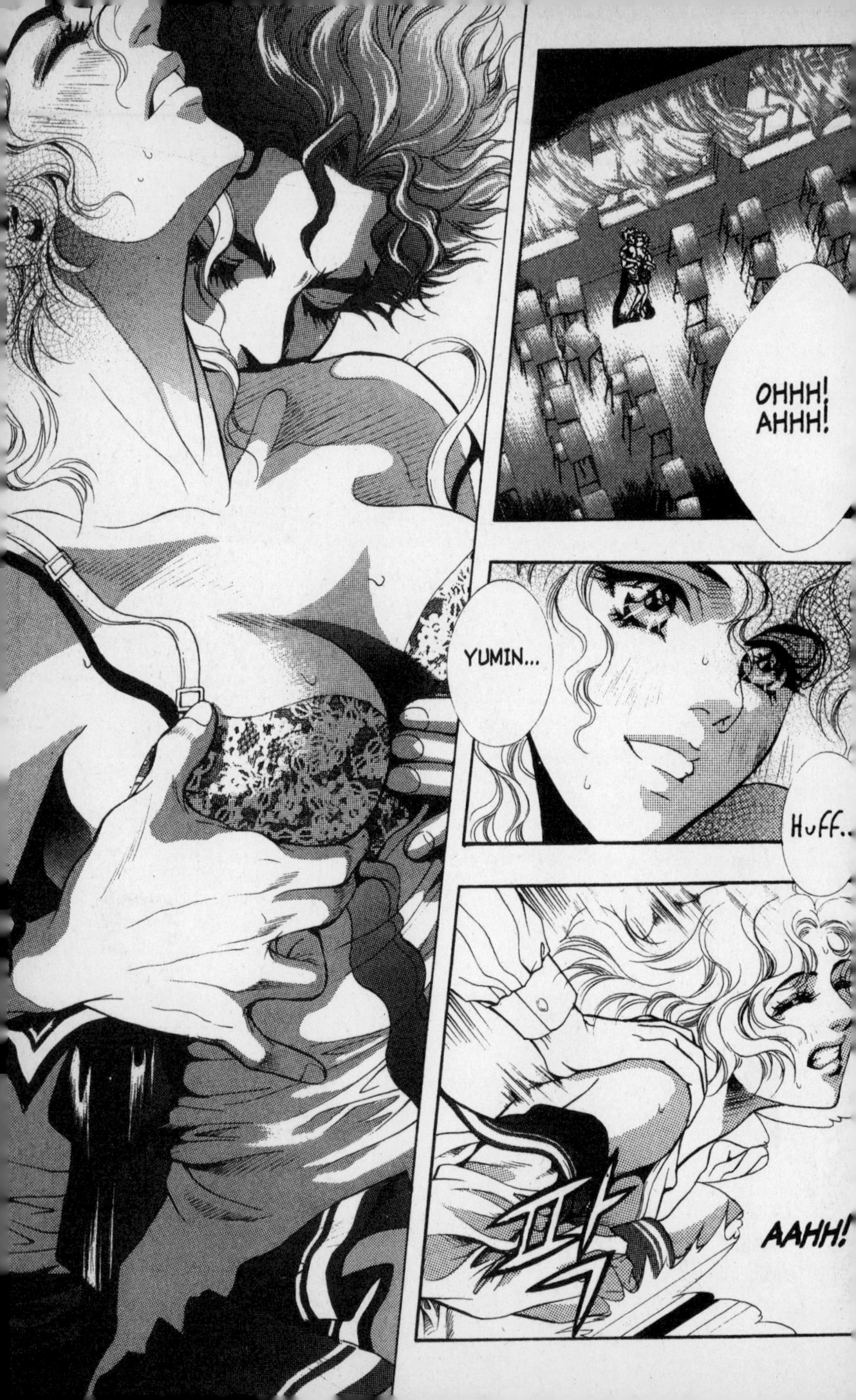
OHHH!
AHHH!
YUMIN...
Huff..
AAHH!

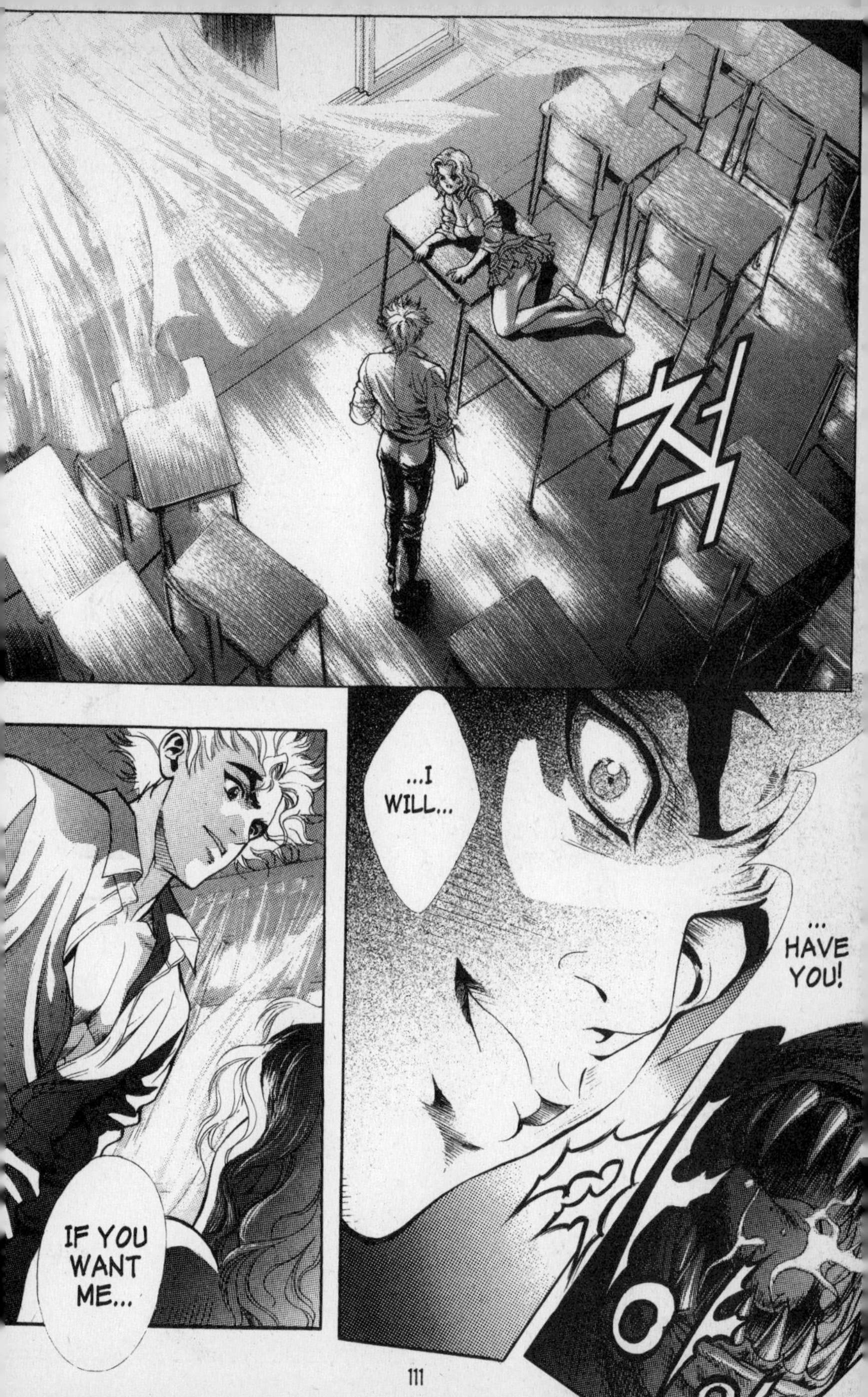
척
IF YOU WANT ME...
...I WILL...
... HAVE YOU!

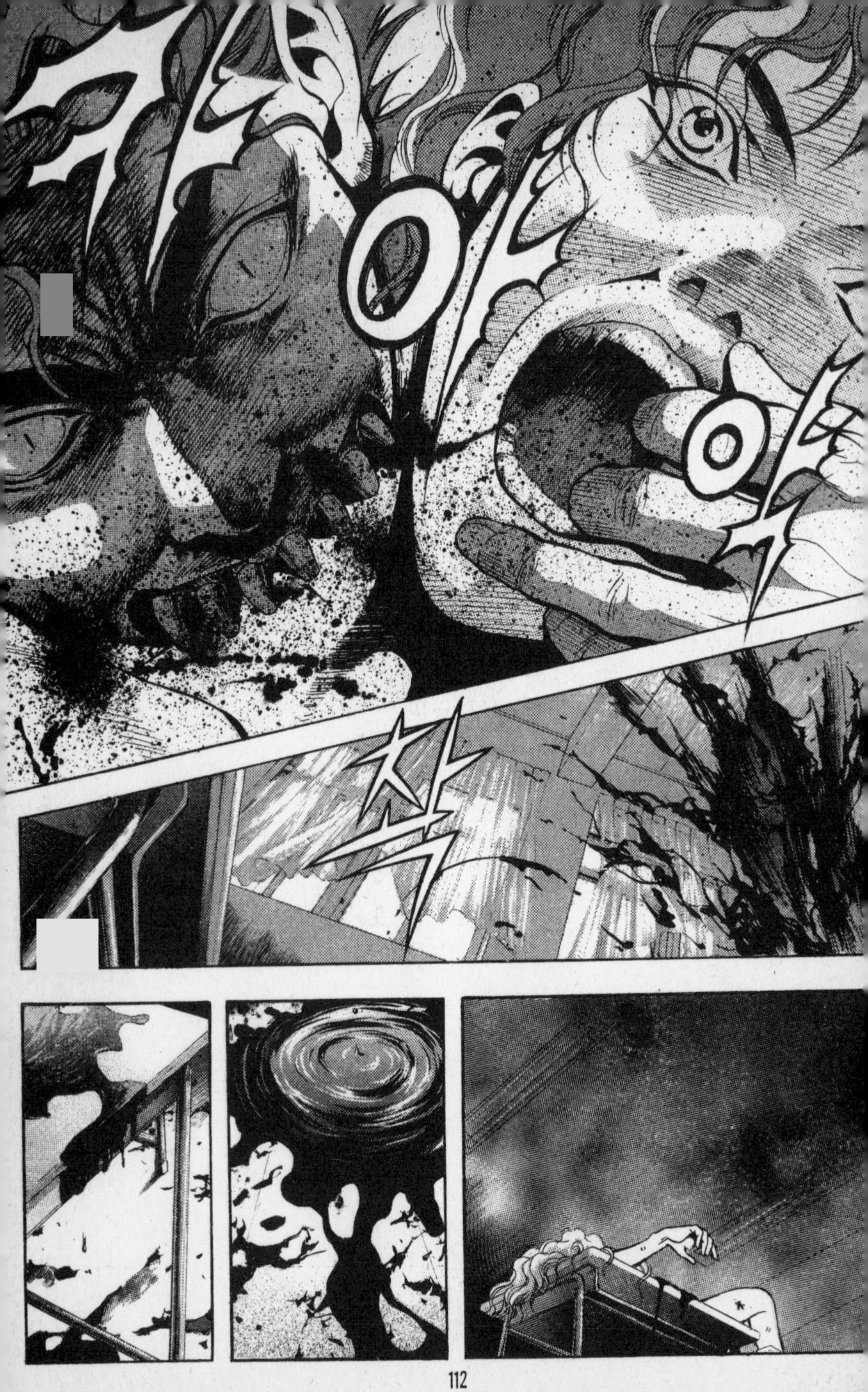

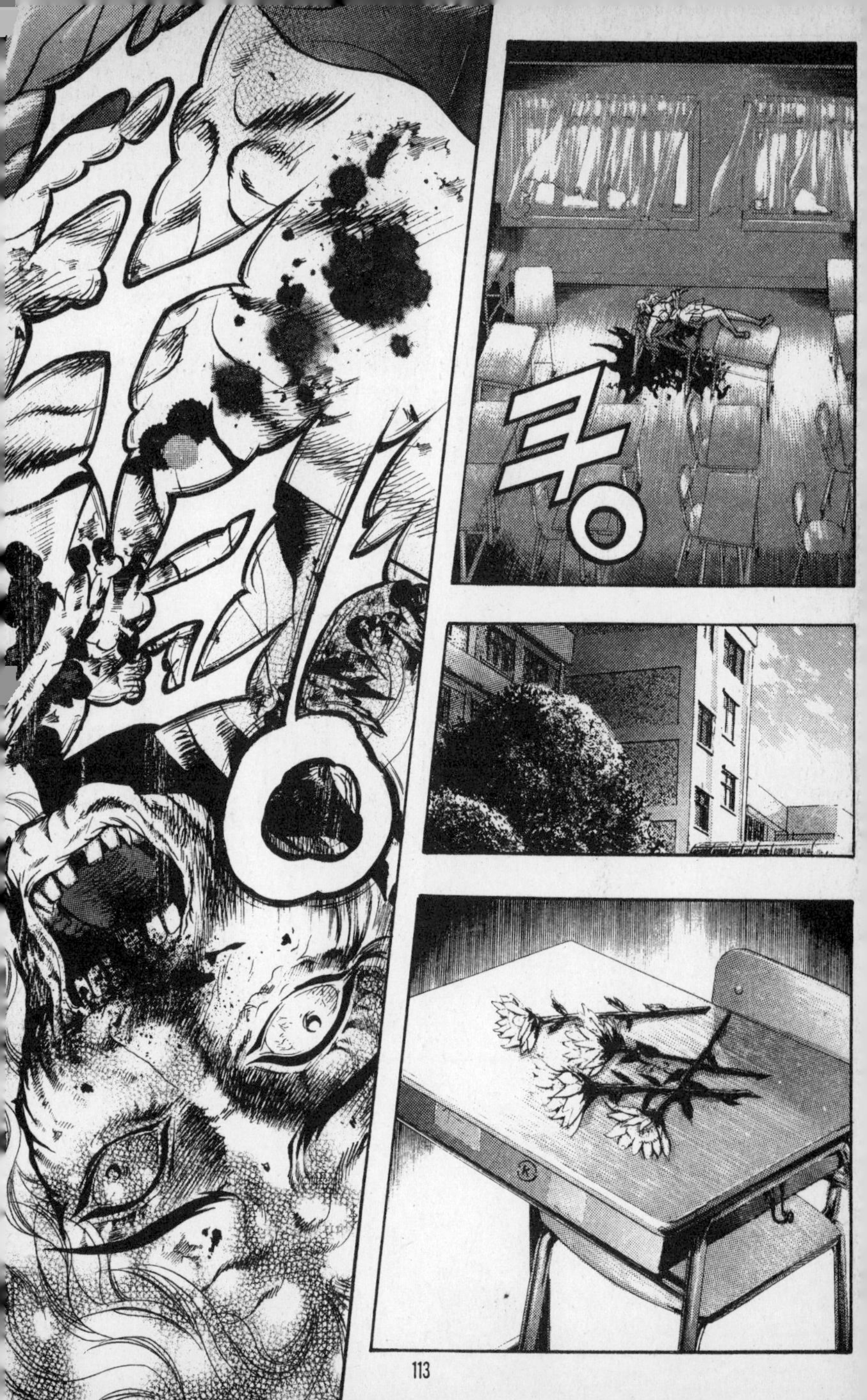
쿠-

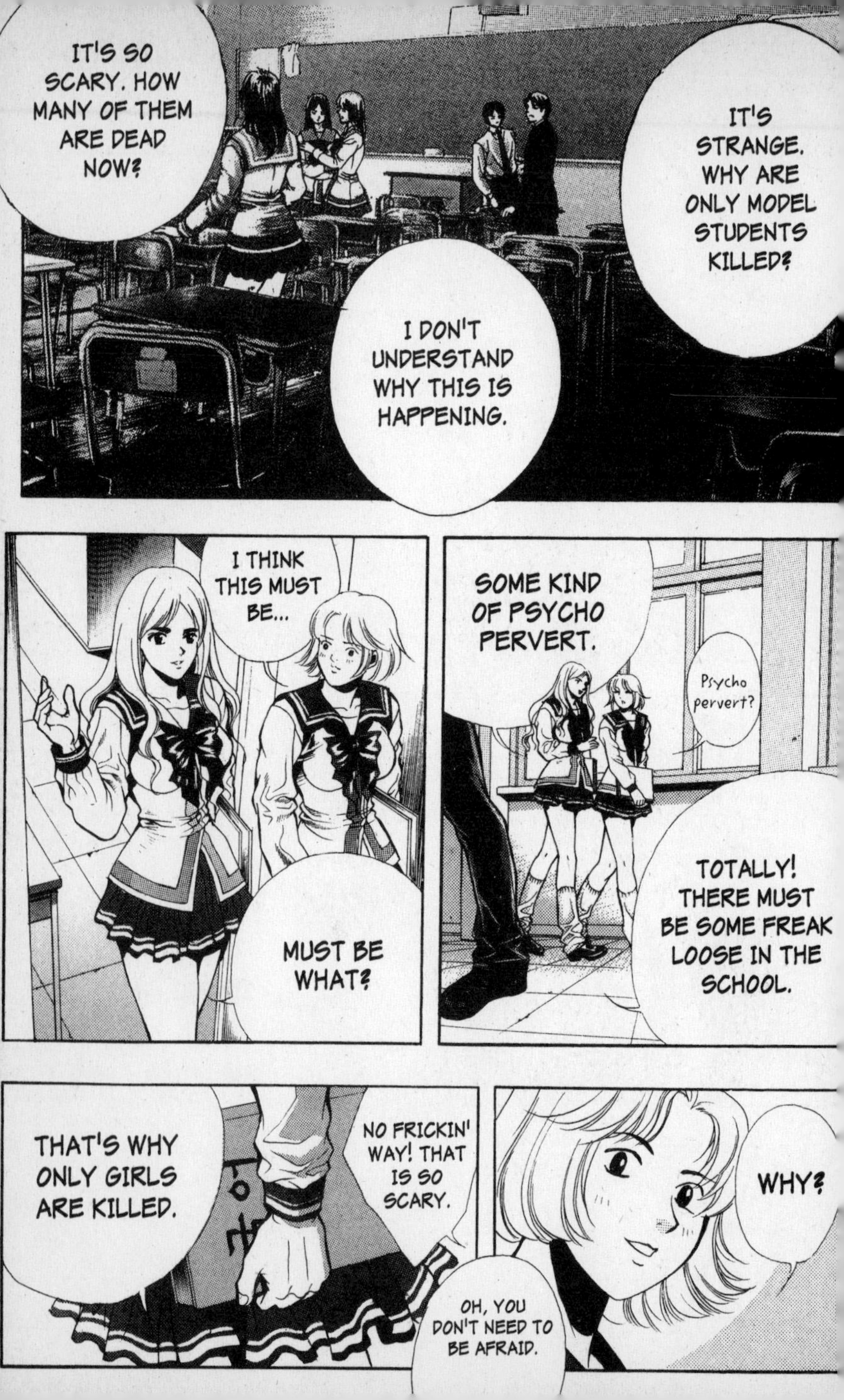
IT'S SO SCARY. HOW MANY OF THEM ARE DEAD NOW?
IT'S STRANGE. WHY ARE ONLY MODEL STUDENTS KILLED?
I DON'T UNDERSTAND WHY THIS IS HAPPENING.
I THINK THIS MUST BE...
MUST BE WHAT?
SOME KIND OF PSYCHO PERVERT.
Psycho pervert?
TOTALLY! THERE MUST BE SOME FREAK LOOSE IN THE SCHOOL.
THAT'S WHY ONLY GIRLS ARE KILLED.
NO FRICKIN' WAY! THAT IS SO SCARY.
OH, YOU DON'T NEED TO BE AFRAID.
WHY?

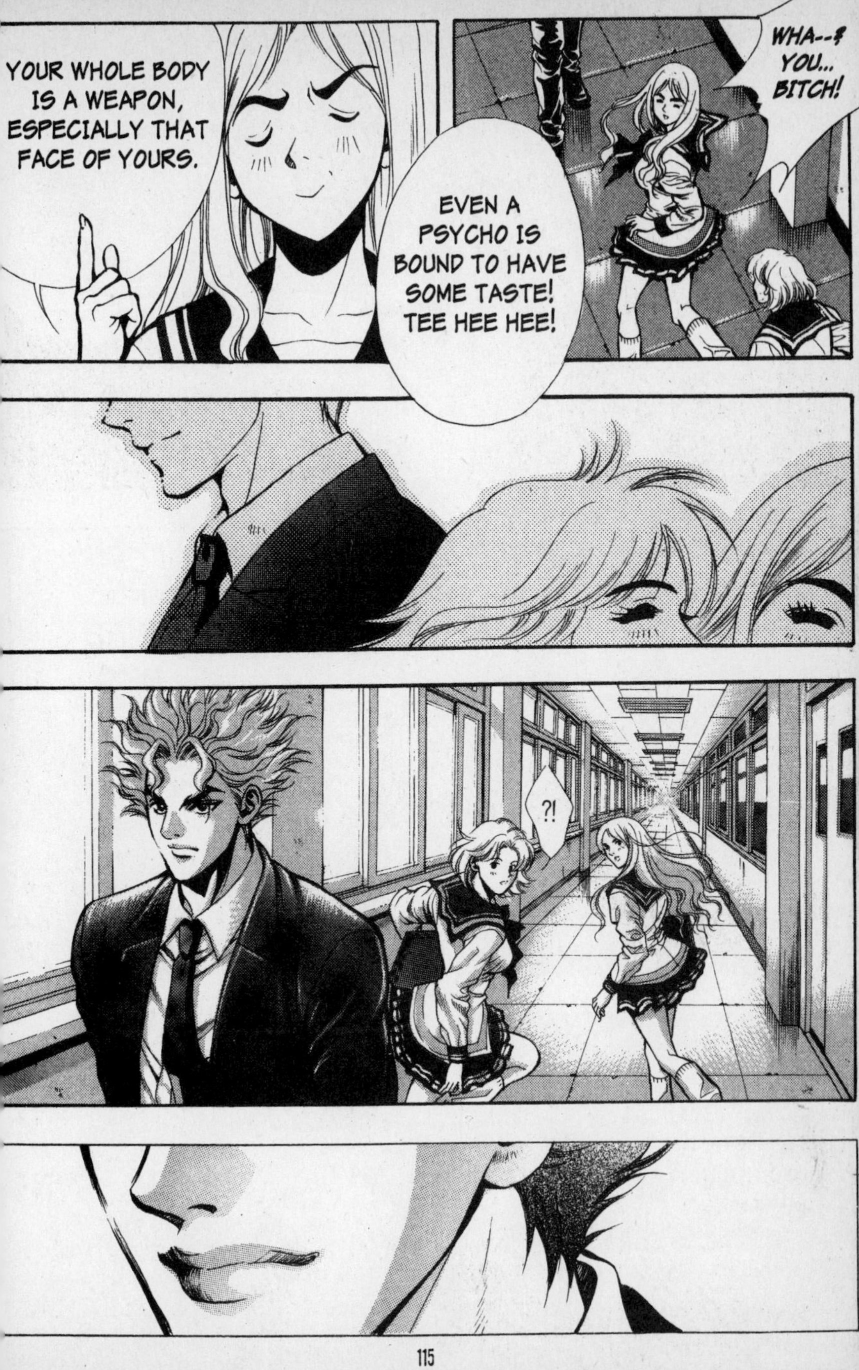
WHA--? YOU... BITCH!
YOUR WHOLE BODY IS A WEAPON, ESPECIALLY THAT FACE OF YOURS.
EVEN A PSYCHO IS BOUND TO HAVE SOME TASTE! TEE HEE HEE!
?!

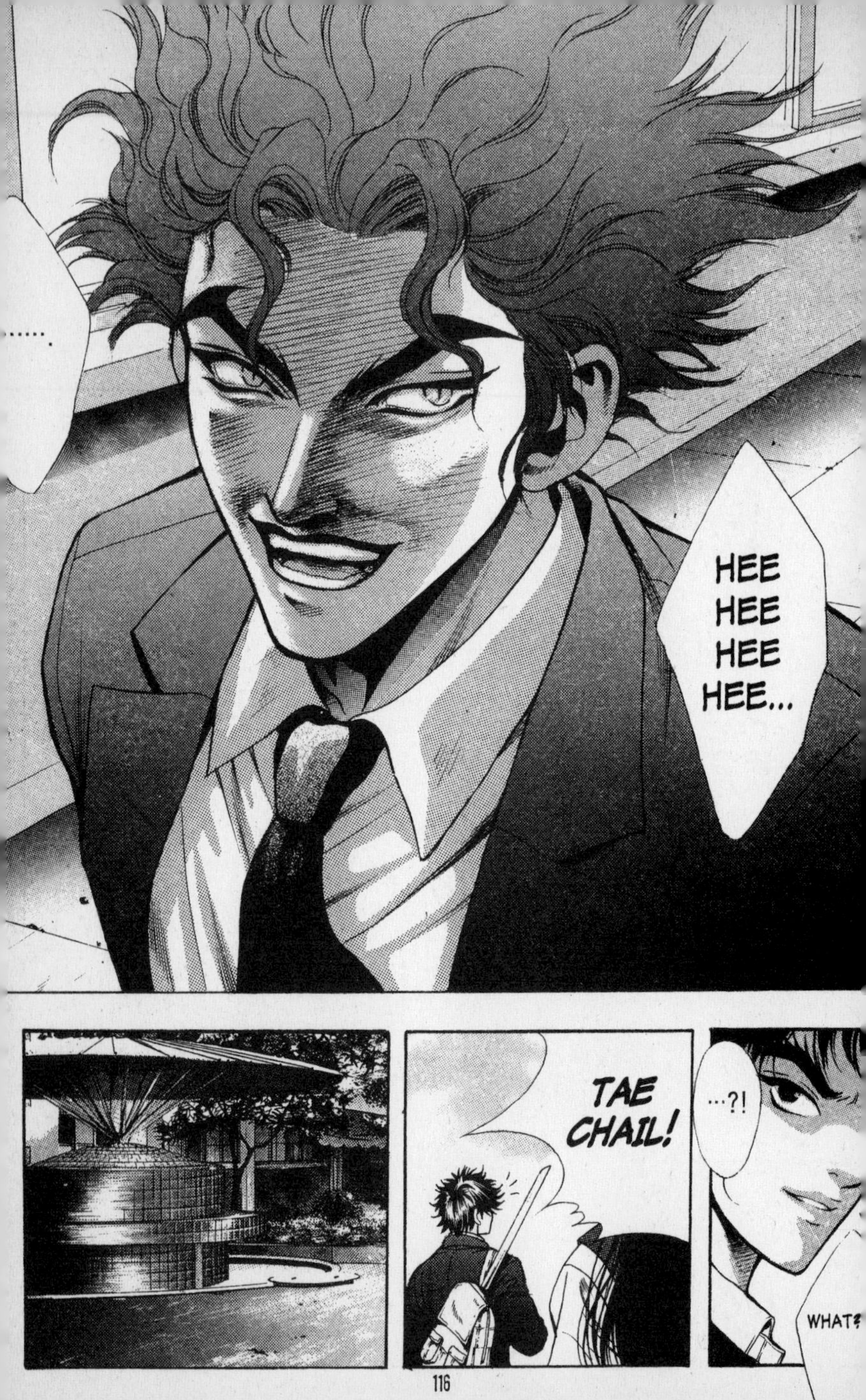
......
HEE HEE HEE HEE...
TAE CHAIL!
...?!
WHAT?!

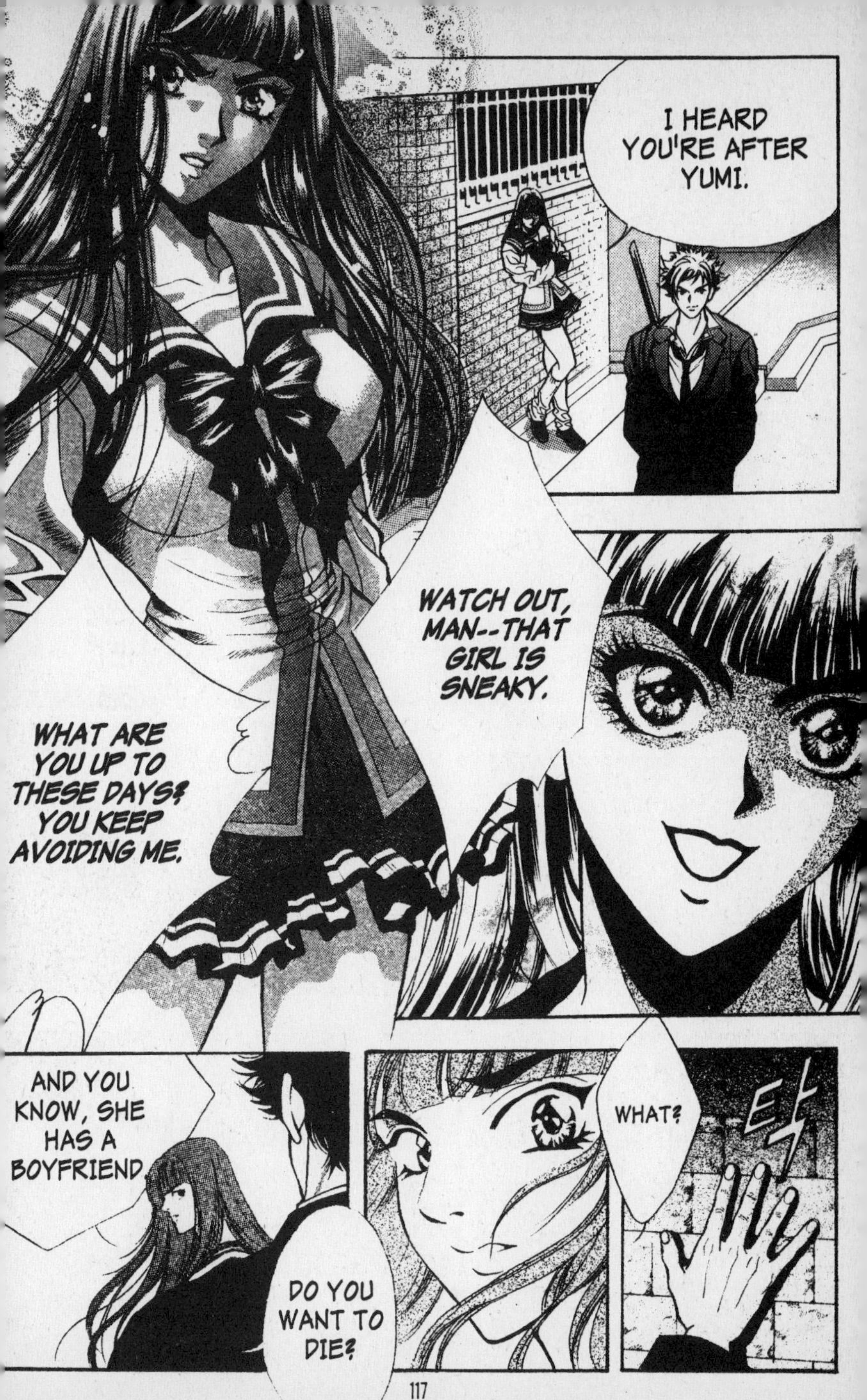
WHAT ARE YOU UP TO THESE DAYS? YOU KEEP AVOIDING ME.
I HEARD YOU'RE AFTER YUMI.
WATCH OUT, MAN--THAT GIRL IS SNEAKY.
AND YOU KNOW, SHE HAS A BOYFRIEND.
DO YOU WANT TO DIE?
WHAT?
탁

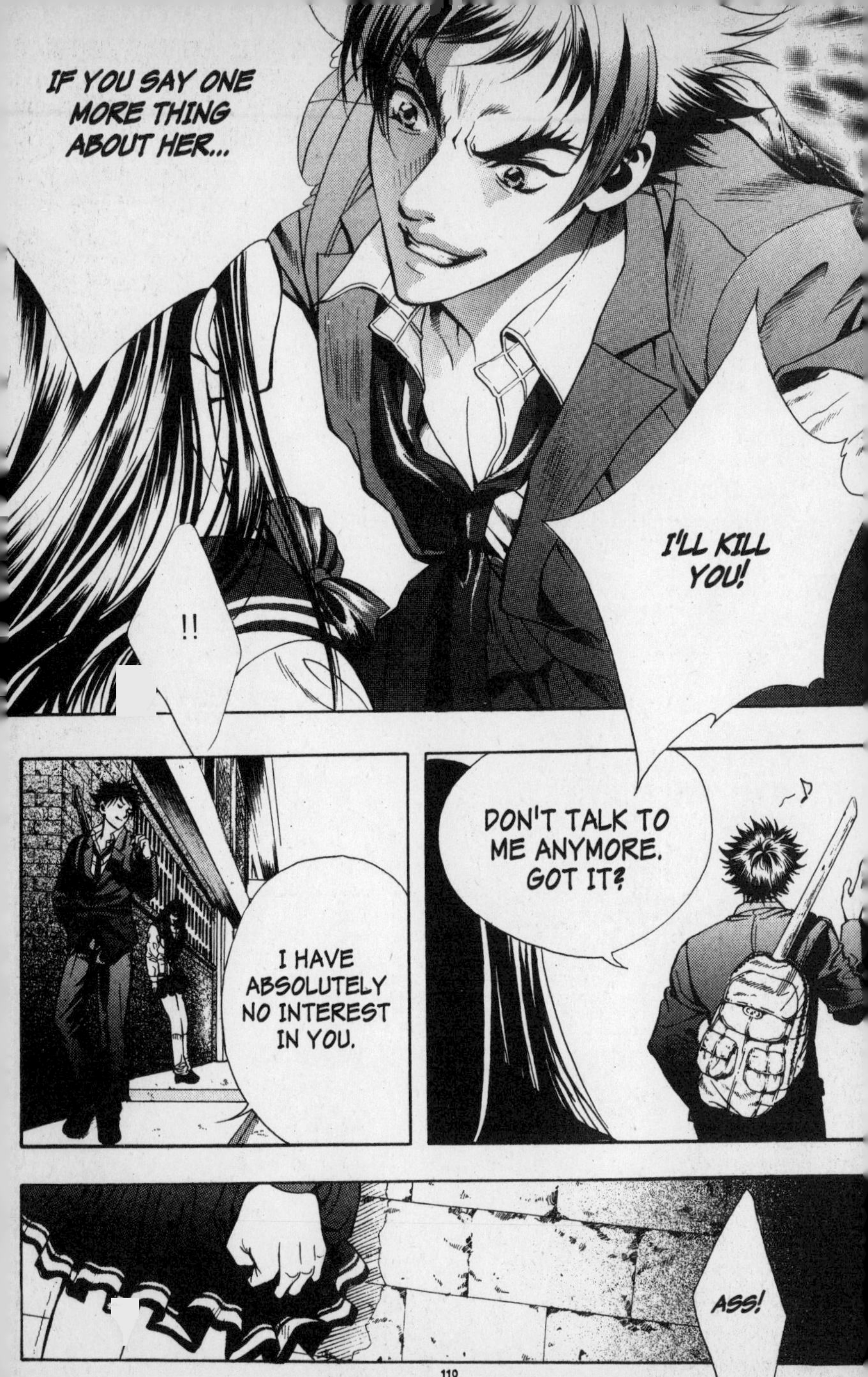
IF YOU SAY ONE MORE THING ABOUT HER...
I'LL KILL YOU!
!!
DON'T TALK TO ME ANYMORE. GOT IT?
I HAVE ABSOLUTELY NO INTEREST IN YOU.
ASS!

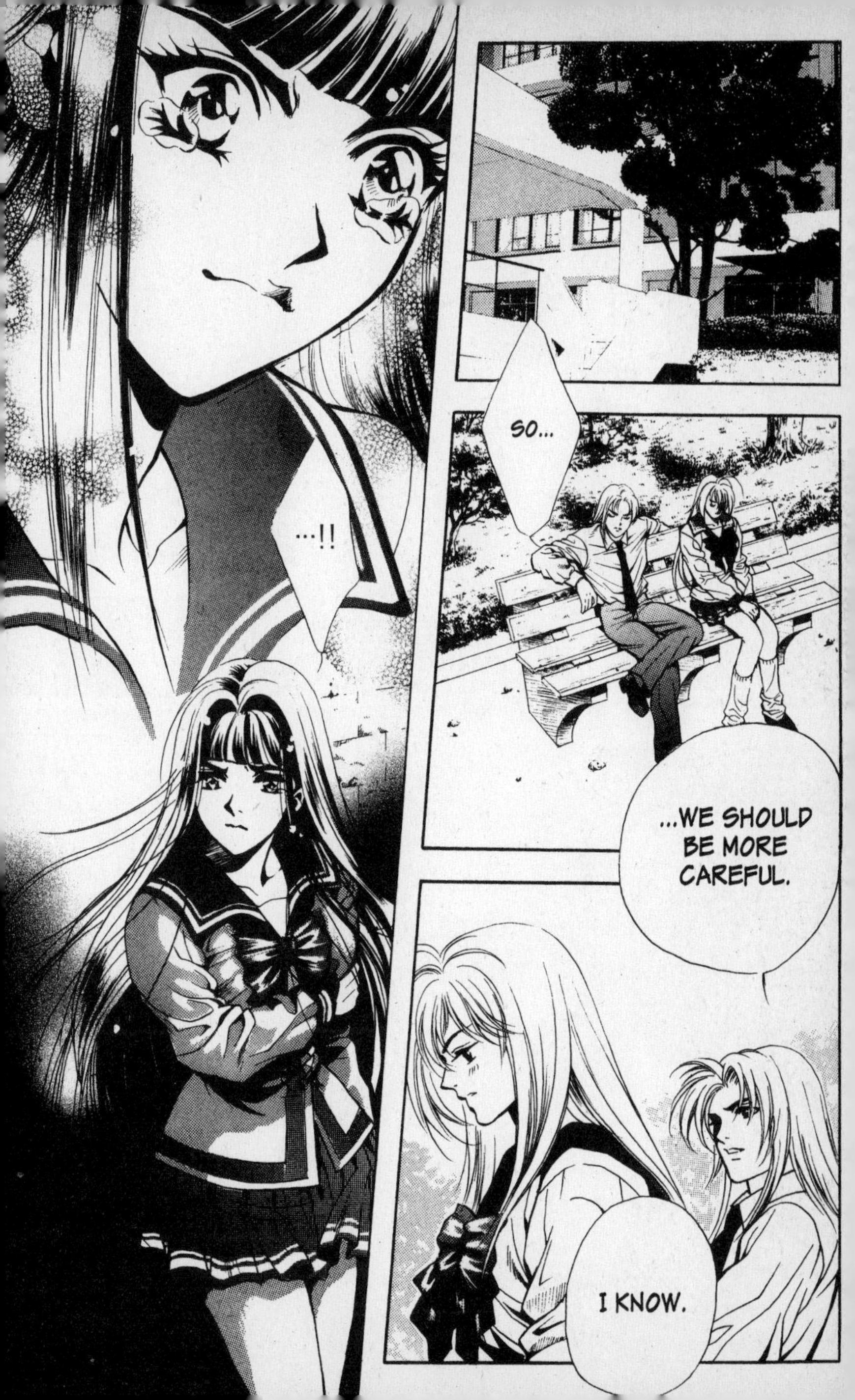

SO...
...!!
...WE SHOULD BE MORE CAREFUL.
I KNOW.

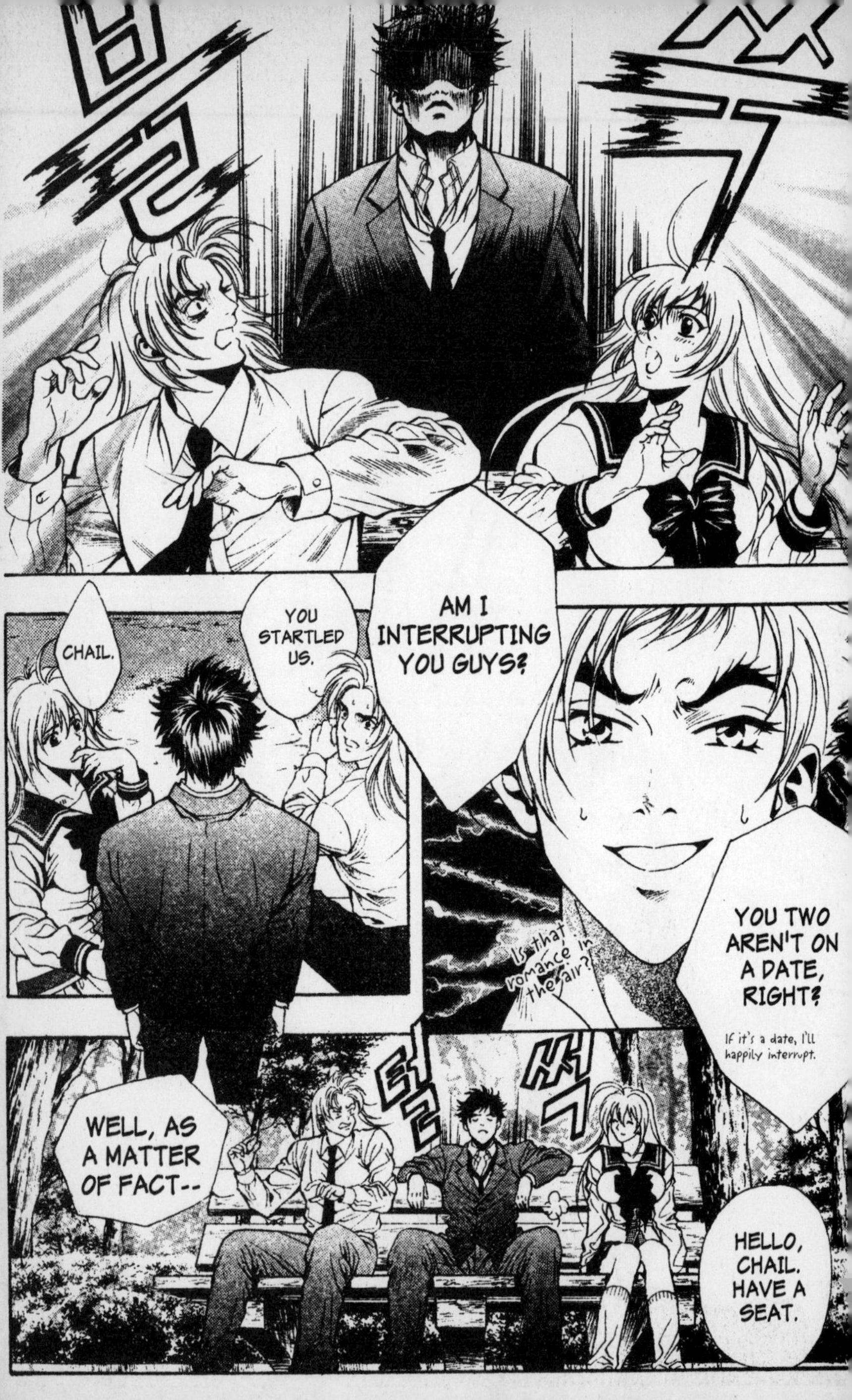

AM I INTERRUPTING YOU GUYS?
YOU STARTLED US.
CHAIL.
Is that romance in the air?
YOU TWO AREN'T ON A DATE, RIGHT?
If it's a date, I'll happily interrupt.
HELLO, CHAIL. HAVE A SEAT.
WELL, AS A MATTER OF FACT--

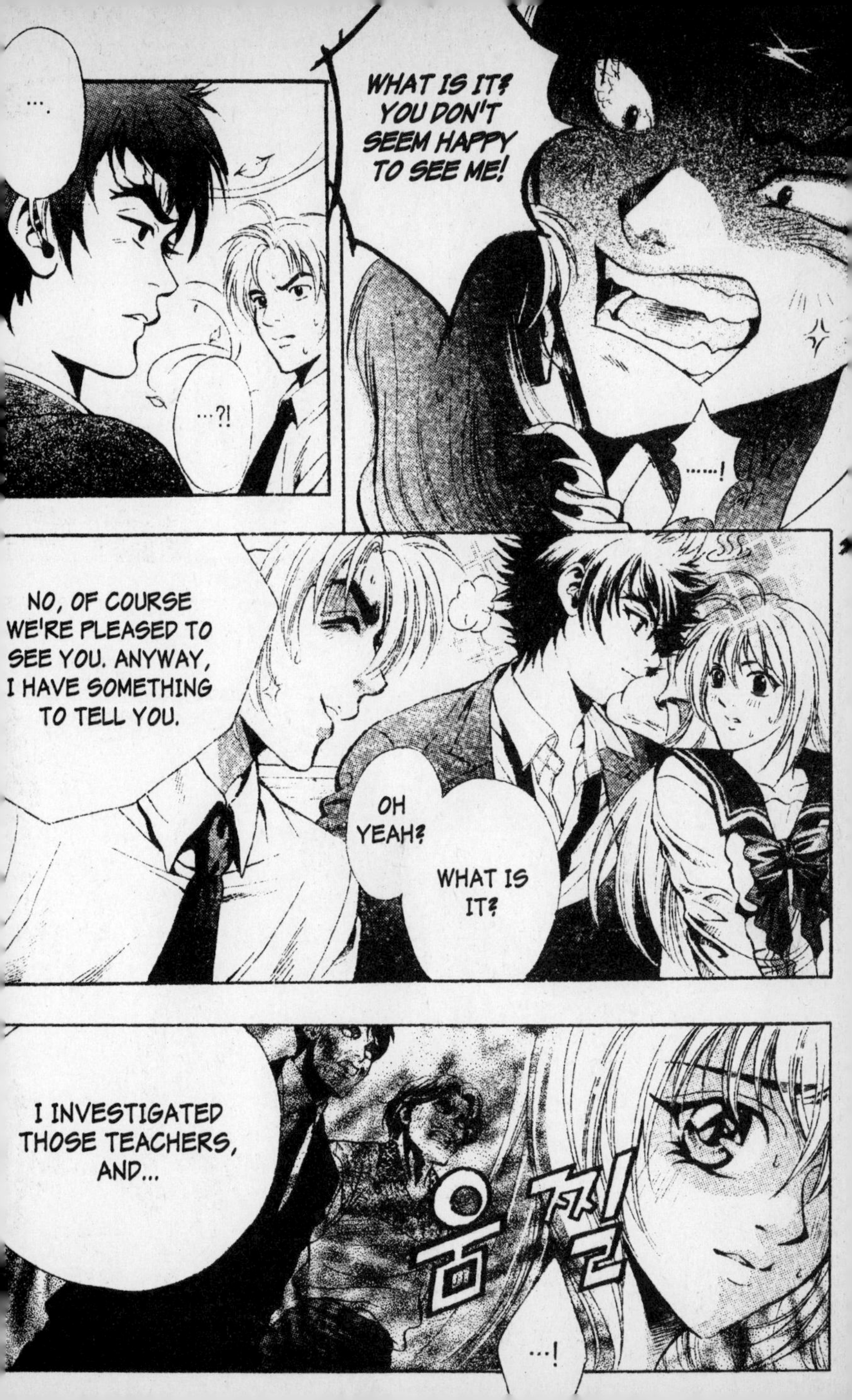
WHAT IS IT? YOU DON'T SEEM HAPPY TO SEE ME!
......!
....
...?!
NO, OF COURSE WE'RE PLEASED TO SEE YOU. ANYWAY, I HAVE SOMETHING TO TELL YOU.
OH YEAH?
WHAT IS IT?
I INVESTIGATED THOSE TEACHERS, AND...
움찔
...!

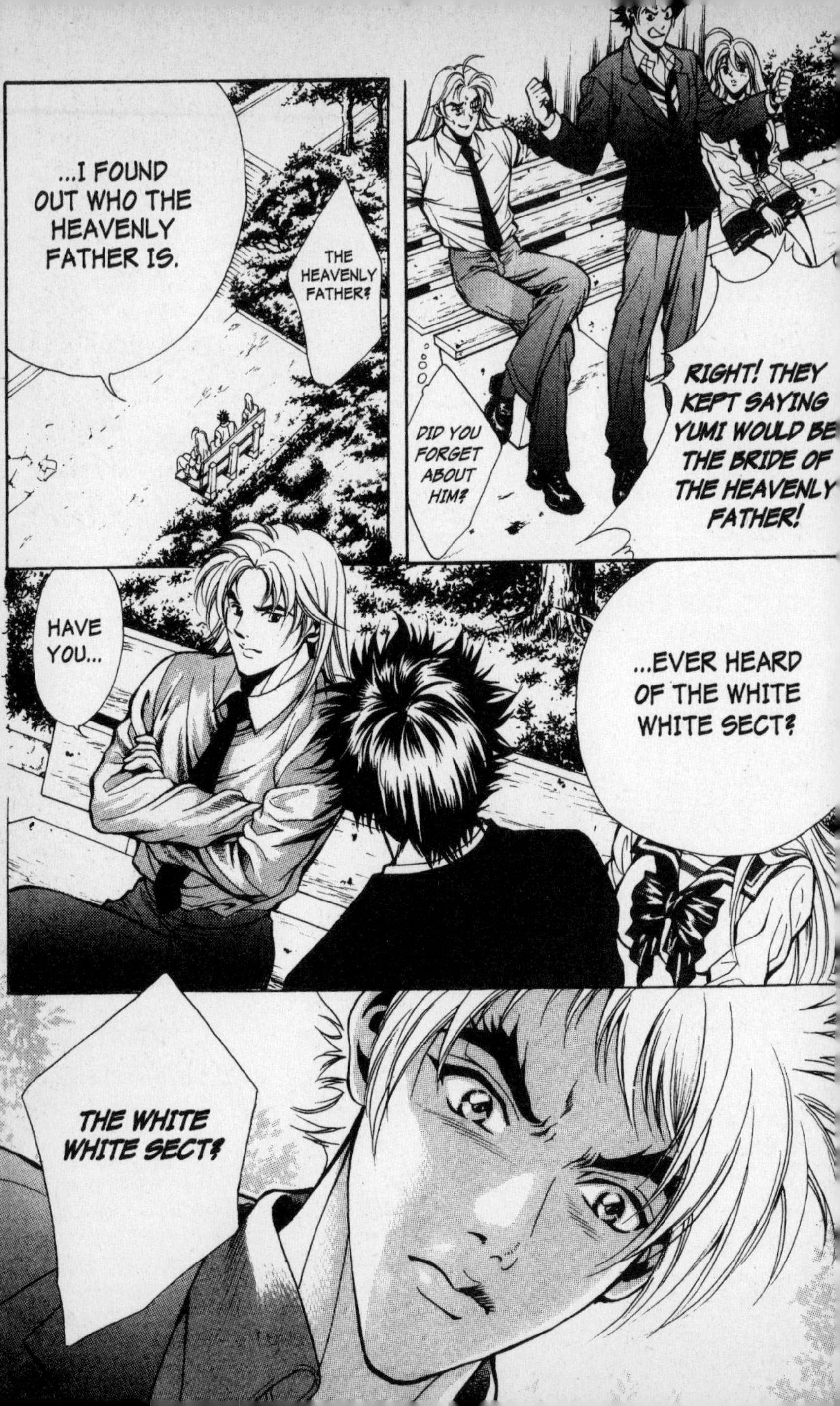

...I FOUND OUT WHO THE HEAVENLY FATHER IS.
THE HEAVENLY FATHER?
DID YOU FORGET ABOUT HIM?
RIGHT! THEY KEPT SAYING YUMI WOULD BE THE BRIDE OF THE HEAVENLY FATHER!
HAVE YOU...
...EVER HEARD OF THE WHITE WHITE SECT?
THE WHITE WHITE SECT?

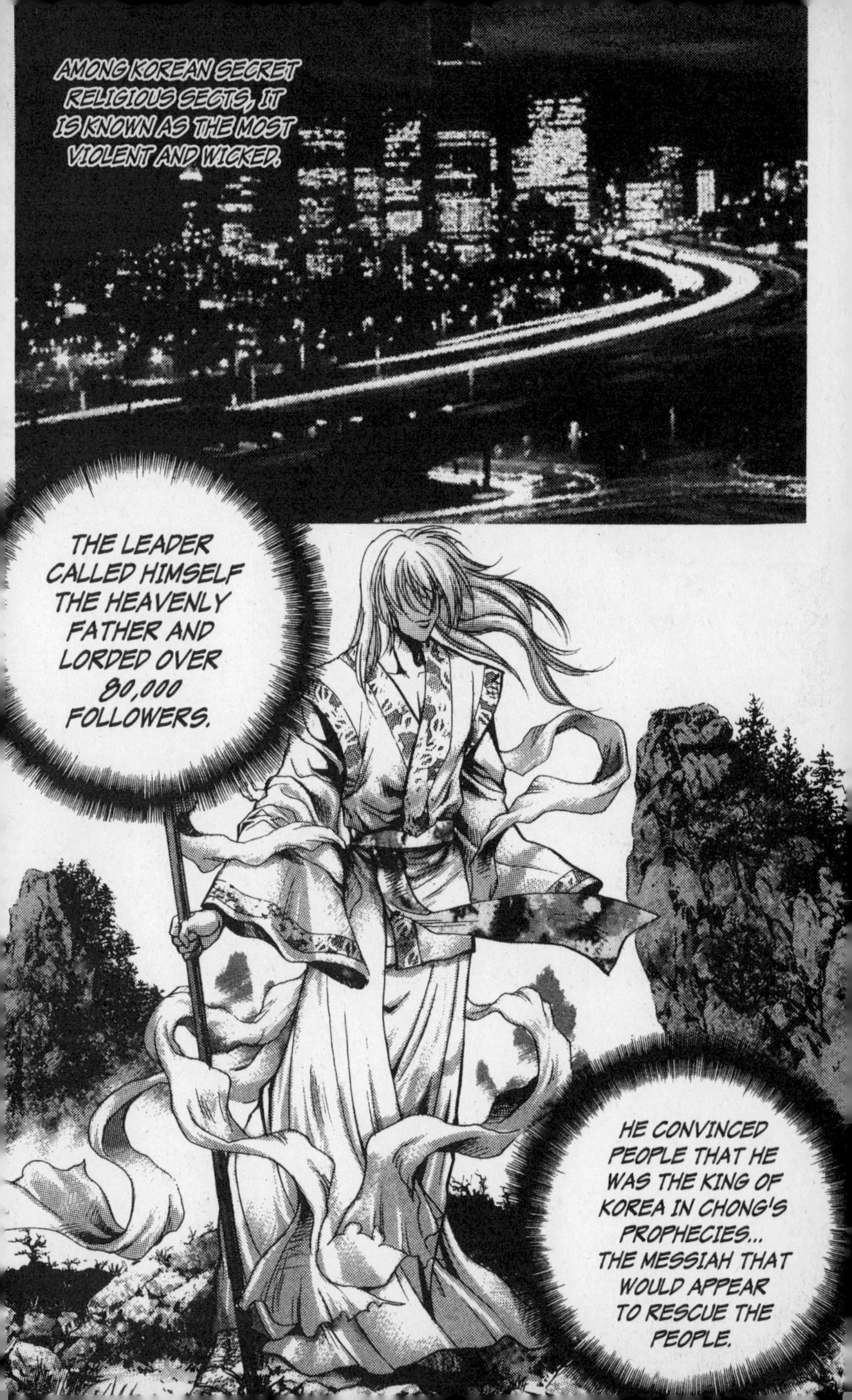
AMONG KOREAN SECRET RELIGIOUS SECTS, IT IS KNOWN AS THE MOST VIOLENT AND WICKED.
THE LEADER CALLED HIMSELF THE HEAVENLY FATHER AND LORDED OVER 80,000 FOLLOWERS.
HE CONVINCED PEOPLE THAT HE WAS THE KING OF KOREA IN CHONG'S PROPHECIES... THE MESSIAH THAT WOULD APPEAR TO RESCUE THE PEOPLE.

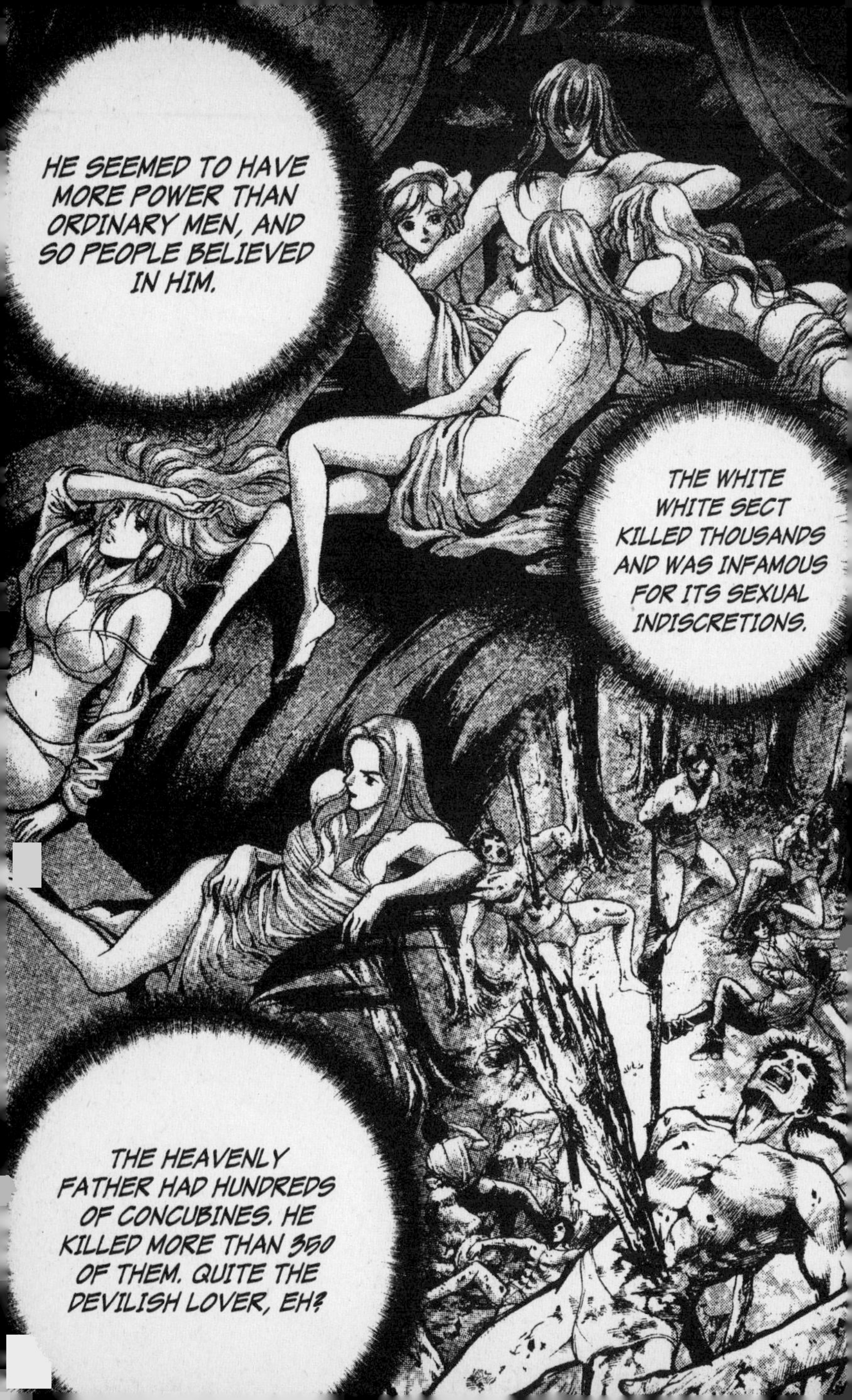
HE SEEMED TO HAVE MORE POWER THAN ORDINARY MEN, AND SO PEOPLE BELIEVED IN HIM.
THE WHITE WHITE SECT KILLED THOUSANDS AND WAS INFAMOUS FOR ITS SEXUAL INDISCRETIONS.
THE HEAVENLY FATHER HAD HUNDREDS OF CONCUBINES. HE KILLED MORE THAN 350 OF THEM. QUITE THE DEVILISH LOVER, EH?

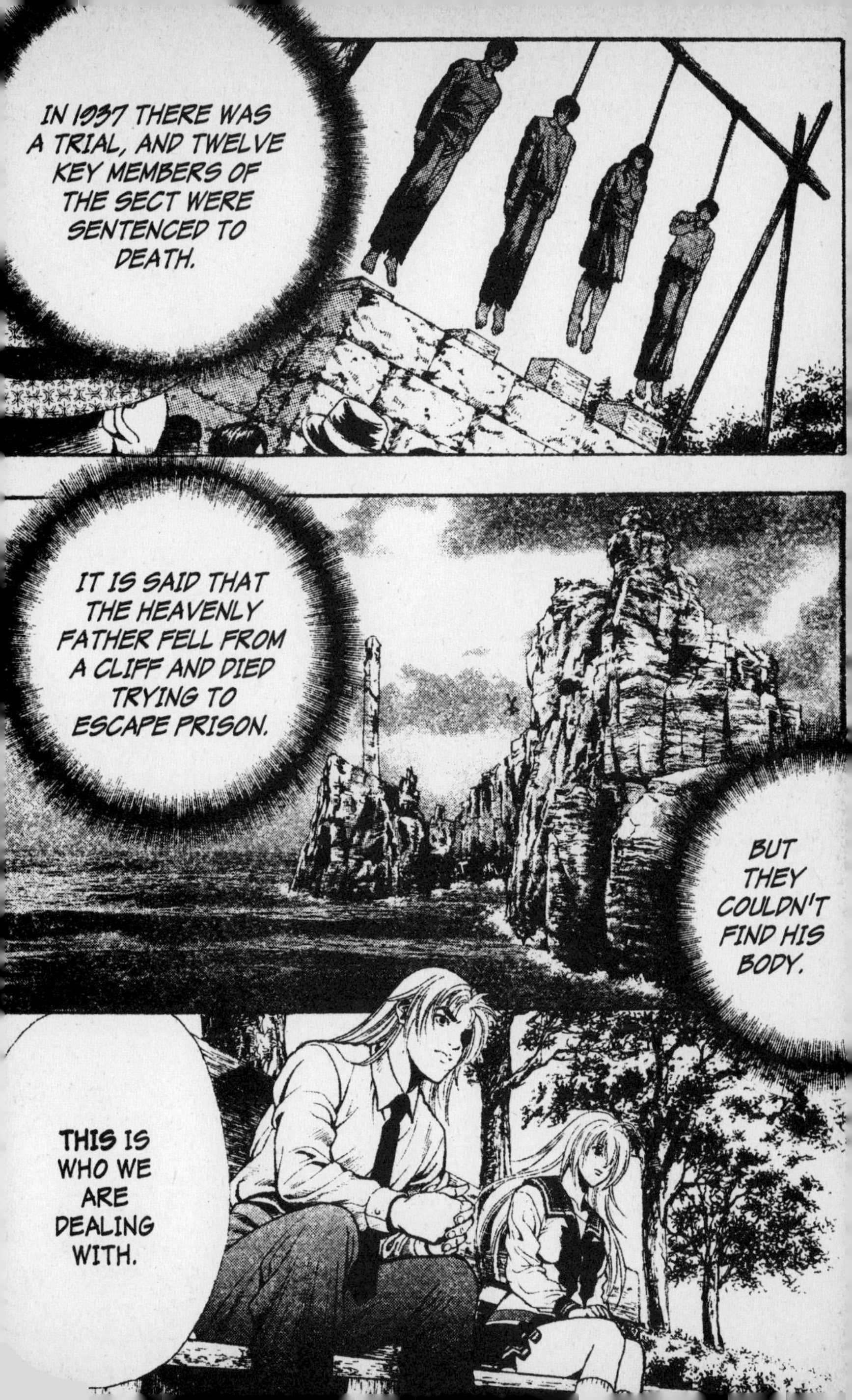
IN 1937 THERE WAS A TRIAL, AND TWELVE KEY MEMBERS OF THE SECT WERE SENTENCED TO DEATH.
IT IS SAID THAT THE HEAVENLY FATHER FELL FROM A CLIFF AND DIED TRYING TO ESCAPE PRISON.
BUT THEY COULDN'T FIND HIS BODY.
THIS IS WHO WE ARE DEALING WITH.

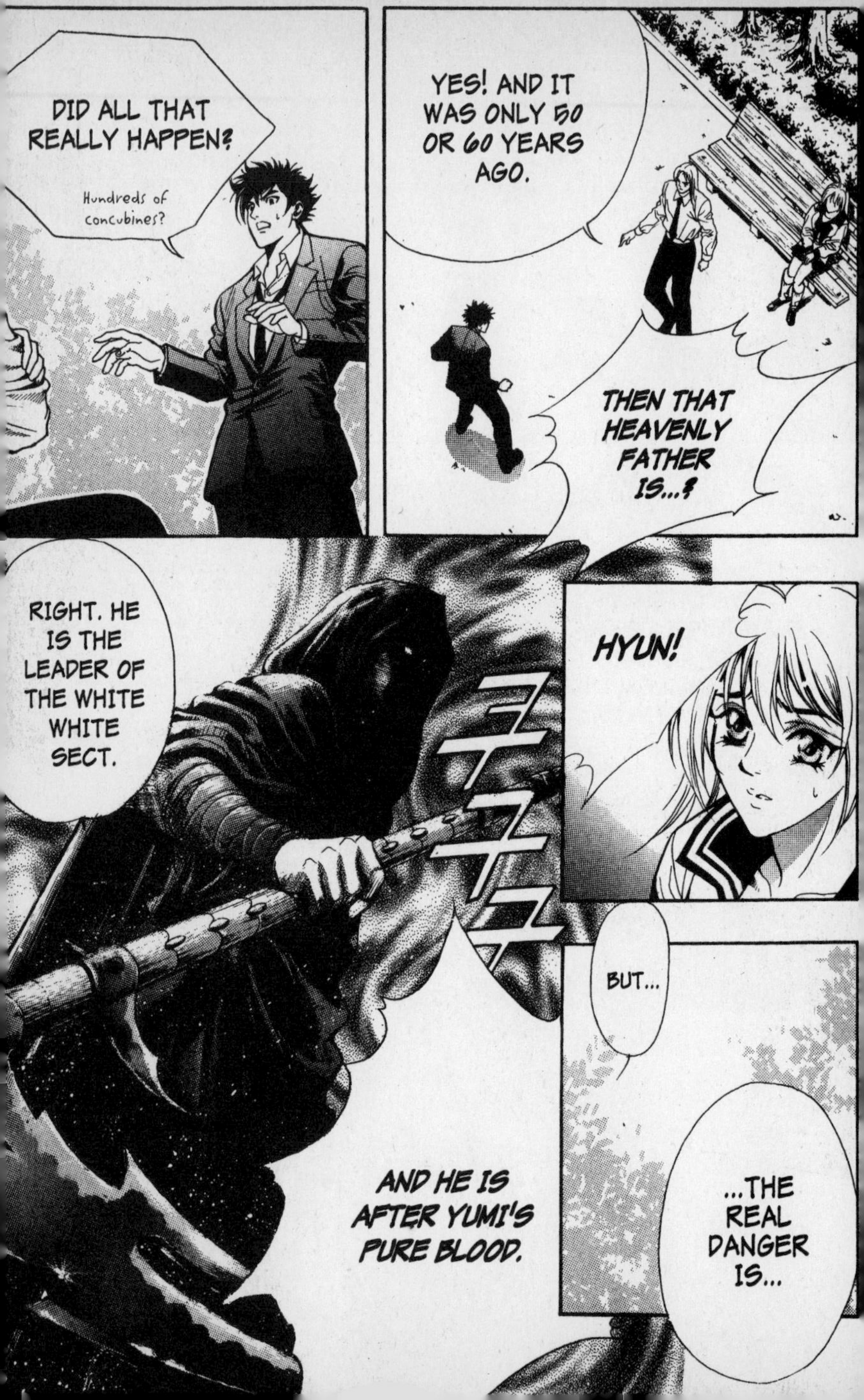
DID ALL THAT REALLY HAPPEN?
Hundreds of concubines?
YES! AND IT WAS ONLY 50 OR 60 YEARS AGO.
THEN THAT HEAVENLY FATHER IS...?
RIGHT. HE IS THE LEADER OF THE WHITE WHITE SECT.
AND HE IS AFTER YUMI'S PURE BLOOD.
HYUN!
BUT...
...THE REAL DANGER IS...

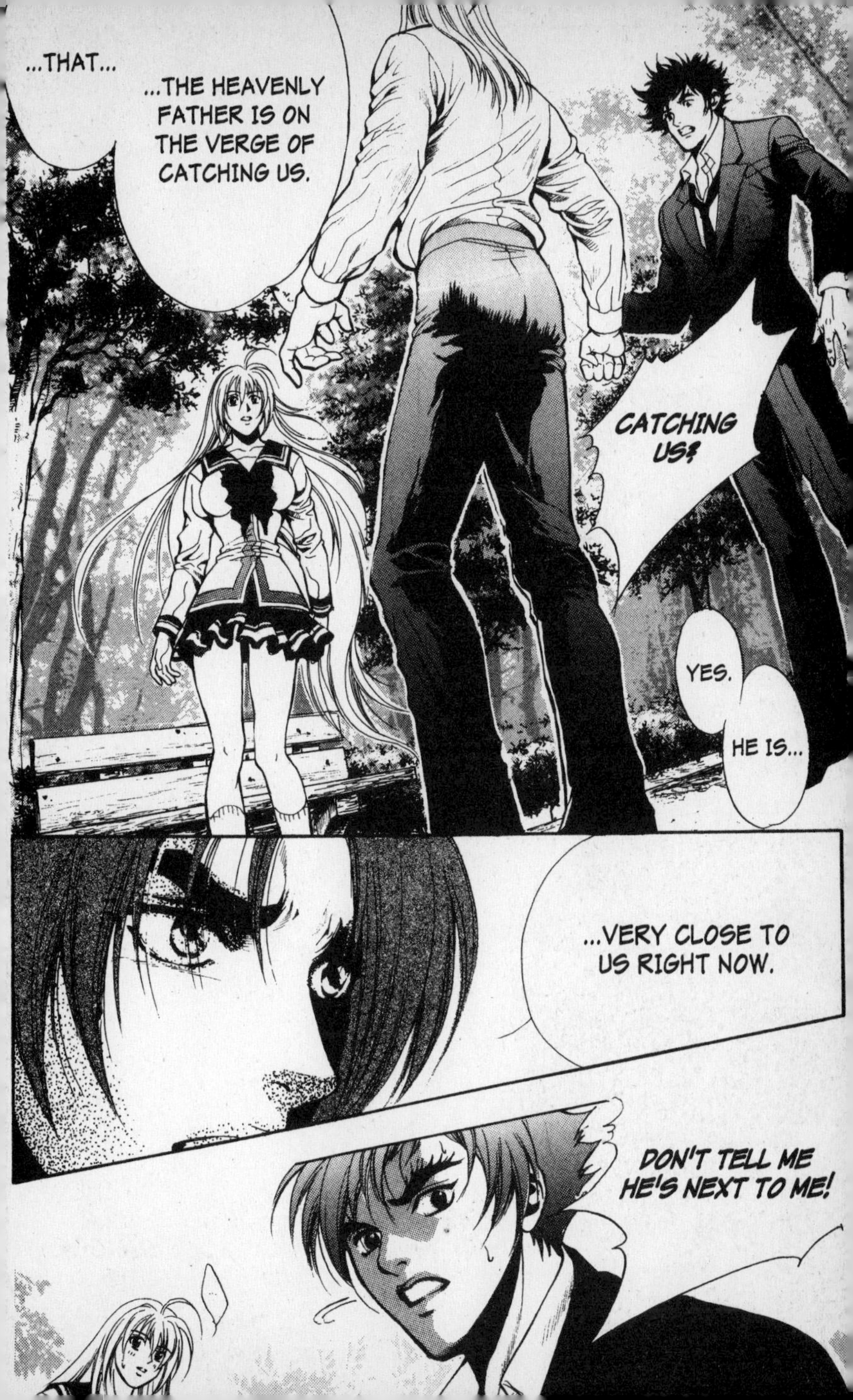
...THAT...
...THE HEAVENLY FATHER IS ON THE VERGE OF CATCHING US.
CATCHING US?
YES.
HE IS...
...VERY CLOSE TO US RIGHT NOW.
DON'T TELL ME HE'S NEXT TO ME!

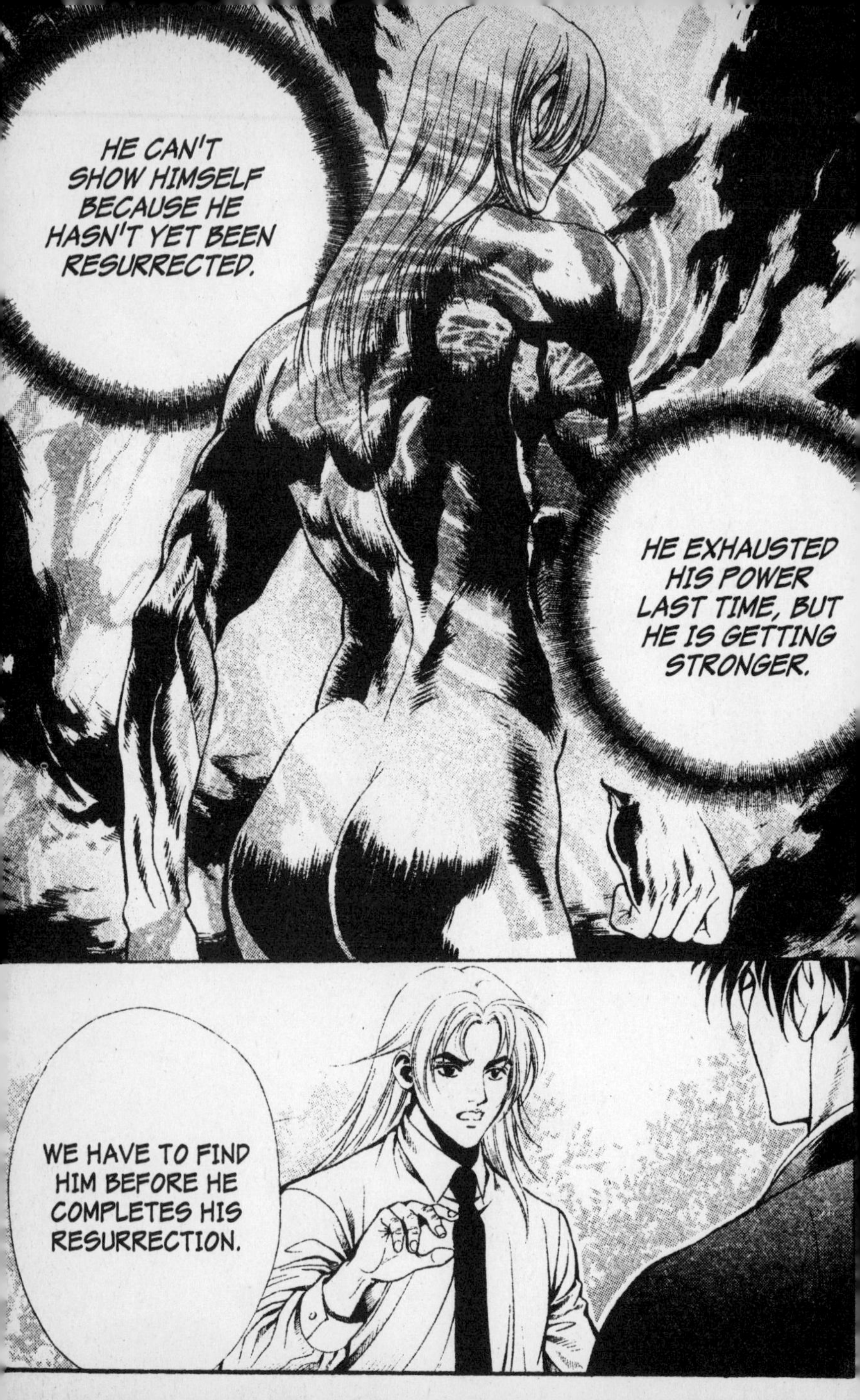
HE CAN'T SHOW HIMSELF BECAUSE HE HASN'T YET BEEN RESURRECTED.
HE EXHAUSTED HIS POWER LAST TIME, BUT HE IS GETTING STRONGER.
WE HAVE TO FIND HIM BEFORE HE COMPLETES HIS RESURRECTION.

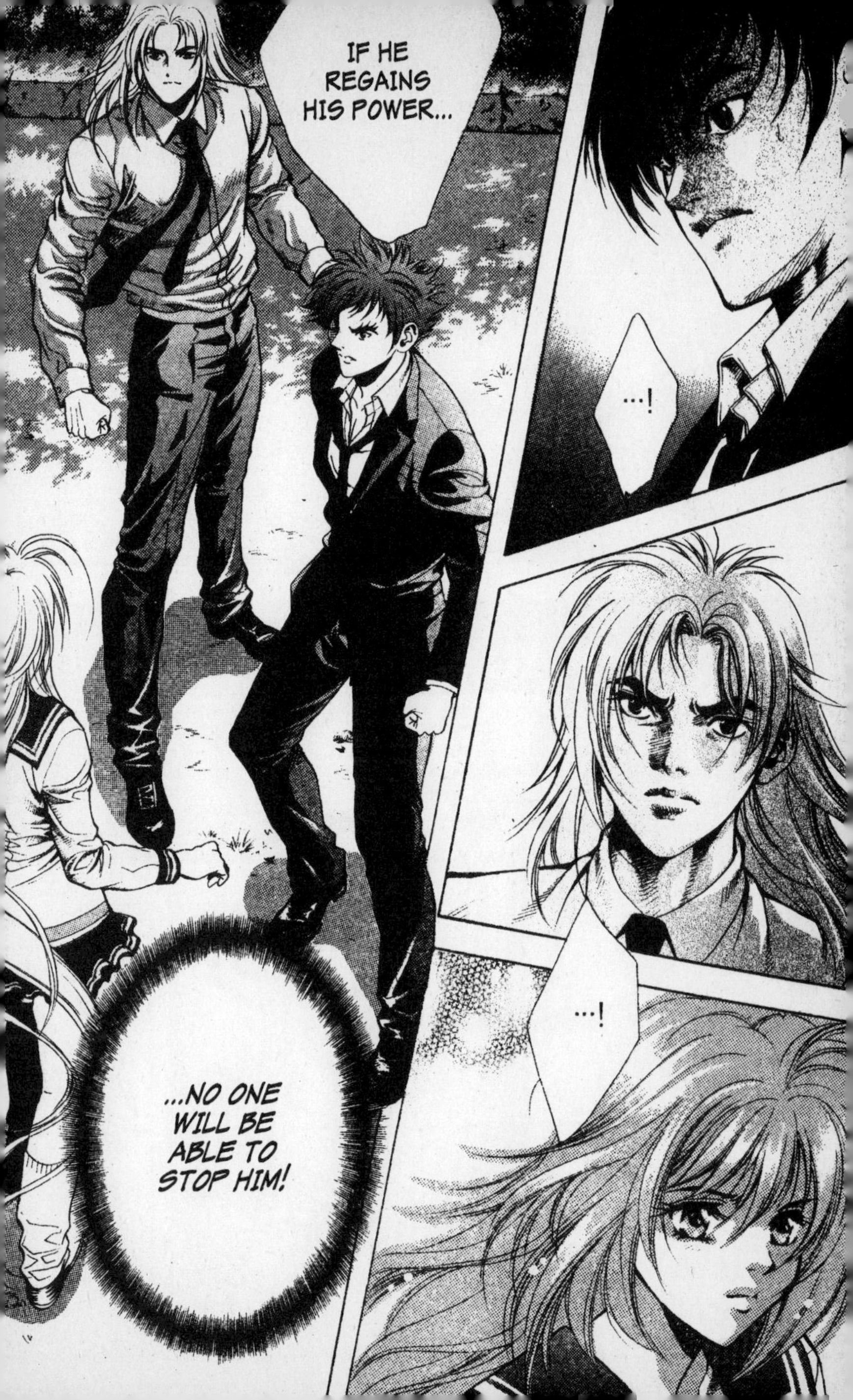
IF HE REGAINS HIS POWER...
...!
...!
...NO ONE WILL BE ABLE TO STOP HIM!

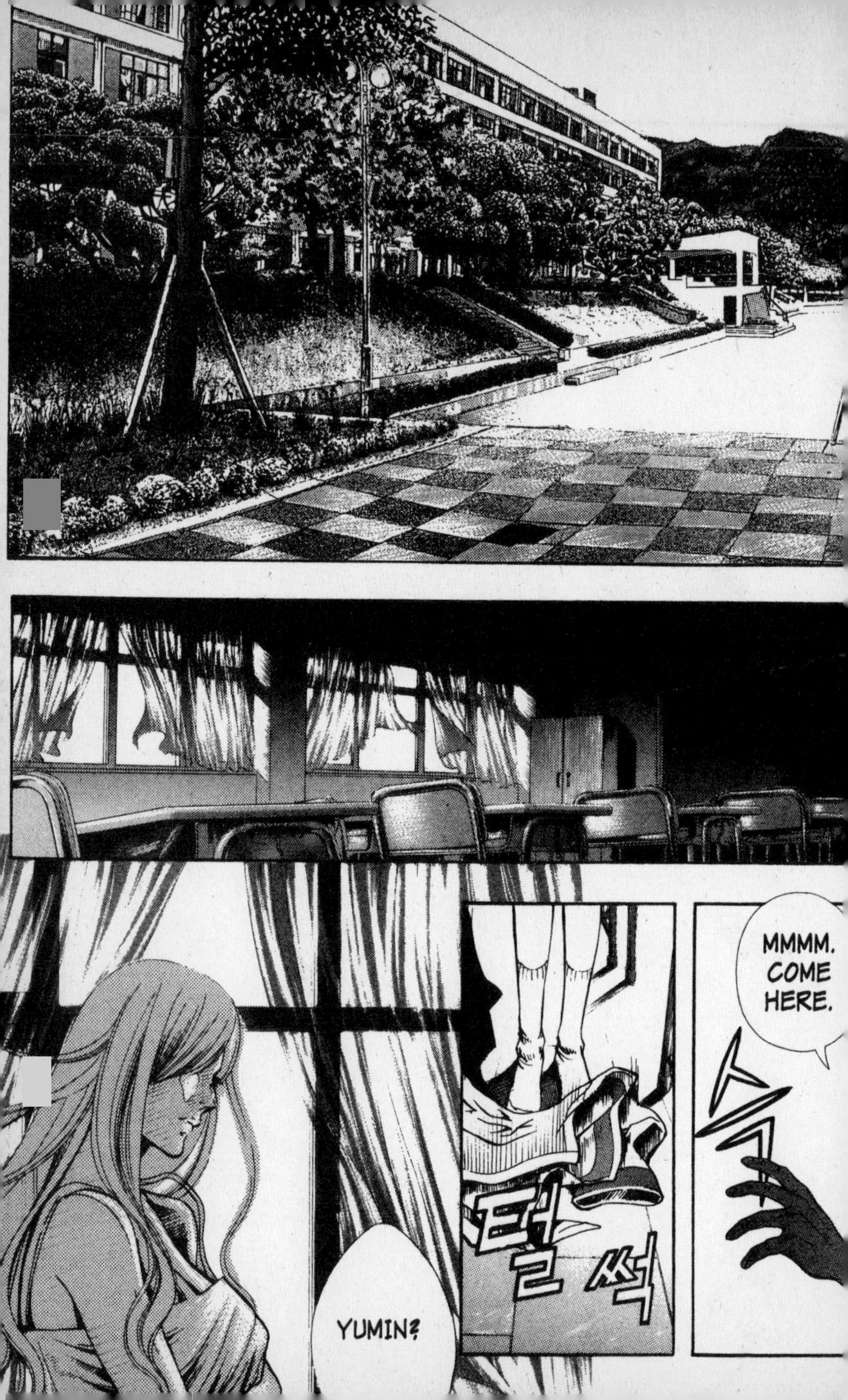
YUMIN?
털썩
MMMM. COME HERE.

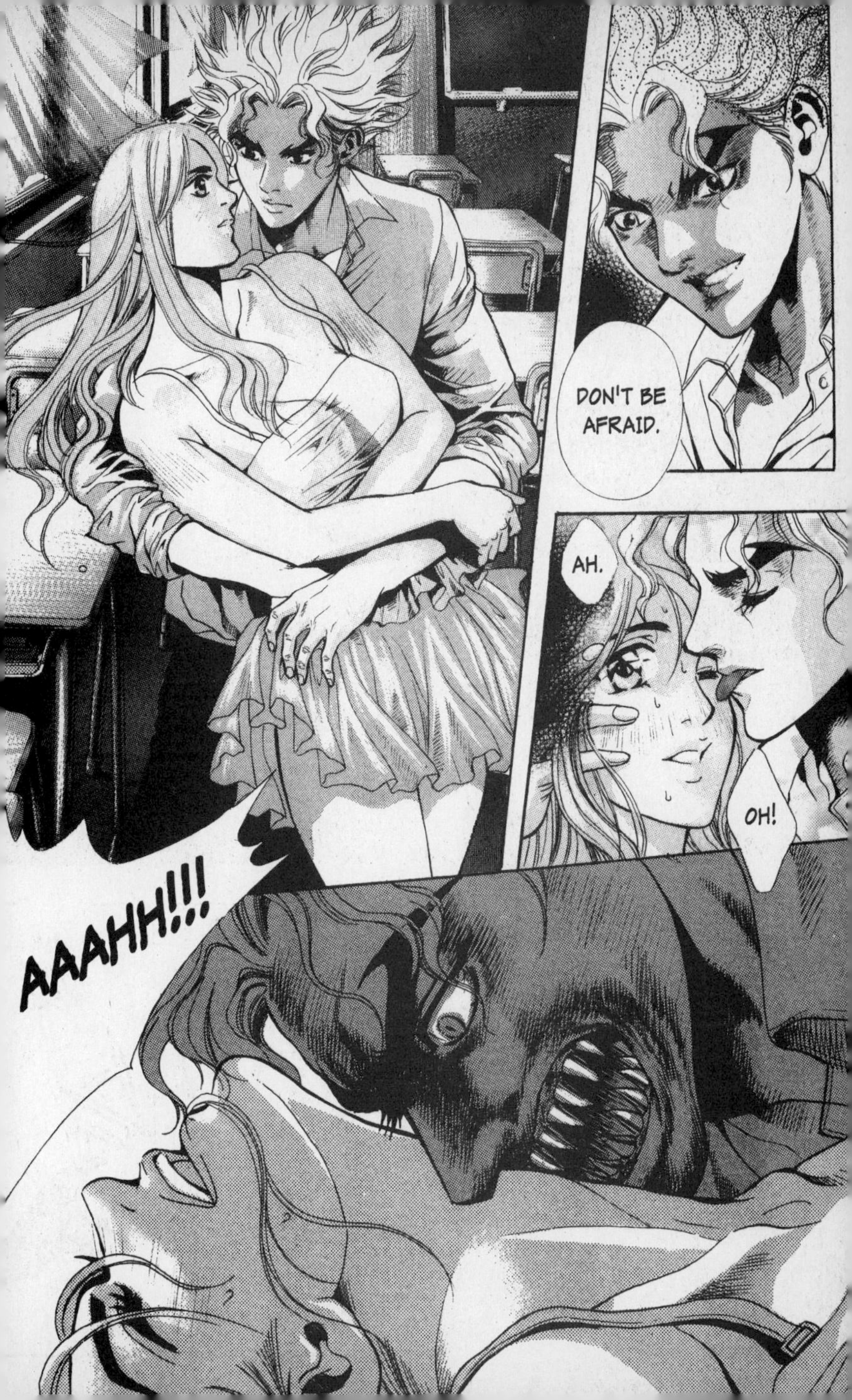
DON'T BE AFRAID.
AH.
OH!
AAAHH!!!

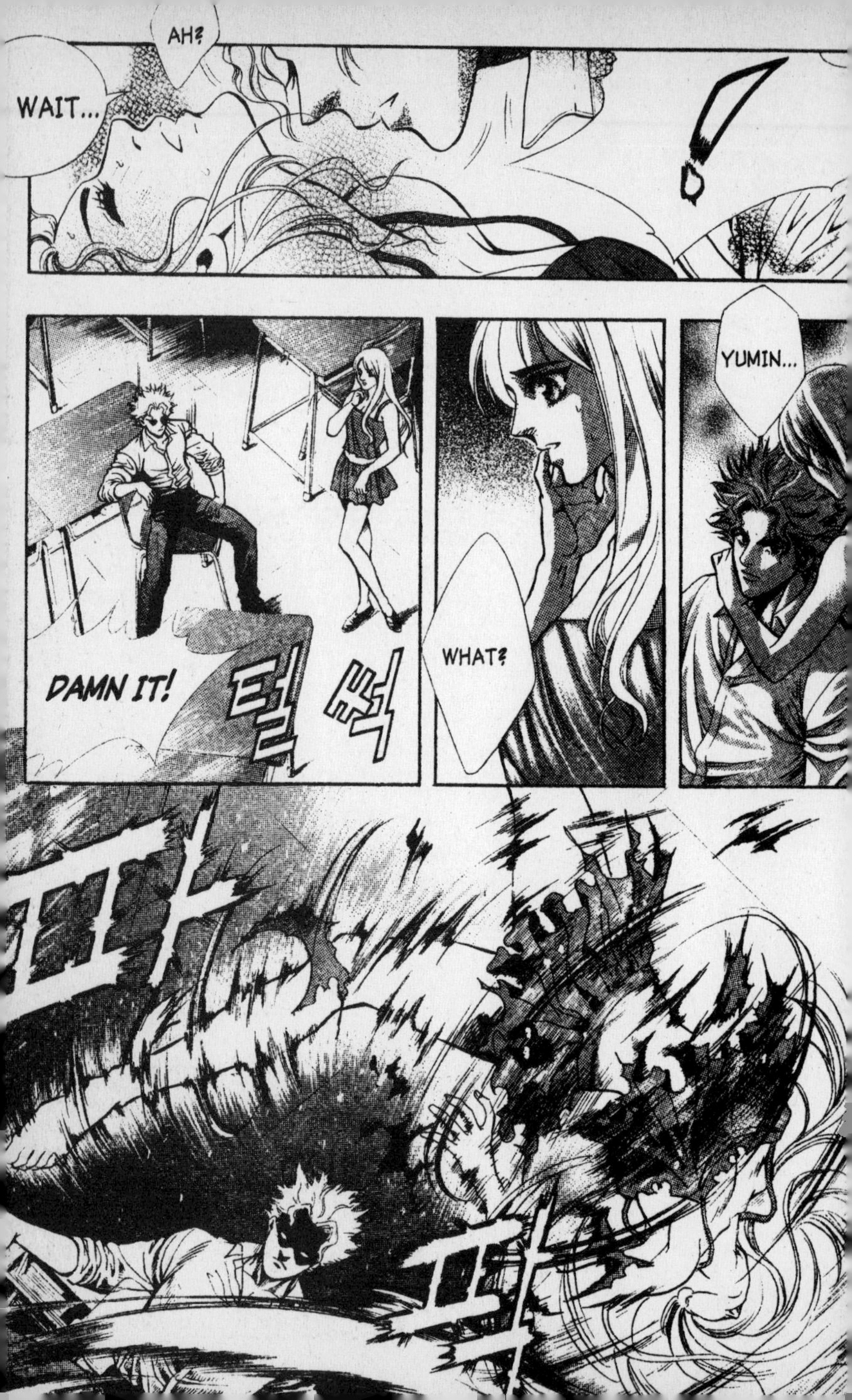
WAIT...
AH?
YUMIN...
WHAT?
DAMN IT!
털썩

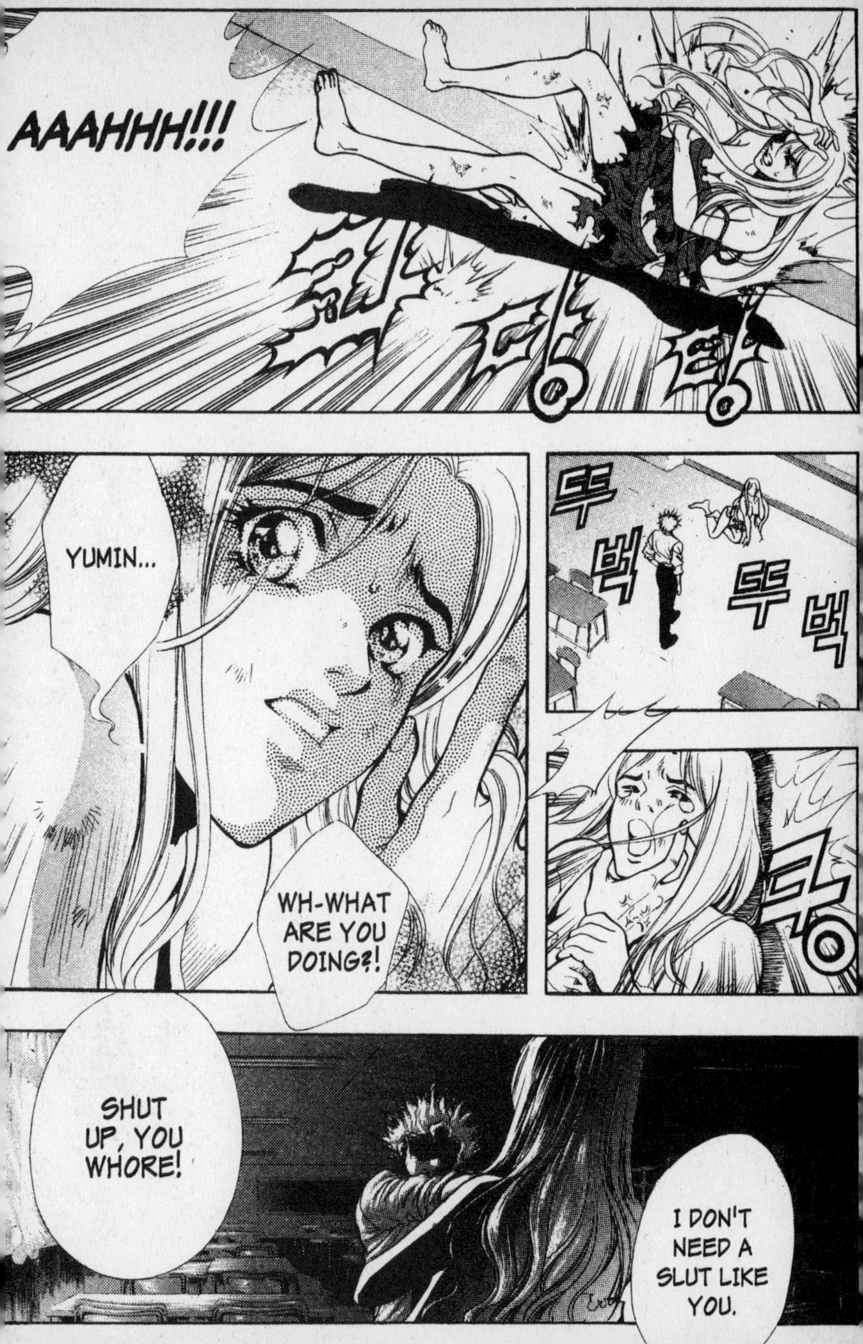
AAAHHH!!!
YUMIN...
WH-WHAT ARE YOU DOING?!
뚜벅 뚜벅
SHUT UP, YOU WHORE!
I DON'T NEED A SLUT LIKE YOU.

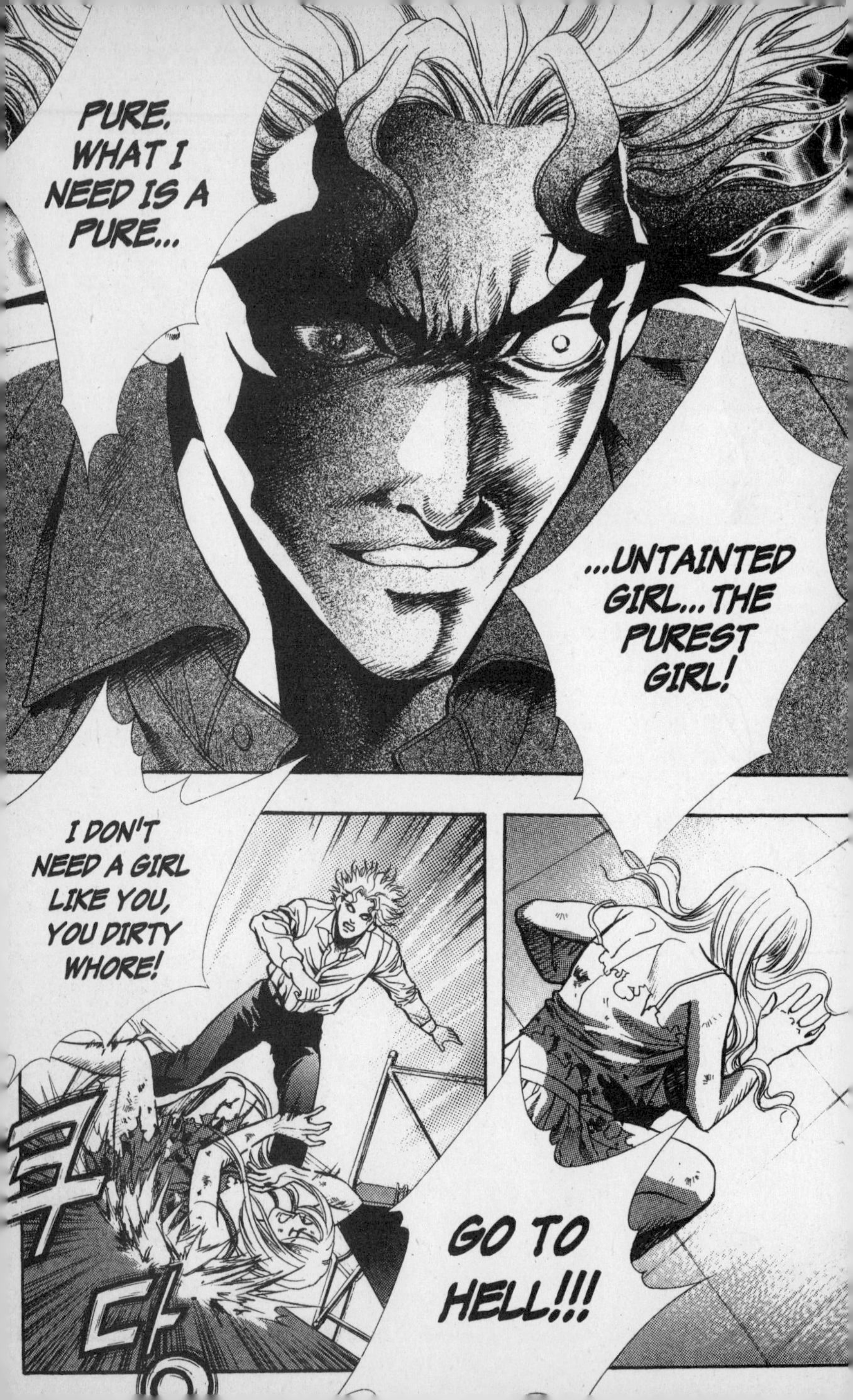
PURE. WHAT I NEED IS A PURE...
...UNTAINTED GIRL...THE PUREST GIRL!
I DON'T NEED A GIRL LIKE YOU, YOU DIRTY WHORE!
GO TO HELL!!!

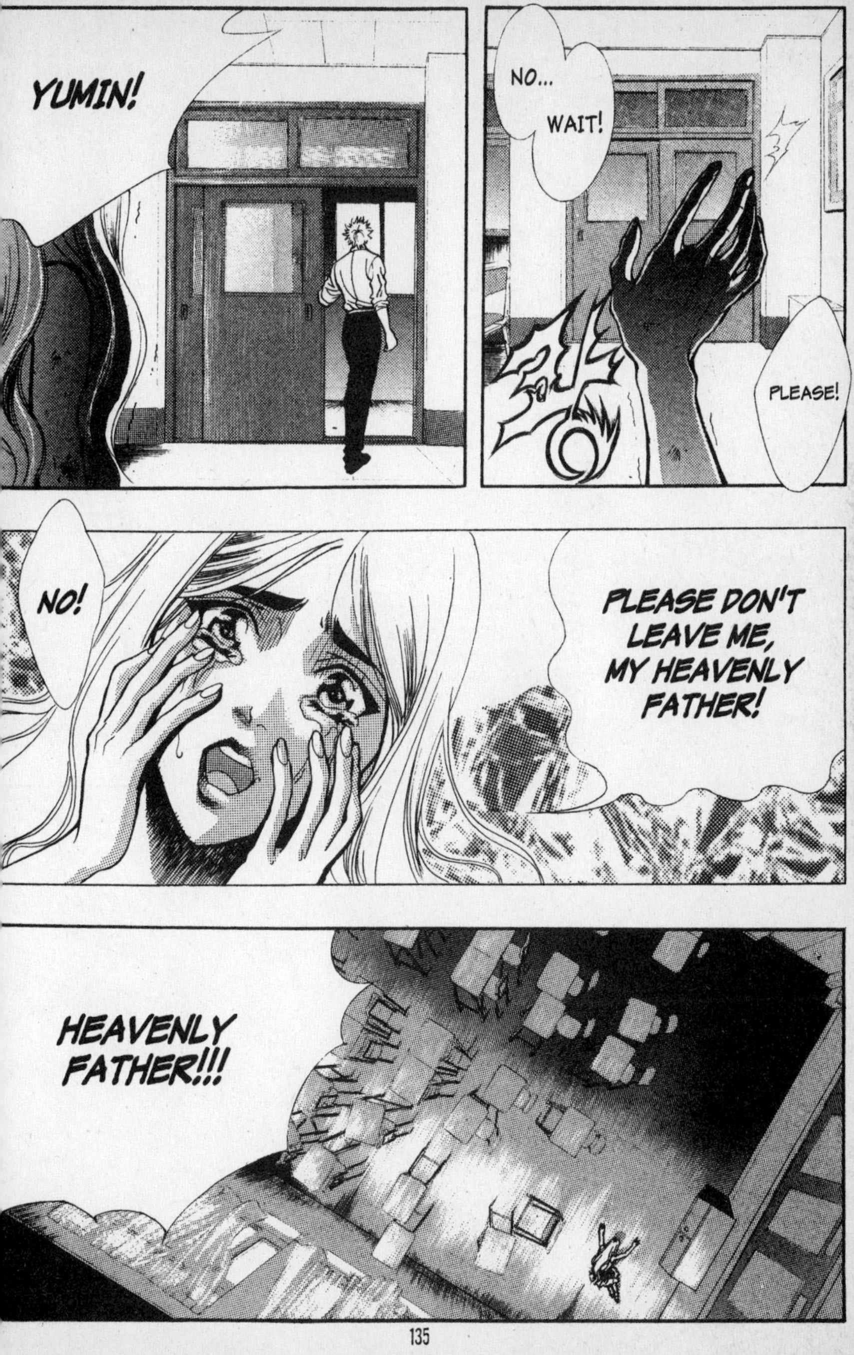
YUMIN!
NO...
WAIT!
PLEASE!
NO!
PLEASE DON'T LEAVE ME, MY HEAVENLY FATHER!
HEAVENLY FATHER!!!

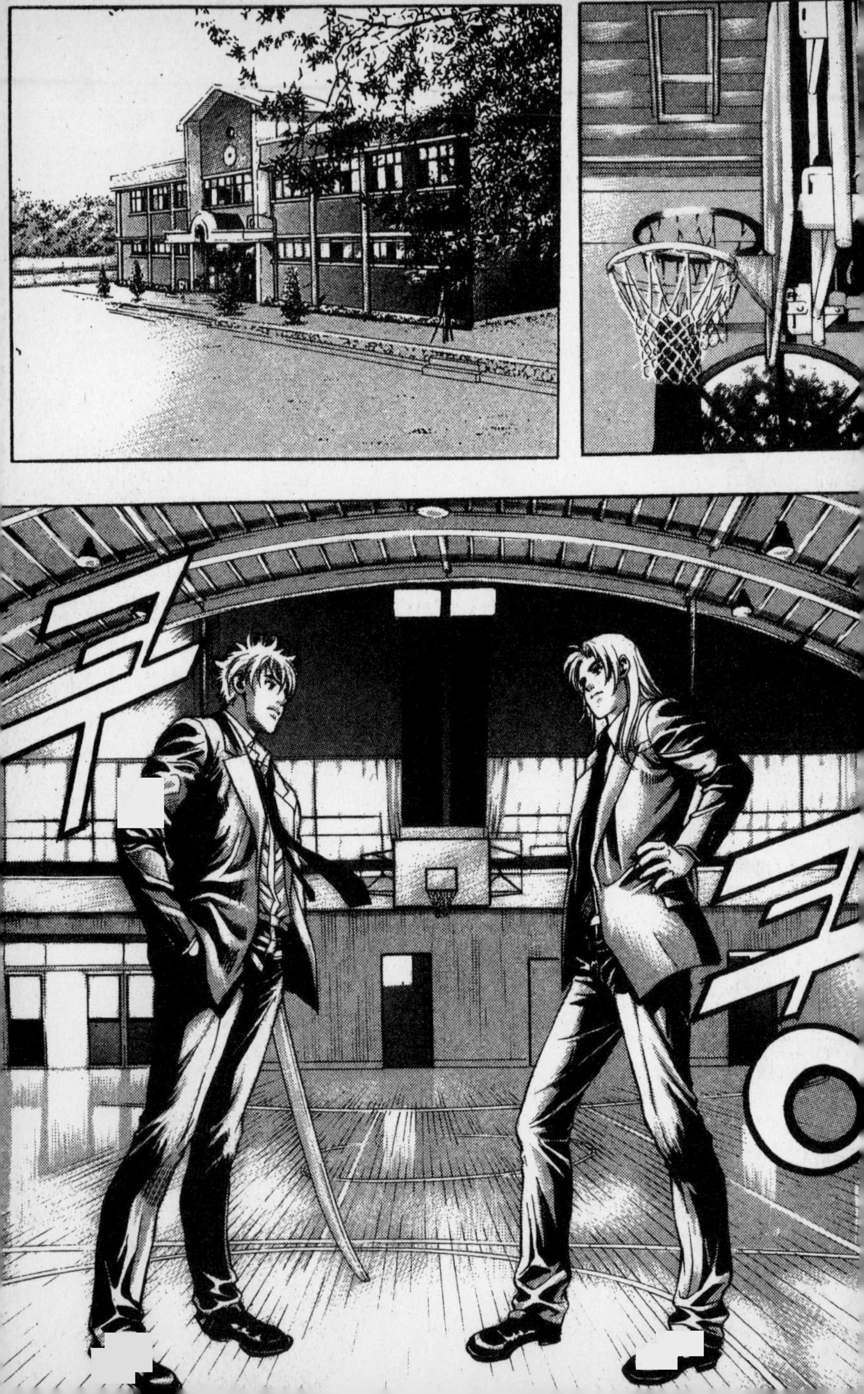

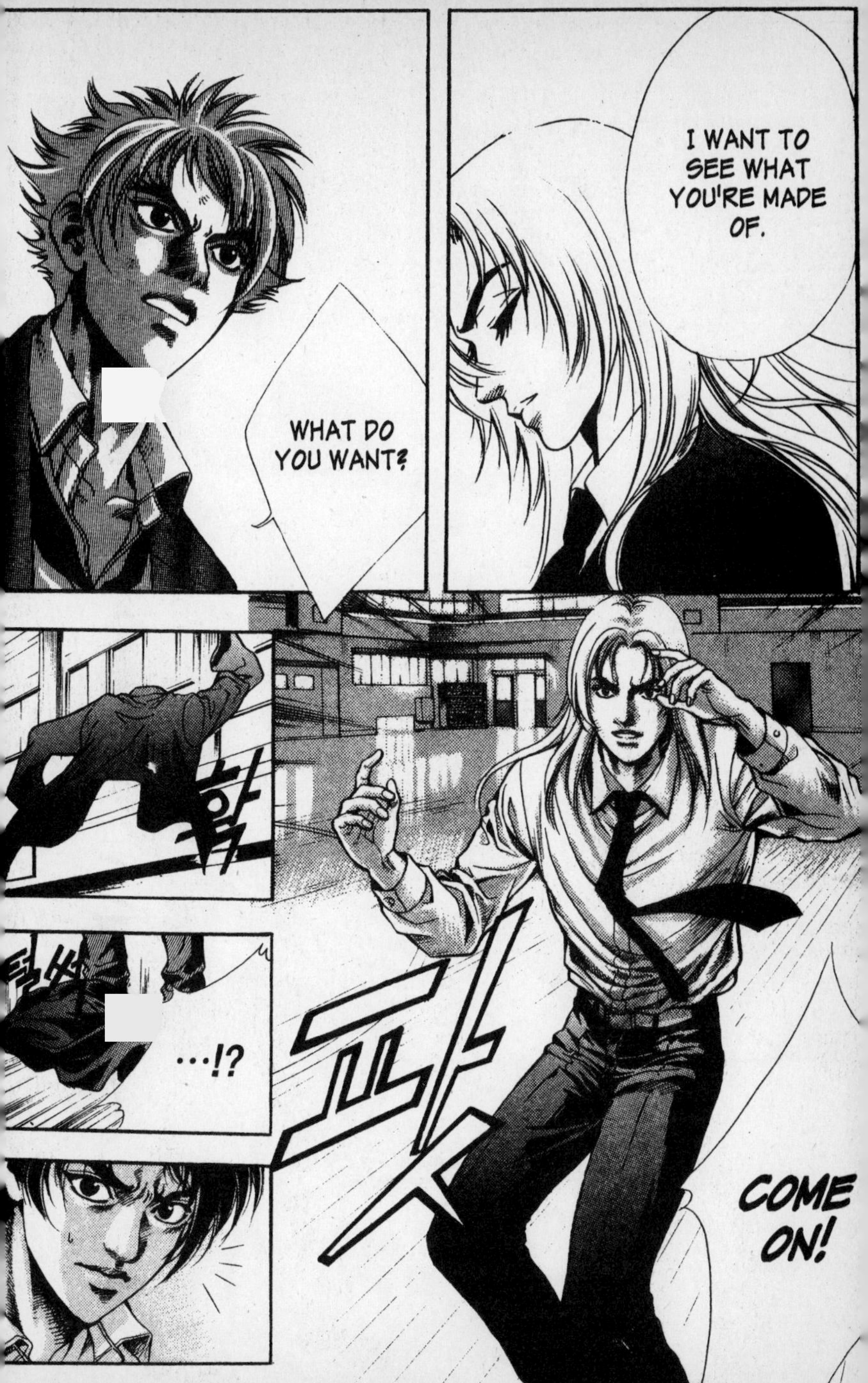
I WANT TO SEE WHAT YOU'RE MADE OF.
WHAT DO YOU WANT?
...!?
COME ON!

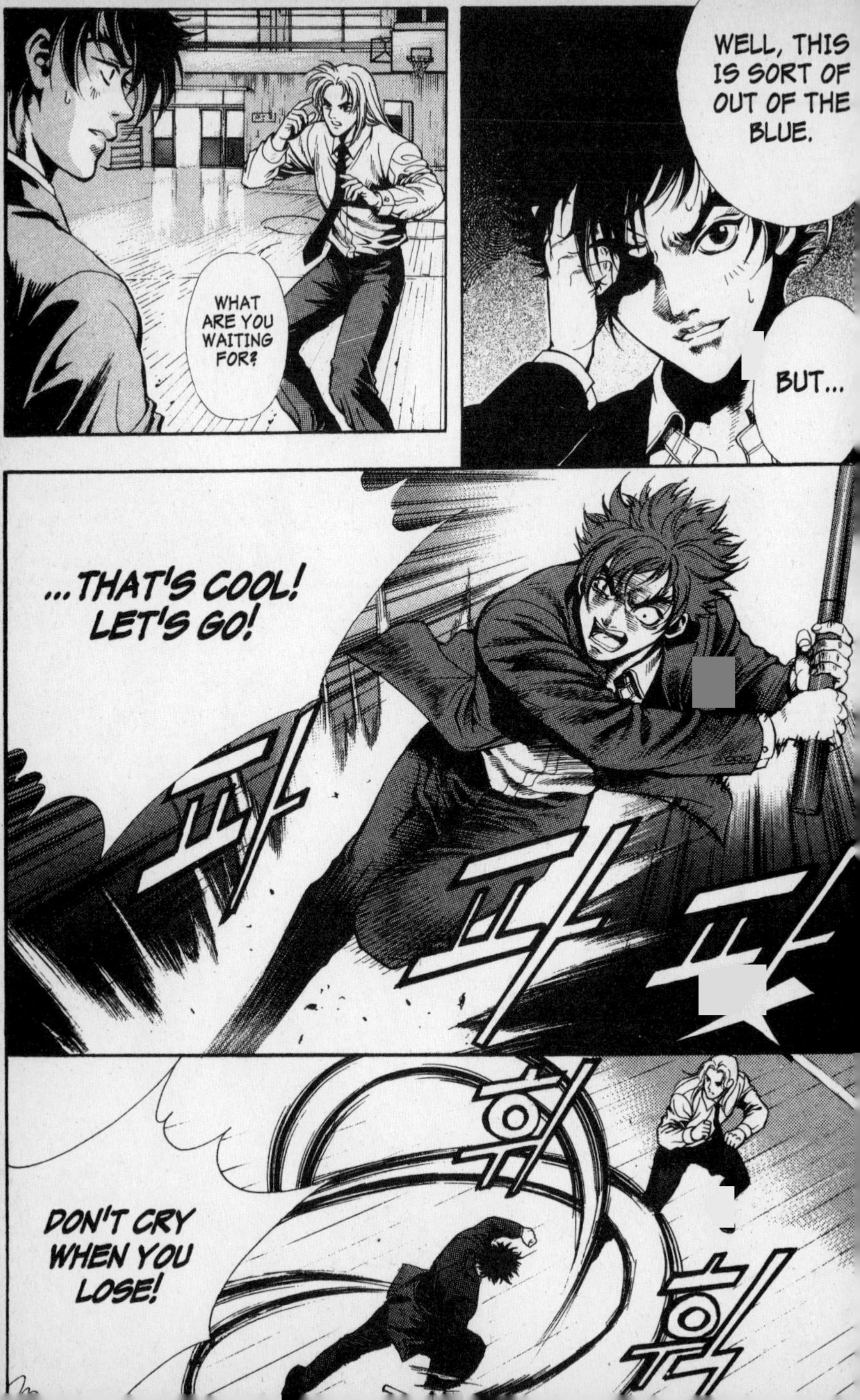
WHAT ARE YOU WAITING FOR?
WELL, THIS IS SORT OF OUT OF THE BLUE.
BUT...
...THAT'S COOL! LET'S GO!
DON'T CRY WHEN YOU LOSE!

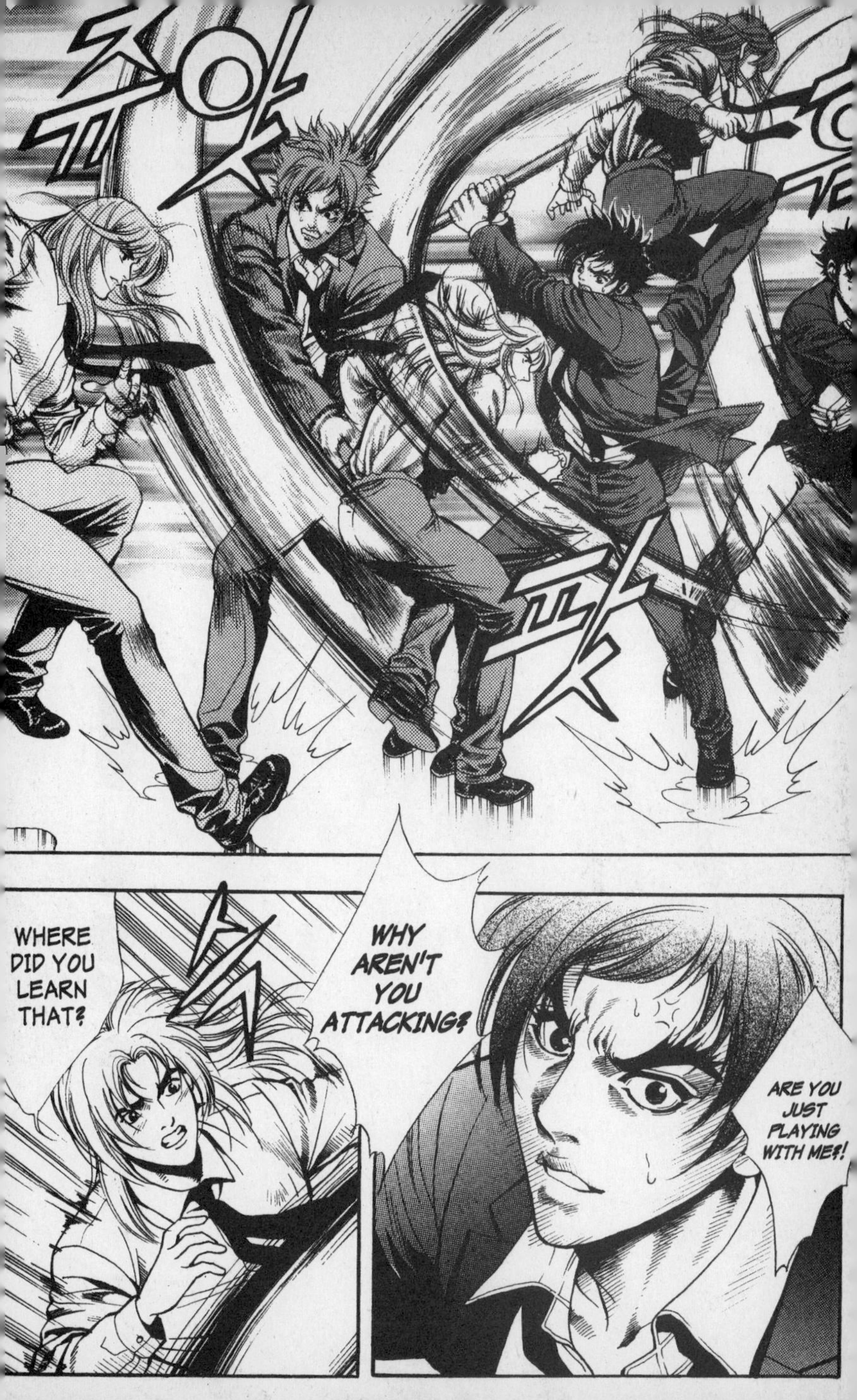
WHERE DID YOU LEARN THAT?
WHY AREN'T YOU ATTACKING?
ARE YOU JUST PLAYING WITH ME?!

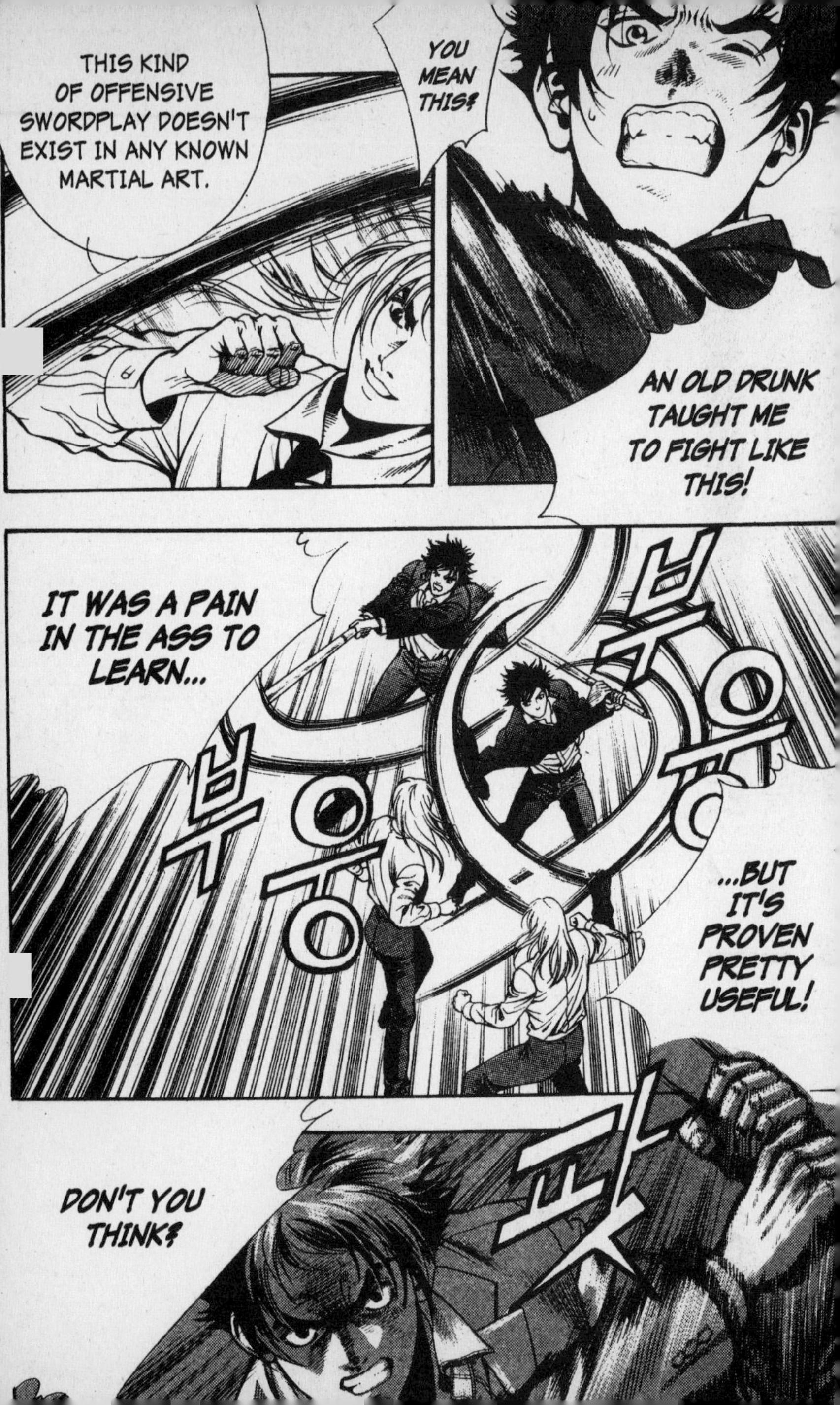
THIS KIND OF OFFENSIVE SWORDPLAY DOESN'T EXIST IN ANY KNOWN MARTIAL ART.
YOU MEAN THIS?
AN OLD DRUNK TAUGHT ME TO FIGHT LIKE THIS!
IT WAS A PAIN IN THE ASS TO LEARN...
...BUT IT'S PROVEN PRETTY USEFUL!
DON'T YOU THINK?

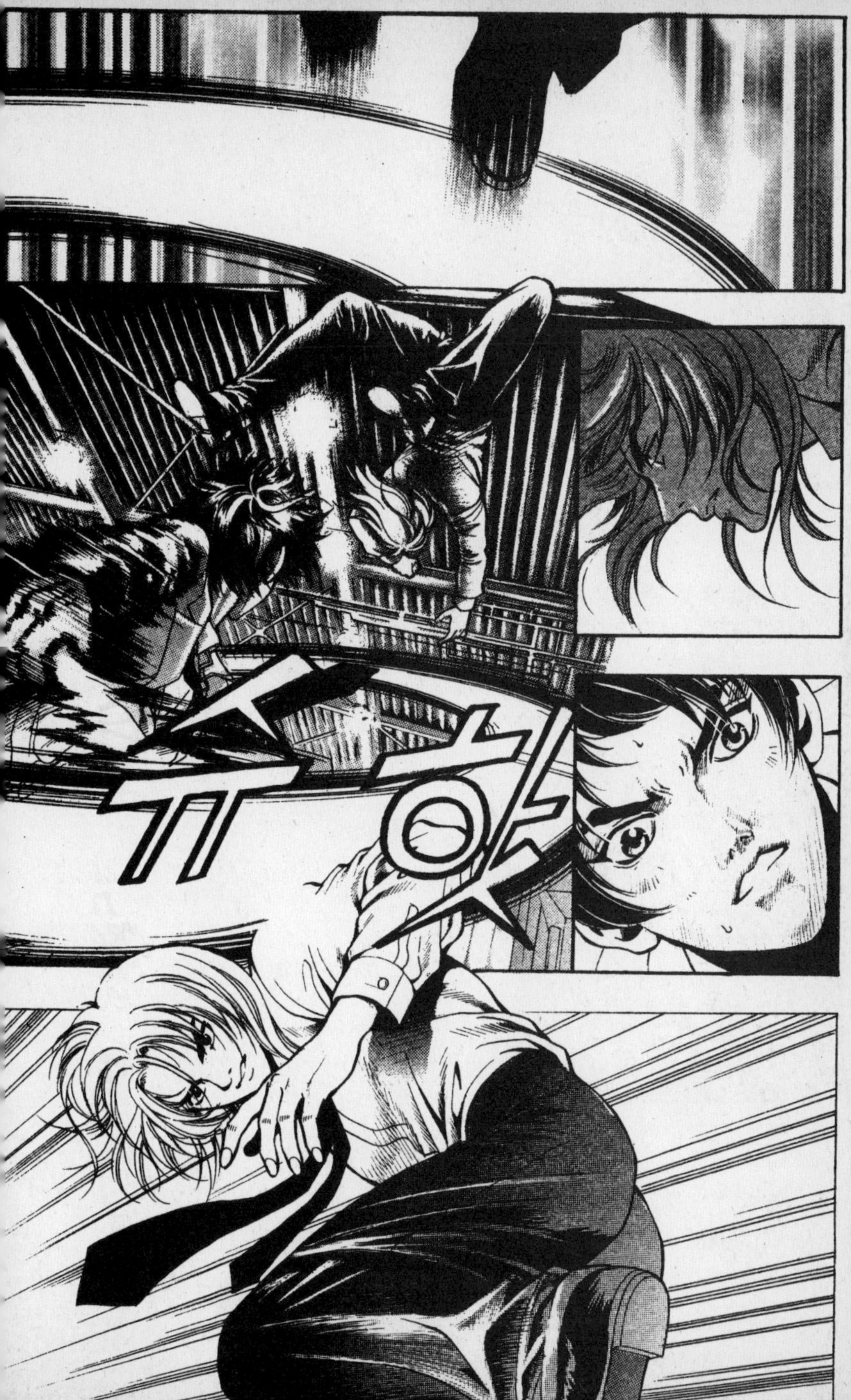

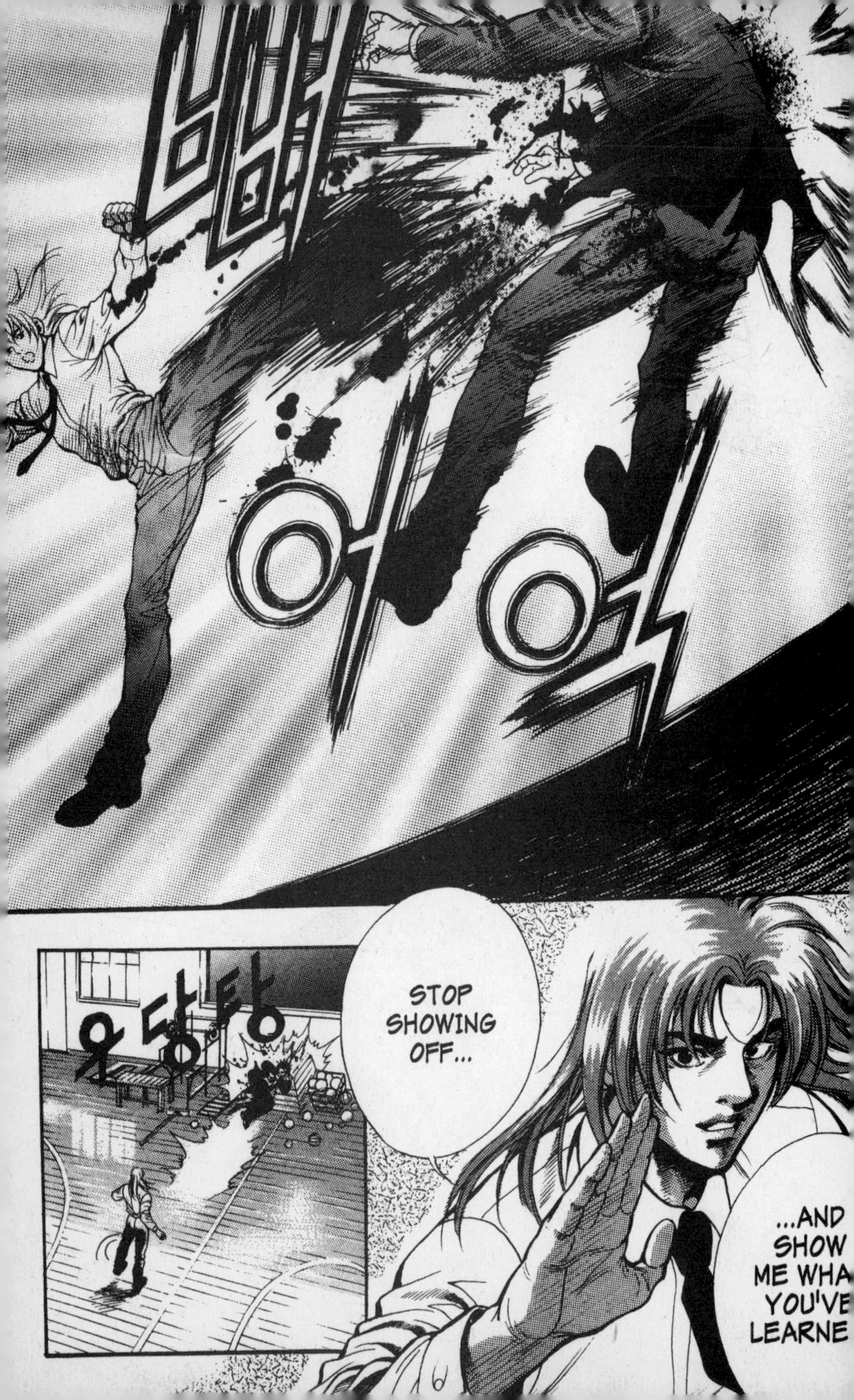
STOP SHOWING OFF...
...AND SHOW ME WHA YOU'VE LEARNE

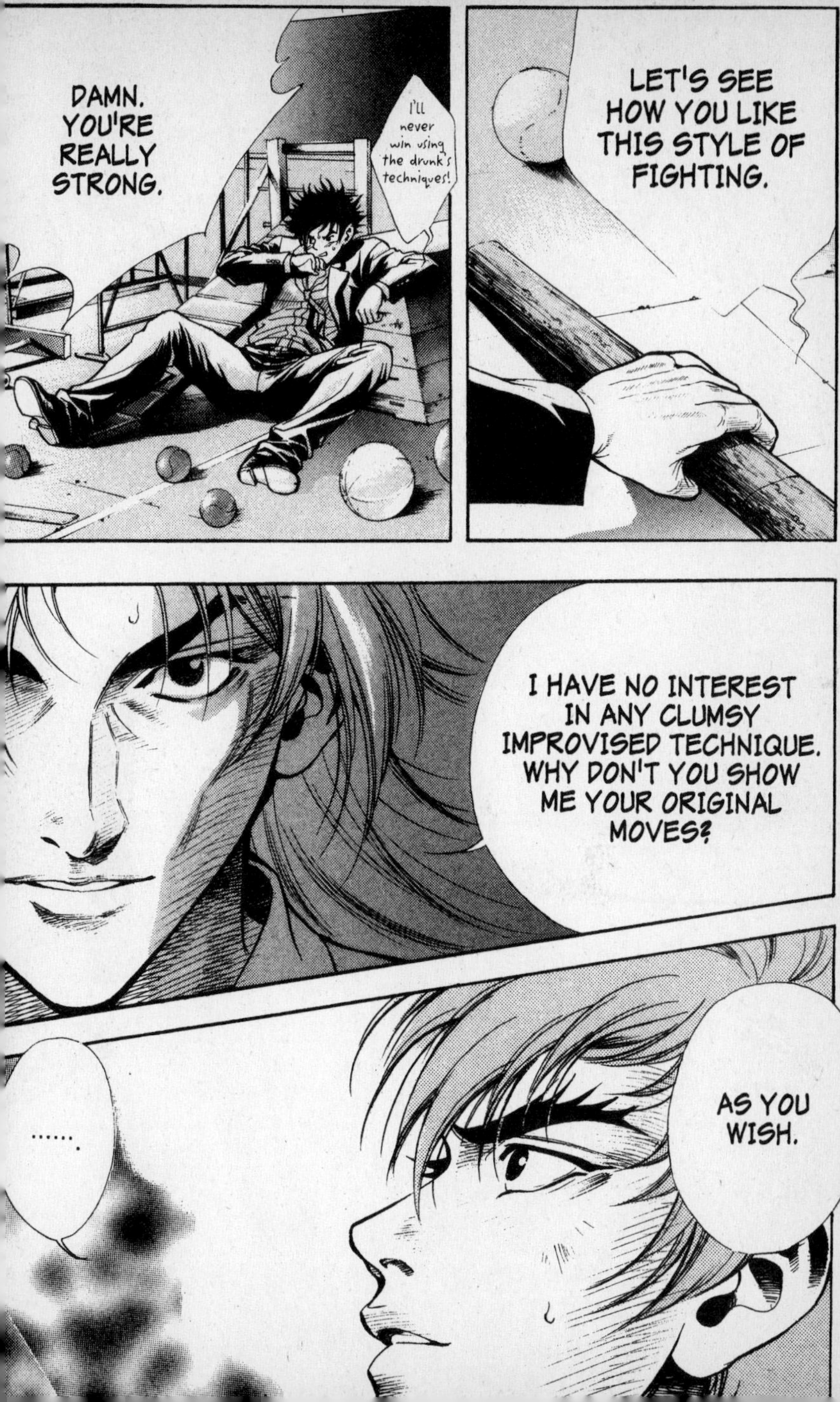

DAMN. YOU'RE REALLY STRONG.
I'll never win using the drunk's techniques!
LET'S SEE HOW YOU LIKE THIS STYLE OF FIGHTING.
I HAVE NO INTEREST IN ANY CLUMSY IMPROVISED TECHNIQUE. WHY DON'T YOU SHOW ME YOUR ORIGINAL MOVES?
....
AS YOU WISH.

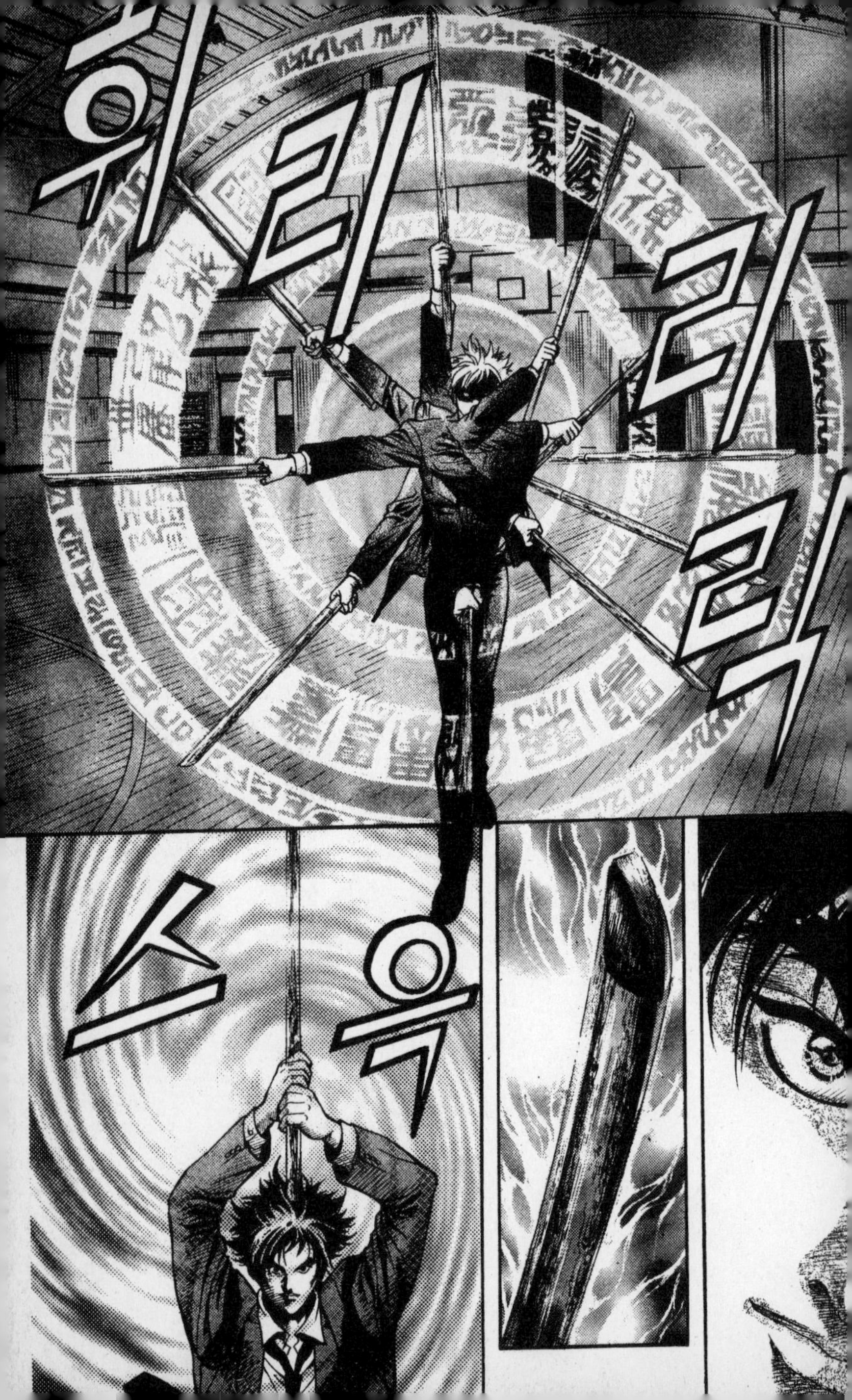
휘리리릭
스윽

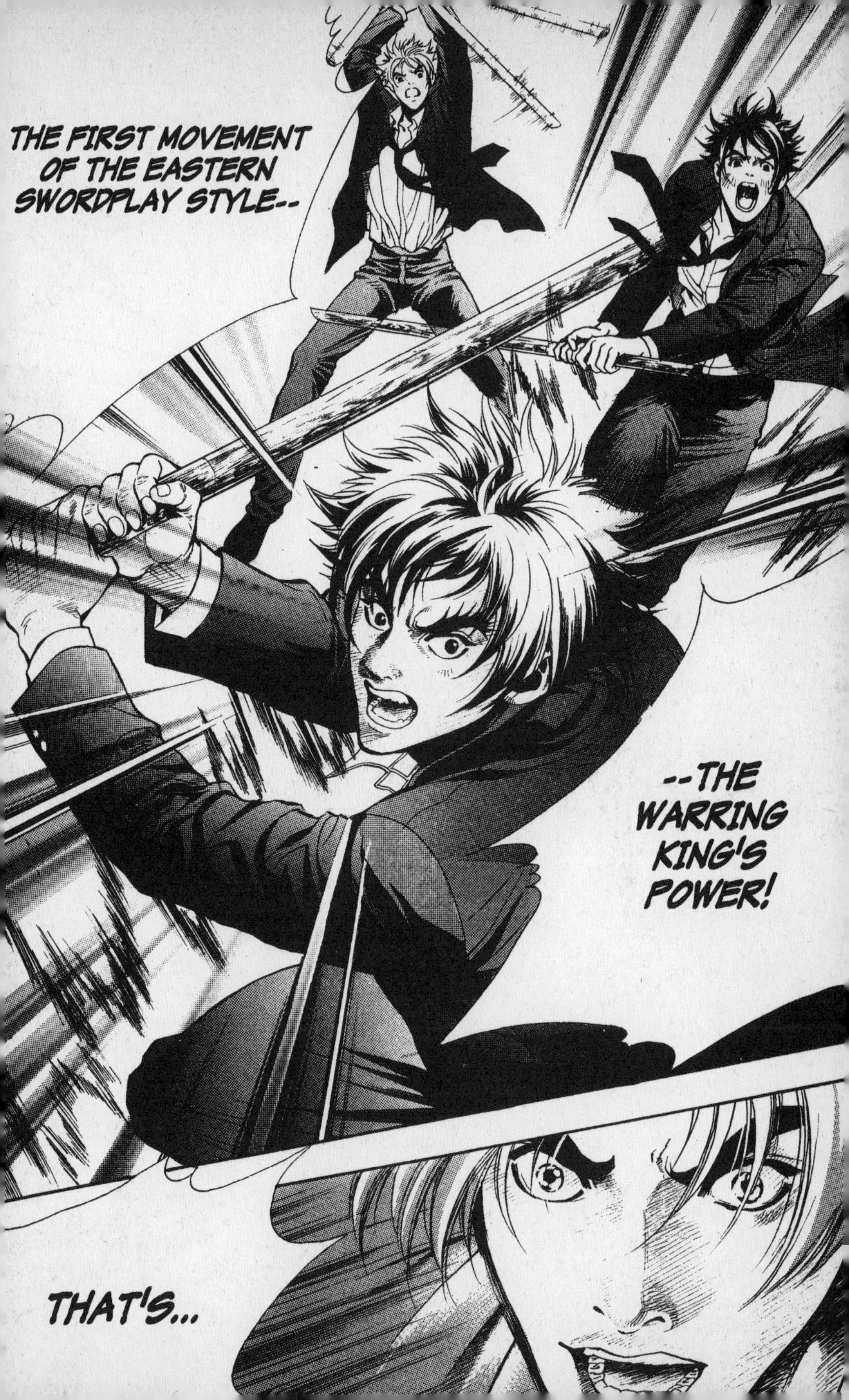
THE FIRST MOVEMENT OF THE EASTERN SWORDPLAY STYLE--
--THE WARRING KING'S POWER!
THAT'S...

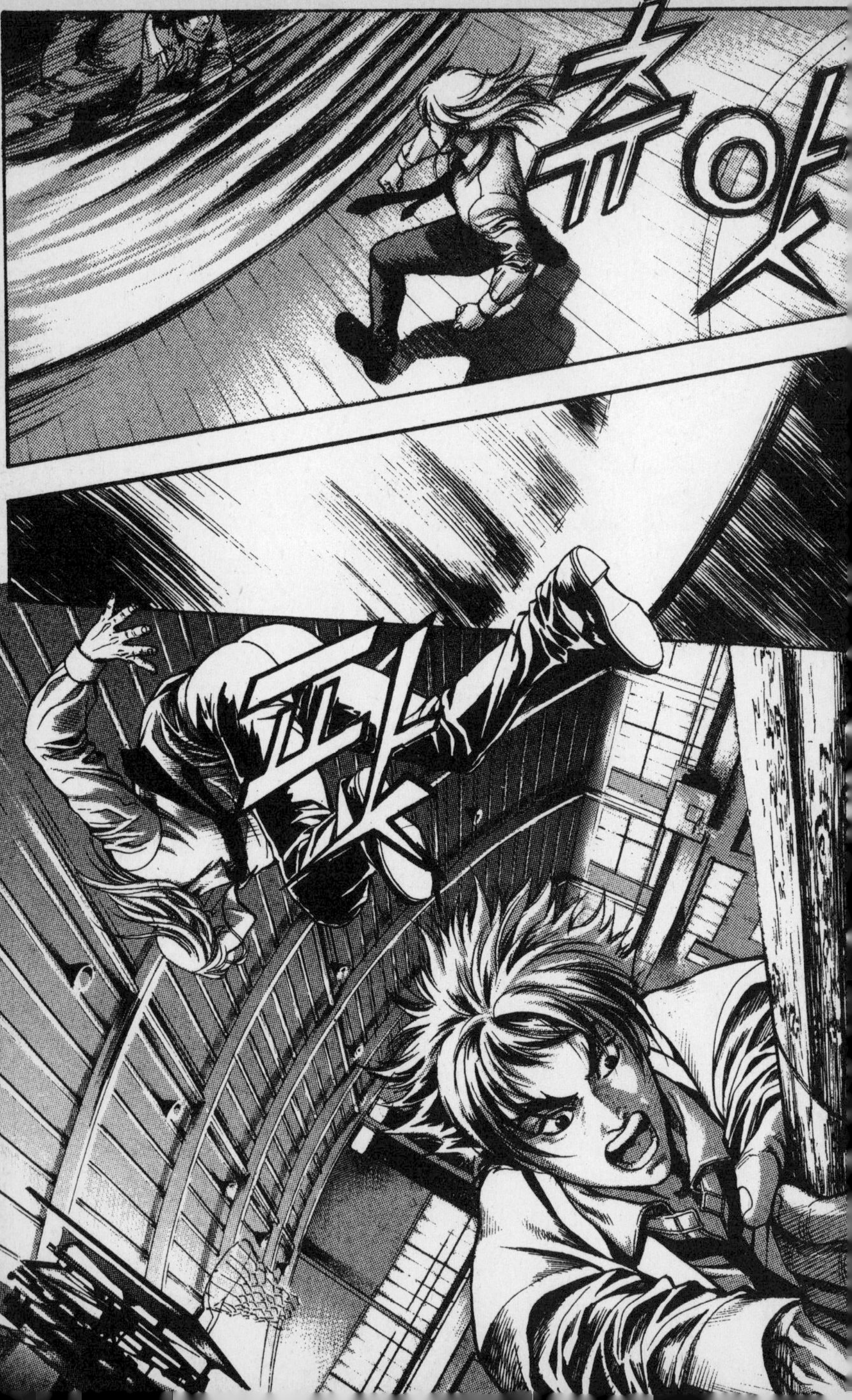

츄앗
팟

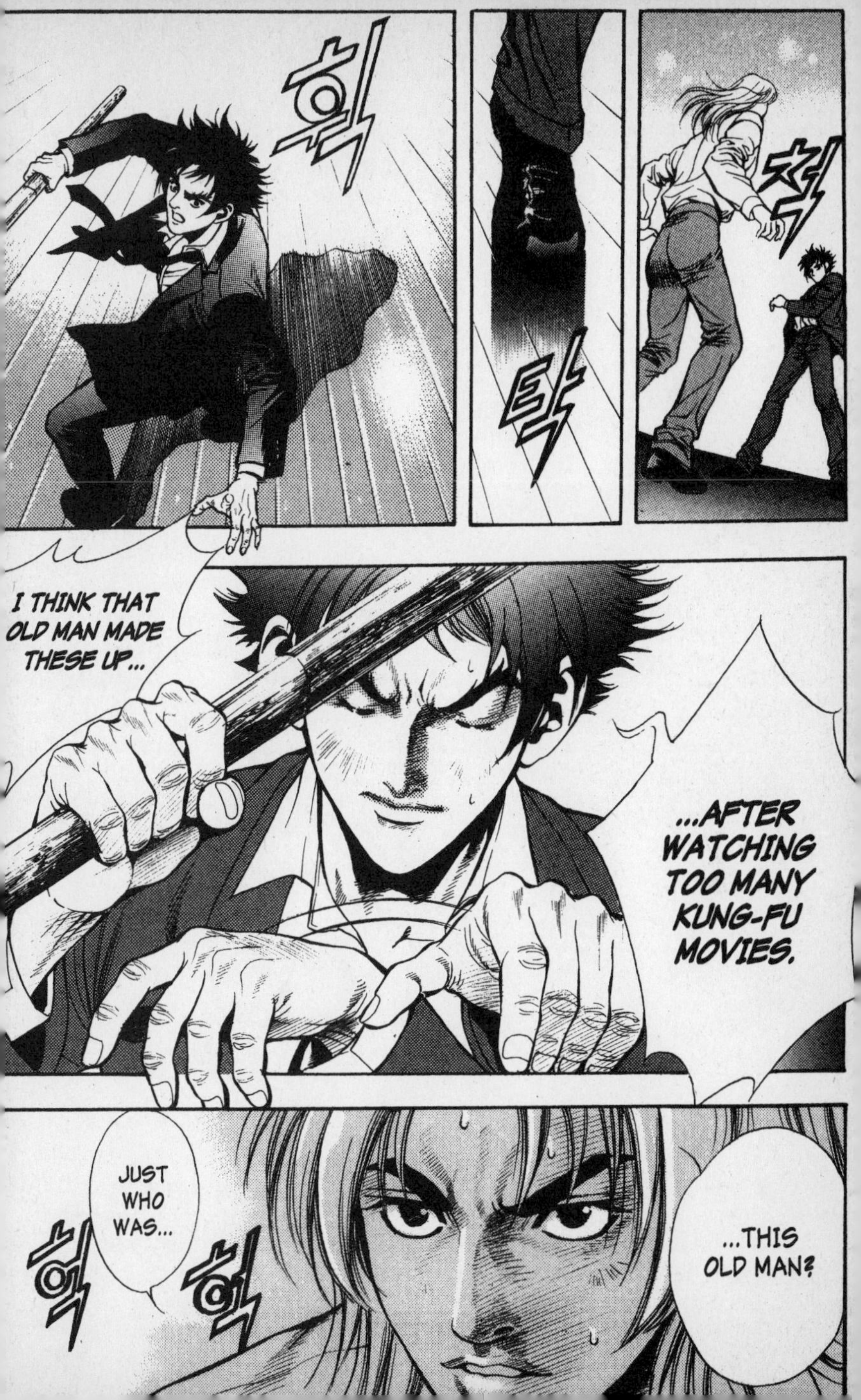
탁
척
I THINK THAT OLD MAN MADE THESE UP...
...AFTER WATCHING TOO MANY KUNG-FU MOVIES.
헉
JUST WHO WAS...
헉
...THIS OLD MAN?

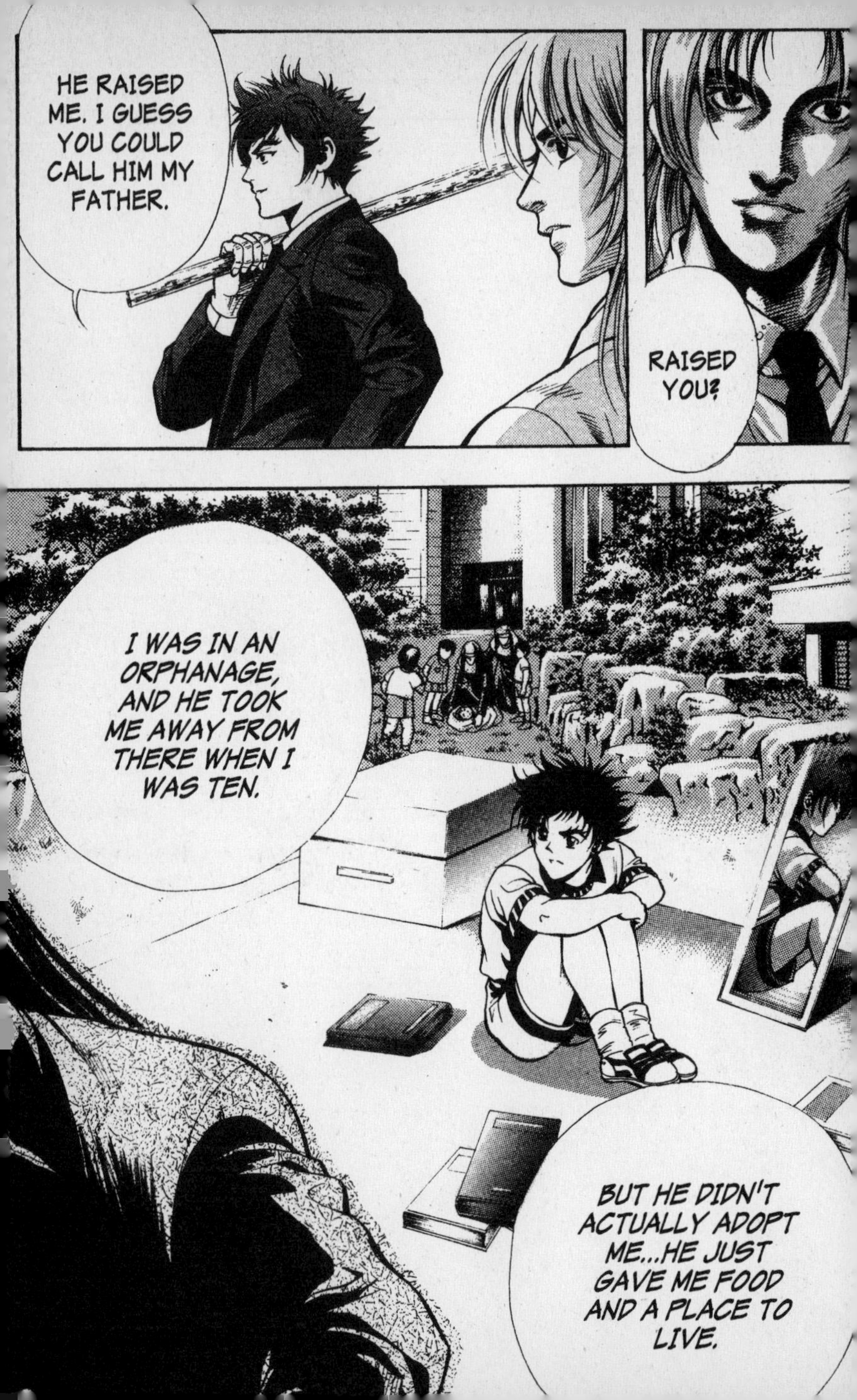

HE RAISED ME. I GUESS YOU COULD CALL HIM MY FATHER.
RAISED YOU?
I WAS IN AN ORPHANAGE, AND HE TOOK ME AWAY FROM THERE WHEN I WAS TEN.
BUT HE DIDN'T ACTUALLY ADOPT ME...HE JUST GAVE ME FOOD AND A PLACE TO LIVE.

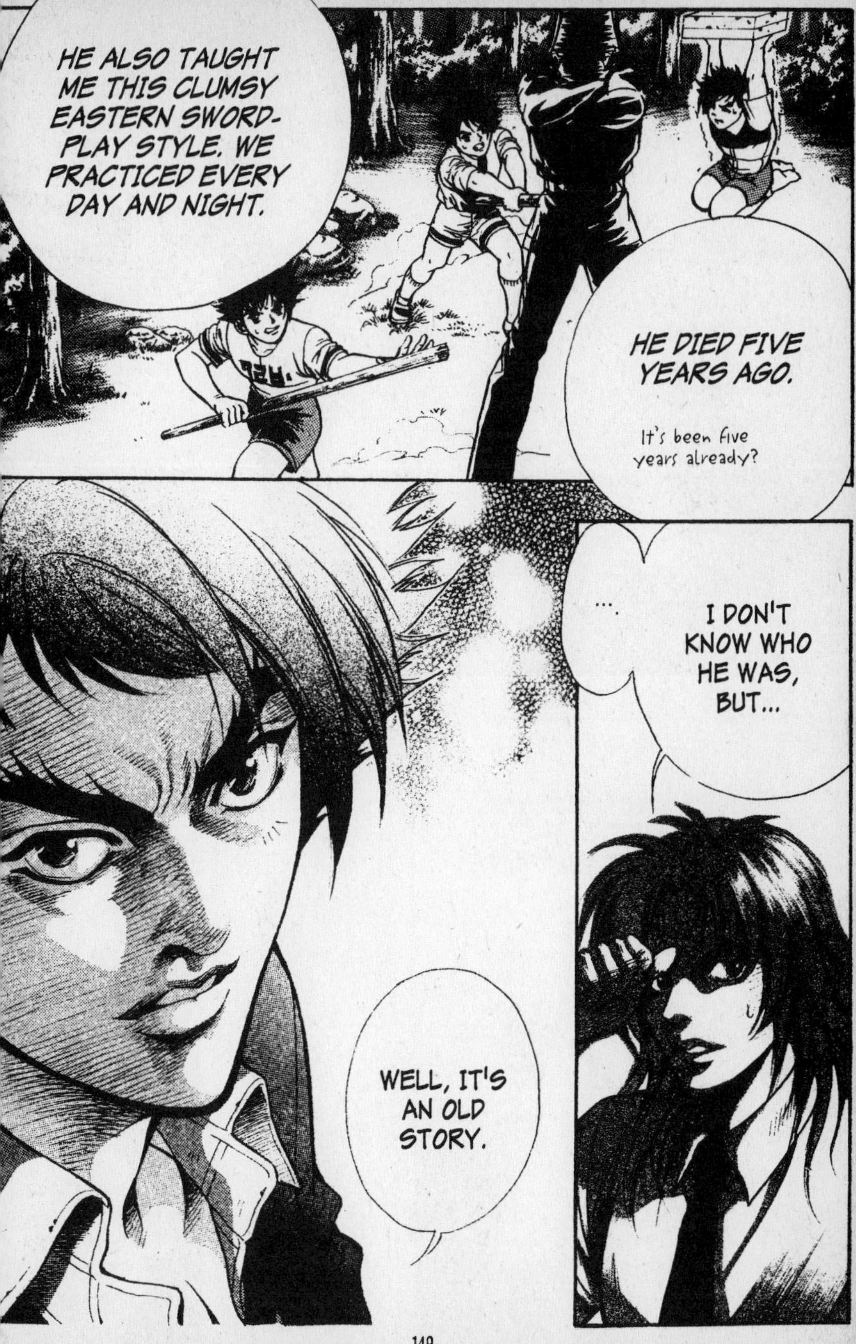

HE ALSO TAUGHT ME THIS CLUMSY EASTERN SWORD-PLAY STYLE. WE PRACTICED EVERY DAY AND NIGHT.
HE DIED FIVE YEARS AGO.
It's been five years already?
...
I DON'T KNOW WHO HE WAS, BUT...
WELL, IT'S AN OLD STORY.

...THAT EASTERN SWORDPLAY STYLE YOU JUST SHOWED ME IS NOT...

...FOR FIGHTING AGAINST HUMAN BEINGS.

WHAT?! WHAT ARE YOU TALKING ABOUT?! IS IT TO FIGHT AGAINST ANIMALS?!

Figures...

ANYTHING'S POSSIBLE WITH THAT OLD FART.

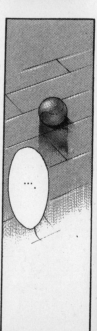

...

IT'S FOR SOMETHING WORSE THAN HUMANS.

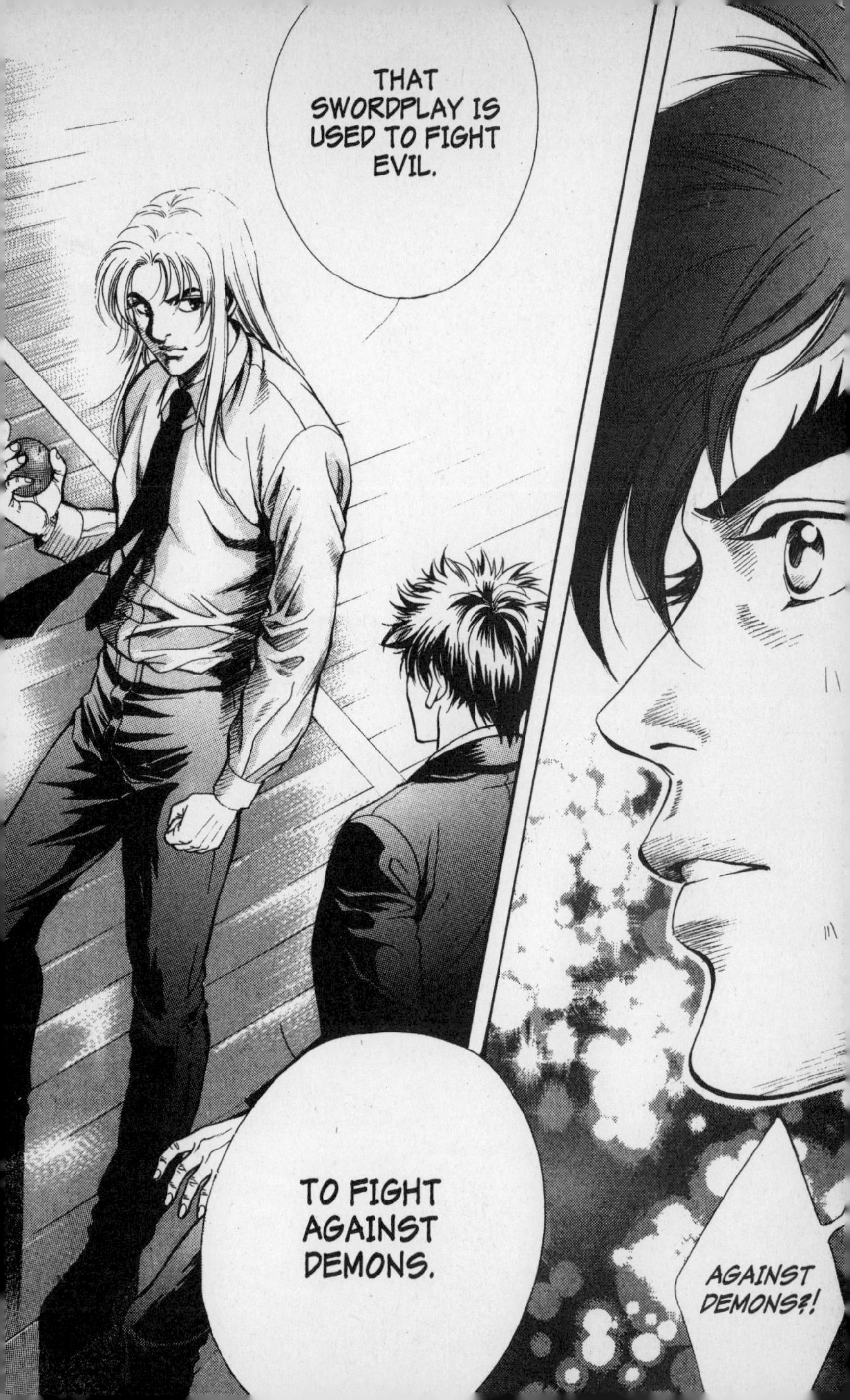
THAT SWORDPLAY IS USED TO FIGHT EVIL.
TO FIGHT AGAINST DEMONS.
AGAINST DEMONS?!

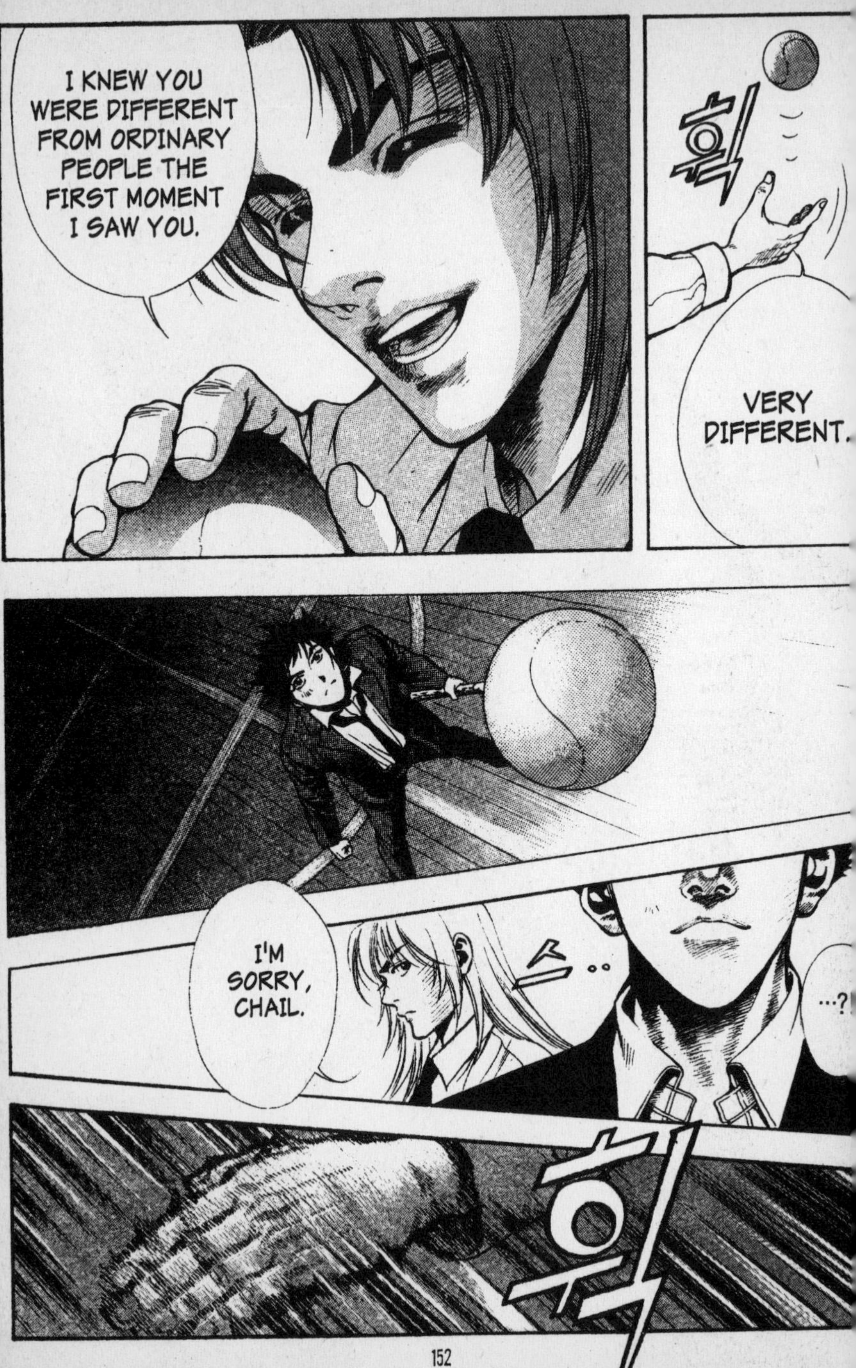

I KNEW YOU WERE DIFFERENT FROM ORDINARY PEOPLE THE FIRST MOMENT I SAW YOU.
휙
VERY DIFFERENT.
I'M SORRY, CHAIL.
...?

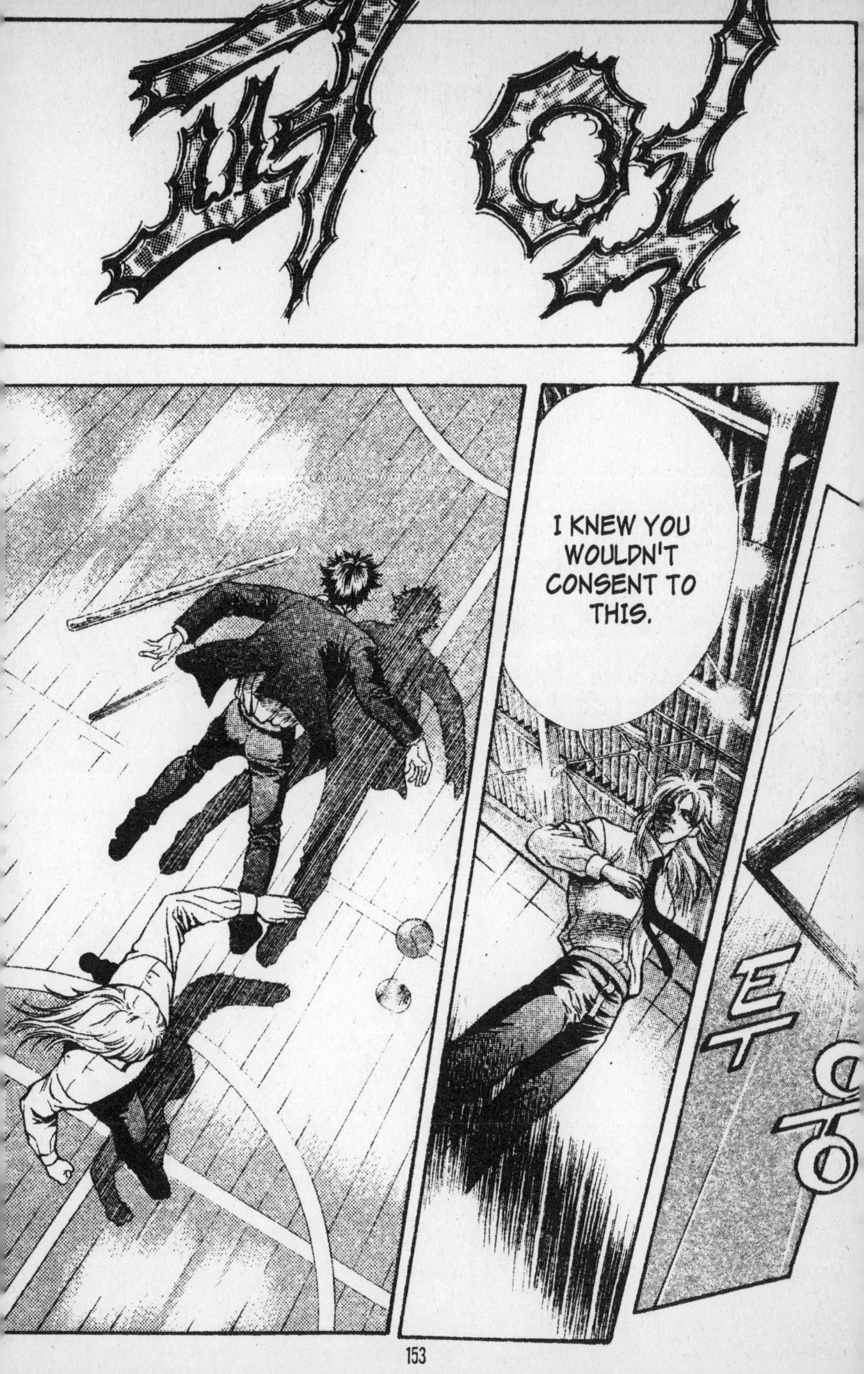
I KNEW YOU WOULDN'T CONSENT TO THIS.

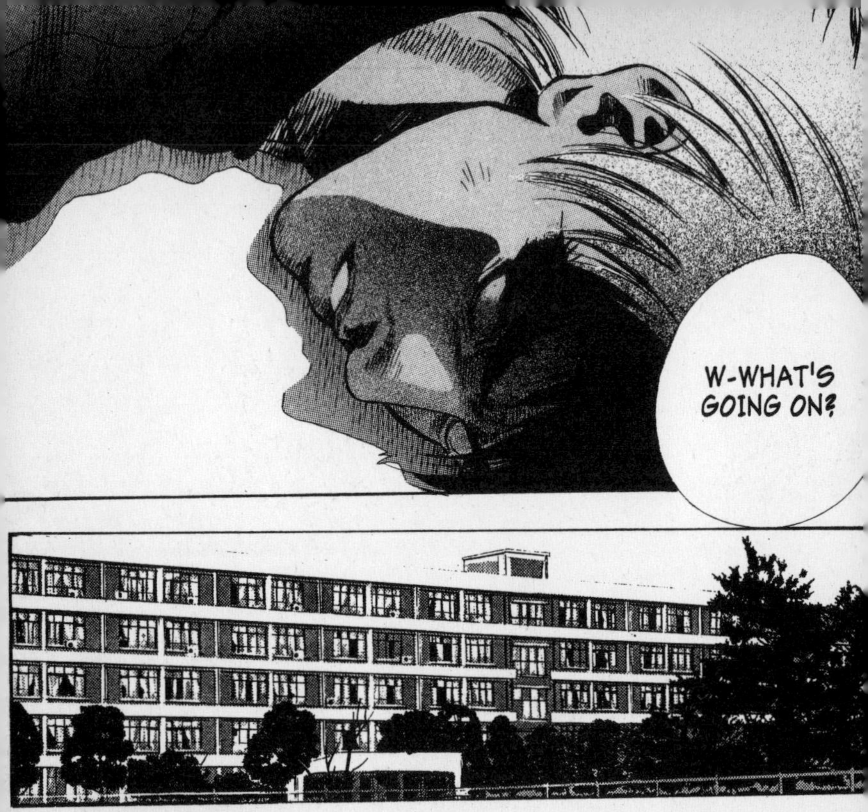
W-WHAT'S GOING ON?

Sign: Science Lab

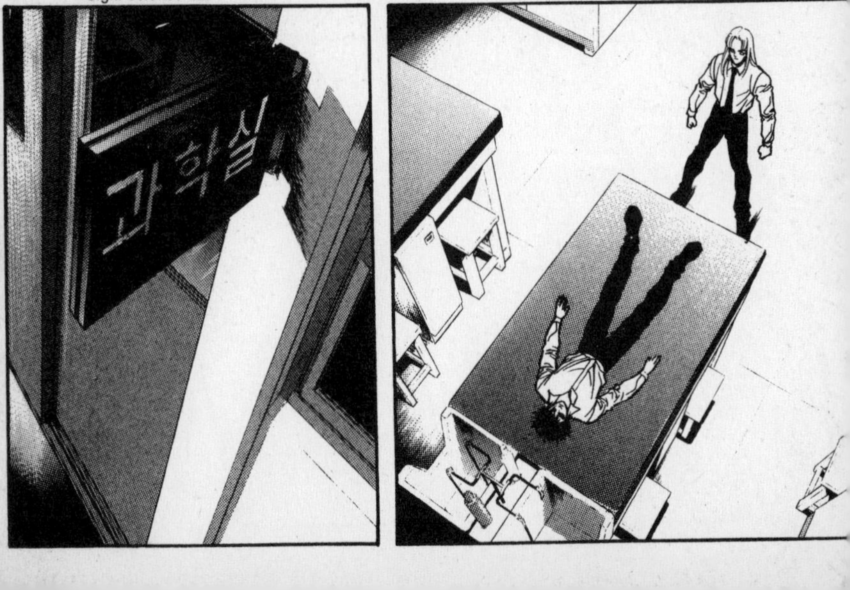
과학실

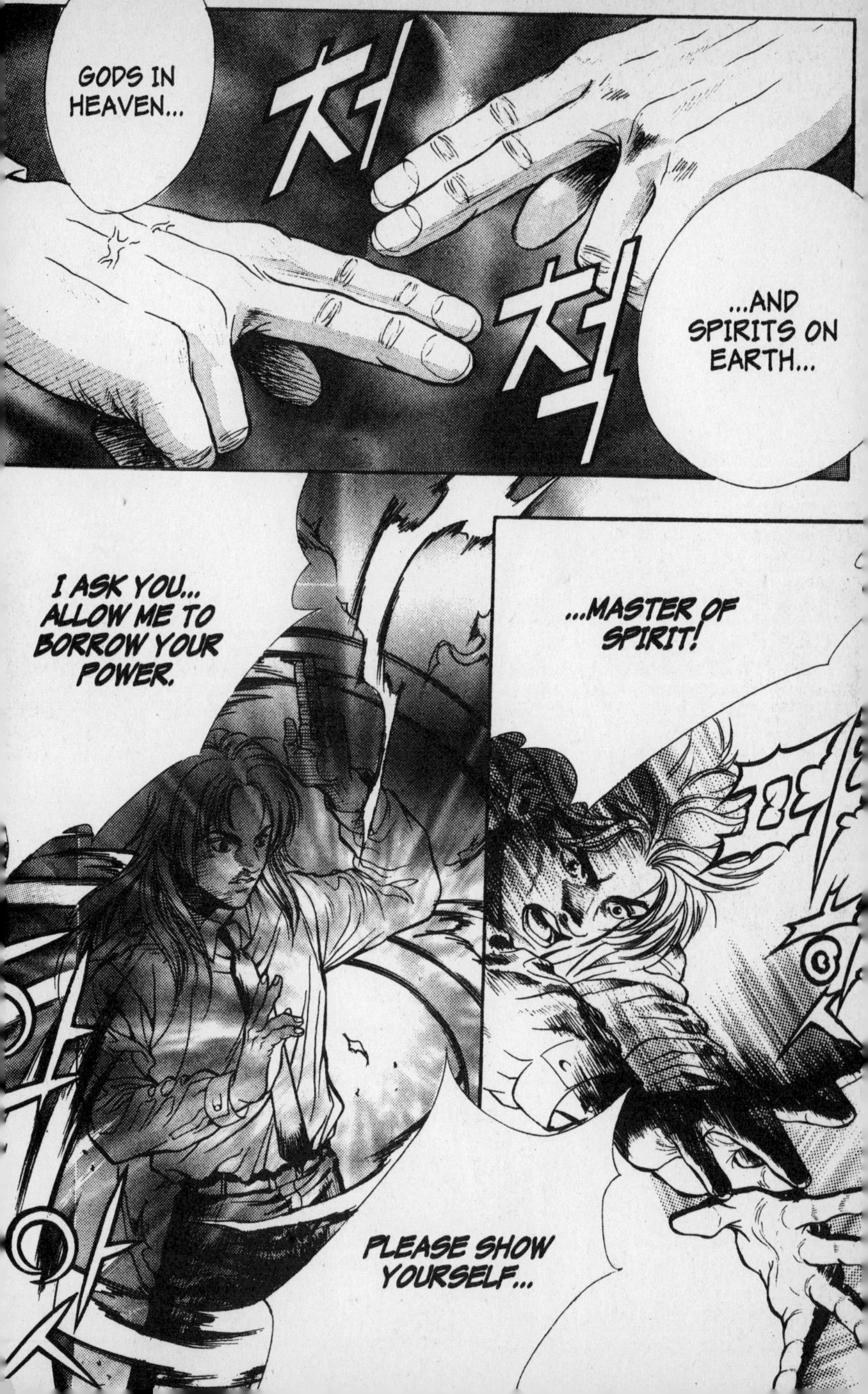
GODS IN HEAVEN...
...AND SPIRITS ON EARTH...
I ASK YOU... ALLOW ME TO BORROW YOUR POWER.
...MASTER OF SPIRIT!
PLEASE SHOW YOURSELF...

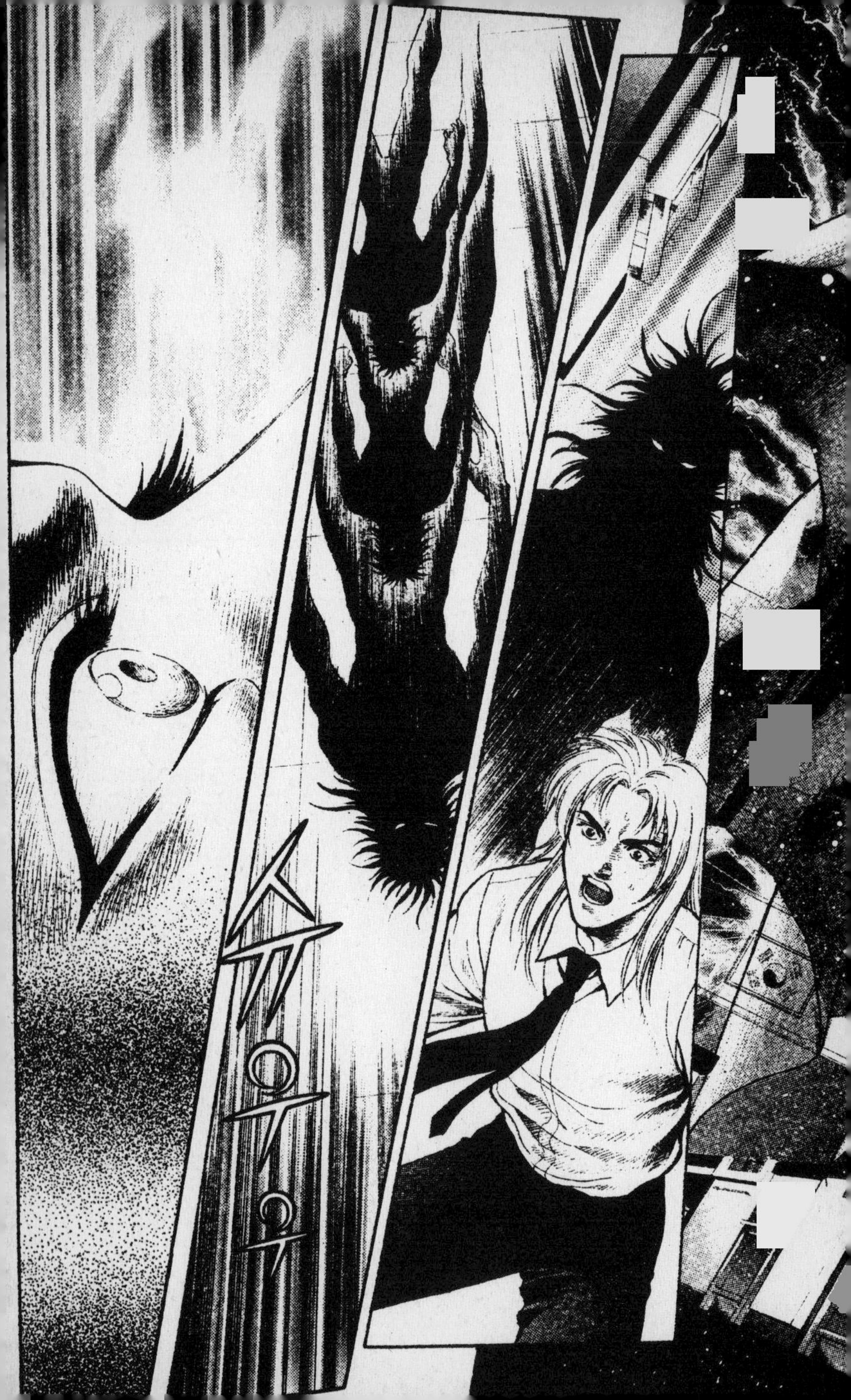

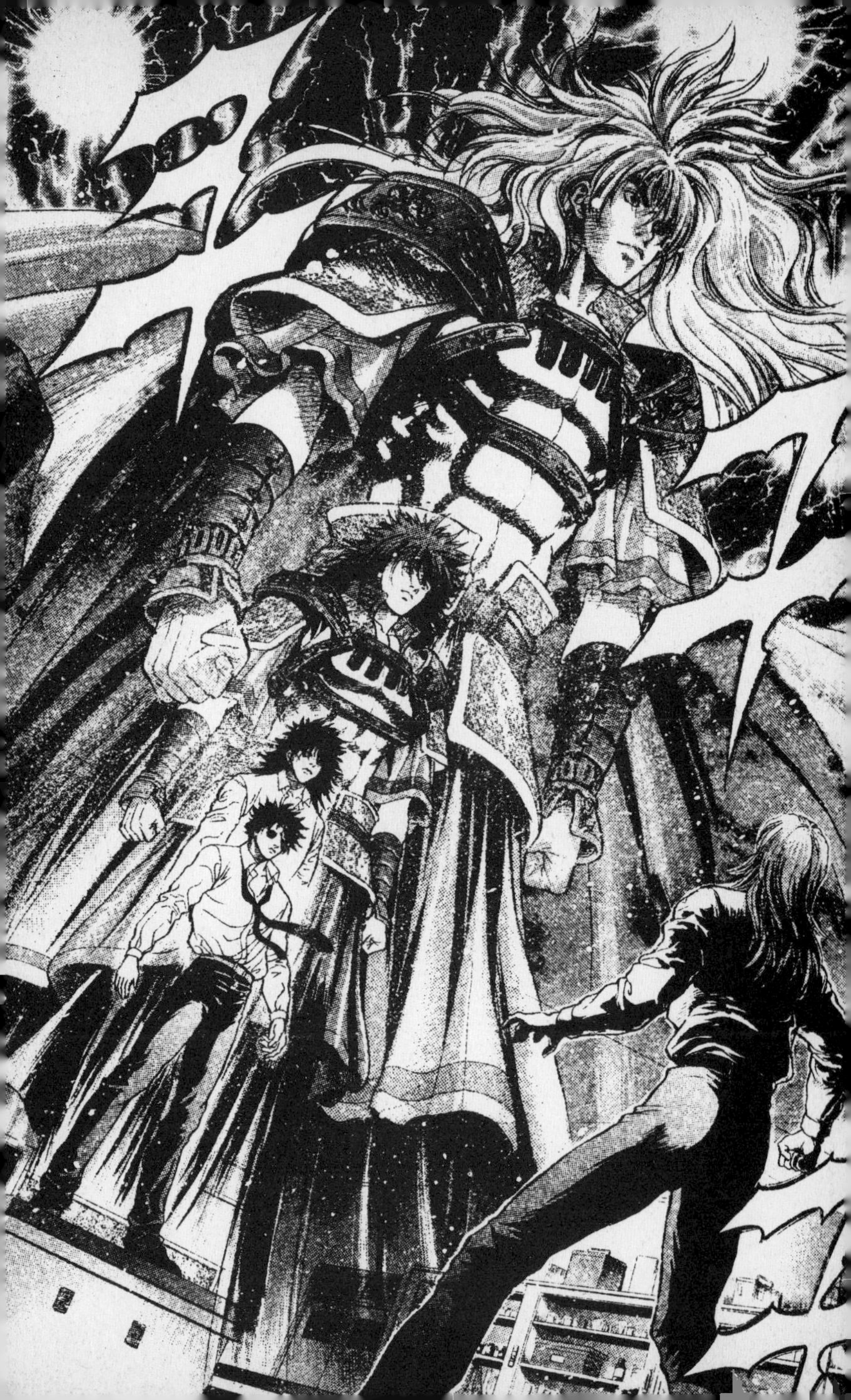

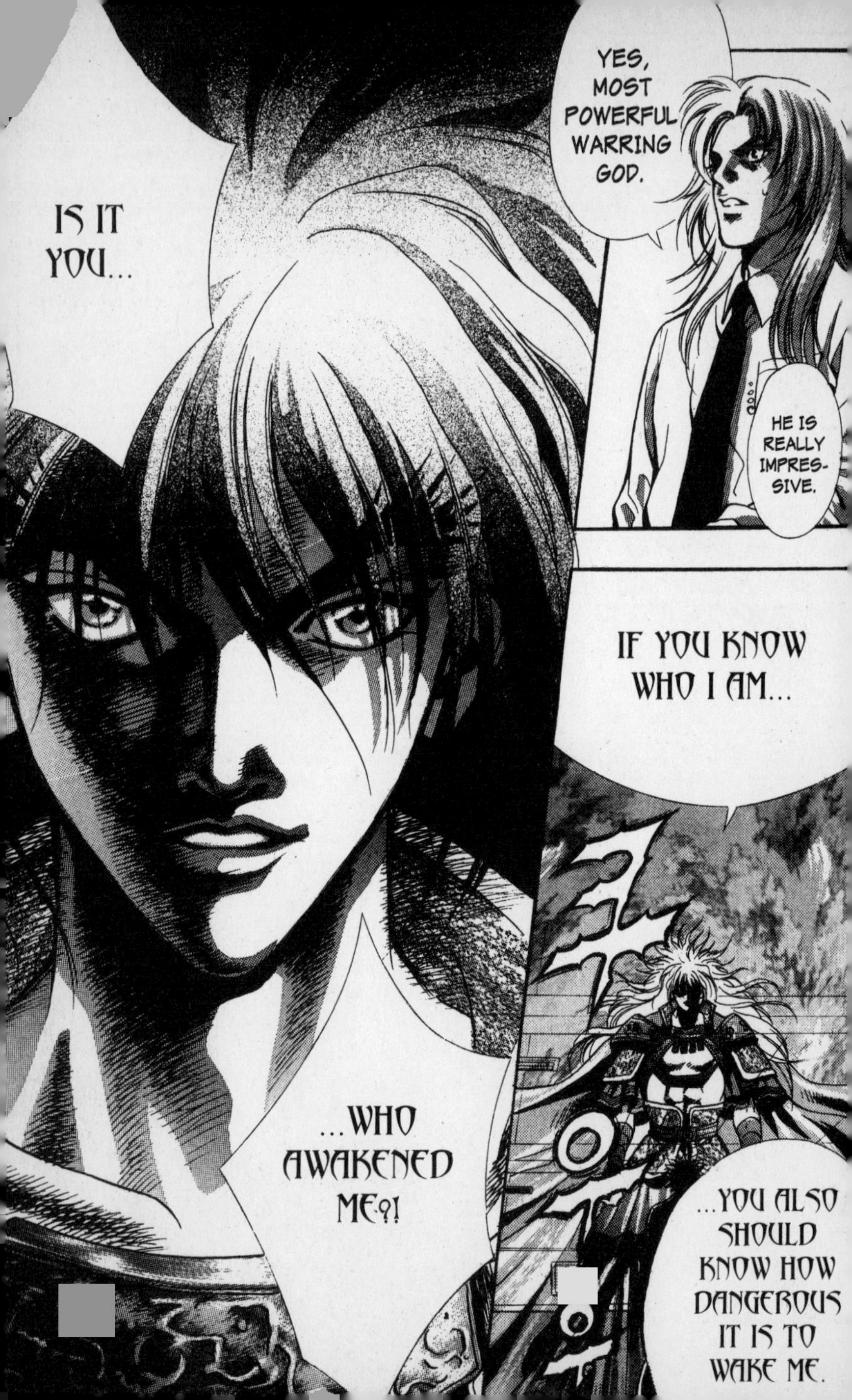
IS IT YOU...
...WHO AWAKENED ME?!
YES, MOST POWERFUL WARRING GOD.
HE IS REALLY IMPRES-SIVE.
IF YOU KNOW WHO I AM...
...YOU ALSO SHOULD KNOW HOW DANGEROUS IT IS TO WAKE ME.

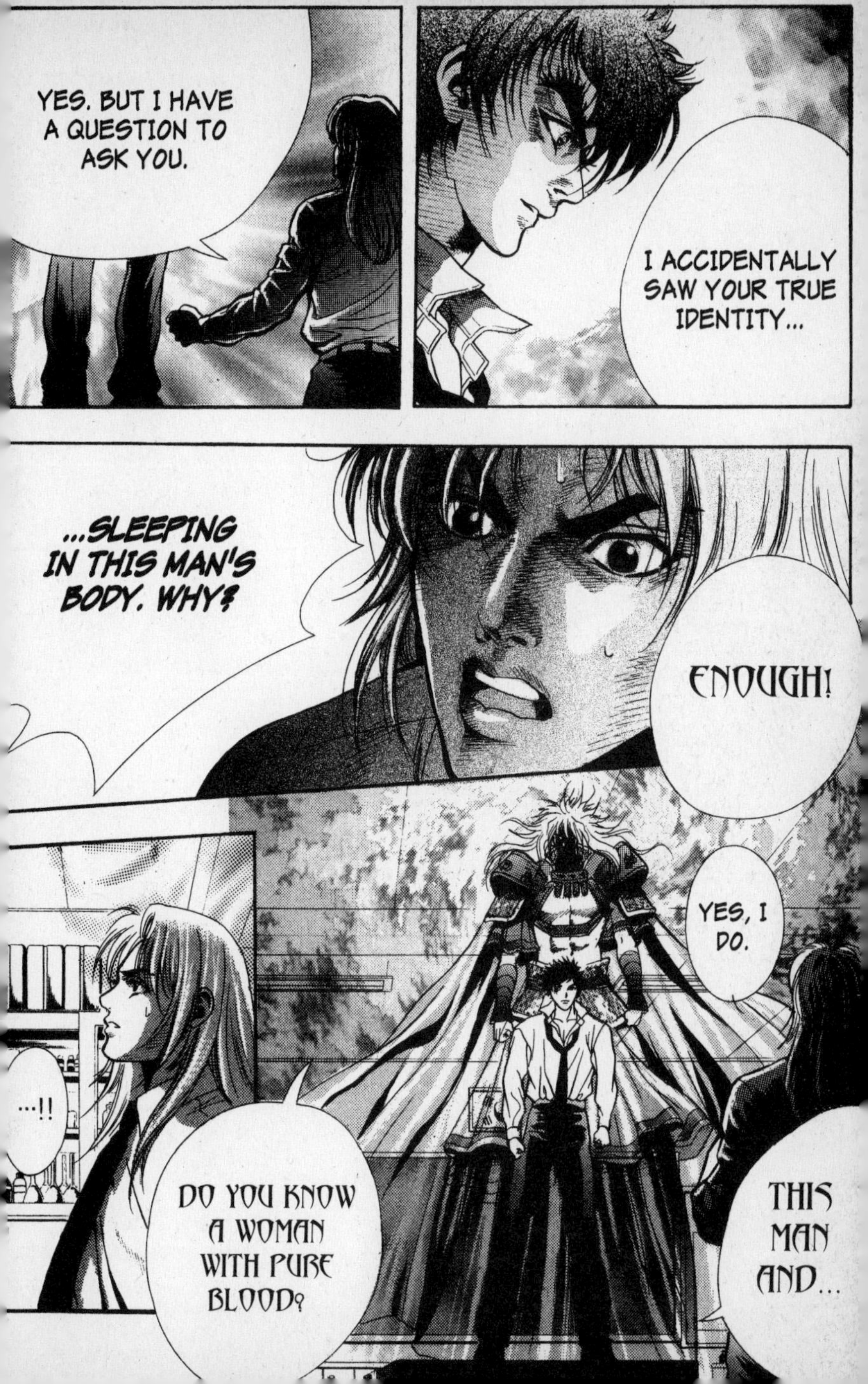
YES. BUT I HAVE A QUESTION TO ASK YOU.
I ACCIDENTALLY SAW YOUR TRUE IDENTITY...
...SLEEPING IN THIS MAN'S BODY. WHY?
ENOUGH!
...!!
DO YOU KNOW A WOMAN WITH PURE BLOOD?
YES, I DO.
THIS MAN AND...

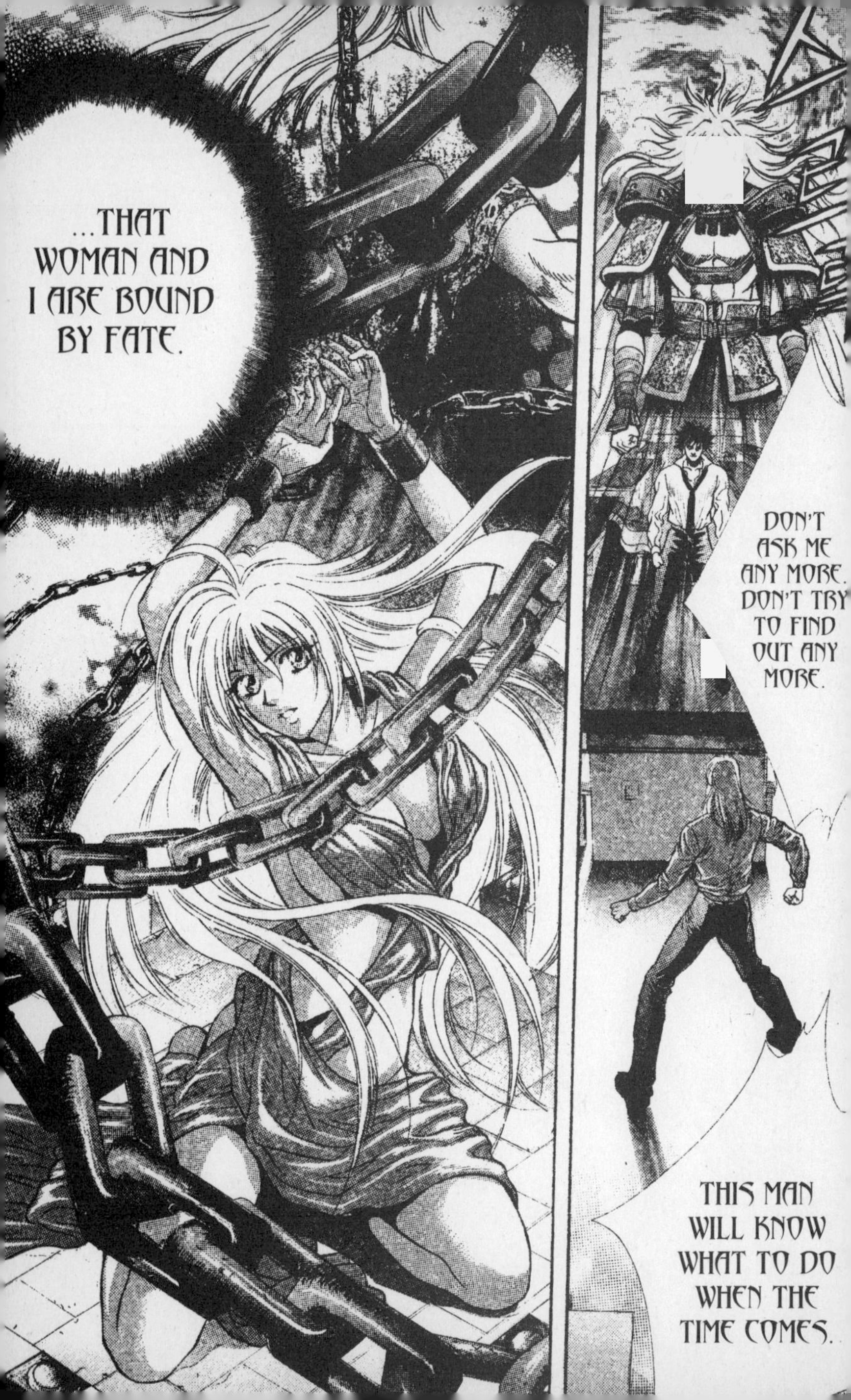
DON'T ASK ME ANY MORE. DON'T TRY TO FIND OUT ANY MORE.
THIS MAN WILL KNOW WHAT TO DO WHEN THE TIME COMES.
...THAT WOMAN AND I ARE BOUND BY FATE.

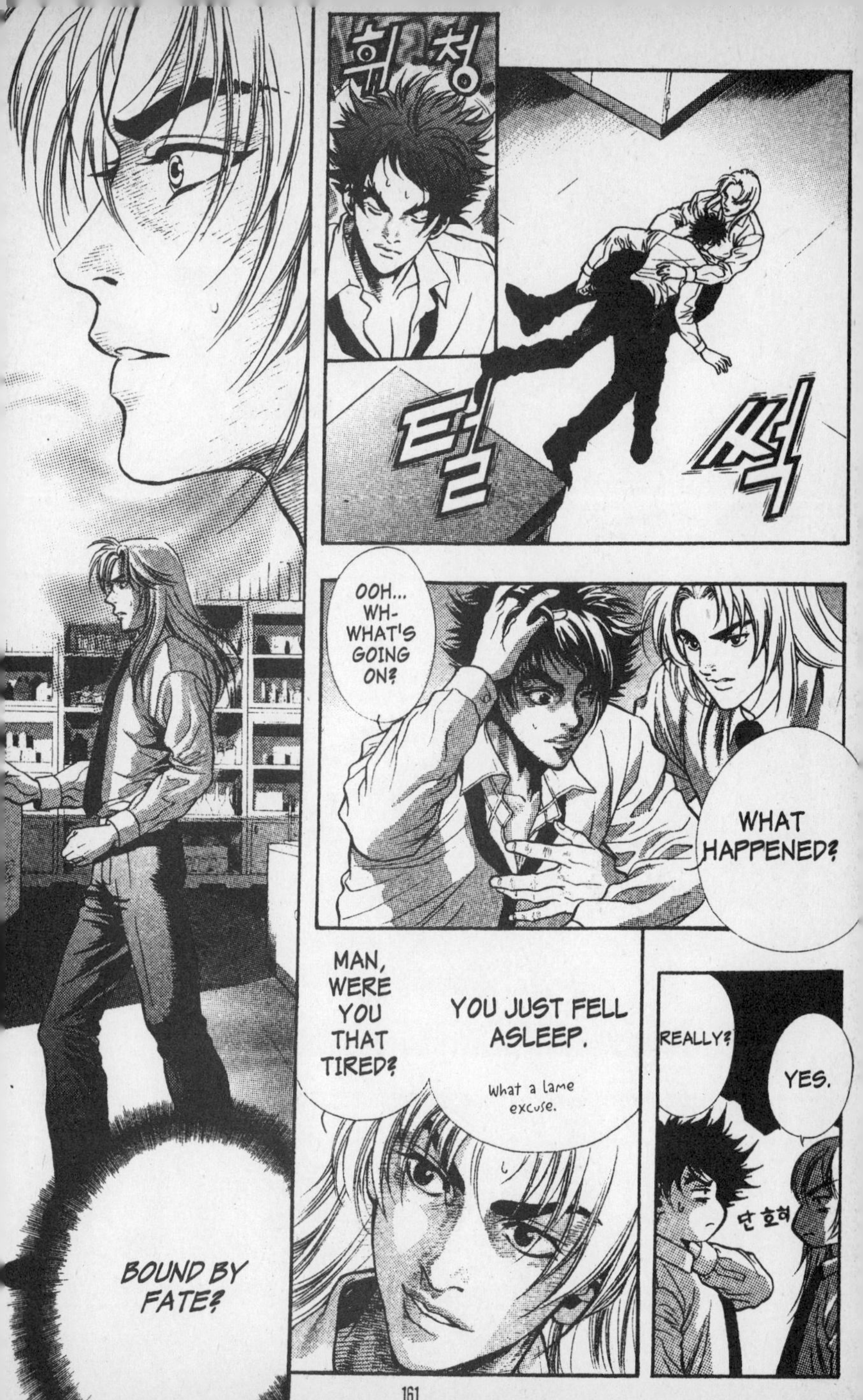
BOUND BY FATE?
휘청
털썩
OOH... WH-WHAT'S GOING ON?
WHAT HAPPENED?
MAN, WERE YOU THAT TIRED?
YOU JUST FELL ASLEEP.
What a lame excuse.
REALLY?
YES.
단호히

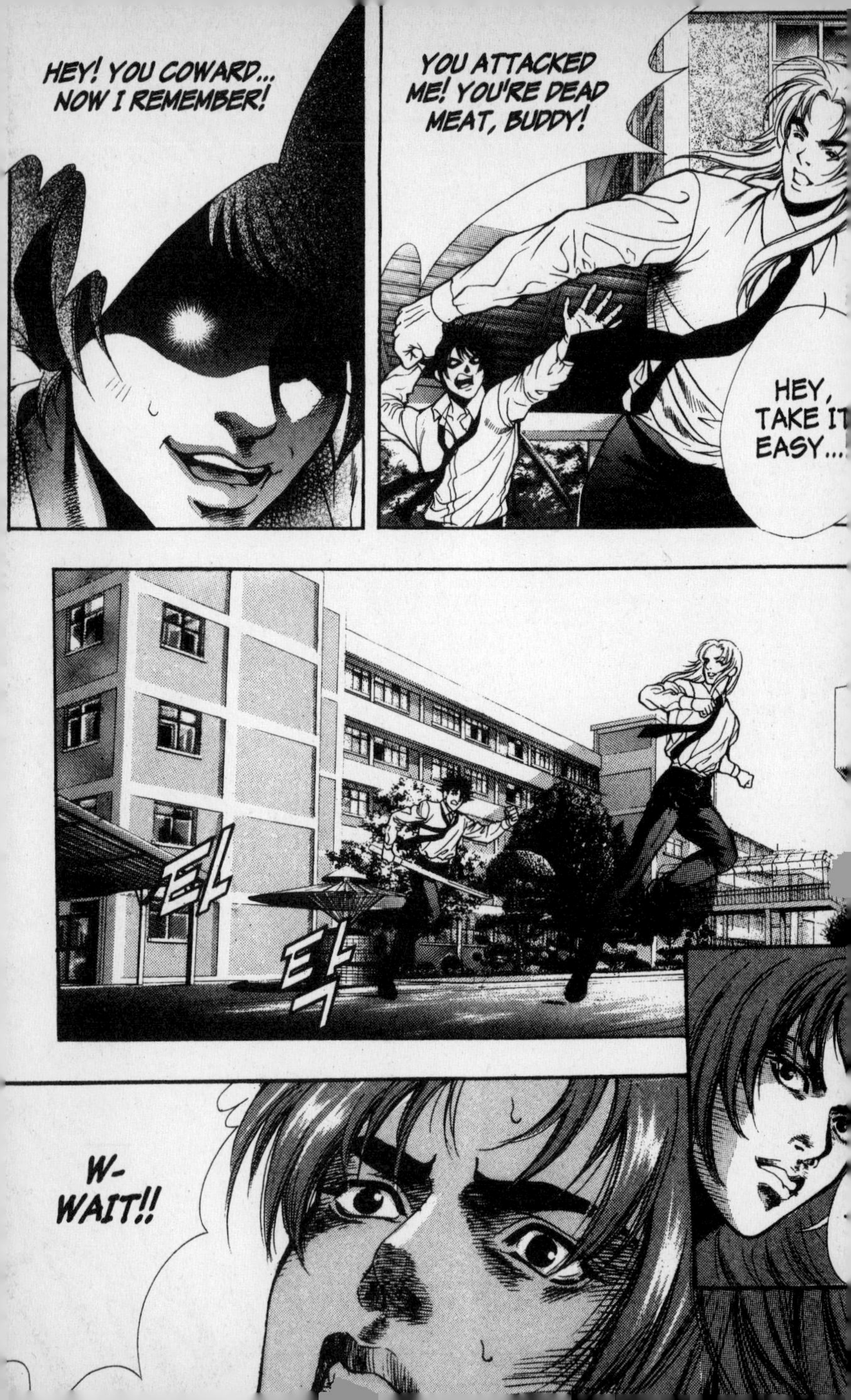
HEY! YOU COWARD... NOW I REMEMBER!
YOU ATTACKED ME! YOU'RE DEAD MEAT, BUDDY!
HEY, TAKE IT EASY...
W- WAIT!!

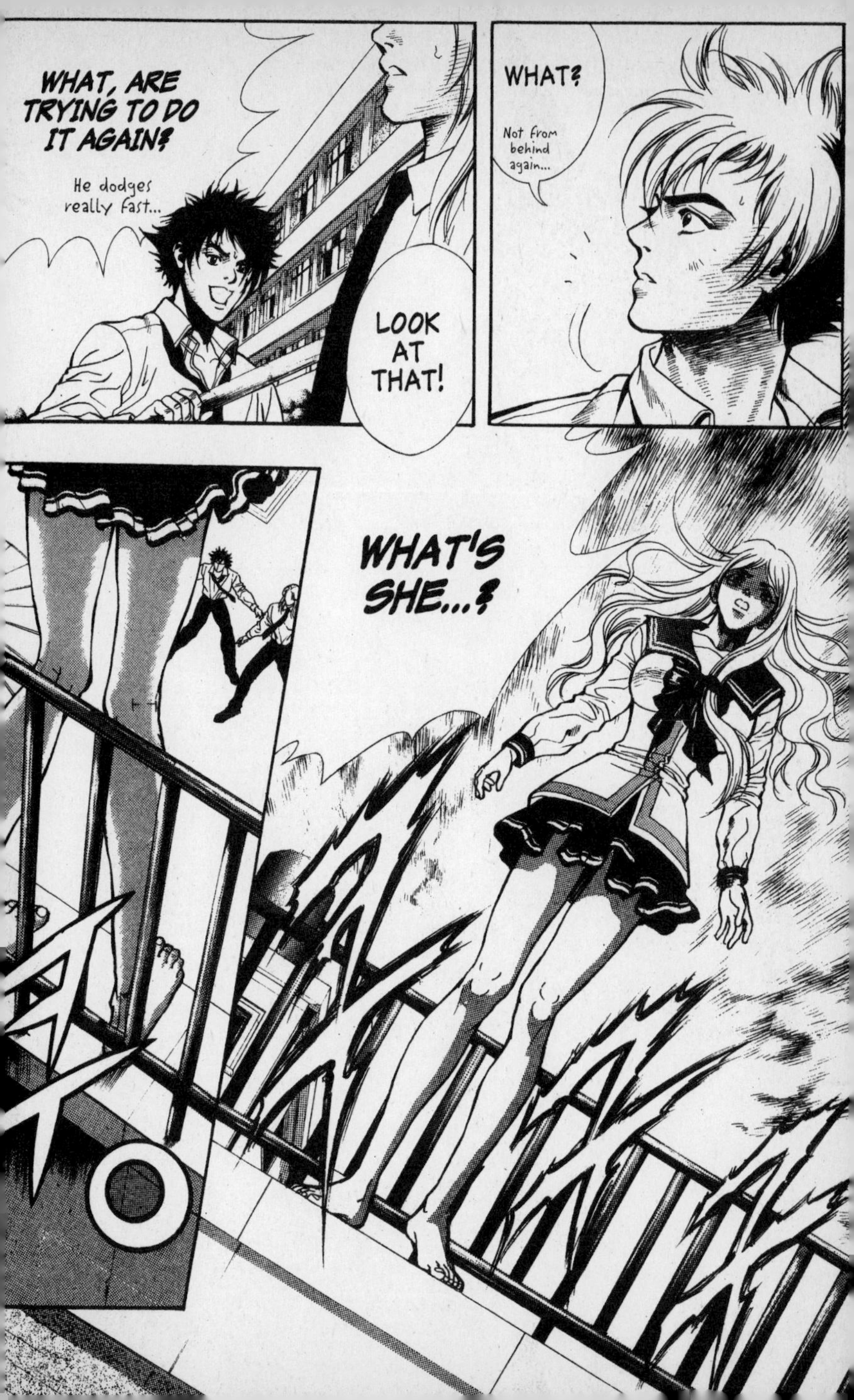
WHAT?
Not from behind again...
WHAT, ARE TRYING TO DO IT AGAIN?
He dodges really fast...
LOOK AT THAT!
WHAT'S SHE...?

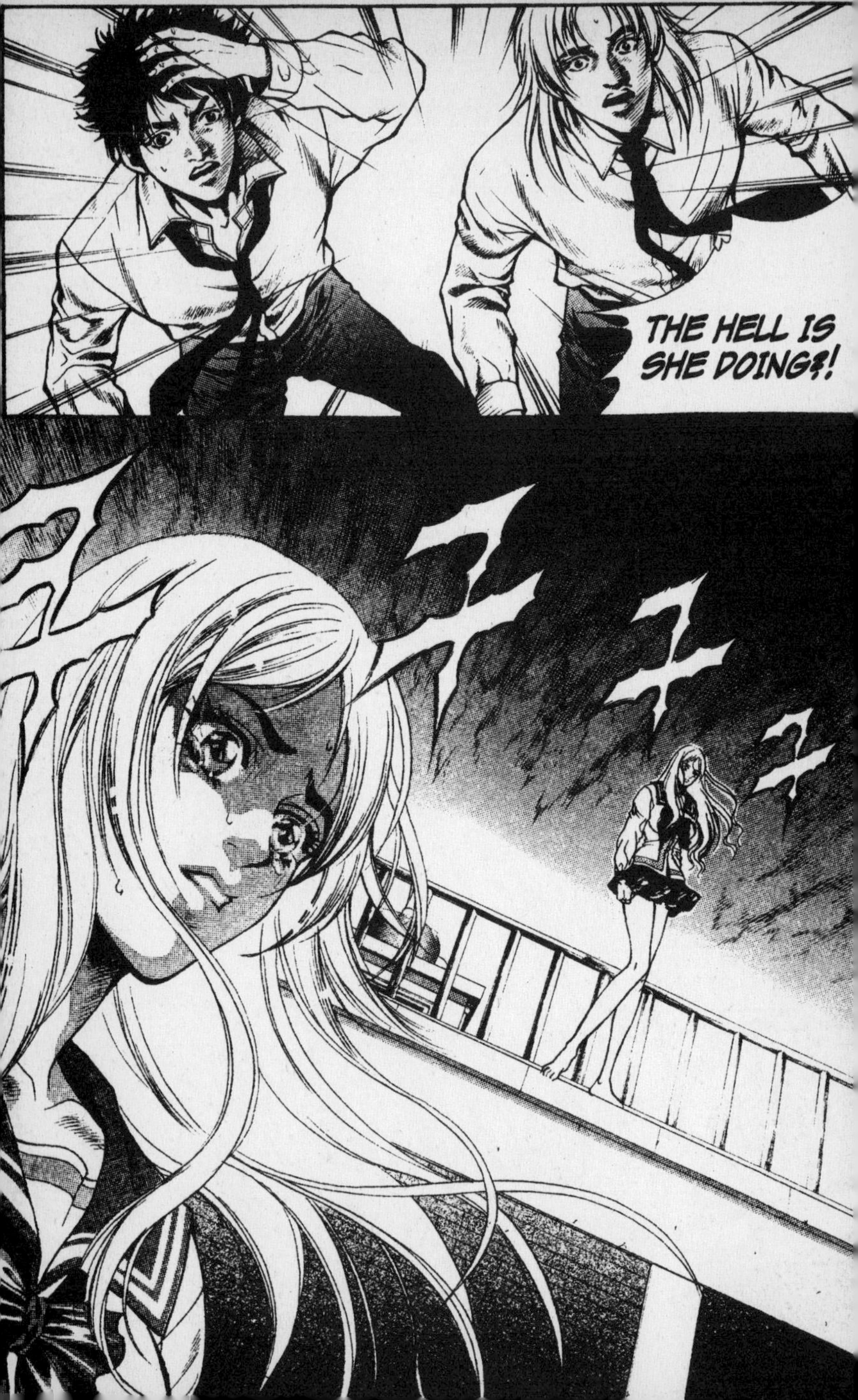
THE HELL IS SHE DOING?!

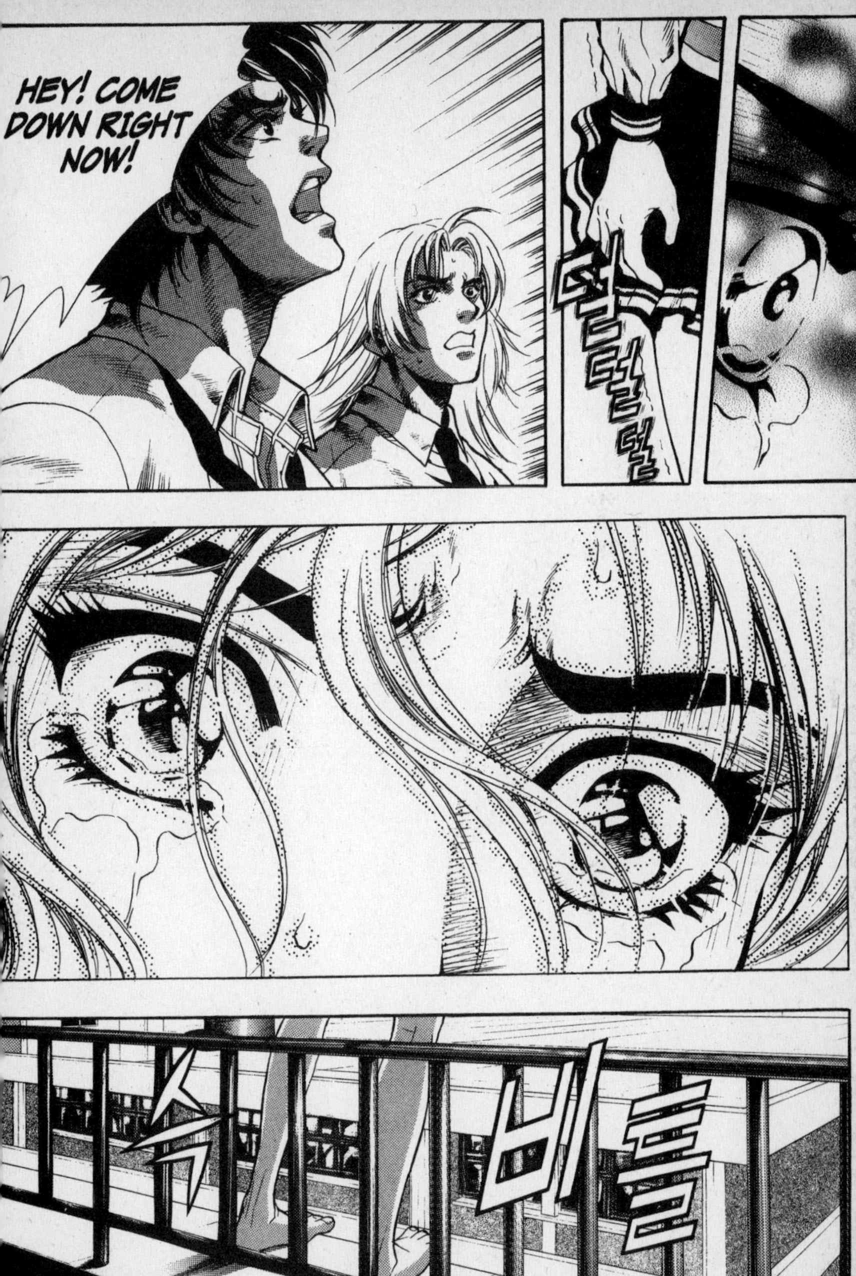
HEY! COME DOWN RIGHT NOW!

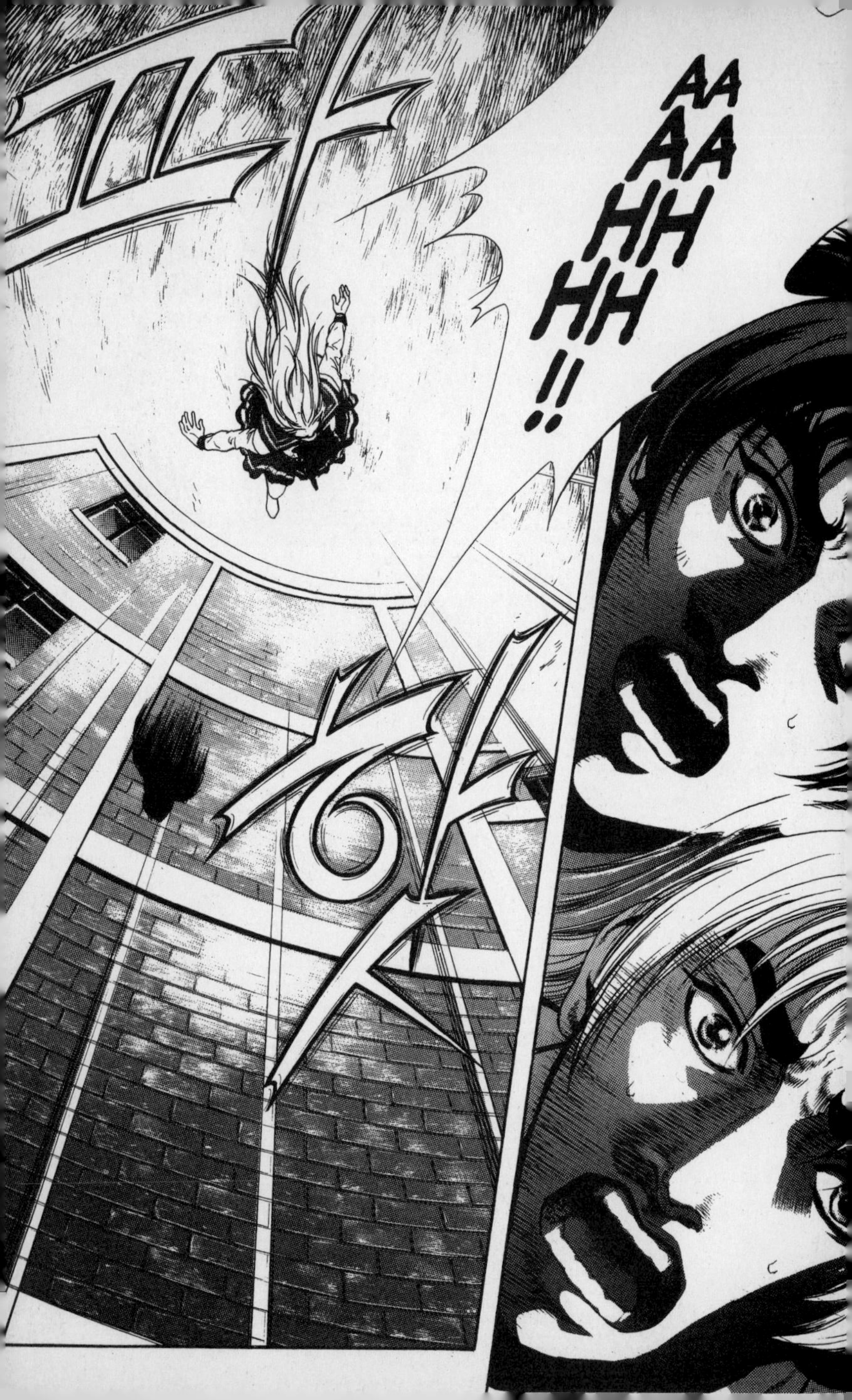

AAAAHHHH!!

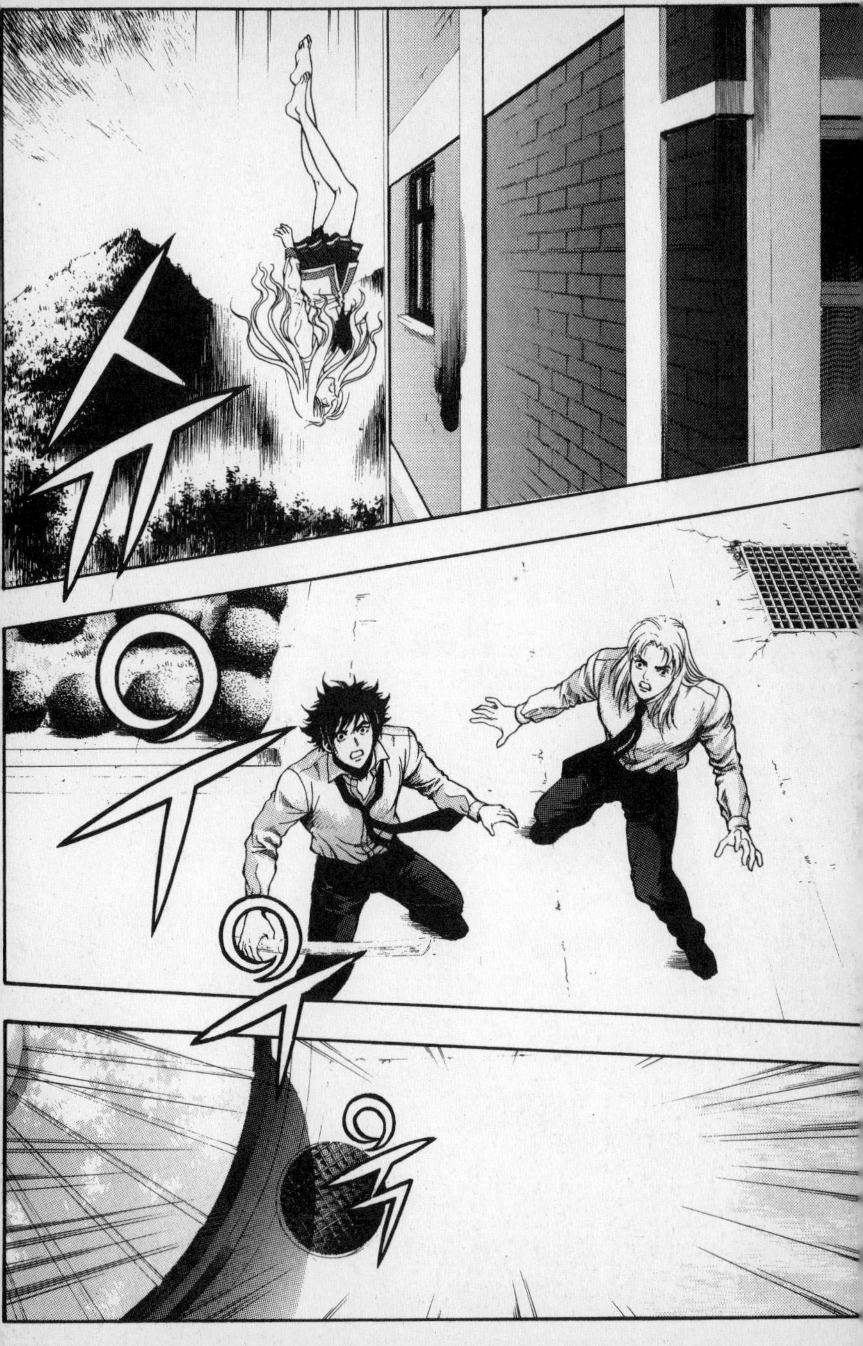

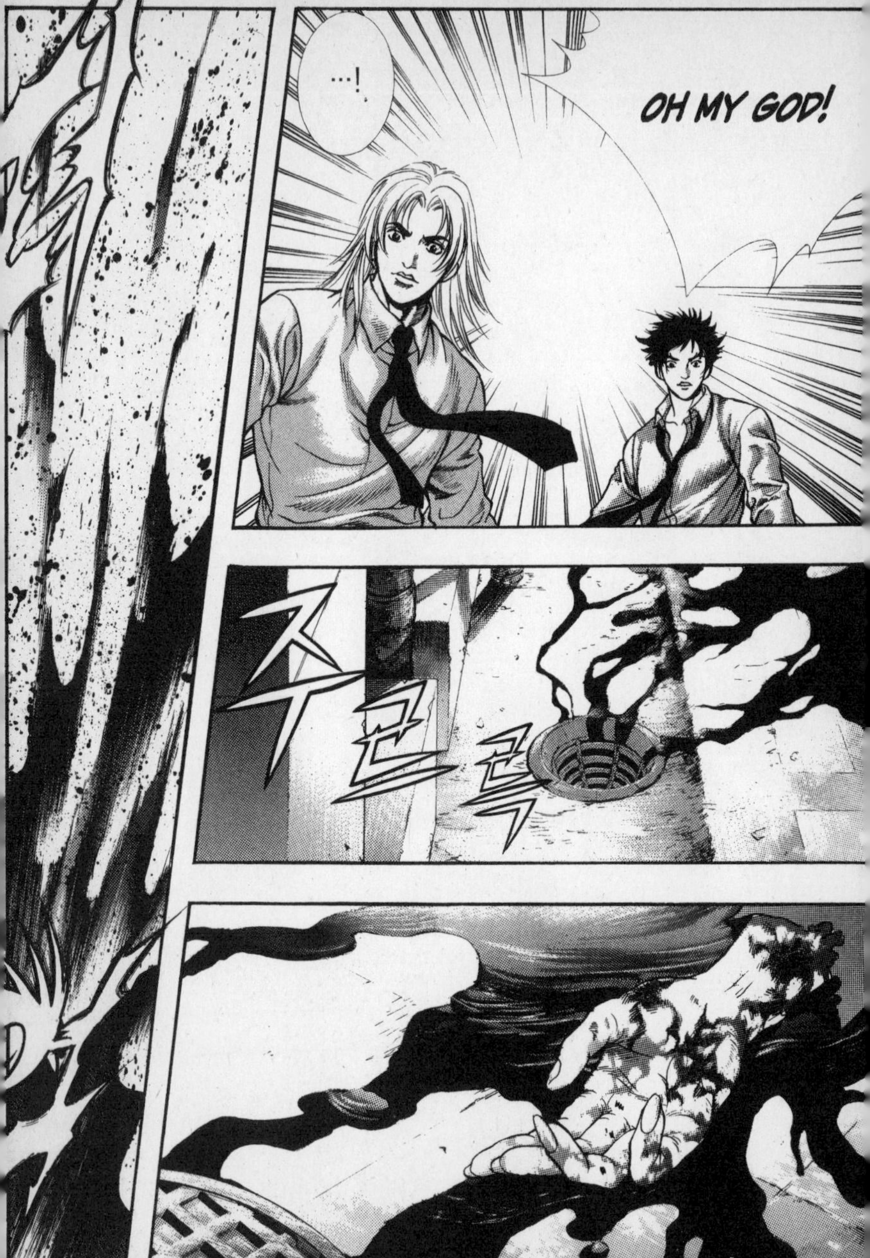
...!
OH MY GOD!

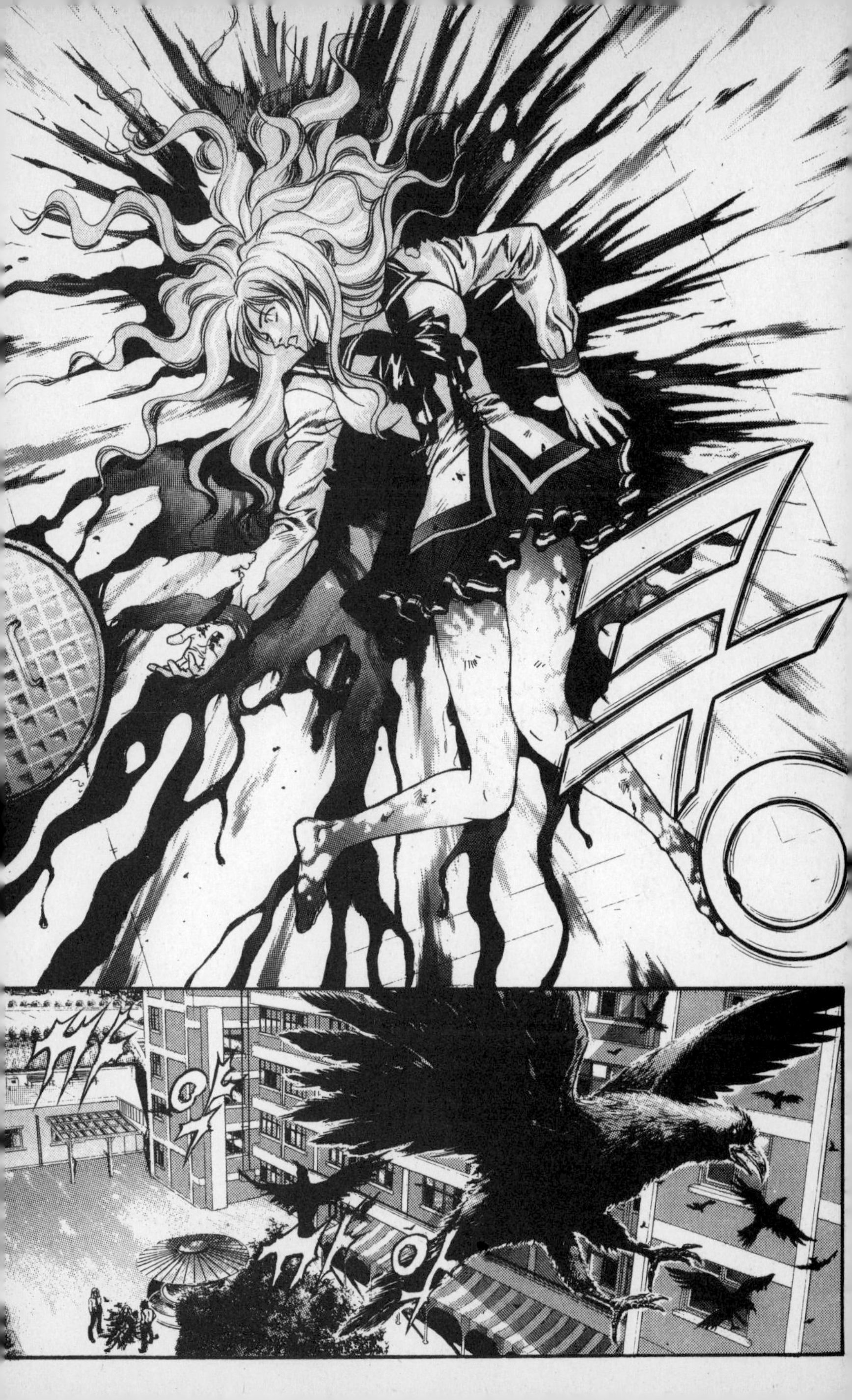
쿵
까악
까악

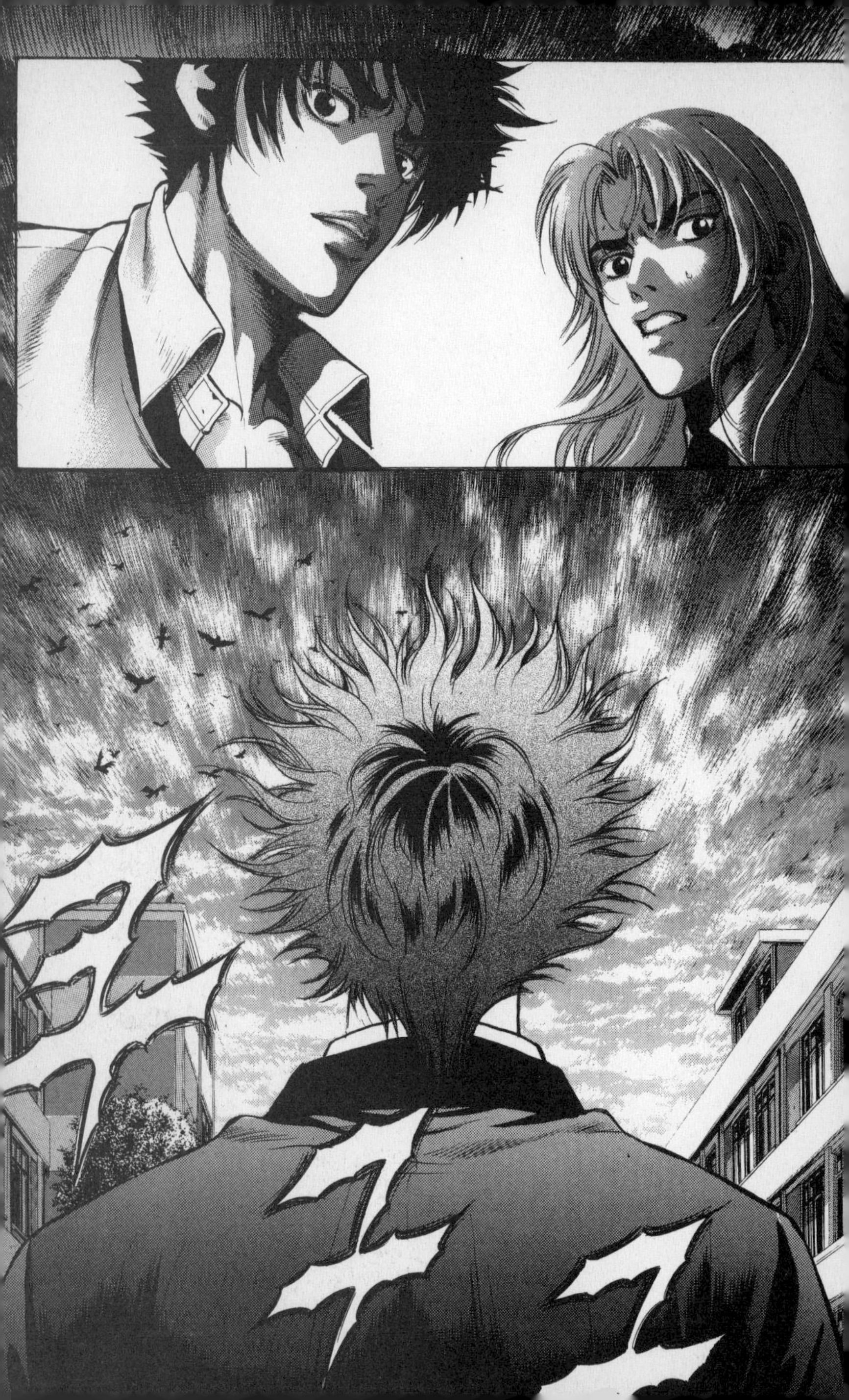

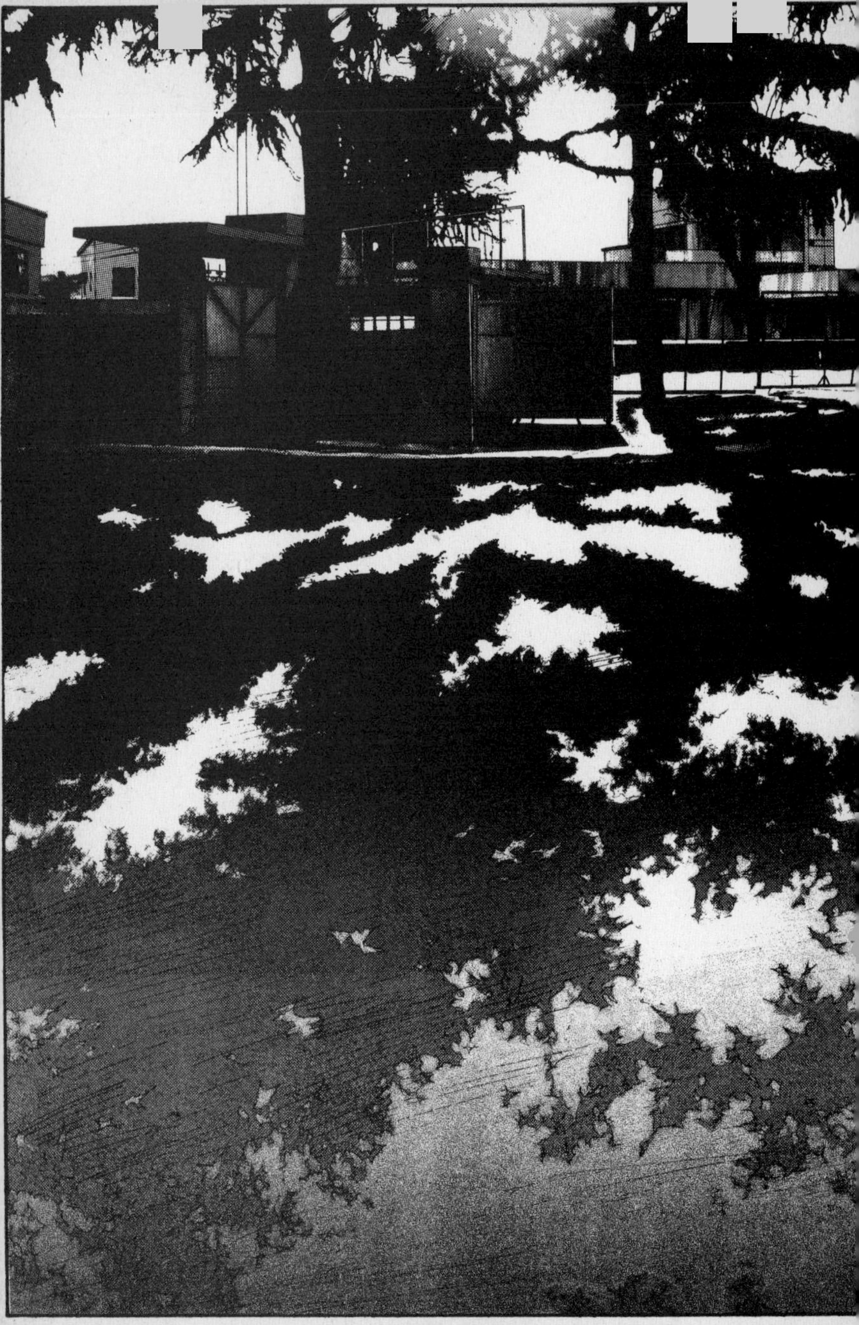

TO BE CONTINUED IN EVIL'S RETURN 3.

EVIL'S RETURN

VOLUME 3 PREVIEW

MIRAE, A VATICAN-TRAINED EXORCIST, JOINS FORCES WITH HYUN AND CHAIL TO PROTECT HER FRIEND YUMI. SHE KNOWS THE UNHOLY HEAVENLY FATHER IS LURKING AROUND CAMPUS, AND THEY ONLY HAVE TO WAIT UNTIL HE KILLS AGAIN TO TRACE HIM AND PUT AN END TO EVIL ONCE AND FOR ALL. BUT WHEN CHAIL IS BADLY INJURED PROTECTING YUMI FROM THE HEAVENLY FATHER HIMSELF, HE MUST RELIVE HIS TRAGIC PAST LIFE IN ORDER TO SAVE HIS PRESENT ONE!

ALSO AVAILABLE FROM TOKYOPOP®

MANGA

.HACK//LEGEND OF THE TWILIGHT
@LARGE
ABENOBASHI: MAGICAL SHOPPING ARCADE
A.I. LOVE YOU
AI YORI AOSHI
ANGELIC LAYER
ARM OF KANNON
BABY BIRTH
BATTLE ROYALE
BATTLE VIXENS
BOYS BE...
BRAIN POWERED
BRIGADOON
B'TX
CANDIDATE FOR GODDESS, THE
CARDCAPTOR SAKURA
CARDCAPTOR SAKURA - MASTER OF THE CLOW
CHOBITS
CHRONICLES OF THE CURSED SWORD
CLAMP SCHOOL DETECTIVES
CLOVER
COMIC PARTY
CONFIDENTIAL CONFESSIONS
CORRECTOR YUI
COWBOY BEBOP
COWBOY BEBOP: SHOOTING STAR
CRAZY LOVE STORY
CRESCENT MOON
CROSS
CULDCEPT
CYBORG 009
D•N•ANGEL
DEMON DIARY
DEMON ORORON, THE
DEUS VITAE
DIABOLO
DIGIMON
DIGIMON TAMERS
DIGIMON ZERO TWO
DOLL
DRAGON HUNTER
DRAGON KNIGHTS
DRAGON VOICE
DREAM SAGA
DUKLYON: CLAMP SCHOOL DEFENDERS
EERIE QUEERIE!
ERICA SAKURAZAWA: COLLECTED WORKS
ET CETERA
ETERNITY
EVIL'S RETURN
FAERIES' LANDING
FAKE
FLCL
FLOWER OF THE DEEP SLEEP, THE
FORBIDDEN DANCE
FRUITS BASKET

G GUNDAM
GATEKEEPERS
GETBACKERS
GIRL GOT GAME
GRAVITATION
GTO
GUNDAM SEED ASTRAY
GUNDAM WING
GUNDAM WING: BATTLEFIELD OF PACIFISTS
GUNDAM WING: ENDLESS WALTZ
GUNDAM WING: THE LAST OUTPOST (G-UNIT)
HANDS OFF!
HAPPY MANIA
HARLEM BEAT
HYPER RUNE
I.N.V.U.
IMMORTAL RAIN
INITIAL D
INSTANT TEEN: JUST ADD NUTS
ISLAND
JING: KING OF BANDITS
JING: KING OF BANDITS - TWILIGHT TALES
JULINE
KARE KANO
KILL ME, KISS ME
KINDAICHI CASE FILES, THE
KING OF HELL
KODOCHA: SANA'S STAGE
LAMENT OF THE LAMB
LEGAL DRUG
LEGEND OF CHUN HYANG, THE
LES BIJOUX
LOVE HINA
LOVE OR MONEY
LUPIN III
LUPIN III: WORLD'S MOST WANTED
MAGIC KNIGHT RAYEARTH I
MAGIC KNIGHT RAYEARTH II
MAHOROMATIC: AUTOMATIC MAIDEN
MAN OF MANY FACES
MARMALADE BOY
MARS
MARS: HORSE WITH NO NAME
MINK
MIRACLE GIRLS
MIYUKI-CHAN IN WONDERLAND
MODEL
MOURYOU KIDEN: LEGEND OF THE NYMPHS
NECK AND NECK
ONE
ONE I LOVE, THE
PARADISE KISS
PARASYTE
PASSION FRUIT
PEACH GIRL
PEACH GIRL: CHANGE OF HEART
PET SHOP OF HORRORS
PITA-TEN

07.15.04T

ALSO AVAILABLE FROM TOKYOPOP®

PLANET LADDER
PLANETES
PRESIDENT DAD
PRIEST
PRINCESS AI
PSYCHIC ACADEMY
QUEEN'S KNIGHT, THE
RAGNAROK
RAVE MASTER
REALITY CHECK
REBIRTH
REBOUND
REMOTE
RISING STARS OF MANGA
SABER MARIONETTE J
SAILOR MOON
SAINT TAIL
SAIYUKI
SAMURAI DEEPER KYO
SAMURAI GIRL REAL BOUT HIGH SCHOOL
SCRYED
SEIKAI TRILOGY, THE
SGT. FROG
SHAOLIN SISTERS
SHIRAHIME-SYO: SNOW GODDESS TALES
SHUTTERBOX
SKULL MAN, THE
SNOW DROP
SORCERER HUNTERS
STONE
SUIKODEN III
SUKI
THREADS OF TIME
TOKYO BABYLON
TOKYO MEW MEW
TOKYO TRIBES
TRAMPS LIKE US
UNDER THE GLASS MOON
VAMPIRE GAME
VISION OF ESCAFLOWNE, THE
WARRIORS OF TAO
WILD ACT
WISH
WORLD OF HARTZ
X-DAY
ZODIAC P.I.

NOVELS

CLAMP SCHOOL PARANORMAL INVESTIGATORS
SAILOR MOON
SLAYERS

ART BOOKS

ART OF CARDCAPTOR SAKURA
ART OF MAGIC KNIGHT RAYEARTH, THE
PEACH: MIWA UEDA ILLUSTRATIONS

ANIME GUIDES

COWBOY BEBOP
GUNDAM TECHNICAL MANUALS
SAILOR MOON SCOUT GUIDES

TOKYOPOP KIDS

STRAY SHEEP

CINE-MANGA™

ALADDIN
CARDCAPTORS
DUEL MASTERS
FAIRLY ODDPARENTS, THE
FAMILY GUY
FINDING NEMO
G.I. JOE SPY TROOPS
GREATEST STARS OF THE NBA: SHAQUILLE O'NEAL
GREATEST STARS OF THE NBA: TIM DUNCAN
JACKIE CHAN ADVENTURES
JIMMY NEUTRON: BOY GENIUS, THE ADVENTURES OF
KIM POSSIBLE
LILO & STITCH: THE SERIES
LIZZIE MCGUIRE
LIZZIE MCGUIRE MOVIE, THE
MALCOLM IN THE MIDDLE
POWER RANGERS: DINO THUNDER
POWER RANGERS: NINJA STORM
PRINCESS DIARIES 2
RAVE MASTER
SHREK 2
SIMPLE LIFE, THE
SPONGEBOB SQUAREPANTS
SPY KIDS 2
SPY KIDS 3-D: GAME OVER
TEENAGE MUTANT NINJA TURTLES
THAT'S SO RAVEN
TOTALLY SPIES
TRANSFORMERS: ARMADA
TRANSFORMERS: ENERGON

You want it? We got it!
A full range of TOKYOPOP
products are available now at:
www.TOKYOPOP.com/shop

07.15.04T

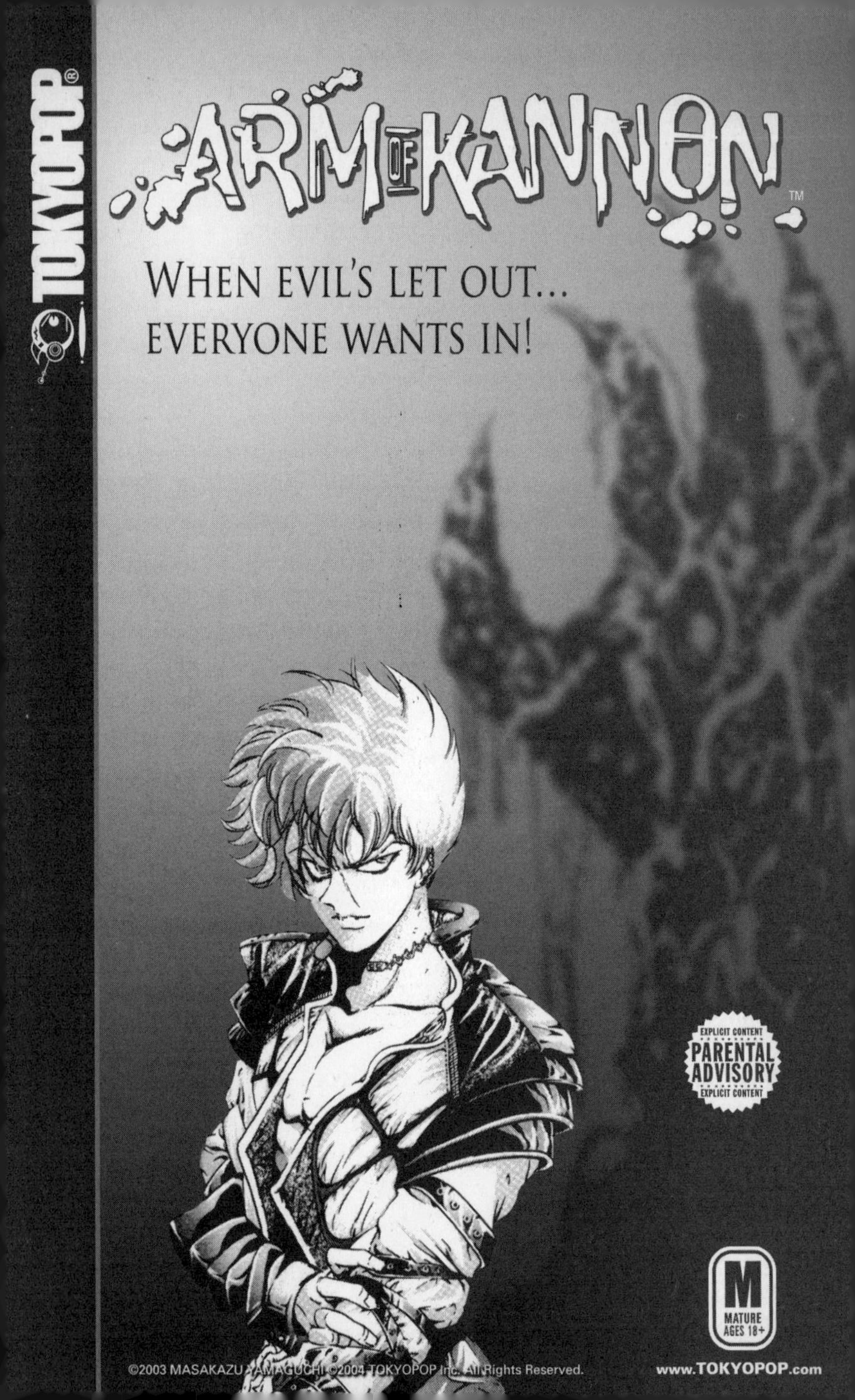
TOKYOPOP
ARM OF KANNON™
WHEN EVIL'S LET OUT...
EVERYONE WANTS IN!
EXPLICIT CONTENT
PARENTAL ADVISORY
EXPLICIT CONTENT
M
MATURE
AGES 18+
©2003 MASAKAZU YAMAGUCHI ©2004 TOKYOPOP Inc. All Rights Reserved.
www.TOKYOPOP.com

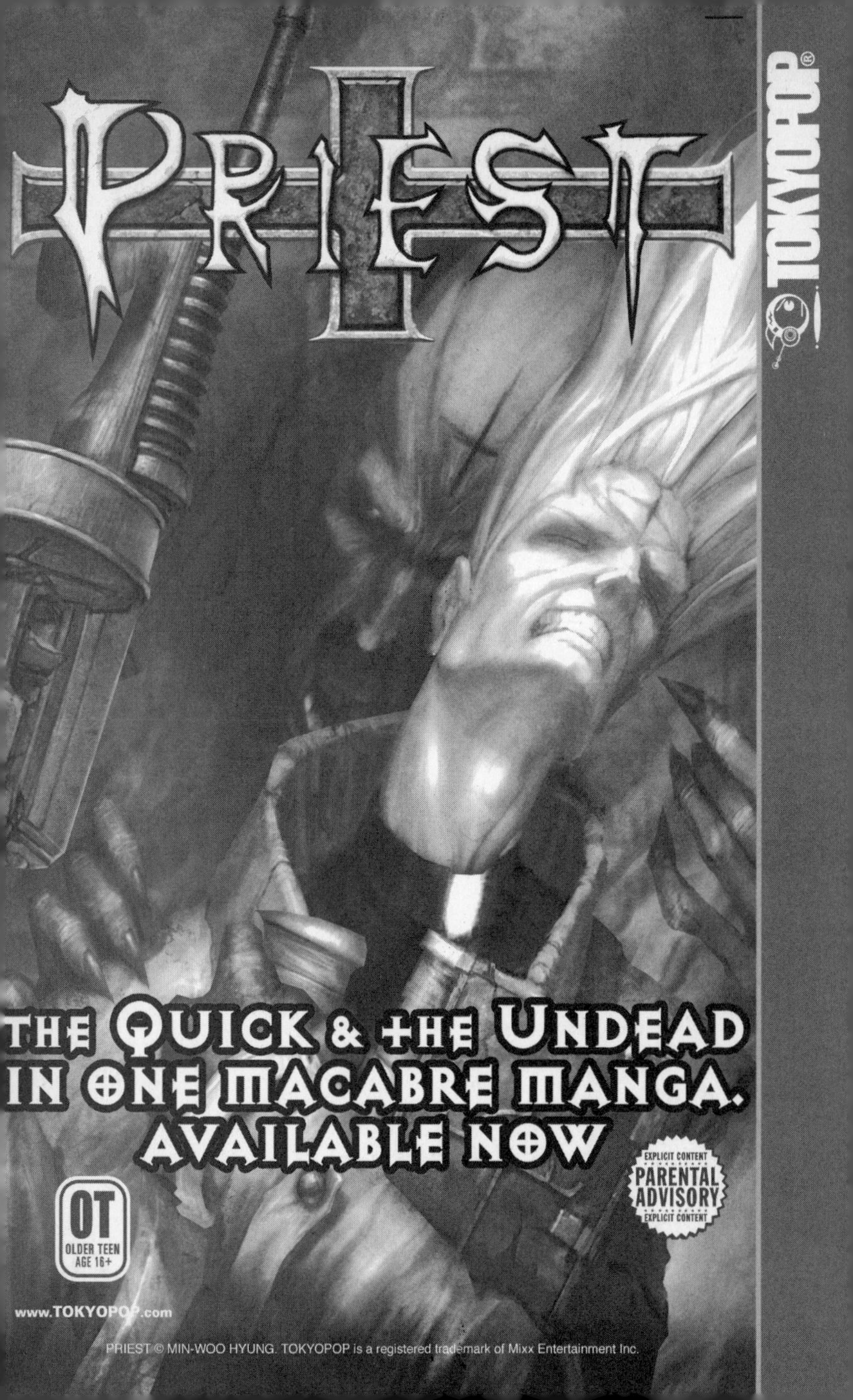
PRIEST
TOKYOPOP®
THE QUICK & THE UNDEAD
IN ONE MACABRE MANGA.
AVAILABLE NOW
OT
OLDER TEEN
AGE 16+
EXPLICIT CONTENT
PARENTAL ADVISORY
EXPLICIT CONTENT
www.TOKYOPOP.com
PRIEST © MIN-WOO HYUNG. TOKYOPOP is a registered trademark of Mixx Entertainment Inc.

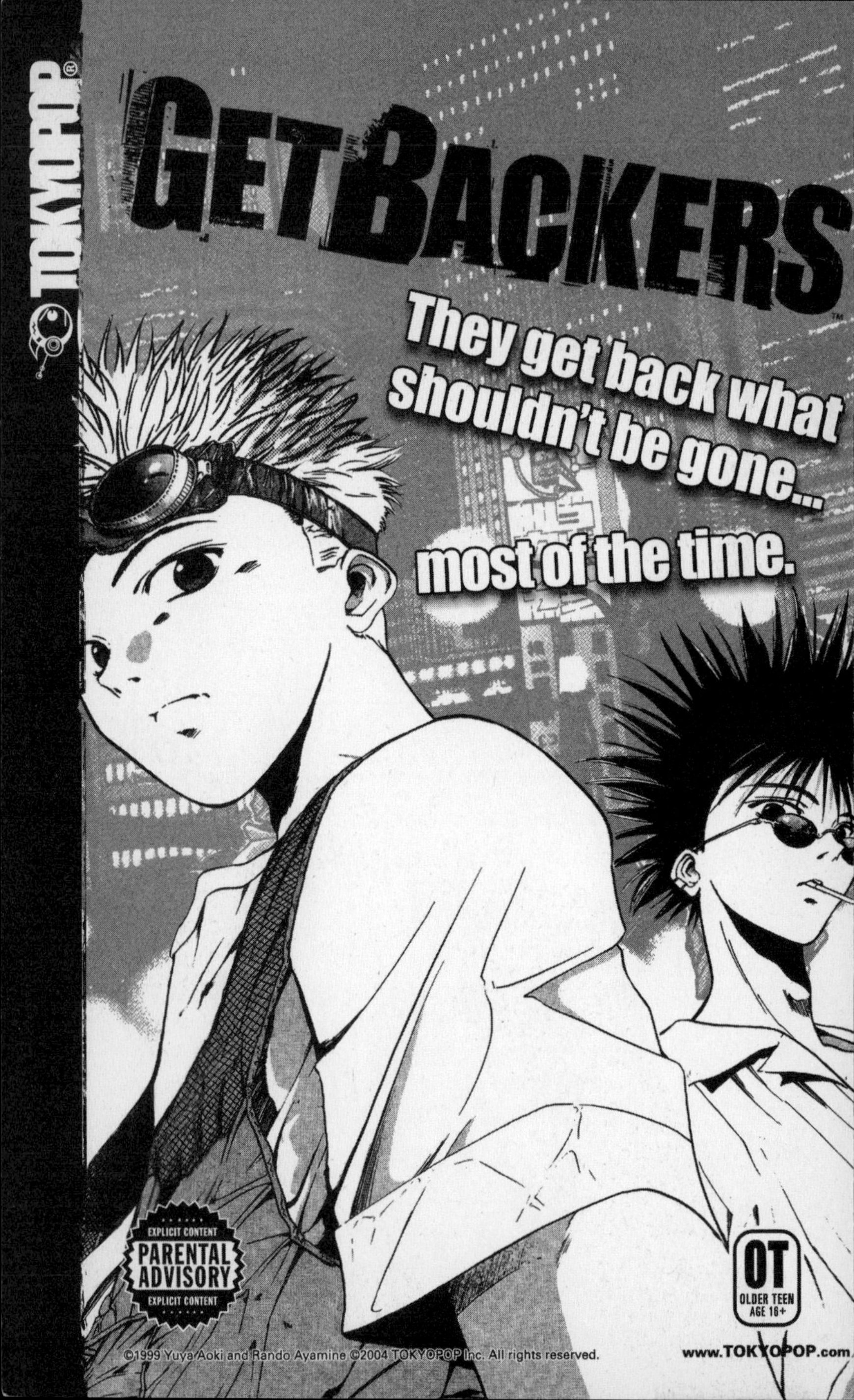
TOKYOPOP®
GETBACKERS™
They get back what shouldn't be gone...
most of the time.
EXPLICIT CONTENT
PARENTAL ADVISORY
EXPLICIT CONTENT
OT
OLDER TEEN AGE 16+
©1999 Yuya Aoki and Rando Ayamine ©2004 TOKYOPOP Inc. All rights reserved.
www.TOKYOPOP.com

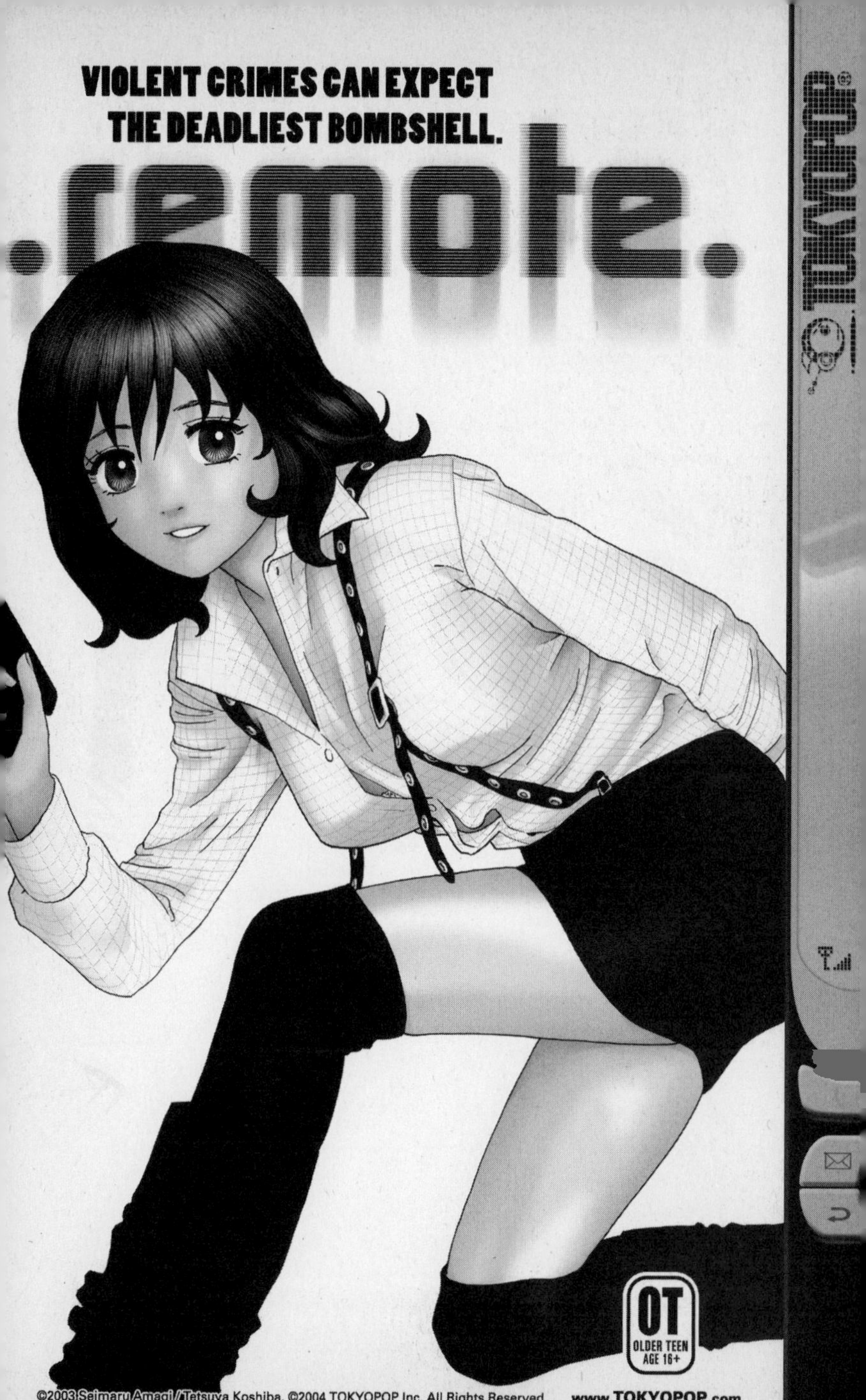
VIOLENT CRIMES CAN EXPECT
THE DEADLIEST BOMBSHELL.
.remote.
TOKYOPOP
OT
OLDER TEEN
AGE 16+

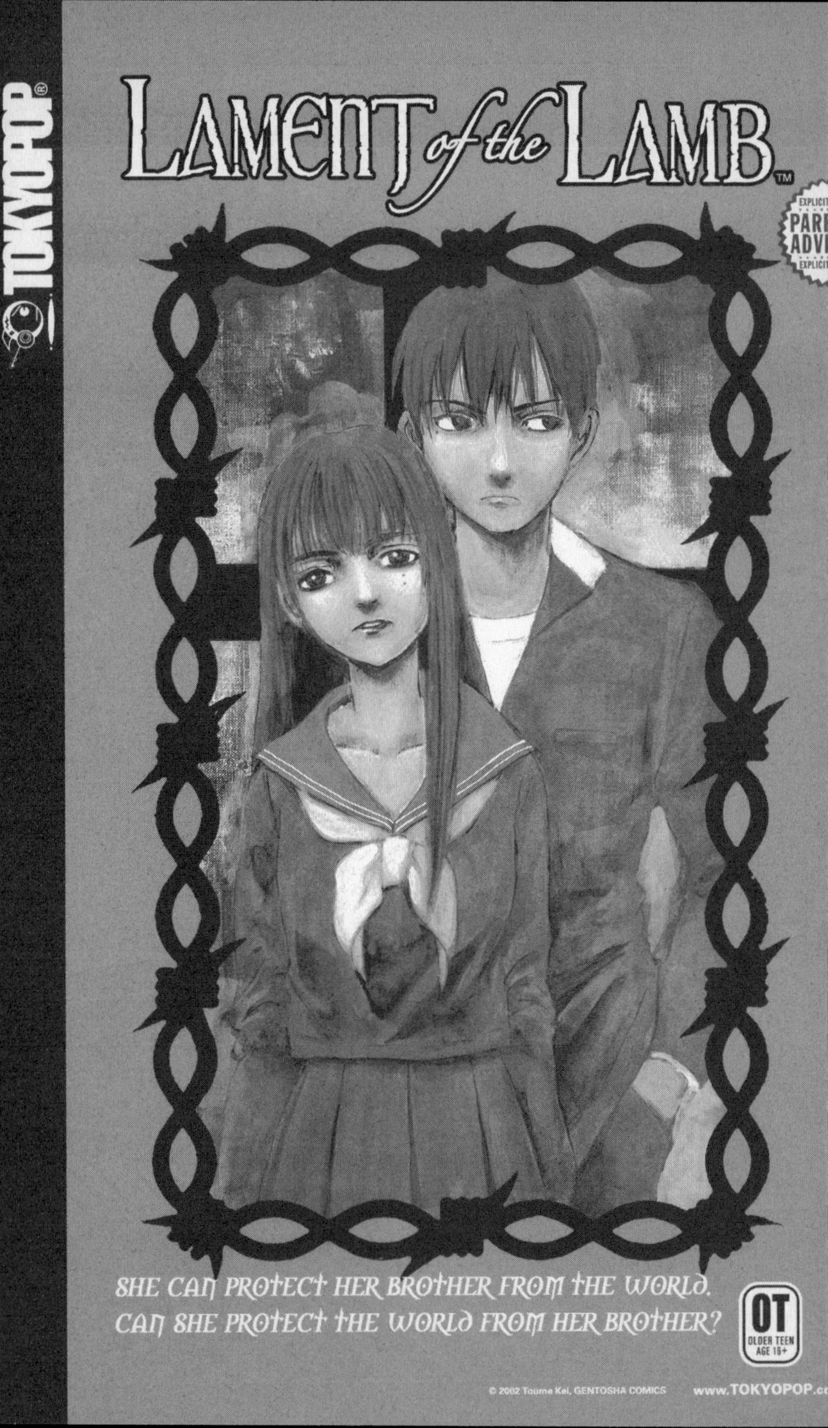

TOKYOPOP®
LAMENT of the LAMB™
SHE CAN PROTECT HER BROTHER FROM THE WORLD.
CAN SHE PROTECT THE WORLD FROM HER BROTHER?
OT
OLDER TEEN AGE 16+
© 2002 Toume Kei, GENTOSHA COMICS
www.TOKYOPOP.co

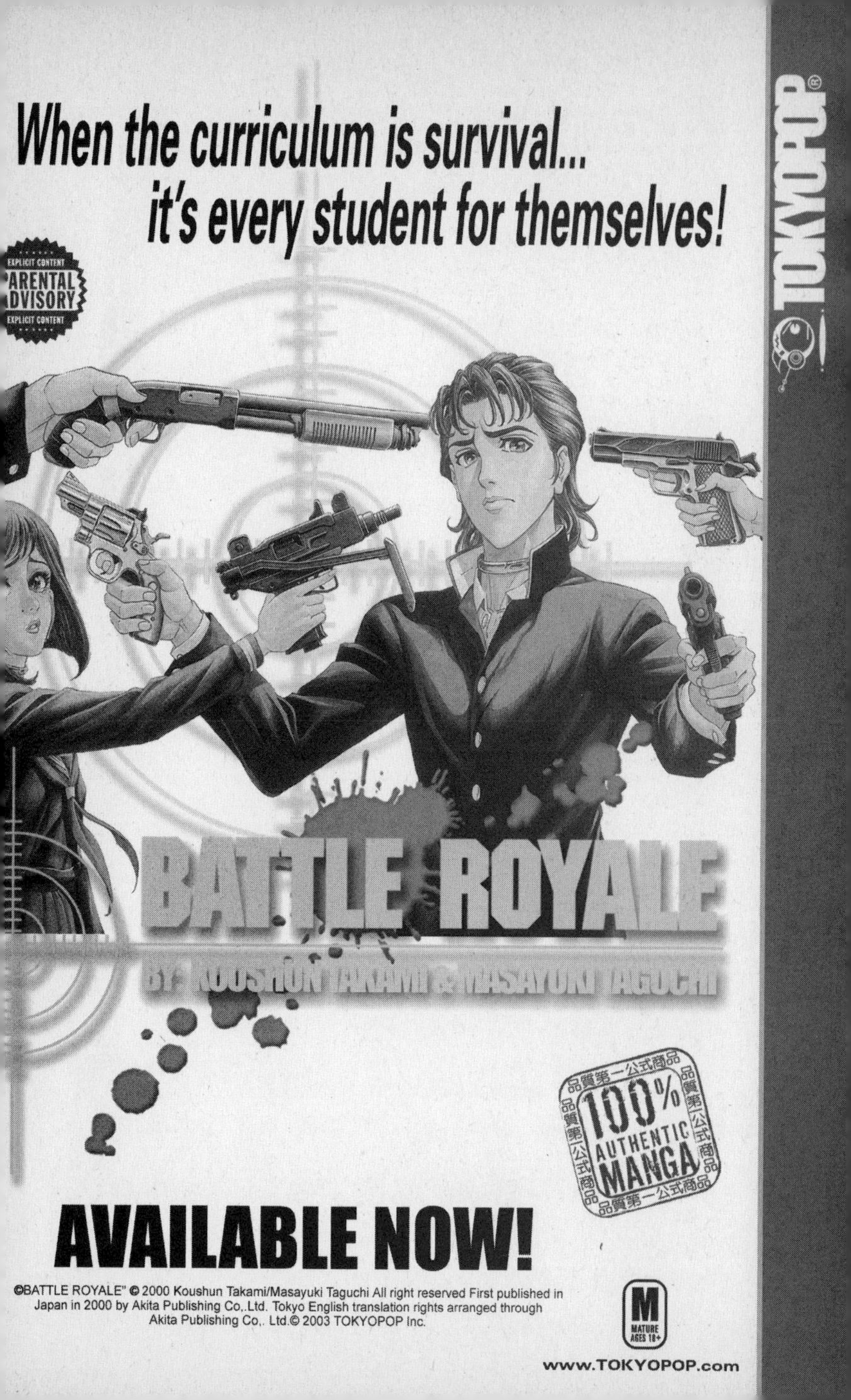

When the curriculum is survival...
it's every student for themselves!
TOKYOPOP®
EXPLICIT CONTENT
ARENTAL
DVISORY
EXPLICIT CONTENT
BATTLE ROYALE
BY: KOUSHUN TAKAMI & MASAYUKI TAGUCHI
品質第一公式商品
100%
AUTHENTIC
MANGA
AVAILABLE NOW!
©BATTLE ROYALE" © 2000 Koushun Takami/Masayuki Taguchi All right reserved First published in Japan in 2000 by Akita Publishing Co,.Ltd. Tokyo English translation rights arranged through Akita Publishing Co,. Ltd.© 2003 TOKYOPOP Inc.
M
MATURE
AGES 18+
www.TOKYOPOP.com

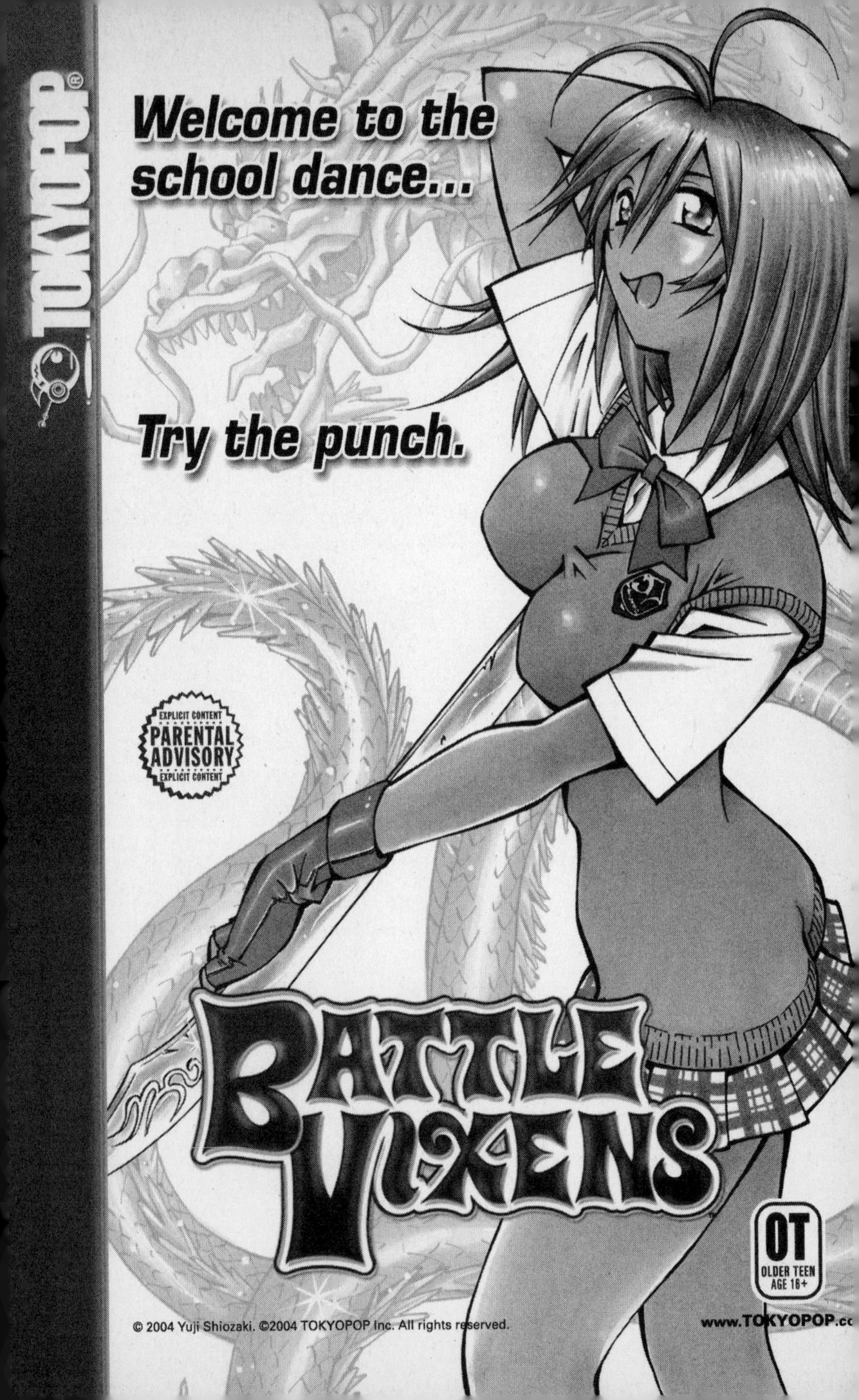
TOKYOPOP®
Welcome to the school dance...
Try the punch.
EXPLICIT CONTENT
PARENTAL ADVISORY
EXPLICIT CONTENT
BATTLE VIXENS
OT
OLDER TEEN AGE 16+
© 2004 Yuji Shiozaki. ©2004 TOKYOPOP Inc. All rights reserved.
www.TOKYOPOP.co

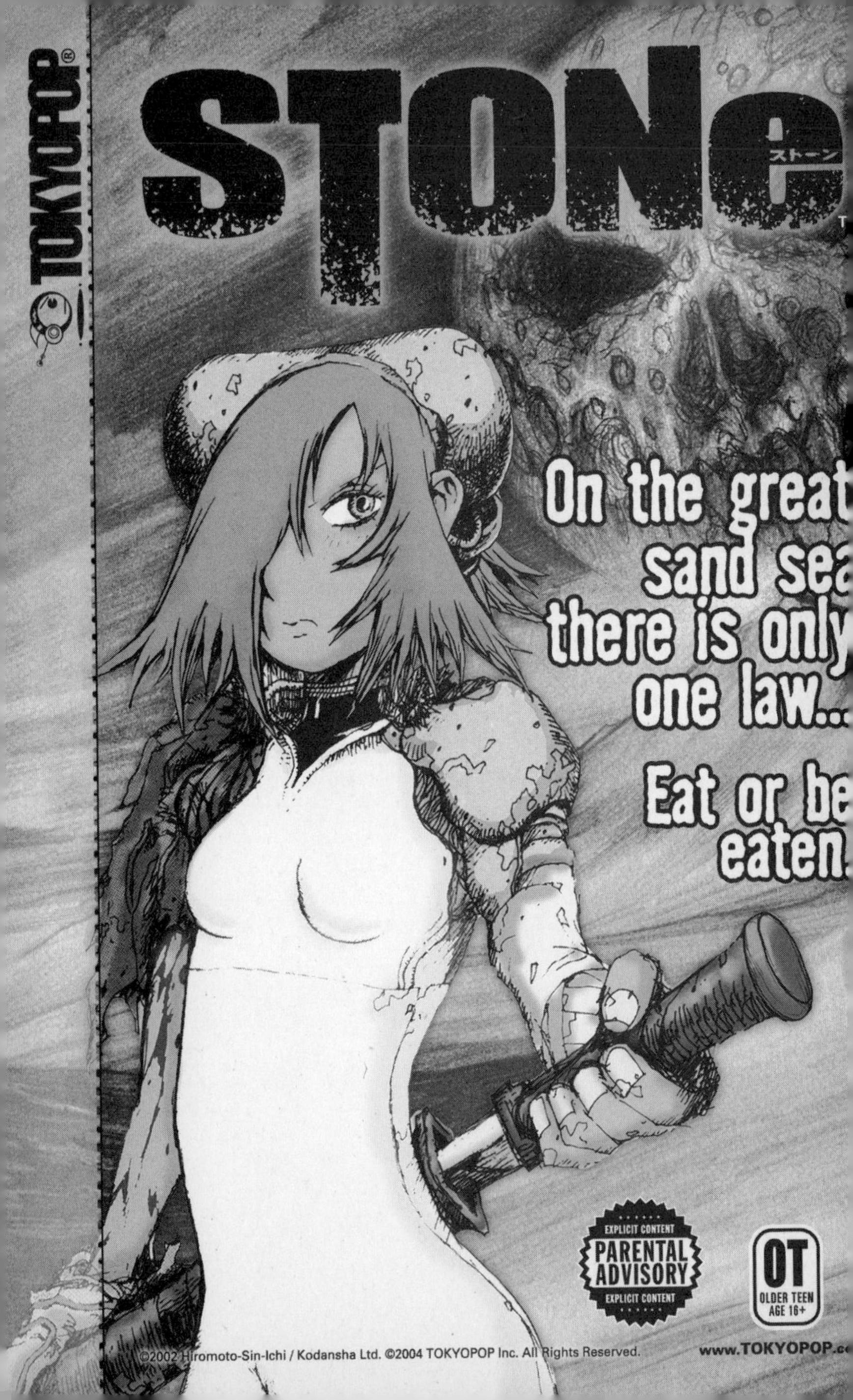
TOKYOPOP®
STONe
ストーン
On the great sand sea there is only one law...
Eat or be eaten.
EXPLICIT CONTENT
PARENTAL ADVISORY
EXPLICIT CONTENT
OT
OLDER TEEN AGE 16+
©2002 Hiromoto-Sin-Ichi / Kodansha Ltd. ©2004 TOKYOPOP Inc. All Rights Reserved.
www.TOKYOPOP.co